ReMembering
Osiris

TOM HARE

ReMembering Osiris

NUMBER, GENDER, AND THE WORD IN ANCIENT EGYPTIAN REPRESENTATIONAL SYSTEMS

STANFORD UNIVERSITY PRESS, STANFORD, CALIFORNIA 1999

Stanford University Press
Stanford, California
© 1999 by the Board of Trustees of the
Leland Stanford Junior University

Printed in the United States of America

CIP data appear at the end of the book

In Memory of My Mother
Phyllis Miriam Hare

CONTENTS

PREFACE viii
CONVENTIONS xvii

　Exergue 1

1. The Reverential Slaughter 10
　　The Passion, 11 Disremembering, 22 Voicings, 27
　　Every Man a King, 34

2. Supplementary: The Language of the Gods 44
　　The Code, 45 Decipherment, 49 What *Différance* Does It
　　Make? 56 Reading Pictures, I, 59 Reading Pictures, II, 64
　　Figural and Spatial Syntax, 74 A Grammar of the Figure, 80
　　A Fine and Private Place, 93

3. Coming and Becoming 106
　　Writing with a Pen(is), 108 The Hand of God, 111 Fathers
　　and Brothers, 124 Two Peas in a Pod, 130 Exotic Erotic, 137
　　Antitype, 148

4. . . . Three, Two, One, Zero 155
　　Lists, 156 The Nature of */'Ne-tjer/, 160 Mind and Body
　　in Memphis, 169 On the Tip of Your Tongue, 184 Pathologies
　　of Monotheism, I, 190 Being and Nothingness, 200

5. Post-ancient Ægyptians 212
   Gift, 215   Habeas Φ? 220   Hide the Sausage, 224
   Pathologies of Monotheism, II, 228   Full-frontal Deity, 233
   Life in the West, 238

NOTES 249

BIBLIOGRAPHY 297

INDEX 311

ILLUSTRATIONS

MAP

Pharaonic and Ptolemaic sites mentioned in the text   xxii

FIGURES

1.1	The *serekh*s of four kings of the Second Dynasty	18
1.2	Horus and Setekh from a papyrus of the *Amduat*	19
1.3	Detail from the "Smaller Hierakonpolis," or "Two Dog" Palette	20
1.4	From the Sixth Dynasty tomb of Idu at Giza	24
1.5	The goddess Ma'at in an inscription from the tomb of Kheruef	30
1.6	The deceased facing judgment in the court of Osiris	34
1.7	The Iykhernofret Stela	36
1.8	Schematic drawing of the Iykhernofret Stela	38
1.9	Detail from the Iykhernofret Stela	40
1.10	Lunette from the Iykhernofret Stela	41
2.1	Details from the Rosetta Stone	48
2.2	The Zodiac of Dendera	54
2.3	Botticelli, *Venus and Mars*	60

ILLUSTRATIONS

2.4	Detail from the Na'rmer Palette	77
2.5	Detail from the "Towns" or "Libya" Palette	77
2.6	Detail from the Battlefield Palette	78
2.7	Detail from the Bull Palette	79
2.8	Stela of King Djet of the First Dynasty	81
2.9	Architrave of Amenemhet III from a temple in the Fayum	84
2.10	The papyrus of the lady Henuttawy	86
2.11	Scene from the papyrus of Mesha'redwyseqeb	87
2.12	Impression from the seal of Queen Neithhotep	91
2.13	Docket for a necklace of Queen Neithhotep	91
2.14	Seal impression showing the deceased receiving offerings	93
2.15	Panel from the tomb of Hesire' at Saqqara	94
2.16	Scene from the tomb of Wepemnefret at Giza	97
2.17	Brewers and sculptors from the tomb of Wepemnefret	100
2.18	Jewelers and bakers from the tomb of Wepemnefret	101
2.19	The royal dais of Osiris from the papyrus of Hunefer	102
3.1	Colossus of Min from Coptos	107
3.2	Egyptian words written with glyphs of the phallus	109
3.3	Detail from the Semna Stela	110
3.4	Senusert I in the embrace of Ptah	113
3.5	Cosmogonic drawing from the papyrus of Nespakashuty	119
3.6	Relief of Isis being impregnated by Osiris	120
3.7	Relief of Sokar-Osiris in his barque	121
3.8	Vignettes from the Papyrus Jumilhac	127
3.9	Joint sovereigns Hatshepsut and Thutmose III	135
3.10	The conception of Amenhotep III	136
3.11	Statuette of a woman from the tomb of Meketre'	140
3.12	Wall painting from the tomb of Nakht in Sheikh Abd'el-Qurna	141
3.13	Wall painting from the tomb of Rekhmire' in Sheikh Abd'el-Qurna	142
3.14	Senusert I running the Heb-Sed course before the "Great God"	146
3.15	Atum leading Senusert I before Amun-Re'	147

3.16	Colossus of Akhenaten found at Karnak	151
4.1	Khnumhotep netting fowl, from Beni Hasan	156
4.2	Khnum, the Great Potter of Mankind	165
4.3	Disposition of text on the Shabaka Stone	176
4.4	Indications of dialogue on the Shabaka Stone	177
4.5	The body and the word on the Shabaka Stone	178
4.6	The glyph *kheper* upon a standard	188
4.7	Binary structures in Egyptian cosmogony, I	189
4.8	Binary structures in Egyptian cosmogony, II	189
4.9	Tut'ankhamun under the hand of Amun	205
5.1	Key, *Pietà*	230
5.2	van Heemskerck, *The Man of Sorrows*	232
5.3	Human-headed scarab beetle of steatite	243

PREFACE

I have been trained as a Japanologist, with a specialization in literary studies. Much of my graduate career was spent in learning to read old Japanese texts (poetry, drama, and *Genji*). I teach Japanese literature and cultural history (as well as comparative literature) at a large research university. So (obviously), "Why have I written a book about Egypt?"

Those who study Japan often ask themselves (or are asked), "hontō ni wakaru no ka ne?" ("I wonder if I/you *really* understand?"). Do you really understand the language? Do you really understand the epistemology, the assumptions concerning the cultural position of the subject, the ontology, that underlies what you are reading? And no matter the culture being studied, there is a line of argument that would evaluate the authenticity of any response to such a question by reference to a putative national, racial, and/or ethnic identity. My very engagement in Japanese studies is proof that I reject out of hand such a framing of the criteria for understanding. All the same, it has seemed to me that any response I make to this question within the context of "Japanology" would be unsettlingly vague and impressionistic. Or that, more reductively still, it might digress to a rehearsal of "facts" or even an apologia, which is not, in the end, what the question of cross-cultural understanding is about.

We are all confronted with the problem of cultural identity and the access and limitation it affords. Claims to special ownership of a cultural legacy are common, but they are often based on the haphazard vagaries of experience, and not on knowledge. Individual experience is, of course, indispensable to culture, but it must not be confounded with knowledge of the broader currents of history; for to do so is to straitjacket understanding inside sociopolitical categories and putative genealogies of the state. Even the heritage of language/s must be understood as contingent and coincidental. The native speaker's very intimacy with his language may occlude his understanding; his very fluency in his culture may fool him into thinking it is his nature, or even universal Nature. Thus it is with a sense of coincidence and contingency that we must examine issues of who "we" are and what we "know" and "understand." Hence Egypt, and hence this book, for Egypt—to be more precise, *ancient* Egypt—is so distant that no one can claim a culturally privileged understanding of it.

At the center of my argument is a chapter on the myth of Osiris. It follows the discussion in the Exergue, which stands apart from the enterprise proper, following instead the line of this Preface. After the Exergue and the chapter on Osiris, there are three technical chapters, the first on language and representation, the second concerning gender, and the third devoted to number. The final chapter would look in some ways like a conclusion, but it is more adequately an opening to considerations of Egypt in and as "the West," considerations I tried to rein in while writing the previous four chapters.

This writing was doubly conceived. It is presented, on the one hand, as a book, with a beginning and an end, with chapter heads and footnotes and a bibliography. The practicalities of publishing at the end of the twentieth century make this material form the most readily processed from my institutional context, and I have, moreover, an attachment to the solidity and clarity of the book (illusory though they may indeed be).

On the other hand, the academic apparatus I have used to write this essay has been, at least in part, an electronically linked "stack of cards" (a "hypercard," to give it its proper commercial due). Since the texts I have been engaged upon belong to no one, or, rather, to everyone, I would wish to disseminate them, as much as I can, "in the original language," in order to lay bare the archaeology of the enterprise as much as possible.

The enterprise as a whole, moreover, should be open to reconstruction and deconstruction by the reader; and so it is already, fundamentally, of course, but the technological capabilities available to us should open it more readily to readings along lines different from those enforced by the format of a conventional book. I have, therefore, created a supplementary collection of material on the World Wide Web, at http://www.stanford.edu/~thare/regypt. There I offer the Egyptian texts around which this book is written, with a panoply of linguistic glosses and notes, bibliographical references, visual aids, asides, definitions, and so on.

My inspiration for such a structure comes from several classics of philology, especially Sir Alan Henderson Gardiner's *Egyptian Grammar*, with its blandishments to scatter the reading around and beyond the page, to the tiny side note listing a reference from the wall of a Theban tomb, back to the sign list for a Thirteenth Dynasty variant of a particular glyph, then to the dictionary or one of the indexes, or to an excursus twenty pages back (which was beyond adequate comprehension the first time you encountered it).

If Sir Alan hoped to contain his subject whole within a single volume and make that single volume a comprehensive initiation to the hieroglyphs, then the meticulously annotated structure he produced defeated his ambition. The result is a splendid monument, arduous and fascinating, but not comprehensive (cock a skeptical eyebrow as you read).

And I myself, I said before, have no ambition to the definitive or comprehensive. I think these words can have only very limited or ironic application today, but I fully embrace the expansive reading that Gardiner envisioned.

I owe thanks to many people for the opportunity to work on this book and for the insights they have provided me along the way. I cannot hope to name all of them here, but I could not proceed without acknowledging at least a few. Sepp (a.k.a. Hans Ulrich) Gumbrecht has been a model colleague in this context, not only for his constructive reading of the manuscript, but also for his encouragement that I was engaged in "what Complit is really about." It was he, as well, who introduced me to Jan Assmann, whose achievements in Egyptology are an inspiration and an (unattainable) example. Assmann and Antonio Loprieno were both generous readers of the manuscript, and I thank them for their comments. Haun Saussy has been a superb interlocutor on the linguistic and literary-critical issues at the heart of this enterprise, and his detailed criticism of the chapter on language and representation saved me from many mistakes even as it pushed me on to a more rigorous consideration of several of the problems at hand. Seth Lerer showed me the forest after I'd been climbing trees for a very long time. John Baines gave warm encouragement and numerous insights, as well as making it possible for me to use the wonderful library of the Griffith Institute, Oxford. Richard Parkinson shared his own excellent work on gender and sexuality in ancient Egypt with me and helped me obtain important materials for publication. David Keightley lectured at Stanford on the earliest Chinese, bringing to my attention a range of cross-cultural problems that proved instructive at a crucial point in my work, and he made many helpful comments about a chunk of the work I unceremoniously dumped in his lap. My student Tomiko Yoda proved herself my teacher as well, and directed my attention to important comparative materials that would otherwise have escaped my notice. A Marta Sutton Weeks research fellowship extended to me through the good offices of the deans of Humanities and Sciences at Stanford made it possible for me to visit important museum collections and acquire materials that would otherwise have remained out of reach, and I thank both Reverend Weeks and my deans, especially John Etchemendy. I am grateful for the expert editorial assistance I have received at Stanford University Press. Helen Tartar and Nathan MacBrien have maintained a creative and cooperative frame of mind in face of the many material complications this book has caused, and Andrew Lewis has suggested countless improvements in the text. Finally, and most deeply, I owe thanks to my wife, Anne, and my children, John, Emma, and William Krishna, for their patience these several years.

CONVENTIONS

The importance of language to the enterprise as a whole demands in certain cases a high degree of technical precision. Thus it has been necessary to use the specialized tools of the Egyptologist even though, at first, they may alienate some readers' eyes and try their patience. My apologies. Whenever I have found it possible, I have aimed to simplify. All the same, it will be helpful to have some familiarity with the complicated and sometimes inconsistent transliteration practices of Egyptologists.

There are two major problems inherent in the English transcription of Egyptian words: Egyptian writing systems did not notate vowels (or notated them only sporadically and obscurely), and Egyptian languages use some consonants that either do not signify or do not occur in English. Thus, the precise reconstruction of Egyptian words in English letters is impossible. Yet it is necessary to refer to Egyptian words in talking about Egyptian matters. In many cases this can be done unobtrusively using accepted compromises, such as "Nefertiti" or "ankh sign." When more precision is required, however, I have adopted the following conventions of transliteration.

The letters below require no special explanations except the practical caveat that g is to be pronounced hard, as in "gate," never soft, as in "genial."

$w, b, p, f, m, n, r, s, h, k, g, t, d, z$

The following letters are marked with diacritics that need to be explained:

ṯ, ḏ, ḫ, ḥ, h, š, q (ḳ)

The letters *ṯ* and *ḏ* produces the sounds "tch" and "dj," as in the words "etch" and "Djibouti" (the latter being more familiar as that soft *g* in "gesture" or as *dg* in "edge"). An *ḫ* signifies a sound similar to "ch" in the German *ich*, whereas *ḥ* indicates the harder "ch" of Scottish "loch" or German *Buch*. An underdot shows emphasis, thus *ḥ* is expressed with more force than *h*, as in the Arabic name Aḥmad. Some Egyptologists similarly use *ḳ* to represent an emphatic *k*, reminiscent of the Arabic *ḳur'ān*, but I use, rather, *q* for this purpose (as in Qur'ān). The letter *š* stands for "sh" as in "shine."

The following letters present some special complexities:

ꜣ, j (i), ꜥ, y

These all have relatives in the Semitic languages and are called by their Hebrew (or Arabic) names, *aleph* (*alif*) for *ꜣ*, *yod* (*ya*) for *j* (some Egyptologists prefer *i*), *'ayin* (*'ain*) for *ꜥ*. Whether these consonants represent the same consonants in ancient Egyptian as they do in modern Arabic or Hebrew is the subject of a lively debate among linguistically oriented Egyptologists. (Some theorize that *aleph* and *'ayin* represented liquids, like *r* and *l*, in Old Egyptian.) By Egyptological convention, however, *aleph* is considered to represent a glottal stop, as in the sound that takes the place of "tt" in the Cockney for "bottle." *'Ayin* does not occur in English, but represents a deeper guttural consonant, perhaps a voiced glottal stop. *Yod* may represent a semiconsonantal glide, like the *y* in "yellow." The Egyptian consonant we transliterate *y* is related to this, and thought to correlate relatively well with English *y*.

The above will be relevant to the discussion in this book only occasionally. The fact is, the scholarly romanization of ancient Egyptian words gives us little hope of pronouncing them. Although it is not actually possible to pronounce Egyptian words as the Egyptians themselves did in any case, it is nonetheless necessary in many contexts to vocalize them, and it is indeed desirable that they should be capable of vocalization even in a silent reading. I will therefore adopt the conventional expedient of inserting vowels (usually "e" or "o") into the consonant clusters of Egyptian words to create more practical if technically less correct romanizations for most Egyptian words cited here, only using the scholarly romanizations explained above when it is important that technical details be conveyed in the text. (When important terms are introduced for the first time, I will give both the scholarly romanization and the more practicable conventional one.)

We will, therefore, speak of "Senusert" rather than "Snwsrt" and "Menkaure'" rather than "Mnk3wrʿ." It is worth noting, however, that this further conventionalization we adopt for most purposes introduces a problem of multiplicity. The selfsame pharaoh, for example, can be variously written "Thutmosis," "Tuthmosis," "Thutmose," "Tethmosis," or even, for purists, "Djehut(y)mose." The problem is compounded by the fact that this is a common personal name, as well as the name of four notable pharaohs in the highly notable Eighteenth Dynasty. I have accepted the convention of distinguishing those four (and other pharaohs sharing the same nomen) with Roman numerals, as "Thutmose I," "Thutmose II," and so on, but on first mention I will give the pharaoh's prenomen as well, which, in this case, produces the following: "'Aakheperkare' Thutmose I," "'Aakheperenre' Thutmose II," "Menkheperre' Thutmose III," and "Menkheperure' Thutmose IV."

Sometimes I prefer to note the presence of my 'ayin with an apostrophe. In such cases the 'ayin is converted either to the English e', as in "Re'" (for $Rʿ$), the principal name of the sun god, or to the English 'a, as in "truth": "ma'at" (for $M3ʿt$). I mark aleph in the usual manner, with an English a, and yod, usually, with an English i except with such important words as jmn, and jtn, the names of the gods commonly rendered as "Amun" (or "Amon") and "Aten" (or "Aton"). I prefer to keep the consonants t and ḥ (which occur in succession in many Egyptian words) distinct, to avoid confusion with "th" as in "thing" or "theology," and have done this by using an underdot with the h. Thus you will find my (picayune?) "Hatḥor" rather than the common "Hathor." These examples all illustrate the inconsistencies we live with in imagining Egyptian vowels.

I include hieroglyphic texts in many cases, insisting on the visual iconicity of the medium, and encourage even those who have no intention of learning to read hieroglyphics to let their eyes play over them for the occasional pleasure of recognizing an ideograph. Such citations are read, as hieroglyphs usually were, from right to left, reading toward the faces of anthropomorphic and theriomorphic signs. (When, however, words in hieroglyphics have been run directly into lines of English text, I have written the hieroglyphic words in English order, from left to right.) I have made all practical effort to present the hieroglyphic texts with due attention to the specific material context from which they come. Thus, nonstandard glyphs are reproduced as they appear in the inscription in question, and defacements or damage to the texts are indicated in my transcriptions as well. I have, however, taken the liberty of transcribing the texts horizontally, except in the case of a brief passage from the Shabaka Stone where the disposition of the glyphs in the inscription is of particular significance for the meaning of the inscription (see p. 178). The texts are identified in the notes as precisely as my epigraphic sources allow. Lowercase "p" affixed to the front of a capitalized word means "papyrus." In referring, when necessary, to dates, I follow the example of Baines and Málek in the *Atlas of Ancient Egypt*. Translations and all drawings are mine unless otherwise noted.

ReMembering
Osiris

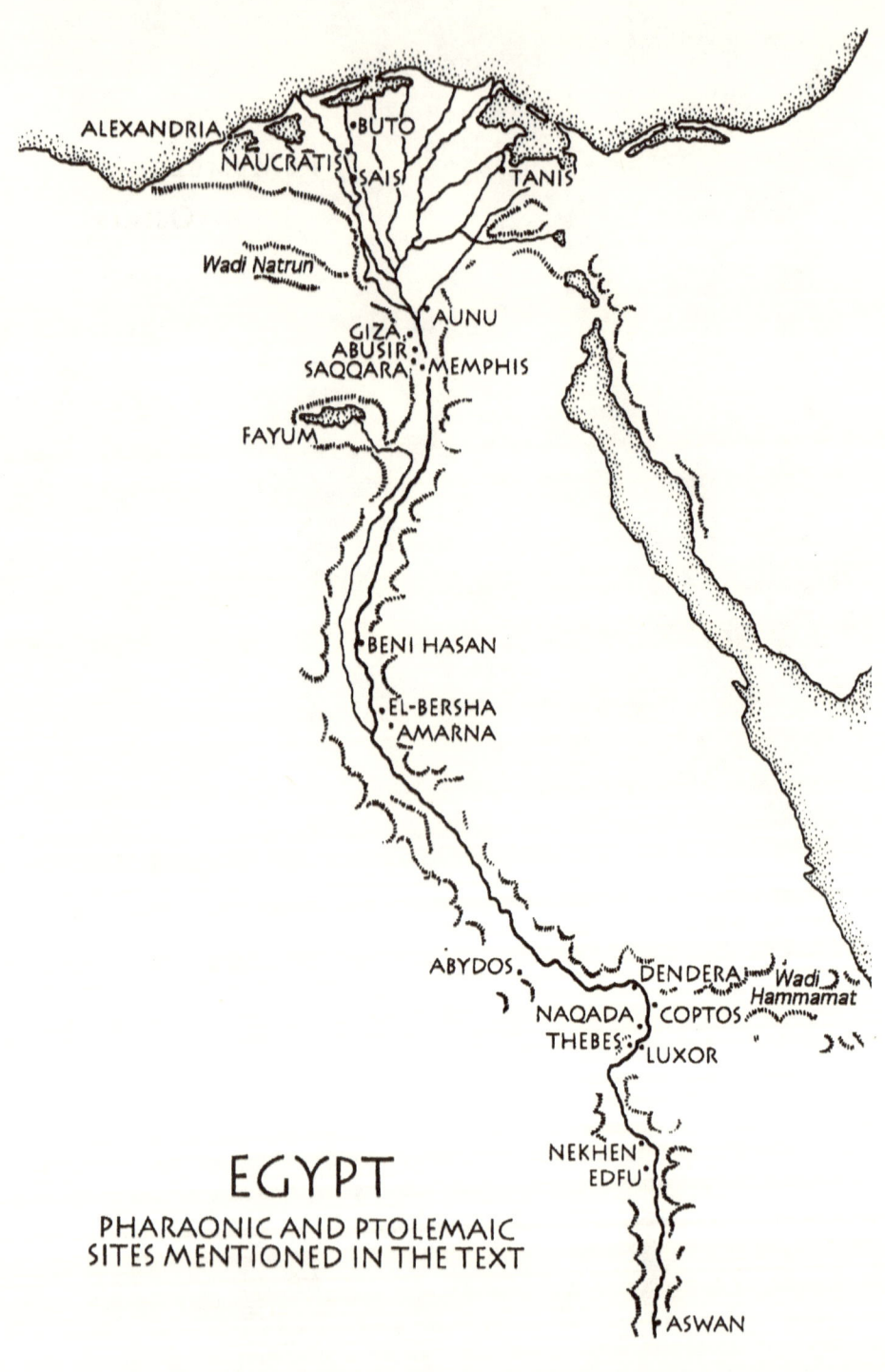

EXERGUE

"Who might we have been," to understand this?
For in reading texts like these, we must first ask who we might have been before we can ask who we are . . . not just because the language is different, the time so remote, bloodlines broken, voices silenced to the faintest whisper, but through a compounded separation, ubiquitous, and for that, less ready to awareness. Less a matter of tense than of aspect, one could say, by which I mean that distance in time, in genealogy of tongue, in "outlook" . . . all these differences are not as important as that other difference which already constitutes any intersubjectivity.

Being in any text (is) already another kind of being, always. In this case the encumbrances of "difficulty" and "significance" award relief, a way to postpone the question of who we are by playing the part of who we might have been. Indeed, to say who we are in this preeminently mediated field of imposition would presume too much. But "who we might have been": that "might" effects the possibility that one might understand at the same time as it stands over the uncertainty of these regimes of understanding, these conjugations, predications, prior authorities, conjectured valences of an other—an other who in writing what we read assumed some common referential field.

This undertaking is, then, explicitly, an operation on the borderlines and a proper opportunity for looking at those borderlines, among them: you/me, them/us, I/Thou, male/female, East/West, then/now. And it is, in consequence of this, a break from the assumption that each of us operates within a complete interiority. Yet the concentration requisite to such a break must acquiesce to routine, tempered and recursive, and disciplined in application, but the ardency of desire cannot be far off in this reading. You come to it to "know thyself," but find in it an other in the textual exigency of otherness, to face on the page the written (by not-you), the word anterior to you and already vested with some intangibility of value. This is différance as an object of desire.

And this is why I say "who we might have been."

My inclination is conservative, in that conserving these texts is at the forefront of my purpose. But I want to be disruptive as well, even though because I am more or less white, male, Anglo-Saxon, heterosexual, and American, I cannot plausibly lay claim to any very acute first-person singular understanding of outsideness.

All the same, having a professional identity in the study of the "non-West" (early Japanese literature), I could hardly have remained unaware of certain dynamics of "the" canon that, in the invention of an "us," have excluded and subordinated the diversity of subjective voices to a presumed great tradition (white, male, mostly Anglo, professedly heterosexual, Western European or North American, usually Christian, if only in some residual sense).

Given the ideological contention of the contemporary critical moment, it seems hardly necessary to challenge the inadequacy of such a characterization of who "we" are. Other formerly dominant discursive regimes, both formal and ideological, have also been weakened in the past decades, and the linear and positivistic presumptions of earlier generations are no longer part of the standard "tool kit" one brings to literary critical endeavors.

Yet the most challenging critical discussions of poststructuralism have remained predominantly Eurocentric and concentrated still further in a few limited areas: Rousseau, Freud, Marx, Heidegger, Romantics, some figures in the Enlightenment, sometimes Plato or the Pre-Socratics. The discourses in opposition to this heavily Eurocentric "Western" intellectual diet, on the other hand, though revolutionary in their attempt to articulate the voices of women, the subaltern, and the disenfranchised, remain in the great majority of cases, engaged on the past century or two, and on languages still spoken and written today. And if some of the work following these trajectories has been insightful and important, nonetheless, our awareness of the blindnesses that go hand in hand with such insights, of the impossibility of a definitive view, of the fluidity of "the" canon—of any canon—these preoccupations redirect my view to the ancient and the faraway, the "non-Western," the muted and the heretofore unintelligible.

That last category, the heretofore unintelligible, is of privileged epistemological focus. For although there have long been experts in the languages and discursive systems of that unintelligible, their enterprise has been institutionally, and often intellectually, contained, circumscribed by and grounded in a hierarchy that assumed, with varying degrees of subtlety, the superiority and centrality of "Western" thought, language, and civilization, of a tradition that was unquestioningly accepted as "ours."

But we can no longer take that little word "our" for granted. The illusion of an integral, rational, and progressive totality which is the legacy of "the West" has given way to more critically rigorous and contentious fields of discourse about culture, civilization, and the first person plural. Egypt holds an important place in this discussion and exemplifies the complexity of border making, of characterizations like the "West" and the "East," even while coaxing on those comparisons relentlessly.

Egyptian, as a semiotic system, had been lost and lay prey to uncomprehending and prejudiced Orientalists, or to Hermetics, who were perhaps more imaginative, but just as uncomprehending. The Decipherment resurrected and reanimated Egyptian, and although it is still "imperfectly understood"—and we must ask ourselves if our English is, even, "perfectly" understood—it can once again beget and misbeget its own discursive progeny.

Egypt has been manipulated to represent a field of difference against which can be posited a "Western" tradition in art, religion, language, and thought; it has been a strategic construction for the differentiation of a presumably monolithic self in the "West" from a presumably monolithic other in the "Orient."

But when you grasp the inconsistency and naïveté of the mongrel category "Orient," can you see that Egypt also represents a field upon which certain crucial strategic decisions were taken, decisions later ratified by Greeks and Romans; Jews, Christians, and Muslims; nation states; and systems of the market.

Edward Said has demonstrated the complicity of intellectual subordination and political subjugation which has characterized relations between the Euro-American world and the modern Near East, and Martin Bernal has analyzed in copious detail the intellectual pathology that fabricated ancient Greece as the fountainhead of "our" civilization.

In a less theoretical frame, Egyptologists like Erik Hornung and Barry Kemp have begun to disengage us from presumptions underlying the construction of Egypt as the other, to show how features of the modern state (and of the modern state of mind) could have been founded in the Nile Valley three or four millennia ago.

As Kemp attests,

> though their status, or the power of their attraction, is much reduced, the ways of thinking that we encounter in ancient sources are still with us. They manifest themselves in many ways. Collectively we may call them "basic thought." We remain sensitive and responsive to symbols, particularly when they relate to group identities: from school ties to national flags and anthems, portraits of leaders, the costumes and architecture of legal courts. In times of stress there rises to the surface of our consciousness the acceptance that sentient power resides in inanimate phenomena and things, from the weather to immovable objects that we curse. And throughout our lives our imagination hovers all the time between taking in and interpreting reality and heading off into worlds of myth and fantasy.[1]

Even, indeed, in the instances where most of us may differ from Egypt in the answers it gave to particular questions, it was still, very often, the Egyptians who formulated the questions themselves and consequently determined the parameters within which any "answer" makes sense.

In this, Egypt lies squarely on the borderlines, of "East" and "West," of life and death, being and nothingness, of stone-hard fact and the breath of imagination, male and female, and the borderlines of I and Thou, as well.

Ancient Egypt is dead. No one can claim a natural ethnic or linguistic privilege with it. But the extraordinary remoteness of its "timelessness" and all the potency of nostalgia raise Egypt from the dead, despite the erosions of tens of centuries and the most assiduous defacements and depredations of Romans, Copts and Muslims, Imperial soldiers, philologists, civic engineers, and tourists. Despite all this, Egypt remains. And in Egypt remains the self.

I make this assumption from the beginning, and I operate, at the most basic level, from this comparative and retrospective stance. Unlike the Egyptologist I just quoted, however, I am not primarily concerned to compare the institutions and material remains of Egypt with contemporary institutions and materialities. I proceed, instead, from an interrogation of comparison, specifically, the comparison of languages and texts. In doing so, I do not assume that this comparison need justify itself in the construction of a narrative history or teleology.

It is not my concern to explain the development of a genre, or demonstrate the evolution of "thought," much less to attest to the progress of the human spirit, or chronicle the rise of the contemporary from the "primitive." I abandon all ambition toward the comprehensive and definitive, toward the expertise of professor or the diachrony of influence and tradition. If whatever Egypt we may know must be assembled from the fragments of its ruin, so my discourse of Egypt must be fragmentary and dispersed, disseminated on the field of now, the subject in its oscillation between the inside and outside.

I take an epistemological lead, once again, from Barry Kemp, but now with elaboration by Jacques Derrida. Kemp articulates the issue with specific regard to ancient Egypt:

> Egyptian thought cannot . . . be recreated as a living intellectual system. This is, however, an accident of history rather than a sign of how being "primitive," it had to be superseded by something else. . . . I am aware as I write this book that I am creating in my own mind images that I hope correspond to the way things were in ancient Egypt. I also know that the more I try to make sense of the facts, the more what I write is speculative and begins to merge with the world of historical fiction, a modern form of myth. My ancient Egypt is very much an imagined world, though I hope that it cannot too readily be shown to be untrue to the original ancient sources. . . .
>
> We underestimate the intellectual grasp of reality in the ancient world if we take myth and symbol only at their face values, as curious images and odd fragments of tales that do not quite make sense. In rejecting the written and symbolic language of ancient myth as having no rational validity, we should not be too quick at the same time to throw out the ideas or sensations which lay behind. They, too, may well be part of basic thought, and universal. . . .
>
> The survival in the modern mind of the same avenues of thought that were open to the ancients supplies part of the mental apparatus by which we can make sense of the past. We can rethink ancient logic. But it creates an interesting pitfall, in that it is hard to know when to stop. . . .
>
> We really have no way of knowing in the end if a set of scholarly guesses which might be quite true to the spirit of ancient thought and well informed of the available sources ever actually passed through the minds of the ancients at all. Modern books and scholarly articles on ancient Egyptian religion are probably adding to the original body of thought as much as simply explaining it in modern western terms. We, as scholars, are now unwittingly and usually unthinkingly carrying forward the evolution of Egyptian religion.[2]

Compare this with the at first seemingly very different standpoint articulated by Derrida in his "Plato's Pharmacy":

> The dissimulation of the woven texture can . . . take centuries to undo its web: a web that envelops a web, undoing the web for centuries; recon-

stituting it too as an organism, indefinitely regenerating its own tissue behind the cutting trace, the decision of each reading. There is always a surprise in store for the anatomy or physiology of any criticism that might think it had mastered the game, surveyed all the threads at once, deluding itself, too, in wanting to look at the text without touching it, without laying a hand on the "object," without risking—which is the only chance of entering into the game, by getting a few fingers caught—the addition of some new thread. Adding, here, is nothing other than giving to read. One must manage to think this out: that it is not a question of embroidering upon a text, unless one considers that to know how to embroider still means to have the ability to follow the given thread. That is, if you follow me, the hidden thread. If reading and writing are one, as is easily thought these days, if reading *is* writing, this oneness designates neither undifferentiated (con)fusion nor identity at perfect rest; the *is* that couples reading with writing must rip apart.[3]

There are always important differences. Kemp's lucidity, his respect for the object of study, his concern to remain true to the original sources, these are all hallmarks of the best traditional work in Egyptology. Lucidity in Derrida, however, would be sleight of hand, a ruse; respect is costumed by play and wit and double entendre; and the notion of "fidelity to an original source" must be, in each of its terms, overturned or undercut or collapsed on itself until the reader-writer swirls too in the vortex(t) where words like "fidelity," "original," and "source" (and perhaps "to" and "an" as well) reside.

All the same, both writers share an awareness of that epistemological promiscuity by which we add to any "original" body of thought with every attempt to explain it. If Kemp's modesty and disciplinary identity hold him back, the extraordinary distance from which he trains his focus serves to magnify to clarity a process otherwise occulted by its very familiarity. And Derrida, for all his subversiveness and originality, is still an archaeologist. Indeed, the epistemology of the archaeologist has become the paradigm for each of us in reading the news, watching television, or any of the other routine and practical transactions through the sign by which we organize our lives.

In engaging any text (whether written properly, or constituted otherwise in the diverse semiotic field of culture), we cannot but father a new brood on it. There is no contraception in reading. Nor is there, in reading, any covenant of marriage, any requirement that one be faithful to a single writer, a single line of writing, a single genre, a single tradition or language.

And so, I do not confine myself to the texts of Egypt. I claim instead the liberty of the widest range of comparisons I can make. What I do here is not, of course, Egyptology of any proper professional pedigree, but rather an *avertissement* to certain myths of beginning near the beginning of our writing. It is provoked by shuffling through old volumes of philology, an enterprise that even now remains as attractive to me as when first I puzzled, decades ago, at how pictures could also be writing. So it is in Egypt, then, and with a focus on Egyptian myths of beginning, that I take a beginning for the discussion of the subject and its construction in language.

The literary subject is a field for interaction—ludic, or strategic, or hermeneutic, whatever you like—interaction that must, in any case, occur on the border between self and other, for many reasons. My focus here is the epistemological, linguistic, and "anthropological" interaction that negotiates the reading of a text.

That interaction entails a variety of operations: some are seemingly straightforward, like the glossing of "I" for *aham* or "love" for *mr(j)*; others are more technically demanding: the observation of degrees of conjecturality, for example, in *poiei* and *poioien*, or the untangling of hearsay, recollection and sudden awareness in *kanashikarikeri*; still others are ramified across a perplexing and frangible tissue of epistemological assumptions—the semantics, for instance, of "mean" or "represent" (*mutatis mutandis*, for any language).

All these cases nonetheless presume, through indeterminate layers of mediation, the imposition of voice on the text, a necessary, yet intricately complicated operation of faith and technical application. Doing so one reads and plays musical chairs with a raucous crowd of constructed subjectivities—characters, narrators, authors, figures of speech, images of self and other—to create and be created by the text.

"Subject," as a single word here, must, therefore, be unpronounceable. It must be constructed across the categories noun, adjective, and verb. In pretending to dominion in a centered consciousness, it will all the same lie subject to the accidental nature of meaning, to allegiances of expediency, threatening betrayal by the merest shift of accent. It will make a macaroni of signification in reaching past the etymological community of Latinate English to Latin exclusivity in SVBIECTVM, "the suborned," "the substituted," "what has been inserted by guile."

Here again, I ask you to consider the "might" of who we might have been. For on the one hand, in imposing the tyranny of our reading, especially on texts so distant and difficult as these, we subject them to our own regimes of understanding, but even as we do so, we stand in for writers long transformed to dust. We are suborned by them; we are, by the guile of the written word, the dummies to their ventriloquy.

Yet for all its subjectivity, this deconstructed subject unlocks and opens the door to the closet of solipsism. Recall our focus on the heretofore unintelligible. It is that "heretofore" which undoes in certain crucial ways the purely subjective in this reading. If a semiotic system lost for fourteen centuries and more can be reanimated, the voices of Egyptians can speak anew, and in the end, the trace of difference will itself be undone.

And so, I remember Osiris. Osiris is everyman, but he's dead. Yet in the figuring of consciousness, he answers back from death:

> What's this I'm bound for? no water there nor breath, twice deep, twice dark, twice vacant. There one lives by peace of heart; sure: no sweet ejaculation happens there.
> To this his interlocutor, the god Atum, responds, "I've given you divinity in place of water, wind, and sweet ejaculation. And peace of mind for bread and beer."[4]

These "Words to be spoken by Osiris" come from the "Spell for Not Dying Again" in the *Book of the Dead*, and the passage, brief though it is, speaks to each of the three main concerns of this book, the word, number, and the phallic body.

In the word resides a hope for and a simulacrum of existence. The written language of Egypt made the name an icon for the thing, the proper name a means whereby the self continued to exist, even if all other effort for immortality were to fail.

This replication of the world in language exemplifies as well the mechanism of number, multiplicity, the plurality of being. In the doubling of Osiris here as "Ani, Royal Scribe, Scribe for Divine Offerings to All the Gods, Overseer of the Granaries of the Lords of Tawer"[5] lies the hope that we might evade the leveling of death and make a claim on the life of god, a claim on making the self a god.

And in the mention of sweet ejaculation is the gendered voice, the indissoluble link, in the male mind, of being to desire to the phallus. Others have translated the word less graphically, and less specifically in male voice, as "sexual pleasure," "love joys," and "love making," but the word in the text, 𓈖𓂸𓂸𓏭𓏭𓇋𓏤 *nedjmemyt*, is clearly the word of a man. It ends with the hieroglyphic determinative picturing an ejaculating phallus, and is derived from the adjective *nedjem*, "sweet." It is a gendered voice, and the inseparability of gender and desire from that voice is an issue that draws our concern as well.

In its query from the shadows, the voice of Osiris is inseparable from the body of Osiris. The threat to his existence is explicitly a threat of dismemberment and disembodiment. His resurrection, his justification under judgment, his connection with the fertility of the land, his link to the power of the throne, all these components of his identity are explicitly matters of the body.

Some of these features of Osiris figure prominently in the Egypt of the popular imagination, the Egypt of magic and the mummy's curse, of extravagant wealth entombed in the desert sand, but this is Egypt as kitsch, a strategy of alienation, the subordination of a superstitious, prodigal, and "effeminate" Other to a scientific, prudent and efficient, masculine Self in the "West."

The constitution and disposition of the other along such Orientalist lines is itself pernicious, but in the case of Egypt, it has done us the double disservice of obscuring the Egyptian paradigms that underlie so many of the assumptions we make even now about male identity, the relationality of self, and the word. Thus must we set about re-membering Osiris.

THE REVERENTIAL SLAUGHTER

1

Telling the tale of Osiris may itself be a way of misunderstanding his significance, for all that his is a tale well worth the telling. There are several versions, even Norman Mailer did one, and Frazer, for example, includes an account in *The Golden Bough*. The most celebrated, and the source of most of the others, is Plutarch's *Peri Isidos kai Osiridos*.

All versions labor under a certain instrumentality, a use to which the tale is being put, which constrains the narrative to a certain closure and distances it from the ready experience of a reader. Mailer's aims must have been commercial, though perhaps "literary" as well. Frazer's concern is, rather, broadly anthropological: he is looking for universal human experience among the myths of the world, at the same time, however, offering up the history of the others as an as yet incomplete or rudimentary approach to something that attains its *telos* in Western civilization.[1]

Plutarch's contextualization is the most sophisticated of those I have mentioned. With an eye for detail, a mastery of narrative, and above all, an enthusiastic interest, he argues that Osiris is an ancient daemon, the likeness of Dionysus, the power of moisture whose efflux creates the Nile, and the principle of generation. He argues vigorously against the idea that Osiris is a simulacrum through whom we might recover an actual ancient king of Egypt, but he sees in the legendary construction of Osiris a rationally comprehensible structure of belief from which history can be extracted, with appropriate care and tact.[2]

But even in looking for "the" legend of Osiris, we are misled: to assume the priority of "a" legend of Osiris over a web of narratives, prayers, topographies, and etymologies in which he is known in Egyptian texts already shrouds and mummifies the king. And if the voices of the Egyptians themselves are hard to make out, we must sharpen our intent upon them all the more, and recall that they had been utterly mute until 170 years ago. The faint and heavily accented murmur we can now discern is itself no small wonder.

The name of Osiris first finds written form in the *Pyramid Texts*, the oldest long texts in the world.[3] His prominence grows in the newer texts we have come upon, on stone monuments and wooden coffins and scrolls of papyrus.

The great majority of these texts were found in tombs or otherwise touched by the culture of death, a fact that shrouds not only our encounter with Osiris, but almost everything we know of Egypt, and we must remain aware that death distorts our readings of Egypt in ways for which there is no compensation.

So, Osiris is called a god of the dead in most of the accounts given in modern reference works, but an oft-repeated hymn of the Middle Kingdom styles him "Ruler of the Living" or "Lord of Life." One of his most common epithets, *Wenennofru* (the Greek *Onnōphris*, and the ancestor of the Italian surname Onofrio), translates to "he in whom good, or beauty, exists" or "he who is permanently in a condition of beneficence."

The paradox is not simply a modern misapprehension of Osiris; it is, rather, the basic condition of his being, a mark of separation from the living as the prior condition of hope for eternal life.

THE PASSION

High over the main entrance to the Egyptian Museum in Cairo, an inscription reads, MONVMENTA PRIORIS AEVI HIS SEDIBUS COLLOCAVIT ABBAS HILMI PRINCEPS,[4] giving testimony, in its incongruous Latin, to the absurdities of European colonialism. On the facade to the west another Latin inscription speaks to a different ideology of power: IMPERIVM HABERVNT THINI, "They held mastery at Thinis," following with a list of kings: OSIRIS, TYPHON, HORVS, MENES, ATHOTHIS, OUSAPHAIS, and so on.

In identifying gods like Osiris, Horus, and Typhon (i.e., Setekh) as the world's first kings, the architects of the Egyptian Museum simply followed the practice of distant Egyptian ancestors, but in the ancient view, the kingship carried back still further, three generations before Osiris, to the primeval Atum. After him, they said, Shu and Geb were sovereigns of a primordial realm. Only then came Osiris and the rest.

Even today, there is an intelligent and plausible line of argument that posits the origin of the Egyptian state around the site of the cult shrine, the inmate of which might well have been *a tribal ancestor*, though not specifically the god Osiris:

> [An] early word for a type of settlement was "seat" or "abode," specifically that of a god; and archaeology as well as early epigraphic records, has underscored the importance of the shrine in predynastic settlements. One should imagine—and now the excavations at Hierakonpolis provide a concrete image—a simple shrine of light material (reeds, boughs, and wood), with a curved roof and horns protruding from the facade. This served not only as a place wherein the service of the god was performed, but also as the center of the administration and as a focus for local markets and festivals. The divine inmate, possibly in origin a tribal ancestor, was "the town god," the protector and liege of all those dwelling in the settlement or its immediate bailiwick. His sphere of activity encompassed the entire range of the community's interest, and thus he was at once creator of the world, founder of the town, sustainer of fertility, mortuary god, and leader in war. Outside the shrine on a pole floated a strip of cloth later to become the hieroglyphic for "god," as well as the god's "emblem," an object or animal enjoying a loose connection with the deity, also elevated for all to see. These emblems, which often seem to identify a predynastic community, as well as its god, begin to proliferate in the decorative arts of the last Neolithic phase, the Gerzean, about 3300 to 3050 B.C.[5]

The life of "the tribal ancestor," like that of Osiris, is little known, but in both cases, he (and it seems clearly *he* rather than she) is credited with the creation of the community, its culture, and its sustenance. The community's existence finds its cause in a genealogy. Historical fact has faded beyond recognition, but agency across many spheres of crucial significance is attributed to a specific subject, once human, now divine.

The reign of Osiris has, indeed, all the marks of prehistory, not in the common sense of a time before the invention of writing, but in the sense of a golden age, unadulterated by change and suffering, a time when the exercise of power was self-possessed and unalienated in a line of paternal transmission. Ironically, though, it is only by dying that Osiris emerges as a focus of religious attention.

The murder of Osiris is, in fact, a precondition for history, a break, a convulsion in the balance that had been creation. As living king, Osiris was, in the words of a celebrated hymn:

Begotten son of his father Geb,
Heritor of kingship through the Two Lands, ...
Into his hand, the land is giv'n,
Its waters and its wind, its herbs, its kine,
Whatever flies, whate'er alights,
Its serpents and its desert beasts.[6]

The death of Osiris, then, leaves a gaping vacancy; the reestablishment of order becomes the burden of his son Horus. In some accounts, death comes by drowning and, in others, under murderous assault. Thereafter, the body is dismembered and the pieces strewn far and wide. Almost all Egyptian references to the murder remain euphemistic and retrospective; the *Pyramid Texts* tell how Osiris was "laid low" by his brother Setekh, and how his sisters found him afterward. In "laid low," an Egyptian homophone names a place, a certain Nedyet, thereby emphasizing a link between the body of Osiris and the land of Egypt itself.[7]

The story of dismemberment and re-collection came to predominate over the story of the death by drowning. You might imagine this to be because the slaughter and disarticulation of the body is more graphic than its mute and clouded disappearance in the Nile; it has more dramatic mythological appeal. But geographical factors and the spread of the cult must also have played an influential role in framing the god this way. For Osiris was not always at the center of Egyptian religion.

In his origins, such as they can be traced from a distance of five millennia, Osiris was not a god of national significance. He was worshiped in cult centers in the towns of PerW'sir (mod. Abusir) in the northern Delta and Abcdju (now Abydos) in Upper Egypt. By late in the Old Kingdom his prominence increased, and during the next millennium and more, his sovereignty spread through the land and into the topography of imagination.

History can, after all, be invoked here. To Egyptians, Osiris was not simply a god; he was, as we have already seen, an early king, so it was not hard to imagine a bond between him and the contemporary world: "Setekh, in his murderous rampage, scattered parts of the dismembered body of Osiris all around Egypt, and even after Isis had come to reclaim the pieces, those places retained the sanctity of his presence: ... and that is why *we* come *here* to pray."

Temples of the Ptolemaic era recorded which parts of his body were left where: the left leg in the first Upper Egyptian nome, the right leg in the sixth nome, the jaw in Eileithyaspolis (the third Upper Egyptian nome), the ear in Athribis (the tenth Lower Egyptian nome), and so on.[8] But the power of his sanctification extended beyond these witnesses to the slaughter, and further sites lay claim to his presence as well, so Osiris became an omnipresent god with residence throughout the Egyptian world and otherworld.

The range of his presence is attested in the litany of titles found in hymns and prayers. An important hymn of the early Eighteenth Dynasty, for example, apostrophizes him: "Hail Osiris, Lord of Eternity, King of the Gods, . . . Revered of the *Ka* Before Djedu, Great Your Portion in Sekhem, Lord of Acclaim in 'Anjety, Foremost of Offerings in Aunu, . . . Sacred in White Walled Memphis, Content in Neni-Nesu . . . Lord of the Mansion of Eight, Great, for the Fear of You, in Shas-hotep, Lord of Eternity, Foremost in Abedju."[9]

Another hymn goes on to name Two-Mounds, Rosetau, Tjenenet, Herwer, Kher-aha, and you begin to see the spread of Osiris throughout the valley of the Nile, and beyond to the world of the gods.[10] The proliferation reaches a peak in Spell 142 from the *Book of the Dead*, where the names of Osiris and all the places he may wish to reside are enumerated in a great litany of more than 140 titles.[11]

So we find address to "Osiris in the sky," "Osiris the commander of the Two Lands [Egypt]," "Osiris among the Aegean islanders, "Osiris in the Two Horizons," "Osiris, Lord of the Universe," and so on. One finds as well the identification of Osiris with other major and minor gods of the Egyptian pantheon, either explicitly—as Osiris Ptah, Lord of Life; Osiris Sokar in the Lake Expanse; Osiris Horus Mighty of Arm; Osiris with the portion of Re'—or by implication.

"Osiris, Lord of Grain," for instance, identifies him with the god of grain, Neper. "Osiris of the Disk" indicates a relation to the sun god, specifically in his manifestation as the solar disk, Aten. Some of his titles, such as "Osiris the begetter" and "Osiris the shrouded one," have no particular geographical significance, either real or imaginary, but many effect a spatial identification on the order of those mentioned in the two hymns, although grander and more comprehensive.

The omnipresence of the god is, in part, both symptom and cause of his popularity, but there are many other reasons for his appeal, and primary among these must be his death and resurrection. For the death of (a) G/god makes a paradoxical incision across the metaphysics of any system in which G/god(s) exist(s). It cannot but threaten the eternity and stability of the system by inserting a flaw into that realm of being(s) which, by its superiority and transcendence, was meant to proffer hope and consolation to its supplicants. And yet a god also, in dying, becomes human and gives a human the hope of being, as well, a god.

The circularity of such a system is inimical to metaphysical constructions based on static absolutes. For Plato, say, the death of a god is as unthinkable as divine immorality and maliciousness. Christianity takes another tack, so that the God-man Christ may die; but he dies uniquely, in a sacrifice for humanity, which must remain eternally different and other from God.

In Egypt, the etiology of the death of god is complex. In the stellar religion of early Egypt, the stars were thought to represent deities, and those which never sank below the horizon were called the imperishable ones. The corollary would assign to those stars which did fall below the horizon a kind of perishing, or death.

The sun, as well, in its daily course across the sky, was a god, born at dawn in the east and aging all the day long until it died at dusk in the west, to proceed through the land of death, through the long night, to be reborn the next day.[12]

The death of Osiris is less explicitly cyclical, and the sequence of events his myth comprises has a stronger sense of uniqueness and linearity, than for instance, the rising and setting of the sun or the stars. In Plutarch's version, the death and its aftermath become the source of an engrossing narrative diversion, but it contains many Hellenistic accretions, and narrative ingenuity tends to confine Osiris to his mythical role and separate him from any immediacy of presence. This is misleading on several counts.

There was, for instance, the flood, that yearly inundation so central to Egypt's fertility and the emergence of its civilization. Each August and September, the Nile used to swell and overflow its banks, depositing throughout the valley a rich bounty of black silt. To us, this was the overflow of heavy rains from the Blue Nile in the highlands of Ethiopia. To the Egyptians, it was (among other things), the sacrifice of a drowned Osiris, who imparted to the waters of the Nile his own magical fecundity in a yearly cycle without which there would have been no Egypt.

So then, the passion of Osiris must come again and again, repeated endlessly, a guarantee of the renewal of life. Here, the association between Osiris and the god of grain, Neper, is signal, and the death of Osiris corresponds, by the economy of metaphor, to the dying back of vegetation after the harvest in preparation for new life next season. Osiris is kin, in this context, not only, of course, to his Egyptian cousin Neper, but to a plenitude of gods and goddesses throughout the world, personifications of the vegetable process in growth and decay.

Yet Osiris is more than just a fertility god; his presence in cult, myth, and legend is unique. He is king of the dead, but his kingship maintains a vital link to the kingship of the living pharaoh. That link is evident on numberless Egyptian monuments and can be seen in almost any museum where Egyptian objects are to be found. It is the raison d'être for the most common performative utterance in Egyptian funerary religion, the offertory.

In its classic formulation, it begins, "an offering which the King makes to Osiris,"[13] then it names the goods to be offered and specifies that they be handed over in turn for the sustenance of the spirit of one deceased, a spirit justified by voice and resident in the here-beyond. The list of goods offered almost always names bread and beer, beef and fowl, clothing, alabaster vessels, and other material goods the deceased might need in the next world.

Many of the named articles have been found in Egyptian tombs alongside the lists naming them, and in some cases, further, and more elaborate, offering lists are found. Given this evidence, it is not difficult to accept the theory that the words of the offering could stand as substitutes should the actual materials be stolen or exhausted.

Some texts name offerings that are not found as well. Consider the following:

Words for recitation: Horus has brought me. He loves (me)
    King N, for (I) have brought Him His eye.
Setekh has brought me. He loves (me) King N, for (I) have
    brought Him His testicles.
Thoth has brought me. He loves (me) King N, for (I) have
    brought Him His wings.
At them, the gods, the gods are atremble,
It is they who bring me, who love (me) King N, and they
    have brought me to the offering.
They will bring (me) King N, to the offering of God.[14]

Eyes, testicles, and arms are not part of an offering list, and the offering proffered herewith finds its place, not in the broader context of funerary practice, but rather in the special circumstances of the murder and reconstitution of the body of Osiris. To come to terms with this, we must consider Osiris in his confraternity with Horus and Setekh, and Osiris in the loving care of Isis and her sister Nephthys. And here, the narrative accounts of Osiris are indispensable, even if they are not seamless.

There is, in fact, a striking omission from most Egyptian accounts of the story: the murder itself. The *Pyramid Text* reference to Osiris having been "laid low" is hardly specified in more detail until Plutarch. As he tells the tale, Setekh has woven a fine deceit in revenge for an adulterous (although apparently mistaken) encounter between Osiris and his own wife, Nephthys. Having designed a beautiful coffin, Setekh brings it to a banquet and offers it to whoever might lie in it and find it a match to his own dimensions. He has, of course, built it expressly for Osiris. After many of the other banqueters have tried the coffin, Osiris falls for the trick and lies down in it himself.

Setekh and some 72 accomplices immediately fall upon him, nail the coffin shut, and seal it with lead. They carry the coffin to the Nile and set it adrift. It eventually floats down the Tanite branch in the delta out into the Mediterranean and along the coast of Palestine as far as Byblos.

Isis, in a frenzy of grief, sets out to search for the coffin, eventually finding it in the royal palace at Byblos. She brings it back to Egypt with the aid of ruses and magical feats ingeniously unfolded in the Greek narrative.

When she has returned to her son Horus in Buto (Arab. Tell el-Fara'in), she hides the body in an out-of-the-way place. Setekh manages all the same to find it. He chops it in fourteen pieces and scatters them throughout Egypt. Isis manages to retrieve them all, except for the phallus, which falls into the Nile where it is devoured by fish.

Plutarch's narrative is filled with intriguing details omitted here—many of them probably accretions to the myth, whether Greek or otherwise—but an Egyptian prototype can be discerned underlying the particularity of Plutarch's version of the story, for throughout the complex of Osirian myths there is a concern with dismemberment and restitution, an economy based on commerce in body parts, as well as a sustained interest in the role played by Isis in recovering and revivifying the body. (Sometimes Isis is assisted in this by her sister Nephthys.)

There can be no ready integration of myth and history here. The death, dismemberment, and resurrection of Osiris cannot be tied to any specific chain of historical events, and the interpretation and contextualization of the story must be mediated by some species of figuration.

One approach to that figuration is contiguous with history in certain demonstrable ways. Consider the sequence of royal titles shown in Figure 1.1. The tall rectangle with a geometric design in the lower third is termed a *serekh*. It is the oldest form of the king's name, dating from the earliest days of the unification of Egypt under a single ruler. (The geometric design is the representation of a palace facade, and the rectangular extension above is a bird's-eye-view of the palace enclosure.) The Horus falcon perches on most *serekh*s, but curiously, in this sequence of names from the end of the Second Dynasty (2770–2649 B.C.E.), the iconography becomes more complicated.

The *serekh* of Ninetjer is orthodox, but note how, in the name of Peribsen, the falcon is replaced by a canine with a forked tail. (This is the totem or tutelary symbol of Setekh.) In the reign of a successor, Kha'sekhemwy, both the falcon and Setekh's canine stand on the *serekh*, suggesting a political struggle, with the dominion of Horus and then Setekh, after which some reconciliation between the two has occurred. What historical reality lies behind this is unclear, and is less important than the dualism

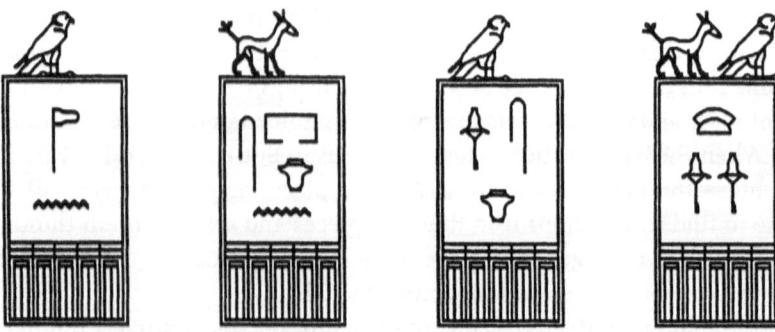

Figure 1.1. The *serekh*s of four kings of the Second Dynasty.

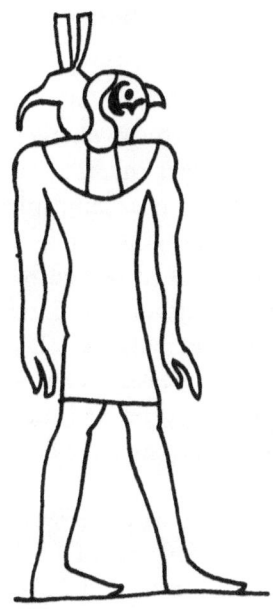

Figure 1.2. A paired representation of Horus and Setekh. Horus and Setekh appear in numerous paired representations, but none, perhaps, so intriguing as this one. From a papyrus of the *Amduat* (a royal funerary text of the Eighteenth Dynasty), this small sketch deploys the semiotic logic of hieroglyphs to construct a unique hieroglyph for the notion of the binary, both oppositional and complementary. In some ways reminiscent of the Daoist symbol of complementarity, it nonetheless betrays a typically hieroglyphic anthropocentrism. A New Kingdom gloss of this character describes him as Two-Headed Horus, "One conveys Ma'at, the other Trespass. He trespasses against one who trespasses and does Ma'at for one who comes with him." Sethe, *Urkunden* 5: 57, 5/8. See Seeber, *Untersuchungen*, p. 162.

for which Horus and Setekh become the primary icons (see Figure 1.2). The iconography of these two is linked with other binary pairs (the red crown and the white, the papyrus and the sedge, etc.) to become the most common semiotic dyad in Egyptian systems of representation.

In Plutarch's characterization—which is common among Hellenistic and Roman interpreters of Egypt—the pair comes to represent good and evil, but earlier, the dualism was not so stark. Setekh, though clearly the enemy of Osiris and Horus, was in other contexts a valued ally of the sun god against the threat of nonexistence. Several pharaohs, moreover, included "Setekh," or a shorter form, "Set," in their names, even the great Menma'atre' Seti I, the builder of a magnificent temple at Abydos. (There, though, since the temple is dedicated to Osiris, Seti was careful to write his name not as *Stẖy*, that is, "the Setekhian," but rather as *Wsjry*, "the Osirian.")

Horus and Setekh are both evident in the culture of Egypt far earlier than Osiris. The pair may well provide the earliest Egyptian figurations of the diversity and multiplicity of being. As Erik Hornung has pointed out,

> The ancient statement that . . . "conflict had not yet come into being" (Pyr. §1040c; 1463d) . . . is a specific allusion to the conflict of Horus and [Setekh], that is, to the figures and situations of myth, but at the same time it is far more generally a negation of all positive struggle, as can be seen from the affirmative description of this state as being "weary" or

20   THE REVERENTIAL SLAUGHTER

"inert": there is nothing that could move or begin to struggle—there is total repose.[15]

The falcon pictured on the celebrated Na'rmer Palette, at the very beginning of the pharaonic state, is none other than Horus as pharaoh; the link between the bird and pharaoh triumphant is clear there. So it may likewise be Setekh who stands playing a flute in uncanny accompaniment to a conflict depicted on another slate palette of similar vintage (Fig. 1.3).[16] The iconographic significance of the pair is fixed very early, and we can see in the vagueness with which Osiris's death is attributed to Setekh, a rough suture where one sequence of myths has been joined to another.

As I said before, it is not possible to identify a single specific narrative in which this first occurred. The myth is too old, too widespread and polyvalent, to fasten to any particular narrative, but it has narrative contours nonetheless.

The common threads are a quarrel over succession, battles resulting in the maiming of the warring parties, and eventually a judgment by tribunal leading to the restoration of order. One finds allusion to the strife between Horus and Setekh throughout Egyptian history, and its virulence spreads sometimes, as a given narrative grows, to overtake Re', Isis, Thoth, and others. Osiris, curiously, never fights. His is the role of scapegoat and victim, receiver of offerings in restitution, and judge, never himself a contender.

In some accounts, Horus and Setekh prosecute an animosity resulting from the murder of Osiris, but in other cases, they fight for a vaguely defined dominion. In the course of the struggle, Setekh may gouge out the eyes of Horus, and Horus squeeze off Setekh's testicles. A cadence is achieved in the restoration of these damaged parts, but the animosity lives

Figure 1.3. Detail from the "Smaller Hierakonpolis," or "Two Dog" Palette, showing an enigmatic figure, perhaps one of the earliest representations of the god Setekh. Ashmolean Museum, Oxford (E 3924).

on, in a long train of battles and deceits until somehow a decisive judgment is pronounced against Setekh, and Horus is celebrated as victor. At this point, the important epithet, *ma'a-kheru* (i.e., *m³ʿ-ḫrw*), "justified of voice," is first mentioned. It is, originally, a characterization of the successful litigant, Horus, but comes to be associated with Osiris more often.

Yet the role of Osiris is ambiguous. As we saw above, Horus and Setekh (and in the case cited, Thoth as well) offer severed parts to Osiris, making him the site of restitution and reconciliation. More often, however, it is Osiris himself who is dismembered. The losses suffered by Horus and Setekh then pale next to the complete dismemberment of the body of Osiris, and the reason for Horus's struggle with Setekh changes.

O Osiris-(Name), be not wanting, do not wail.
Geb has brought Horus to you, he claims their hearts for you.
He has brought all the gods at once, they do not remain afar from him.
Horus has taken care of you, it has not taken long for him to take
    care of you.
Horus has wrested his eye from Setekh. He has given it to you.
This, his sweet eye, he offers it to you,
Lay claim to it, ho, it is yours by rights.
He gives over the throne to you.
Horus is joyful because of you, in your name of Foremost of Westerners.
Horus himself will make good what Setekh has done to you.[17]

Horus, thus, becomes the avenger of his murdered father, but of equal or greater significance in the passion is Isis, the mother of Horus and sister of Osiris. Her role is to search out and collect the pieces of Osiris's body, and, more important still, to resuscitate him and conceive of him a child.

Several inconsistencies mark this spot where the story of Osiris is joined with that of Horus and Setekh and suggest the emergence and spread of the cult of Osiris at some point well after the Horus-Setekh dyad was established.

Connection is made through the agency of a miracle, that of engenderment. The engenderment itself is hardly surprising, but the explicitly sexual nature of that engenderment, in that the son is the only begotten son of a god, bears a more striking likeness to events in the New Testament. But that, for the moment, is a digression.

DISREMEMBERING

There are other miraculous moments in the tales of Osiris, but most striking of all is this ejaculatory link, effected in Egyptian sources, note well, upon a kite, not a woman, for Isis is woman as mother, woman as faithful and miraculously efficacious sister, but she is not a wife in any sexual sense. She has no explicitly sexual being at all, much less a sexuality equal to the extravagant phallocentrism of Osiris (scion after all, of a god who masturbated the cosmos into existence). She is the vessel and bower of male identity, itself most explicitly marked by the phallus, erect.

This would seem a deep mystery among the miracles of Osirian religion. The scene is not well attested, and in its best exemplum lies hidden and unique among the many nearly identical offering tableaux of Seti's monument in Abydos.[18] But if in Osirian religion, it is a secret moment, hidden away from general view, in other divine and androcentric cults in Egypt, there are abundant celebrations of the phallus. The walls of Karnak are peopled with a crowd of ithyphallic representations of Amun, and Min has explicitly phallic cults in Coptos and Akhmim.

What is unique in the Osirian cult is the coupling of the phallus with death. The other phallic cults make no such connection. This brokers a differential of strength and weakness simultaneously. Thus Osiris is "the weary one" and clearly the victim of his narratives, but he is victorious as well, overcoming, not merely exhaustion, but death itself, ejaculating his identity into the living king through the instrumentality of a keening bird. When the link reverses, and the living king dies to become Osiris, it is in his voice as *Osiris* that he finds justification, while some new Horus rises to the royal throne. A chain of transformations enables the bridging of life and death in a way unexampled elsewhere.[19]

Only in the version recorded by Plutarch, and thereafter, does Osiris lose his phallus to the fish of the Nile. In Egyptian sources, the dismemberment extends to the full body of the dead king—or we should more precisely say, to a particularly Egyptian construction of the full body: favoring this limb or that organ, ignoring others. Nonetheless, the phallus is clearly of central significance, for it links Osiris both to the temporal power of Horus the King and to the archetype of sovereign consciousness, which is figured through the phallus.

The dismemberment serves on the one hand to "rationalize" or "historicize" the passion of the dead king in his relation to the land, but it also identifies the land as the body of Osiris, linking its fertility to the divine presence. The resurrection of the god is multiplied into vegetable growth on a broad spatial and temporal scale; this too finds place among the transformations of Osiris. But such transformations hardly circumscribe the range of figuration whereby Osiris attains his cultural potency in Egypt. He is, even in dismemberment, a figural representation of consciousness, a figure of the subject itself.

The dead king (whether, for example, the "Osiris Unas," or "Osiris Menma'atre'," or "Osiris Nakhtnebef")—eventually, indeed, any decedent (the "Osiris Ani," the "Osiris Rekhmire'," the "Osiris 'Ankhnesneferibre'") —overcomes his symbolic dismemberment in death and mummification, attaining to a multiple individuality in the afterlife, endowed with the specifically Egyptian posthumous spirits known as the *ka* and *ba*,[20] as well as with name, body, heart, shadow, sculptural doubles, painted representations, and the rest: all of which are additional "transformations." In one example, from the tomb of Idu at Giza, we see the deceased transformed into a limestone figure with arms open for the receipt of offerings (see Fig. 1.4)

To better understand this, consider the differential of fragmentation and integration that operates at the level of myth in direct reference to Osiris, at the level of funerary technology in the process of mummification, and at the level of subject position in the Egyptian construction of a posthumous identity.

The mythical dismemberment of Osiris mimics psychological and semiotic dismemberments constituting (even as they threaten) Egyptian constructions of subjective consciousness. Egyptian systems of eschatology, myth, psychology, and written language find a nexus here in a particularly revealing way, linking the economy of mummification with the economy of written Egyptian.

Thus the identification and specification of the individual aspects of

24 THE REVERENTIAL SLAUGHTER

Figure 1.4. From the Sixth Dynasty tomb of Idu. Giza (G 7102). After the photograph in Forman and Quirke, *Hieroglyphs and the Afterlife,* p. 30.

the subject suggest their separability, even as pointing to separate parts of the body with logographs in itself suggests the possibility of dismemberment.[21] Already we see the diffusion of the subject in several directions. That this diffusion can also be seen as dismemberment becomes clear when we consider the anatomization of the individual into constituent parts.

Explicitly corporal elements of the anatomized subject reveal more clearly how the diffusion of the person is also its dismemberment. Start with the whole body, represented by the mummy lying on its back or on a bier or standing upright. The corpse thus meticulously preserved, wrapped, and reconstructed, in its resemblance to its living antecedent, exemplifies one of the greatest triumphs of Egyptian art; in its difference from that antecedent, it is as well one of the most poignant failures of human science. It was important to preserve the body in its appearance (the Egyptian word for image or likeness is, indeed, written with the mummy glyph as determinative).

Although mummification of some form or another was practiced for the full three millennia of Egyptian civilization, and techniques varied considerably in that vast span of time, we can see throughout that the attempt to preserve the body, or at least its image, could not but engage its active destruction as well. The very effort to preserve the image entails a certain amount of dismemberment. The viscera were characteristically removed, either through an incision in the side or abdomen, or by the insertion of oil through the anus, which would flow out again with the better part of the decomposed viscera.

In the accounts given by Herodotus and Diodorus Siculus, the violence of mummification is ritually counteracted by a ritual or dramatic recasting of the funerary technicians in two categories. The Greeks irreverently termed the pair "slitters" (Gk. *paraskhistai*) and "picklers" (Gk. *tarikheutai*).[22]

Egyptian terminology for the process is more positive, and reverent, and discusses mummification in the language of healing.[23] Yet whatever the language invoked, the effort to preserve engages, perforce, the process of dismembering. To be preserved "completely," the body must be supplemented by a trousseau of substitutes. Already in the Old Kingdom, for example, "reserve heads" were sculpted to leave near the mummy, should some incorporeal element of the deceased fail to recognize the body to which it belonged.

Some have theorized that as more self-conscious methods of mummification evolved to replace simple interment of the body in the fetal position in the desert, the bodies of the deceased were actually cut in pieces for individual wrapping before the body was reassembled for burial.[24] And in many burials at the peak of Egyptian proficiency in the process, the liver, lungs, intestines, and stomach were separated from the rest of the viscera and afforded special preparation. They were removed and embalmed individually, and as early as the Fifth or Sixth Dynasty, the practice of interring them in vessels of their own ("canopic jars") was practiced even by some of lower social status. In the Middle and New Kingdoms, their placement in canopic jars affords the differentiated protection of the four sons of Horus.[25]

The heart was also given special treatment. If separately embalmed, it was nonetheless replaced in the body when the corpse was wrapped, but with the supplementary provision of a heart scarab, carefully inscribed with a specific spell to control the testimony the heart should be called upon to give. (The kidneys may have been left in the body simply because access to them is difficult.)

Other parts of the body were also carefully wrapped or padded to simulate life. Thus the cheeks are sometimes found packed to mitigate shrinkage; the fingernails and toenails sometimes bound to the bone to prevent their loss after the desiccation of the flesh or sheathed to contain them with the fingers and toes. The phallus was carefully bound up to simulate erection: as we have seen, the resurrection of the flesh was most tangibly demonstrated in the case of Osiris by his posthumous erection, and there is an important link here as well to one of the Egyptian creation myths, but the realization of male sexual desire so trenchantly exemplified in the Egyptian glyph of the phallus, erect or erect and ejaculating, is itself implicated in the paradox of dissemination and dispersal of the self, as we shall see.

We cannot overlook here an important link between writing and the violence of dismemberment.[26] In the hieroglyphic system, exterior human body parts are frequently represented by drawings of the part in question. Internal organs are more frequently represented by analogy with the organs of animals. Here the vocabulary of sacrifice and butchery comes into play, introducing a difficult negotiation between similarity and difference, for as much as the slaughter of animals occupied an important place in the economy of offerings, the idea of "slaughtering" human beings (even in the ambivalent reconstitutive process of mummification) identified the corpse with Osiris and the embalmers with Setekh. (Thus, Diodorus Siculus's "slitters" were enjoined to play the role of Setekh. They were harried and chased off on completing their operation by the "picklers," who were cast as the partisans of Horus.)[27]

Language and writing play an important reconstitutive role as well, however. The name becomes the name tag; it too, a fraction of the subject, was maintained with all possible care beyond the depredations of death and entombment. What is in a name? In the end, perhaps everything. For in the sad eventuality that the offerings cease, the tomb is violated, the sculpted likeness disfigured out of fear or iconoclasm, the mummy hacked to pieces for its jewels, or ground to powder to feed the apothecary's stores, if then all physical trace of the subject disappears, the name might still remain.

Expressions of the importance of the name are common enough in Egyptian texts,[28] and even were they not, one could still hardly fail to recognize their importance on the stelae expressing aspirations to immortality on the part of countless Egyptians from the earliest days of the pharaonic state through the Roman occupation.

Serge Sauneron explains the significance of the name in the overall context of Egyptian philosophies of language:

> To pronounce a word, a name, is not only a technique creating in the mind of the hearer the picture which haunts that of the speaker, it is to act on the thing or being mentioned, it is to repeat the initial act of the creator.[29]

For Egyptians, the name partakes of a reality difficult to accede to in our post-Saussurean age. Pascal Vernus speaks through the difference when he points out that

There is nothing arbitrary about the sign among the Egyptians; on the contrary, there is a belief in an essential bond between the signifier and signified, between the name (*rn*) and what it designates. This holds true for all reality, objects, institutions, plants, animals, men, kings, and divinities. Even in Coptic, *rn* can be constructed with the possessive suffix, as is the case with names designating that which is innate and which cannot be acquired.... Correspondingly, the name of a person participates in his being and constitutes a manifestation of him, parallel to his body, in the manner of the *ka*, with which it sometimes identifies.[30]

There is an interesting complication here, in that the subject desires to have his or her name known to future generations, perhaps written in numerous variant forms, but if there are different ways to write it, then the recognizability or identity (i.e., self-sameness and distinction from others) must reside in the vocalization of the name, its sound. (And what irony that the Egyptian writing system takes insufficient account of how that vocalization is to be accomplished, by failing to notate vowels!)

Yet a further perplexity arises from the fact that the name, though it belongs to you, is primarily for the use of others, a token by which they may designate you, a filter between your subjective interiority and the uses and abuses of the outside; here again, the subject faces a potential for dismemberment. In myth this is exemplified in a New Kingdom story in which Isis gains power over Re' by learning his secret name.[31] Similarly, in an ethnographic context, Egyptians seem to have believed that one could harm an enemy by writing his name on a pottery bowl and then shattering the bowl.[32] Yet clearly the name, in particular the voicing of the name, plays a role in Egyptian thought analogous (and likely antecedent) to later Western formulations of personal identity. It is perhaps the most stable marker of identity, and in combination with its epithet, *ma'a-kheru* ($m3^c$-hrw), "justified of voice," centers the performativity of Egyptian religion in the written memorialization of the deceased.

VOICINGS

If the performative context of the offertory or other more elaborate funerary texts suggests the possibility of a reconstitution in closure through the funerary cult, it cannot fully disarm the threat of dismemberment. We find, indeed, that at the very heart of the problem, we are dogged by a persistent fragmentation.

This problem extends, via the alchemy of metonymy and metaphor, beyond a concern for violence to the body proper to violence in the psychic realm. For if we must negotiate the border between human and animal in hieroglyphic writing, analogizing from the heart of an animal to the heart of a human being, then we must as well image the subject in the dismembered corporeality of the heart. This is a serious threat to the integrity of the individual, because the heart has a mind of its own.

Consider the example from an aphorism in the *Sayings of Kha'kheperre'seneb*,

When a heart is steadfast in tribulation, then it is the equal of its lord.[33]

The equation, in its paradoxical bifurcation of the subject, producing the heart apart, exemplifies a dispersion of the subject which we have examined already. But in the case of the heart, the dispersion, or dismemberment, becomes yet more threatening because of a perceived opposition between the self and the heart. The heart for the Egyptians was not a muscle to pump blood but rather the seat of intellective and moral discrimination, that other self which knows what you ought to do even as you do something entirely different. The heart has, then, an oppositional potential which the *ba* or *ka* or body or shadow does not attain. (And this bifurcation can proceed further, can it not, splitting the heart itself into consciousness and conscience?)

This accounts for the precaution taken in mummification during the New Kingdom to provide the corpse with a heart scarab, a large stone scarab beetle on the underside of which is characteristically inscribed the following injunction:

> My heart of my mother, my heart of my mother,
> My heart of my transformations,
> Do not stand up against me as a witness,
> Do not oppose me in the magistracy of gods,
> Do not make enmity against me in the presence of the
>   keeper of the scales,
> You are my *ka* in my body, which is suffused throughout
>   my limbs and which sustains them.[34]

There is indeed a capacity for betrayal in the heart. For if it threatens to provide a record of your conduct and moral quality in the crisis of judgment after death, it may, in life, have been the very tempter who led you into trouble.[35] But if the self cannot be made to cohere about the heart, is there any possibility of finding a stable center of individual identity? Given the vast sweep of Egyptian history, there can be no single answer to such a question. The situation clearly changes over time, and there is reason to surmise that beliefs varied in some degree in accordance with proximity to or distance from the center of power. We are, moreover, in almost every case, limited in our view to that class of Egyptians who were wealthy, powerful, and lucky enough to have some artifact from their lives survive, a stela, a papyrus, a mummy case, or the like.

Acknowledging these limitations, we are nonetheless able to identify a certain performativity underpinning the majority of Egyptian texts, which suggests that the problems of fragmentation and dismemberment, which were so much a part of Egyptian thought, found answers in the phenomenality of voice. This is most obvious and most explicit in the ubiquitous epithet, *ma'a-kheru*.

In the oldest texts in which it appears, the term applies to Horus, characterizing him as truthful in his claim to the throne of Osiris, and victorious, therefore, over his uncle Setekh. The term retains a judicial or legal connotation throughout Egyptian history, but it is most specific here in its vindication of Horus as royal heir before the assembled pantheon. The specificity of usage in this case, however, makes for a close and rather narrow association between the term and the narrative of Horus's contentions with Setekh. This cannot account for the broad application to which we find the term put in other ancient Egyptian texts. To understand that broader application, we must examine in detail the first term in the compound, *ma'a* ($m3^c$), and the abstract noun derived from it, *Ma'at* ($M3^ct$).

Jan Assmann shows the way in his 1988 lectures at the Collège de France. *Ma'a*, as he points out, is a verb or an adjective we might translate provisionally with English words like "true," "real," "rightful," and "ordered." It is perhaps etymologically linked with verbal and adjectival homonyms meaning "present" or "offer," "fit to be offered," "lead," "direct," and with a noun meaning "the temples (of the head)." *Ma'at* is, then, an abstract nominal derivation from *ma'a*.

Ma'at is personified as a goddess and often expressed in a theomorphic icon, the figure of a slender girl, usually seated peacefully with a feather standing upright atop her head as in Figure 1.5. The abstract term is in some ways difficult to pin down, but it is crucially important, as Assmann points out,

If one desires to enlarge the limits of our cultural memory and regain a part of this submerged intellectual continent [of Egyptian ethical thought], it is through the notion of Ma'at that one ought to make a hermeneutic approach. The analysis of texts and images in which this notion is developed can give us a "view from the interior" of the pharaonic world, and can teach us the manner in which the ancient Egyptians themselves lived and interpreted their vision of the world.[36]

Conventional translations may suggest truth, righteousness, justice, order, harmony, balance, right, straightness, sacrifice, and the like.[37] In any given context, one might justify recourse to one or another of these, but there is, of course, no one-to-one correspondence possible between languages, and it is one of the many virtues of Assmann's lecture that he engages and situates the word in numerous contexts in thick description. We can do no better in furthering our discussion here than to rehearse his.

It is important, for one thing, to realize what *ma'at* is not and how we might glean what it is by contrast:

> The great advantage of a textual analysis (reckoning from discourses) over a semiological analysis (reckoning from references) is that one does not risk missing passages which treat of *ma'at* without mentioning the word. This is the case, for example, with texts which speak of *ma'at a contrario*, which is to say, where it is a case of lying, injustice, iniquity, disorder, ingratitude, rebellion, egoism, greediness, etc.[38]

It is also important to ground the discussion historically, especially in the formative periods of the Old and Middle Kingdoms. Assmann's discus-

Figure 1.5. The name of the goddess Ma'at in an inscription from the tomb of Kheruef (TT 192) in El-Khokha on the West Bank opposite Thebes. The name is finely carved in limestone with four phonetic glyphs at the top, followed at the bottom with a determinative picturing the goddess holding an 'ankh sign and with the feather of truth on her head. Author's photograph.

sion, therefore, takes a chronological framework and first relies on the biographies of Old Kingdom officials, in which he finds a grounding for that aspect of *ma'at* which he identifies with social solidarity:

> The aim of an Egyptian education is the man who knows how to listen, homo auditor, the man who hears, who obeys, the man attentive, benevolent, and docile, who bows before one who speaks and accepts the counsel which one gives him. The entirety of Egyptian civilization seems to be founded upon and animated by this faculty of listening to one another. The whole of social life depends on the faculty of understanding one another.[39]

In this context, the tomb and the feast days celebrated there are a means of integrating the self into life and the social memory. The tomb is then, "by its monumentality, its visibility and visitability, a means of remaining present in the life of society."[40] Of great importance, however—and contrary to the common misconception that the civilization of Egypt was static and basically unchanging for its three millennia—is the fact that the individual's mode of survival in and beyond the tomb, and his (or her) relation to *ma'at*, underwent a crucial transformation from the Old Kingdom into the Middle Kingdom.

> Under the Old Kingdom there are always two ways which lead to the state of [blessedness after death], and thereby, to survival: *ma'at* and a career. Each is indispensable. By the former, one obtains affective integration into the social memory; by the latter, one obtains the distinction of an important man. To live on, one needs both: integration and distinction, conformity to *ma'at* and the importance of a social position.
>
> We have said that under the Old Kingdom, *ma'at* was identified with the will of the king. Now, it seems paradoxical that it is not the career, that is to say, in service to the king, where *ma'at* is accomplished, but in service to men. In fact, there is no contradiction. In this epoch, one did not distinguish between the state and society; the king desires that one serve men, he loves solidarity, because solidarity is the foundation of the state. There is no need of a prescriptive ethic in service of the king. It is not a requirement, but a privilege. The advantages are too evident for it to be necessary to make appeal to solidarity. It is not a question of altruism, but of ambition, which, contrary to altruism, is natural and has no need of being aroused. This is, moreover, precisely what changes with the Middle Kingdom, where the dynasty . . . has a clear necessity for propaganda.[41]

In the new view of the ideal individual life, previously separate aspects of the official's life were combined. The distinction of a fine career was integrated with the promotion of social solidarity through individual action:

This new vision is the base of what one might call "the invention of virtue"... a means of integrating the self as well as distinguishing the self.... As successor to the two former paths, *ma'at* and merit, the arrival of virtue is evident in a new vocabulary. The more general term is *nfrw*, "beauty, goodness,'" which corresponds—and would later be translated by—the Greek *aretē*. Other terms are more specialized, such as *jwn nfr*, "good disposition," *qdjt*, "quality," *bj3*, "character," *j3mt*, "grace, gentility," *w3ḥ-jb* "patience, benevolence," etc.[42]

That the concept of *ma'at* is so crucial in judgment after death brings us back to our grounding in the myth of Osiris. For although *ma'at* is the central social and political virtue during the life of an Egyptian, it is also the mark of passage that creates the possibility of divinity in the hereafter.

> The idea of the judgment of the dead is therefore not only a new speculation of magico-theologian scribes on the beyond: it translates a new image which has been made of man, a new anthropological, and even political, conception. Indeed, the man guided by his heart—which will be weighed upon the balance—is no longer dependent upon the initiative and the orders of the king to act..., but receives henceforward orders from his own heart, which therefore takes on responsibility itself. This is a self-directed man—as opposed to the man of the Old Kingdom who was directed by external authority—which is shown by all the discourses which we have studied, inscriptions from tombs, wisdom texts, and even magico-funerary literature.[43]

This has direct relevance to the evolution of funerary belief as we see it in the fragments of Egypt upon which we are so completely dependent. There, in connection with *ma'at*, we find the link between (the related verb/adjective) *ma'a* and voice. On first run-through, take the adjective *ma'a* to mean "straight" or "true," and the following noun, "voice," as an expression of manner, for "true of voice" or "true with regard to voice."

The long conflict between Horus and Setekh is at last resolved only when Horus is declared *"ma'a-kheru"* in the court of his grandsire Geb. He is "true of voice" when he claims his father's kingdom, and he is therefore "justified" (another common translation for the phrase).

In the mortal world, too, the designation *"ma'a-kheru"* seems first to have referred to litigation and the justification of *A* versus *B*, a judgment replacing combat with the institution of a social contract. The designation of one party to a given conflict as justified, even "triumphant" (yet another translation), necessarily rendered the other culpable. That the *voice* is specified here is central to our enterprise, and a logical consequence of the legal context from which the expression *ma'a-kheru* developed.

As Jan Assmann has pointed out, however, a crucial change takes place in the semantic field of *ma'a-kheru* as the symptom of a transformation in consciousness of profound consequences.

> The individual is no longer confronted before the divine tribunal with an adversary, but with Ma'at herself. The confrontation assumes from this fact a significance altogether different, which translates itself by the image of a balance and the action of the weighing of the heart.[44]

Already as early as the *Pyramid Texts*, we find the designation *ma'a-kheru* attached to the names of Horus and deceased kings.[45] The references attest to (and perhaps, even, perform) divine consent for royal dominion and are not, at first, associated with Osiris. Stephen Quirke explains:

> The justification of Horus before the tribunal of the gods gave meaning and form also to the world beyond the grave. In the Middle Kingdom the tribunal of the afterlife is cited in the Coffin Texts only as a regular Egyptian court where petition could be made concerning any affair that one wished to settle in the public domain, anything that we might call a legal case. In the transition from the Middle to the New Kingdom the tribunal suddenly became not an arbitration board within the next life but a passport control point for permission to enter that life at all. The deceased was led by Horus to his father Osiris and a tribunal of forty-two assessor deities who witnessed the weighing of his heart against the figure of Right. If the heart did not prove full of goodness but was instead shown to be wracked with wrongs committed against society and against the divine order, then the person could not enter the underworld, the kingdom of Osiris. If the deceased passed the test, he or she would be declared to be like Horus, "true of voice," that is "justified" in the eyes of the tribunal; this tag of "justification" permitted entry into the company of the blessed dead. The deceased thus acquired both an identity as Osiris, guaranteeing resurrection with Osiris in his Underworld, and the quality of Horus, as "true of voice," and from the New Kingdom to the Roman Period those two designations almost invariably occur respectively before and after the name of the person in funerary contexts.[46]

The distinction Quirke makes between the *quality* of Horus and *identity* as Osiris is important. Only pharaohs are identified with Horus, but Osiris becomes the standard focus of personal identity after death for private individuals as well (see Fig. 1.6). So we find that the characterization *ma'a-kheru* is expanded beyond the adversarial context of the law court to a broader statement about the moral integrity of the individual, and the epithet moves from Horus to his father Osiris, and to each "Osiris Such-and-such" who comes justified in his being to the life beyond.

34   THE REVERENTIAL SLAUGHTER

Figure 1.6. The deceased facing judgment in the court of Osiris. To the left sits Osiris flanked by Isis. The four sons of Horus (who have special roles in the funerary cult) stand before Osiris on the petals of a lotus. The deceased makes obeisance to Osiris. A beast waits to devour the deceased should he prove morally unfit for eternal life. Ibis-headed Thoth stands to the right, and before him, the scales on which the deceased's heart is to be weighed. This representation is from the demotic papyrus of Pamonthes (pBerlin P3135) from the year 63 C.E. It attests to the survival of Egyptian funerary belief well into the common era. After Seeber, *Untersuchungen*, p. 52.

EVERY MAN A KING

The genealogy of voice in the reintegration of the body of Egypt finds straightforward political figuration in the struggle and reconciliation of Horus and Setekh, as we saw earlier, but such a figuration, enclosed by royal monopoly and bound to the cyclical eruption and containment of antagonism, leaves little room for any voice other than the apocalyptic voice of the god king. Yet it is, paradoxically, voice which most intimately and effectively situates Osiris as a personal subject of knowledge, and it is only through voice that we might ourselves come to an awareness of such presence in the worship of the dead. We must approach the question of voice again, then, on a different tack, not to find our object in the story of a victory, but rather through the instantiation of a voice in reading, a voice that speaks to personal justification.

Some of the difficulties such an approach entails can be seen in a reading of the stela of a Twelfth Dynasty grandee named Iykhernofret (Fig. 1.7).[47] We can only situate reading/s of such a text as a chain of engagements among which there is no recoverable authoritative moment. It is certainly significant that this stela is the grandest of a set of eleven. Clearly, it was taken from the Middle Kingdom cemetery at Abydos, but the circumstances of its excavation were not adequately recorded. Whether the collection of stelae was intended to accompany the burials of some or all the individuals to whom they are dedicated is open to question. They may rather have represented an Abydene presence for people actually buried elsewhere. In either case, the site of Abydos, near the reputed tomb of Osiris, is central to any understanding of them.

The text of the Iykhernofret Stela consists of 24 lines of text covering the surface of a large round-topped stela of limestone with a lunette of emblematic hieroglyphs and a scene at the bottom representing the principal, Iykhernofret, receiving offerings from his surviving relatives. "The" text on the stela is, however, not one text, but several, and although the interrelation among these texts as a whole must eventually be considered, it is also necessary to consider the fragmentation—even the degree of mutual effacement—these texts effect one upon another as one reads them. Titularies abound, and they are given pride of place on the physical surface, occupying the raised border of the stela as well as the lunette. The full fivefold titulary of Kha'kaure', Senusert III, appears only once, but four of the names therein are repeated several times in prominent positions. Iykhernofret's titulary appears four times, in different variants.[48] Osiris and Horus are named repeatedly, with various epithets, and the vignettes on the stela contain captions sometimes giving merely the name of the individual pictured, sometimes more information.

There is a part of reading something that consists in not reading, which is to say that even in recognizing the diverse kinds of texts on this surface (as on the surface of a soup can or a book cover) we give precedence to some over others. The titularies are heavily formulaic and predictable in content, so despite their physical prominence, a focused reading might be inclined to skip over them to get to what is not formulaic, what is unique about this particular stela, and it is here that we see why the Iykhernofret Stela has attracted the attention of several generations of scholars (see Fig. 1.8).

Proceeding in this manner ourselves we look beyond most of the titles to the concentrated body of hieroglyphs below the lunette and above the representation of Iykhernofret before an offering table. This main text is itself two texts. The first is a legal document, a royal decree proclaiming the privilege and responsibility of Iykhernofret to act as the king's surrogate in the mysteries of Osiris, performed upriver from the royal capital, at Abydos. The second text gives an account of what it was Iykhernofret accomplished.

The first text is spoken from the person of pharaoh and not only relates the specific commission to Iykhernofret, but gives as well an intriguing

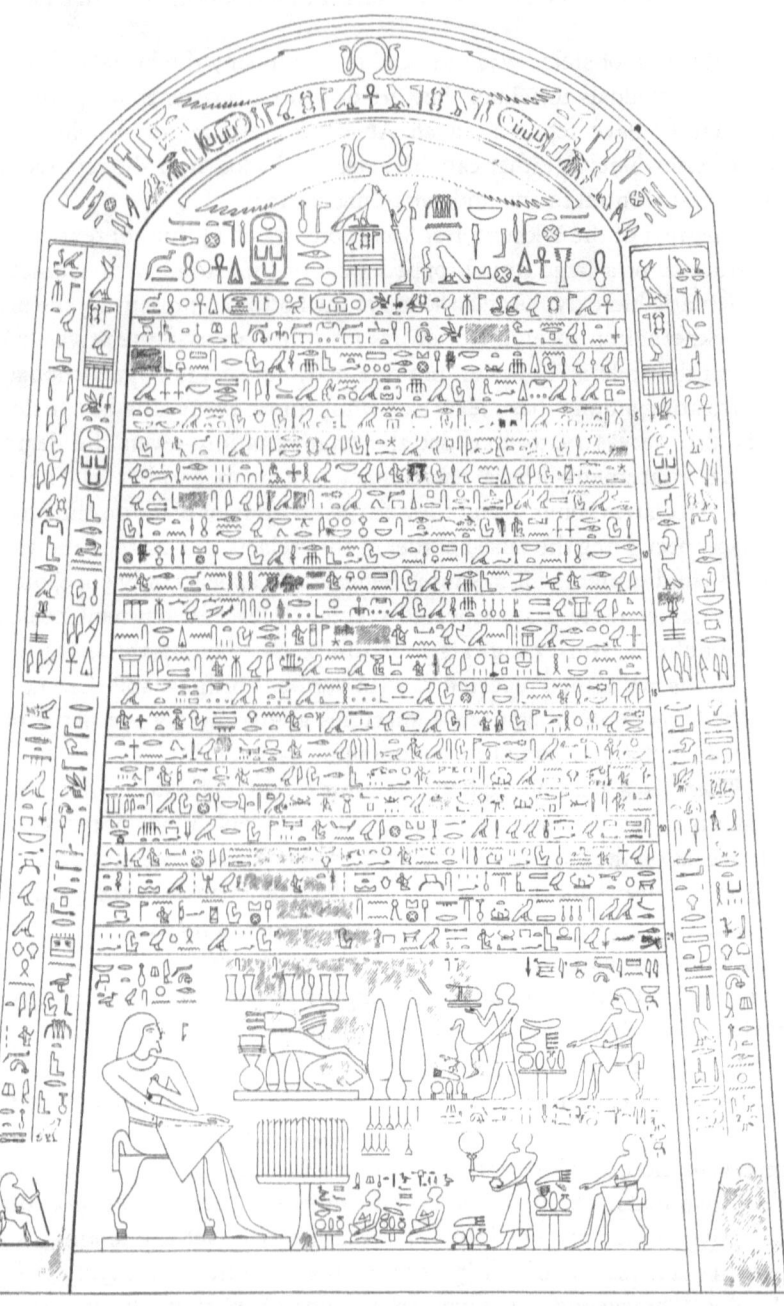

Figure 1.7. The Iykhernofret Stela. Though now chipped and pitted, the stela is a unique account of rituals associated with the cult of Osiris at Abydos in the Twelfth Dynasty. Ägyptisches Museum, Berlin (1204). Line drawing after Schäfer, *Mysterien des Osiris*, pl. 1.

account of the reasons he has been chosen to undertake this task. The passage is awkwardly encumbered by dependent clauses and peppered with the exclusive prerogative of the first person royal pronoun. It seems only fair in translating it to counterfeit the English of a royal decree:

King's Decree to Hereditary Noble and Prince of the Region, Royal Treasurer, Unique Friend, Master of the Houses of Gold and the Houses of Silver, Master of Sealbearers, Iykhernofret, Justified of Voice.

We deign to grant herewith that thou embark for Abydos in Tawer, there to stablish monuments for Our Father Osiris, First of Westerners, and to effect His Secret Likeness in fine gold, the which He granted Us, Triumphant Victor, to bring forth from the land of Nubia,
and in this consequence it is to thee to undertake such in the manner most effective for Our Father Osiris;
and We send thee confident thou wilt fulfil this to Our Pleasure in that thou wert brought unto Us, Our Disciple, and wert become Our Foster Child, Unique Disciple of Our Palace; and We created thee, moreover, Companion Royal when thou wert but six and twenty; and We did this, discerning in thee one excellent of counsel, articulate in speech, one come with prudence from the very womb,
Thus do We dispatch thee to accomplish this, in cognizance that there be no man else who should accomplish this entire.

Go then, and return to Us when thou hast accomplished in entirety the likeness of This Our Command.

Only now does Iykhernofret himself speak, and it is worth noting that he does so from the perspective of completed action. "I have acted in accord with His Majesty's every command," he says,[49] giving a detailed account of some of the tasks he accomplished at Abydos. It is this portion of the stela that has attracted the most attention from Egyptologists, because it gives the best extant account, from pharaonic Egypt, of the rituals and celebrations of the festival of Osiris.[50] That account is, all the same, frustratingly selective, and grants the reader specificity in mainly peripheral matters, the description of the materials used for ritual objects, and so on. The festival, like most Egyptian religious celebrations, included an important procession on the Nile—three different boats or barques are mentioned—and there was clearly some sort of reenactment of the battle between Setekh and the forces of Osiris. Iykhernofret makes clear that he himself directed the climactic part of the festival. Full translations of the

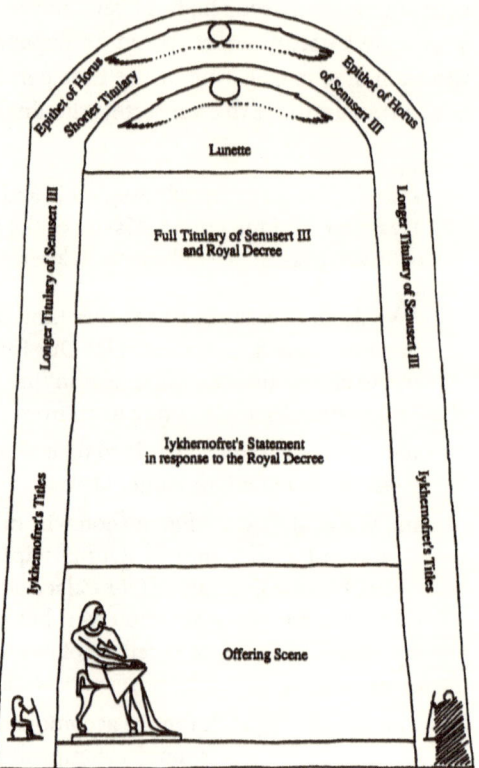

Figure 1.8. Schematic drawing of the Iykhernofret Stela showing the placement of different texts.

account can be found elsewhere,[51] but excerpts from it will serve to lay the groundwork for further discussion.

> I performed "His Beloved Son" for Osiris Foremost of Westerners, I fit out His great [Barque] of ever and always, I made for Him a portable shrine to display the beauty of the Foremost of Westerners, with gold and silver, lapis and bronze, and *sesnedjem* wood and cedar. . . .
>
> I supervised construction of the Neshmet Barque and made the cabin myself. I adorned the breast of the god of Abydos with lapis, turquoise, fine gold, and all manner of precious stones: ornaments for the limbs of god. . . .
>
> I had Wepwawet go forth, setting out in the protection of His Father, I drove the enemy away from the Neshmet Barque, I defeated the foes of Osiris. I made the great procession. I had the god's ship set sail with Thoth at the helm. . . . I consecrated the way of the Lord to His western mansion in Peqer. . . . I gave counsel to Wenennofru on that day of the great battle and vanquished all His enemies on the sandbanks of Nedyet. I caused that

He proceed into the Great Barque; it raised His beauty high. I gladdened the hearts of those in the Eastern Desert and brought joy to those in the Western Desert when they saw the beauty of the Neshmet Barque.

The god is returned to his palace after his manifestation to "those in the Eastern Desert" and "those in the Western Desert": namely, the blessed dead in the necropolises on both sides of the Nile. Living participants also, presumably, found this a festive and celebratory occasion, but the events of the festival proper are of less cogency to our current line of inquiry than the economy of subjective voice in the passage, and that is what we must come back to now. Note, first of all, the assumption of a role on Iykhernofret's part. He performs "His Beloved Son" for Osiris. This of course reads at one level as an acknowledgment of Iykhernofret's portrayal of Horus in the rituals, symbolically vanquishing the enemy of Osiris. Another substitution is suggested in the end of the citation, where Iykhernofret takes credit for making the blessed dead joyful, even though it is the "beauty" or "goodness" (the Egyptian *nfrw* is ambiguous) of Osiris that arouses them.

Iykhernofret's participation in the event represents, in itself, yet a further form of substitution: theoretically, it was pharaoh who, as god king, was sole celebrant for all state religious ritual, but this being a practical impossibility given the ubiquity of temples and the frequency of religious offices, pharaoh very typically delegated his authority in a wide variety of religious performances to favored courtiers. This too, however, must be viewed in another context, that of myth, where the living pharaoh is, after all, Horus. Thus the present occasion produces a chain of substitutions whereby "His Beloved Son" = Horus = Pharaoh = Iykhernofret. It is at this point that we must come back to a consideration of the subject in Egyptian thought, because we are witness here to one of the most potent and dynamic paradoxes of the theocratic nature of the Egyptian subject. And we must now return from the specific focus on the texts we have just considered to look at how these texts take their place among the other, more formulaic ones in their disposition across the surface of the stela. Not only do these texts compete with one another for the reader's attention, in their interaction, they also create the reading subject.

The reading occurs under the aegis of Horus, precisely, Horus of Behdet, the victorious son represented by the winged solar disk. This disk crowns the stela, centered at the top of the entire composition. The wings of Hor-Behdet are augmented and extended by symmetrical writings of his epithets, which are shadowed by royal titularies tracing the same curve at the top of the stela, just under the winged disk.

Figure 1.9. Detail from the Iykhernofret Stela. The subject, Iykhernofret, receives offerings. From the relief at the bottom of the stela.

The lines of the winged disk are echoed in the curve of the top of the stela and in an attenuated glyph of the sky encircling it. There below, on the lateral border of the stela, we find fourfold titularies of the king stretching halfway down the sides, giving way at the bottom of each half to titularies of Iykhernofret himself. In the lower corners of the stela, we find small figures of Iykhernofret, determinatives for his name; on the left he is seated, on the right he stands with a staff of office (see Fig. 1.9). This raised frame, then, encircles with larger glyphs the royal decree and ritual narrative in the central body of the stela.

But we must notice the vignettes that lie between the frame and the central text as well (see Fig. 1.10). In the lunette at the top, we again find the winged disk of Horus of Behdet, mirroring the winged disk at the top of the stela. Here it shelters an emblematic text in which a statue of Osiris (note the plinth) bestows life and power upon the royal falcon in one of the titles of Senusert III. Reaching to the right and left of this central emblem are, respectively, epithets of Osiris and epithets of Senusert, as well as his prenomen, Kha'kaure'. After Osiris's epithets comes the formula, "He gives life and stability like Re'," while after the pharaoh's epithets and titles comes the formula, "given life like Re' forever."

If the titles and epithets that surround the reading of the unique texts on the Iykhernofret Stela are utterly predictable and formulaic, they are,

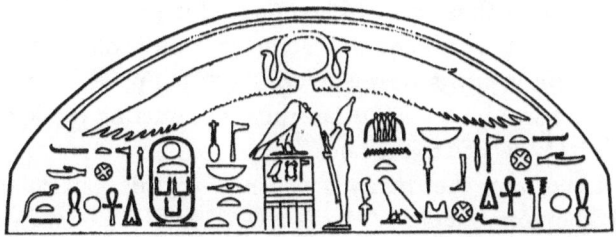

Figure 1.10. Lunette from the Iykhernofret Stela. Emblematic hieroglyphs place the ritual under the protection of Horus of Behdet, indicated by the winged disk at the top. Underneath, Osiris offers life and dominion to the *serekh* of Senusert III.

nonetheless, indispensable to the textual performance the stela enables. Surrounding the unique texts, these formulas seem a kind of protective matrix within which the individual accomplishment of Iykhernofret can be acknowledged. Yet the dependence of Iykhernofret's biography is itself mirrored in a complex and fascinating way by the dependence of the titles, epithets, the royal prerogatives, and divine embraces on the identity of Iykhernofret. Their mutual implication is achieved in an eloquent balance in this particular case, but it is, nonetheless, the most characteristic element in even the most hackneyed and clumsily executed offering formula; this mutual implication is, indeed, the central performative myth of Egyptian funerary religion and its central paradox.

As we saw earlier while considering the offering formula, the situation of the funerary cult proposes that the offerings proffered in the memorial chapel of the deceased are "an offering which the king gives" to Osiris (and perhaps other deities), which are in turn to be passed on for the eventual benefit of the *ka* of the deceased. The process so far might be schematized as follows:

Pharaoh → Osiris → the *ka* of the Deceased

but this must be bracketed further to acknowledge the material economy of offerings, resulting in the following:

Descendents (in the name of pharaoh) → Osiris → the *ka* of the Deceased

The fuller implications of this performance are not readily apparent with a bare offering formula. There are, at least, two problems that obscure the cyclicality of relations, but the Iykhernofret Stela when considered from the point of view of both its texts and its figural representations, fills out the economy of the performance in an important way. Thus, although the entire stela is written under the aegis of Horus of

Behdet, and would thus seem to be "under his protection," as it were, when we consider the emblematic statement at the center of the lunette it is, on the contrary, Osiris who is offering life and power to the pharaoh, not the other way around. Thus far, then, the offering the king gives to Osiris finds its way back to the king.

More important, the dramatis personae in this particular context, wherein Iykhernofret acts as "His Beloved Son" for pharaoh, allow the insertion of the private subject, Iykhernofret himself, in the space of the royal subject. This is, moreover, altered in consideration of Iykhernofret as Osiris-Iykhernofret, who then, as Osiris, returns the blessings of offering to the divinity of pharaoh, under whose protection he acts.

The movement in the locus of subject from the top of the stela to its bottom echoes the transposition of the subject from the royal center to the individual and personal center of Iykhernofret as recipient of offerings. The whole is, incidentally, all the while observed by the small figures in the lower right and left corners of the stela, lexical determinatives for Iykhernofret and representatives of his identity.

The subject Iykhernofret is ramified across the surface of the stela, then, explicitly pictured three times at the bottom, but aspiring to the position of Osiris himself, even as he also stands in for the king as "His Beloved Son [Horus]." The subject's position literally spreads over and across the stela, not requiring a single focal point from without, even as the eye, in reading an Egyptian painting, is not constrained to a single exterior point of observation.[52] So also, the subject, as one of the blessed dead, exists within a multiplicity of "transformations" between this world and eternity.

Here we should recall again the formula of offering, which also operates through many levels of substitution. It is literally "an offering which the king gives" for the eventual sustenance of the beloved deceased, but it is, of course, not the king himself who brings the food and drink to the tomb in all but the rarest cases. Here the individual private subject enacts the king to set off a chain of giving from himself (or herself) through the king to Osiris (most usually, it is Osiris, but other gods may be named either in addition to, or in place of, him). Osiris is then expected to transfer the offerings to the *ka* of the deceased, but that deceased, from at least as early as the Middle Kingdom, is him- or herself explicitly named as "Osiris Such-and-such," a conventional designation of the decedent. So the filters of identity through which the gift passes come to suggest filters of a subject who enacts the king (whether the living king, Horus, or the dead king, Osiris) even as his private individual identity is preserved.

One can sometimes observe royalist tendencies among Egyptologists, and there are those who take this economy of substitution as evidence of the usurpation of royal prerogatives, first by the nobility, and then by anyone who can lay claim to a tomb or funerary stela. There is, it is true, a historical process involved here, and the spread of the subject, in the voice of the king, to an increasingly broad cross section of Egyptian society can be observed from the First Intermediate Period, through the Middle Kingdom, New Kingdom, and so on. This historical trajectory, however, is secondary to an epistemological stance that is not about usurpation but rather about the framing of the subject within the myth of royal identity: every man a king.

Here, indeed, lies the most important thing about Osiris. He appears not as the object of a narrative construct but rather in a figuring of subjective voice.

SUPPLEMENTARY: THE LANGUAGE OF THE GODS

2

In speaking of the letter, Derrida chooses death. He inserts the letter *a* in place of the letter *e* to make a *différance* in difference, discreetly, ingeniously, perhaps disingenuously, suggesting the "necessity" of such a (mis)formation.

"This discrete graphic intervention, which is made neither in the first place nor simply to shock," he says,

> This marked difference between two apparently vocal notations, between two vowels, remains purely graphic: it is written or read, but it is not heard. One cannot hear it, and we will see wherein it surpasses as well the order of the understood. It is posited as a mute mark, a tacit monument, I should even say as a pyramid, thinking thus not only of the form of the letter when it is printed as a capital, but of that passage in Hegel's *Encyclopedia* where the body of the sign is compared to the Egyptian pyramid. The *a* of the difference, therefore, is not heard, it remains silent, secret and discrete as a tomb: *oikēsis*. Thus let us mark this place, in anticipation, the familial residence and tomb of the proper where is produced, in *différance*, the economy of death. This stone, provided one knows how to decipher the legend, is not far from signaling the death of the dynast.[1]

For all its lip service to sound, to the phonetic quality of language which registers no difference even while writing "*différance*," this passage is visual in its logic. It presents a string of substitutions, icons of the letter, leading from the apparent insignificance of the mute intrusion of *a* in the place of *e*, to a change of case in *A*, then to the monumental *A*, of the *pyramid*, to the image of *death* (shall we say a skull?), the founder(ing) of the line.

The essay so begun proceeds with brilliance and obsessiveness into the heart of *différance*, a seminal example of the agon of presence in language, which will come before us again. For the time being, I would pull at merely one thread of its significance: the link (of course) with Egypt and Egyptian. The engagement is already acknowledged in Derrida's reference to Hegel, a choice site of bewilderment and misapprehension before the hieroglyphs.

In this Hegelian context, Derrida comes with boldness and precision to the heart of a problem long bedeviling the reading of "Oriental" languages. He baffles the phonocentrism of Saussurean linguistics with the simplest of means, a single letter, but his deconstruction itself remains boxed within an Orientalism equating the "tacit monument" of the pyramid with death, the death, specifically, of the ruler. (Derrida's "dynaste," comes from the Greek *dynastēs*, implicitly an Oriental despot.) And the intrusive *a*, in its obstinate refusal to sound, speaks as much to the death of a possibility (Gk. *dynamis*) as the death of a master.

THE CODE

The myth that Egyptian writing is somehow "other" is woven from a warp of fantasies about the death of Egyptian as a readable language and a weft of the erroneous assertion that alphabetic writing is a full, perfect, and sufficient representation of the spoken word. Already among the Greeks, misconceptions about hieroglyphs encouraged a charade, a willful misunderstanding of a language they could have naturally mastered (while there were still millions of native speakers of Egyptian). To be fair, in fact, some Greeks did manage to learn to speak Egyptian, even the Cleopatra of legend. Note well, however: she was the seventh Cleopatra, the last of the three-hundred-year-long Ptolemaic line, but the first of those Ptolemies who learned how to speak Egyptian.[2]

Some Greeks went further, even learning to read and write in Egyptian as well, but generally only in pursuit of a specific purpose, a skill, or domain of knowledge, and not for the broader understanding of Egyptian civilization. The language was clearly stigmatized among the Greeks, and there were cases in which people manifestly able to write Egyptian were declared to be illiterate.[3]

In general, Egyptian writing was beyond not the capacity of the Greeks but rather their will. They did not open their minds to its principles. In the first century B.C.E., for instance, Diodorus Siculus makes the following assessment of the hieroglyphs:

> I should say something about the letters . . . called by the Egyptians hieroglyphs—so as not to omit anything from their antiquities. It happens that the shapes of these [letters] of theirs are like those of all sorts of animals and of the extremities of humans, and even of tools and artificial things. For among them the art of writing [*hē grammatikē*] does not transmit the underlying meaning through the combination of syllables, but rather out of the appearance of the things transcribed there, and by metaphor allied to memory. For they draw the hawk and the crocodile, moreover the serpent and, among human body parts, the eye, the hand, the face and other things of this kind. Now the hawk signifies for them anything that happens quickly, because this animal is more or less the swiftest of all winged things. By means of suitable metaphors, this meaning is transferred onto all other swift things, and so it is done for all the things that are related to the objects I just mentioned. The crocodile is significant of every kind of baseness; the eye is the watchman of justice and the guardian of the whole body. Of the extremities, the right hand with its fingers outstretched signifies the getting of a livelihood, and the left hand drawn in on itself signifies the watching and guardianship of possessions. And the same rule holds for the other sign-types, those taken from the body, from tools and from all other things: by following the appearances lodged in each of these, and after having exercised their souls with many years of effort and memory, the [scribes] are able to read all their writings fluently.[4]

Diodorus is not completely incorrect,[5] but he takes as his point of departure a dissimilarity with Greek (in the apparent iconicity of hieroglyphs). By failing to account for that aspect of Egyptian writing which is *like* Greek, its phoneticism, he oversimplifies, even as he mystifies, the hieroglyphs.

Intellectuals of the Roman empire seem to have misunderstood the simple phonetic use of hieroglyphs utterly, even though it is preponderant in even the most ideographically rich Egyptian texts.[6] In his *Hieroglyphika* (ca. 4–5 C.E.), "Horapollo" reflected this general misunderstanding by seeing in written Egyptian nothing but symbols entailed in, and owing all their significance to, chains of metaphor and strings of imagistic association, which, he asserts, could only be mastered after long study as a member of an alien priestly class.

At about the same time, Ammianus Marcellinus spoke of Egyptian as follows:

> Not as nowadays, when fixed and easy series of letters express whatever the mind of man may conceive, did the ancient Egyptians also write; but

individual characters stood for individual nouns and verbs; and sometimes they meant whole phrases. The principle of this thing for a time it will suffice to illustrate with these two examples: by a vulture they represent the word "nature," because as natural history records, no males can be found among these birds; and under the figure of a bee making honey they designate "a king," showing by this imagery that in a ruler sweetness should be combined with a sting as well.[7]

In medieval Europe, Egypt retained a reputation as the most ancient source of wisdom and science, and there may well have been an extensive folklore of Egypt. But knowledge of Egypt (not to mention the Egyptian language) came only through the Bible and the slender and exclusive thread of Hermeticism, until finally, in the Renaissance, with renewed access to classical writing, Europe began to regain some sense of Nile civilization. Misconceptions colored everything, but contact with a broader world brought a new interest in Egyptian.

The seventeenth-century German scholar Athanasius Kircher displayed a brilliant curiosity about the language, proposing the use of Coptic as a key to its decipherment (*Prodomus coptus sive ægyptiacus*, 1636) and quite correctly perceived a conceptual similarity behind the Egyptian and Chinese systems of writing. Kircher was, however, bizarrely wrongheaded in his fantastic "readings" of Egyptian texts. During the Enlightenment, an increasing awareness of China and Chinese helped to spur on attempts to decipher Egyptian. The French Orientalist C. Joseph de Guignes, for example, believed China to have once been a colony of Egypt and tried in 1785 to demonstrate the unity of Chinese and Egyptian. In this he was of course mistaken, but he did make certain contributions to the study of Coptic, the last surviving descendant of Egyptian. His colleague, the abbé Jean-Jacques Barthélemy, not only first suggested the link between hieroglyphs and the alphabet, but also first enunciated the significance of the cartouche, a crucial step in the decipherment.[8]

Near the end of the eighteenth century, comparisons between Egyptian and Chinese diminished in favor of a contrastive pairing of Egyptian with Sanskrit. The political entanglements of Britain and France went hand in hand with academic enterprise, with profound consequences for the ways in which Europe constructed itself vis-à-vis "the Orient" and Oriental languages; if the British and the French were rivals for control of the Nile Valley, so also were they in competition in India, and Indian culture had recently risen steeply in the esteem of European intellectuals, even as their regard for China had declined.[9] It was, then, in these last decades of the eighteenth century, that the jurist and philologist Sir William Jones "discovered" Sanskrit, and discovered as well the Indo-European language family through the observation of deep lexical, syntactic, and morphological similarities between Greek and Latin, on the one hand, and Sanskrit, on the other.

Jones's demonstration of the common stock of Greek, Latin, Germanic, Slavic, and Indic languages in Indo-European was an extraordinary milestone in the development of linguistics and our understanding of human prehistory, but in virulent combination with newly emerging theories of race and racial difference and the emergence of Orientalism as an epistemic domain, it provided an intellectual ground for the imperialist and colonialist expansion of the great powers of Europe. In such a context, the rivalry of France and Britain prefigures the decipherment of Egyptian, and the Rosetta Stone, housed securely in the British Museum in

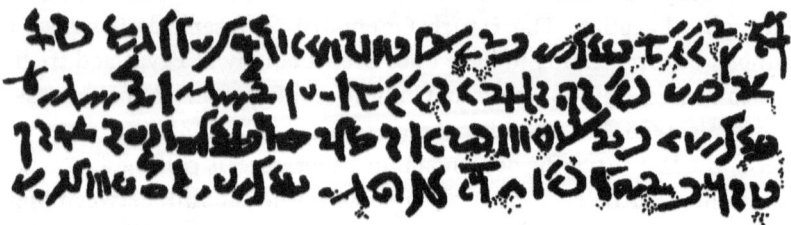

Figure 2.1. Details from the Rosetta Stone showing passages from the (top) hieroglyphic, (center) demotic, and (bottom) Greek texts inscribed on the stone. British Museum, London (EA 24). After Quirke and Andrews, *The Rosetta Stone*.

London—even though it was discovered by French soldiers in the western Nile Delta—stands in concretely both for that rivalry and for the decipherment of Egyptian. (See Fig. 2.1.)

DECIPHERMENT

An account of the decipherment of the hieroglyphs should begin with Jean-François Champollion, because it was he who crossed a certain threshold in the (mis)understanding of ancient Egyptian. Reshuffling the assumptions of his mystified forefathers in this enterprise, he made advance enough in the writing of Egypt that he could conventionally be said to read the language.

"Conventionally," I say, though, because the threshold at which one "reads" is conventionally determined (and surprisingly indeterminate). Champollion was never able to "read" Egyptian the way you and I read English—which is to take nothing away from his achievement. One point is, of course, that none of us can read Egyptian the way we read English, because Egyptian can no longer be pronounced (as we shall see below). Yet we *can* "read" Egyptian better than Champollion, not merely because of technical advances in the lexical and grammatical analysis of the language, but because we live in a more diverse world, a world in which "knowledge" can be more broadly constructed.

Even today, moreover, a pall of controversy and scandal hangs over the assertion that it was Champollion who first made the "great leap" in deciphering the hieroglyphs. Wasn't it, rather, the English polymath Thomas Young (1773–1829) or the Swedish diplomat Johan Åkerblad (1763–1819)? Indeed, the idea of a "great leap" is itself suspiciously romantic. It would suggest that a genius, Champollion, happened along and single-handedly, in a flash of otherworldy brilliance, hit upon a fundamental secret, thereby lifting the pall of centuries and making Egyptian comprehensible.

Such a tale does inadequate justice to Champollion's untiring struggle to read the language and rests on the same prejudice about Egyptian that bedeviled Horapollo, Kircher, and the others, the assumption that Egyptian is, as a written language, somehow alien to the "normal" operations of writing. Holding such a view may lead one to fantasize that hieroglyphics allow a direct inscription of ideas, immediately accessible to the mind without the intervention of sound and are, hence, superior to writing systems that use alphabets. Or it may lead one to consider hieroglyphics a primitive evolutionary stage on the way to the alphabetic telos, hence inferior to writing systems that use alphabets. Either way, the argument hinges on a claim of difference; in its simplest form, on a crude dichotomy between sound, on the one hand, and symbol, figure, or idea, on the other.

Lexically, the dichotomy is constructed between the words "phonogram" and "ideogram" (or "ideograph"). Thus, a lexical binarism is assumed to reflect a polarity in the means at our disposal for writing.[10] (Whether or not this is merely a matter of semantics, we shall see later, but for now it will be useful to review certain etymological details.)

"Ideogram" derives from (1) *ideo-*, a form of "idea" used in combination with a second element, also seen in the word "ideology," and (2) *-gram*, an element used in combination to create words relating to either (a) writing or (b) units of measure (here, the former is more appropriate).

"Phonogram" derives from (1) *phono-*, an element used in combination to impart the notion "sound," "speech," or "tone," and (2) *-gram*, as above.

The resulting polarity relies on the contrast between *ideo-* and *phono-*, so it will suffice to limit subsequent etymological inquiry to those two lexical strains.

In that context, it is worth noting that *phono-* can be traced back to the Greek words *phōnē*, "speech," "tone," "voice," and *phanai*, "speak."

The word "idea," from the Greek *idea*, requires more explication, since the latter carries with it the heavy philosophical baggage of the Platonic "Idea," but not the common contemporary English meaning, "plan," "scheme," or "errant thought" (as in "It's just an idea I had" or "What a great idea!").

More important still is the rooting of *idea* in *idein*, the infinitive of a defective verb meaning "see" and "know." This word is believed to be derived from an Indo-European root *weid-*, which has cognates in Latin, Balto-Slavic, Celtic, Germanic, and Indo-Iranian as well as Greek. In many of those language families it relates to the verb "know" as well as to the verb "see."

At heart, then, the polarity between ideogram and phonogram parallels that between sight and sound, but the cohabitation of knowledge and sight in Indo-European *weid-* has seriously confused the issue. "Phonogram" remains, by contrast, a relatively simple notion relating to "sound" without the inconvenient obtrusion of "knowledge."

A third term, "logogram," must be brought into the discussion here. As before, the element *-gram* in "logogram" indicates writing. The element *logo-* derives from the Greek *logos*, at its most basic, a word that sometimes means "word." The term is not coextensive with the English "word," however; and among its meanings we must also recognize a long list of English terms relating to spoken discourse and thought: talk, speech, discourse, promise, consent, story, language, proverb, narrative, oration, proposition, ration, reason, opinion, and analogy, not to mention the complex metaphysical constructions of the Platonic *logos* and Christian *Logos*. "Logogram," therefore, has a range of meaning as complex as that of "ideogram," but extending through the association of sound with thought even as "ideogram" extends through the association of sight with thought.

One of the great contributions of Champollion and Young was the identification of phonograms, that is to say, phonetically deployed glyphs in the hieroglyphic inscription on the Rosetta Stone. (Åkerblad had already identified phonetic renderings of several names in the demotic section of the inscription.)

In 1819, Young became the first to publish the transcription of a Ptolemaic royal name from the hieroglyphic inscription, and while it remains controversial whether Champollion built upon this achievement or arrived at the same insight independently, it is clear that the name both men first identified in their investigations was "Ptolemy" (or, more correctly, "Ptolemaios").

This name had been taken by generations of Greek rulers of Egypt after Alexander's conquest of 332 B.C.E. On the Rosetta Stone it was found enclosed in an oval called a cartouche, as are all royal names in hieroglyphic script, conveniently setting the text contained therein apart from its surroundings. In the case of PTOLEMAIOS, the glyphs inside the cartouche are read as below:

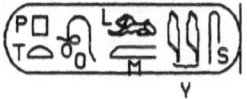

In early 1822, Champollion proceeded to identify the name of Cleopatra on an obelisk that had just been transported to Europe, and before long, he had confirmed the readings of other names as well:

This was, indeed, a very important milestone in the decipherment, but it has all too often been portrayed as the decisive moment. Champollion himself realized, however, that this was simply a first step. Because the names he had identified were all Greek names, he felt for some time that he had merely stumbled upon the Egyptian way of transcribing foreign words, as the subtitle of his celebrated *Lettre à M. Dacier* declares: *"on the alphabet of phonetic hieroglyphs employed by the Egyptians to inscribe the names, surnames, and titles of Greek and Roman sovereigns upon their monuments."*[11]

The decipherment of "Ptolemy," "Cleopatra," "Berenike," and so on, has also been characterized as a breakthrough based solely on the discovery of the phonogram in Egyptian, but it could not have happened without the equally important recognition of the cartouche, and the cartouche, having no pronunciation in this case, remains an exclusively visual device for indicating difference in the textual environment, an "ideogram," in one sense of the word.[12]

Champollion, in proving decisively that the hieroglyphs contained important phonetic elements, struck the most powerful blow to his day against the "ideographic" fallacy that they allowed direct access to "ideas" without the mediation of language. But his success in this particular sphere also contributed to a notion that writing was, at its best, nothing other than the phonetic transcription of a natural language. To this day, the common assumption holds that the alphabet is the normative and exemplary way to write, that the one-to-one correspondence between abstract written forms and the sounds of a natural language is the goal toward which higher civilizations progress, given time, and that, thus, in their invention of the alphabet, the Greeks had (yet again) demonstrated their superiority to the other ancient civilizations of the Near East.

There are a number of problems with such an assumption, however. First, the alphabet does not in fact entail a one-to-one correspondence between abstract written signs and the sounds of a natural language. (In Greek alone there are, even at the most elementary level, cases where the correspondence is not between one sign and one sound, but rather between one sign and two sounds: Ψ, for example, might just as well have been written with two signs, as it was in the so-called red alphabets: whether as ΦΣ or ΠΣ.[13]

This example is trivial, a mere inconsistency, you might say, and it is true that classical Greek seems, from our current remove, to have maintained an admirable degree of consistency between its written forms and pronunciation. This is simply speculation, however, and to come back to the point we began with, it is merely an illusion that a one-to-one correspondence exists between the forms of an alphabetic writing system and the sounds of the language it purports to represent. If this were, in fact, the ideal toward which languages progressed, then modern alphabet-based systems should be more consistent than their hoary ancestor, classical Greek.

In fact, however, there is in modern Greek a far less "logical" or transparent relation between the letters of the alphabet and the way a given word sounds than was (apparently) the case in the days of Sophocles and Plato. And this fact is even more pronounced in the case of languages like, say, English and French. (Consider, for instance, the complex and illogical relationship between the spelling and the pronunciation of words like "thought" and "beaucoup.")

Many elements of speech, moreover, are not notated by any writing system, even the most phonetically consistent and efficient sort of alphabet. No system can completely spell out an intonation or a tone of voice or the context of irony; so we supplement inadequacy by the provision of pointings and punctuation marks, yet these are blunt instruments at best, and suffer a heavy attrition under the assault of grammatical convention. There is, indeed, something about speech, the potential for irony, for polyvalency in the intersubjectivity of lived lives, which holds out against the full disclosure of the spoken voice on the page, and this inadequacy may well make us, in the end, more like the Egyptians in their writing than different from them.

Since Champollion's persistent and determined efforts to demonstrate the phonetic element in Egyptian writing, it has become all too easy to assume that this insight was sufficient, that once the phonetic basis had been established, the rest was merely a matter of uncovering the link between the glyphs and the phonetic structure of Egyptian. This simplification colludes with the desire for a closure that would prematurely make Champollion *the* great genius who finally completed a task that generations of his predecessors could not even begin. Such a view ignores the laborious process that followed these early steps.

Into the summer of 1822, Champollion continued his work on Coptic, the most recent lineal descendent of ancient Egyptian—work he had begun years earlier. Perhaps this is when he came to an understanding of the hybrid nature of Egyptian: he seems to have identified the relation between certain phonetic elements and the ideographic designation "star" on the Zodiac of Dendera, only recently stolen from its place in an Upper Egyptian temple to be installed in the Louvre (Fig. 2.2).[14]

In September of the same year, he managed to decipher the first cartouche of a native ruler of Egypt. Examining copies of some of the bas-reliefs of the rock temple at Abu Simbel, he came to a crucial insight. Again, he worked from a royal name, recognizing therein phonetic glyphs he had identified in his earlier decipherments:

He took a leap here, interpreting the circle near the upper middle of the cartouche as a picture of the sun. In his studies of the last descendant of the Egyptian language, Coptic, he had learned that the Coptic word for sun was PH, i.e., "re." The sequence E———RE—SS, then might be understood to terminate in the royal name Ramesses or Rameses, known well to Champollion from the Bible. Some corroboration was needed, however to confirm a reading of "me" or "mes" for the intervening glyph: 𓏥

This, Champollion found in another cartouche:

He reasoned that the bird at the head of the cartouche could well be an ibis, and the ibis, as he knew, was sacred to the Egyptian god Thoth. Champollion knew as well that one of the few classical sources on

Figure 2.2. The Zodiac of Dendera as rendered in the *Déscription de l'Égypte*, vol. 4, pl. 21.

Egyptian history, the fragmented account of the priest Manetho, made reference to a pharaoh called Touthmōsis.[15]

Looking back at the Rosetta Stone, he found the glyph in question in a group that corresponded to a part of the Greek text containing the word *genethlia*, "birthday feast, birthday offerings." His study of Coptic reinforced this evidence because he knew the Coptic verb "to give birth" was ⲘⲒⲤⲒ "misi" or ⲘⲞⲤⲈ "mose," depending on the dialect.

Champollion thereby adequately demonstrated that the glyph 𓐑 was indeed the phonetic link he needed to construct "——Ramesses" from

and in the bargain, he came to a reading as well for

The decipherment of these two pharaonic cartouches led in the opposite direction from that of the cartouches of Greek and Roman rulers of Egypt, that is to say, it suggested that during the period of native rule, hieroglyphic writing might well have been entirely *ideographic*.

Champollion was finally disabused of this notion only by his methodical, long-term work on hieratic.[16] This genre of Egyptian writing was not attested on the Rosetta Stone, and only sparsely available to Champollion (in selections from the *Déscription de l'Égypte* resulting from Napoléon's Egyptian expedition, and in a limited number of hieratic papyri that had begun to appear in Europe, especially those in the hands of the collector Sallier in Aix-en-Provence).

Hieratic was obviously different from hieroglyphic. It was executed not in stone or on carefully painted tomb walls, but written rather with a reed stylus on papyrus, leather, linen, potsherds, or limestone flakes, and although some had ventured to suggest that it was merely a cursivized form of the hieroglyphic writing system, such an opinion was far from widely accepted in the early 1820s.

Champollion's painstaking comparison of hieroglyphic and hieratic forms, especially from two versions of the same text from the *Book of the Dead* in these scripts, eventually proved that the two writing systems were entirely transposable: that each character in a hieratic text can be reconstituted into its hieroglyphic form (as is standard scholarly practice today). (Such is not the case with demotic.)

This discovery was far more significant than it may seem to us now, because it confirmed for Champollion that even in the time of the pharaohs, the hieroglyphic system had used the same phonograms he had identified in the transcription of Greek and Roman names.

The great majority of the work Champollion published during his life concerned the writing systems of ancient Egypt. It was only after his death, from 1836 to 1841, that his study of Egyptian, *Grammaire égyptienne ou principes généraux de l'écriture sacrée égyptienne*, was published.[17] Understandably, the story of the decipherment as it relates to the writing system has garnered far more attention than the laborious efforts of generations of scholars to understand the grammar and morphology of the Egyptian language,[18] but it is grammar which brings us back to the controversy about ideograms and phonograms, because it is in the question of grammatical relations and syntax that the problem of the ideogram becomes most acute. This may indeed be the crux of the dispute between those who accept the notion of the ideogram in the written representation of language and those who reject it.

It is not difficult to understand the representation of objects from the real world by means of pictures of those objects. It is difficult, however, to express notions of a more abstract sort, especially notions attached to various types of action (verbs and adverbs, say) and syntactic relation (particles, conjunctions, verbal and substantival inflection).

These problems put us face to face with the question of what language is and have philosophical, psychological, and physiological ramifications of the broadest significance and difficulty, which we cannot pretend to approach here. We can, however, return to the ideogram-phonogram distinction from a somewhat different perspective, not to consider *what* language is, but to consider how meaning is constructed in written language in two distinct, and seemingly opposing, modes, the differential and the figural.

WHAT DIFFÉRANCE DOES IT MAKE?

The name perhaps most closely associated with the notion of differential meaning is that of Ferdinand de Saussure, a Swiss linguist whose theories of meaning have had a lasting and profound influence on not only twentieth-century linguistics but also contemporary literary criticism and theory. Saussure was instrumental in separating the "science" of linguistics from the humanistic and philological studies that had been so closely associated with the emergence of linguistics as a discipline in the nineteenth century.

In this project, Saussure is careful to distinguish the elements of language from the phenomenal or conceptual worlds they are commonly purported to represent. He also makes a careful discrimination between the system of language (*la langue*) and its manifestation in the speech of any individual or group of individuals (*la parole*).

Postulating a schema whereby the linguistic sign is composed of two parts, one of them a concept in the mind of a speaker (the signified), and the other a sound-image of that concept (the signifier), which is part of the system of the language shared by all its competent speakers.[19] For Saussure, meaning in language is constructed solely on the basis of differences. As he says, "*In language there is nothing but differences*. What's more: a difference generally presumes positive terms between which it is constituted; but in language there are only differences *without positive terms*."[20] The statement was revolutionary because it severed the link between the natural world and the social phenomenon of language.

> All conventional values exhibit this characteristic of not being confused with the tangible element which serves as their support. Thus it is not the metal of a coin which fixes its value; an ecu nominally worth five francs contains but a portion of that amount in silver; it is worth more or less with such and such an effigy, more or less on this side or that of a political frontier. This is truer still of the linguistic signifier; in its essence, it is not phonetic at all, it is incorporeal, constituted, not by its material substance, but uniquely by the differences which separate its sound image from all others.[21]

These differences are socially agreed-upon distinctions grounded in the phonological capacities of human voices. Simply stated: We attribute meaning to the vocalization of the sequence of sounds [c]-[a]-[t] not because it has any relation to a feline actually existing in the world, but because it is a different sequence of sounds from [r]-[a]-[t], [h]-[a]-[t], [c]-[a]-[ll], or [c]-[u]-[t], and in the system of conventions which English speakers comply with, it is arbitrarily assigned to the domestic feline.

This leads to the characterization of Saussurean linguistics as based on negative difference, because according to it what characterizes the elements of spoken language (phonemes) "is not, as one might believe, their own positive quality, but simply the fact that they remain distinct. Phonemes are above all, oppositional entities, relative and negative."[22] Language is, consequently, a matter of formal relations, not a matter of a natural link between sound patterns and elements of thought or elements of the real world.

The Saussurean system heavily favors the spoken word over the written because of this emphasis on the relation between sound and language, and also because, for Saussure, the synchronic (system-oriented, contemporaneous) study of language is to be completely separated from the diachronic (evolutionarily or historically oriented) study thereof. The Saussurean recontextualization of linguistic study provided a much-needed impetus to the "democratization" of linguistic theory, to the study of diverse means of linguistic expression in diverse communities of speakers, and to the principle that any one native speaker's speech is as authentic a manifestation of the language in question as any other's.

The social consequences of this theory are far-reaching and extraordinarily important, but it has its weak points as well, particularly in its insistence on the absolutely arbitrary nature of the linguistic sign and the heavy privileging of speech over all other manifestations of language. These problems become apparent in Saussure's discussion of the "word." He admits from the start that "every definition of a word is vain; starting with words to define things is a poor method."[23] The word is not identical with the phonetic structure by which it comes to be realized in language: "It is essential to note that the word-image is distinct from the sound itself and that it is just as psychological as the concept with which it is associated."[24]

Saussure maintains, moreover, that phonetic structure can be accurately transposed into graphic form:

> [Language] is a system of signs in which nothing is essential except the union of sense and sound image, and in which both parts of the sign are equally psychological.... In language, ... there is nothing other than the sound image, and it can be translated into a fixed visual image.... Each sound image is, as we shall see, nothing other than the sum of a limited number of elements or phonemes, that can in turn be called to mind by a corresponding number of written signs.[25]

The admission to limits in the sound structure and the assertion that this structure can be "called to mind by a corresponding number of written signs" throws open to doubt the necessary link between the word and sound itself, for given such possibility, the sound structure might be dispensed with. More significant still, the suggestion that a word and a sound structure are separate entities opens up the possibility of words without reference to sound whatsoever.

Such words can be observed in contemporary life in sign language, by which I do not mean to say the manipulation of the fingers to produce an alphabet and spell words (which is simply a transposition of phonetic letters into visually perceptible movement), but rather to indicate "signing," the communication through manual "symbols" of concepts. Such systems, exemplified by, say, American Sign Language (ASL), have their own syntax and grammar, are not grounded in the phonetic structures of natural languages, and demonstrate concretely that the link between language and sound is not absolute or indispensable.

In the context of the current discussion, they point to the other means for constructing meaning relevant to our inquiry, the figural.

READING PICTURES, I

How can a picture "have meaning"? In other words, how do pictures reliably communicate content to people of diverse linguistic backgrounds with authority, clarity, objectivity, and immediacy?

Some answers to the question of how a picture can "have meaning" would involve us in the most abstract and complex reflections on the value and significance of the visual arts in "culture" considered in the broadest possible terms: how is it that a particular combination of colors, textures, and forms on a flat surface elicits the reverence and fascination of generations of people from the most diverse backgrounds?

The social dimension of this question, which implicates meaning in an intricate web of assumptions about taste and cultural value, is clearly relevant to the reconsideration of "our" Egyptian heritage, but it is not a dimension that can be addressed in the context of the current argument about the "ideograph," and we must for the moment resign ourselves to limiting our investigation of how a picture can "have meaning" to a drier and less impassioned range of understanding. Any answers given here to the question of how a picture might have meaning must be circumscribed by the task at hand, the investigation of meaning in a logographic writing system.

With that caveat in mind, consider, then, the *Venus and Mars* of Botticelli, in the National Gallery of London (Fig. 2.3). What categories of meaning might we construct to make some tentative gesture toward the question, how does this painting "have meaning"?

There is certainly a historical significance to the work. It was painted in egg tempera between 1480 and 1490, at the height of the Italian Renaissance, apparently as part of a bedroom decoration, perhaps on commission to the Vespucci family.[26] It was purchased by the National Gallery in 1874, at a time of Pre-Raphaelite enthusiasm for the color, the fluent line, and the detail Botticelli deploys in tempera with unparalleled virtuosity.

Matters such as these, while basic to a knowledge of the place of *Venus and Mars* in a social construction of meaning, are not particularly

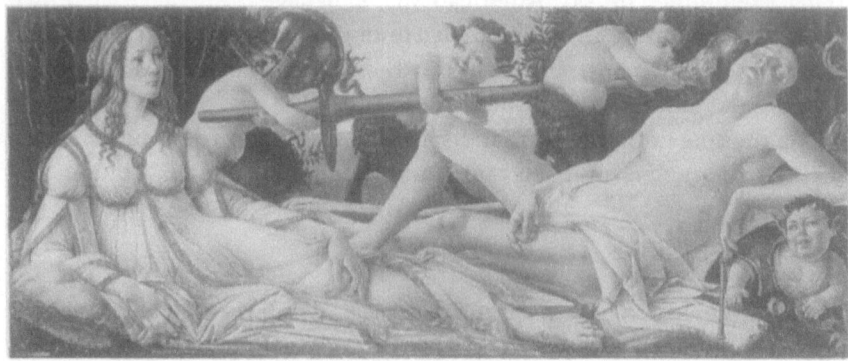

Figure 2.3. Sandro Botticelli, *Venus and Mars*. Courtesy of the Trustees of the National Gallery, London (NG 915).

informative for us. To address the problem of meaning in writing, we must proceed from a less specific and individualized understanding. Thus, historical facts pertaining to the production of the picture are of relatively limited relevance. The intellectual- and cultural-historical contexts in which the painting was created are more cogent. The question of allegory is especially suggestive.

The allegorical meaning of the painting, baldly stated, is perhaps the triumph of love over war. It is crucial to such an interpretation that one understand the male figure to be the classical god of war, Mars, and his female companion to be Venus, the goddess of love. Such a recognition is not immediate, but would follow from a familiarity with the Renaissance predilection for Greek and Roman mythology. Such a register of meaning is, moreover, reinforced by the four little satyrs and the weapons of war they have appropriated while Mars sleeps.[27]

The identification of the female figure as Venus is dependent upon that of the male as Mars. The picture contains no objects iconographically specific to Venus, and the fact that she is a beautiful young woman is hardly specific enough to tell us this is the goddess herself. Though epistemologically problematic, the allegorical interpretation of the painting is widely accepted, and the allegorical intent of Renaissance artists such as Botticelli can be attested with copious textual references.[28]

The importance of allegorical meaning in our discussion resides in its capability to use one thing to represent another. Thus we may see a young woman and young man lying on the ground, the former awake, the latter asleep, but we are licensed to understand in these two figures the abstract concept of a victory of love over war. Venus, representing love, has sexually exhausted Mars, representing war, and he sleeps in such obliviousness that the four infant satyrs can toy heedlessly with his lance, helmet, and breastplate.

Allegory, however, is not the only way to use one thing to represent another, and within the broader range of figural meaning, we might also consider two other terms of common occurrence and great importance, metaphor and metonymy. These, too, are ways of making one thing serve for another. The terms are not static and must be accommodated to the specifics of any discussion in which they play a significant role, so the attempt to define them generally entangles us in many complications, as we will see later in specific consideration of the figural capabilities of hieroglyphic writing. For the present, however, it will serve to rehearse brief conventional accounts, if at least to hint thereby at the limits of allegory.

Metaphor is generally spoken of as the making of one thing into another by means of similarity or analogy. One thing is like another because of a resemblance of certain aspects of the first to those of the second. We might broaden, then, the allegorical meaning of Venus in the painting into a metaphor that takes the beautiful young woman as a material expression for a reasoned love, with eyes wide open; her graceful proportions, gentleness, modesty, and clarity of vision controlling and directing the lovely body just discernible beneath her pleated gown, just as reason, sense of proportion, morality, and decorum might control the voluptuous sensuality that motivates passion.

Such a metaphorical reading is by no means exhaustive, and many important questions about the alchemy of metaphor are left in abeyance by our acceptance of it, but for the time being, it may show how metaphor extends and transforms meanings with a much freer hand than allegory. Metonymy is a more constricted and less ambitious figure than metaphor, and is said to allow a transfer of meaning based on contiguity rather than analogy. Thus, "the crown" is understood to mean "the king" or "royal authority," not because the king is like a crown, but because kings are imagined to wear crowns.

Metonymy is more difficult to extricate from the painting because of the irony implicit in the situation, but we might consider, say, Mars's lance as a metonym for force, violence, or war, because it is a tool of war, because it is in the arsenal of those who impose their will violently in the world of the painting, and so on.

As soon as one ranges allegory against these other figures, metaphor and metonymy, one becomes aware of the specificity and constriction of the former in contrast to the vagueness and freedom of the latter. Allegory tends to be much more directly tied to the interests and understanding of a specific group and may indeed be policed by that group so that such and such an allegory is to be interpreted within very limited and authoritarian constraints. This is plainly exemplified by certain medieval Christian allegories.[29] Metaphor and metonymy, on the other hand, are open to manipulation and recontextualization that might, in some cases, seem almost promiscuous. (They are, at the same time, so very basic to operations of thought and understanding that it becomes difficult to distinguish "plain language" from metaphor and metonymy, and indeed impossible to draw a definitive line between the two figures themselves, in some instances.)

We can see the promiscuity of the figure by returning to the painting: that Venus was taken by Renaissance viewers to represent reason as well as love here introduces a crucial problematic into the question of the painting's meaning. For the Greek antecedent to this Venus, Aphrodite, was the very goddess who provoked the most famous (although mythical) war in history, the Trojan War. This Aphrodite hardly defeated War, on the contrary, she titillated him.

This dissonance between the received interpretation of the painting and another received tradition of the identity of Venus must alert us to the problematics of figuration, especially allegory, and return us to a consideration of differential meaning, for it is not in language alone that difference is important for the construction of meaning, and the meanings of Mars and Venus are not restricted to the figural.

Allegorical meaning accomplishes (or fails to accomplish) its ends by analogy with a narrative already known to the viewer. Differential meaning relies rather on formal perceptual differences structurally or semiotically disposed upon a field. The formal character of differential meaning suggests a far broader and more open range of possibilities for meaning than allegory can, because "form" can be conceived so variously. By the differential nature of such meaning, we acknowledge the importance of difference in opposition, usually in paired opposites, for the construction of meaning. Here one set of oppositions can be inaugurated in a consideration of space. Venus is on the left, Mars on the right. This spatial difference suggests and mimics a list of other, potentially significant oppositions: male/female, asleep/awake, naked/clothed, oblivious/aware, and so on.

A secondary differential might be constructed as well, between the infant satyrs and the adults in the picture. The oppositions such a differential suggests would include young/adult, moving/still, and playful/serious. This secondary differential can interact with the first differential to identify

Mars and the satyrs on the one hand, in opposition to Venus on the other because the former are all male and the latter female, and because the spatial disposition of the satyrs reinforces that of Mars.[30] An opposition that ranges Venus with the satyrs in the category "awake," versus Mars, who is alone asleep, is also apparent in the painting, and it generates a further opposition still: that between the somber reflection of Venus and the playful, or even mischievous, satyrs.

Yet another differential might be suggested between the animate and the inanimate, ranging Venus, Mars, and the satyrs on the one hand against, most significantly, the weapons on the other hand. Here though, we must see in the differential the suggestion of a similarity as well. The lance now deployed by the satyrs is phallic and echoes with irony the empty open grasp of Mars's right hand, a grasp only recently released from his own phallus.

I would remind those who feel resistance to such a suggestion of the mythological context of an act of intercourse whereby Venus "disarms" Mars, precipitating his orgasm and enabling the "little death" of sleep he now enjoys. This is central to the allegorical reading of the painting, but also problematic in that context, because even as Mars has been disarmed, as it were, he lies satisfied, and his phallus, though displaced to the lance, remains, by this displacement, in the possession of the males in the picture.

An allegorical reading proposes that Venus is victorious here, and Mars defeated. But I question the construction of such a network of gender relations, which allows for the sexual satisfaction of the male, and reads it as defeat, while the female looks for all the world melancholy and unsatisfied. The allegorical reading of the painting suggests that her wakefulness is a "victory" (however temporary) over her male counterpart. But it is also a wakeful frustration that ranges her repressed sexuality against the expressed and expended sexuality of Mars.

Such a validation of male sexuality extends as well to the binary opposition naked/clothed, for Mars lies nearly naked in the loving idealization of classical homoeroticism, whereas Venus is decorously clothed and coifed. That Venus remains clothed and wakeful allows the surprising equation between her and Reason, but it uncovers as well the long history of repressed sexuality and oppositionality between body and mind we have seen so often elsewhere.

This is a subtle revision of the idea of love, which, in exalting the association of love with all things bright and beautiful, also accepts the humiliation of the body. Such a defacing of the image of Venus/Aphrodite must have found ready acquiescence among the Christian neoclassicists of Botticelli's day, but is itself the aftershock of an ambivalence about the body and the word which might be traced as far back as Osiris, who has exchanged sweet ejaculation for a state of beatitude.[31]

If the phallocentrism of such a view of the picture is familiar in its devaluation of female sexuality for a quasi-courtly feminization of "Reason," it is nonetheless a Pyrrhic victory, which separates the female from sexuality even as it alienates the male subject, in his phallic body, from the logos. (The equation of male sexuality with violence is corollary to this difference, but to pursue it further immediately would take us away from our immediate concern.)

Recall, then, that we were trying to identify how a picture could have meaning, and we had considered the construction of meaning in a differential model and in a figural model. The awkward word "model" is unavoidable here, because when we considered meaning in *Venus and Mars*, we kept crossing over from the one construction of meaning to the other. In the end, indeed, it seems questionable whether these different constructions of meaning can ever be separate; are they not always already mutually implicated, and our "models," imperfect polarities with a certain mutual impenetrability.

Or does this merely seem so because we were considering a painting, something very different from "language" (whether written or spoken). A more detailed consideration of Egyptian writing is clearly in order.

READING PICTURES, II

Look back, then, at the cartouches that first gave Young and Champollion their insights:

These four cartouches together suggest phonetic readings, which were transcribed with the following letters: *a, b, e, k, l, m, n, o, p, r, s, t,* and *y.* Questions remain. Why, for instance are the sounds [*e*] and [*y*] both represented by this glyph: 𓇌? Why are the sounds [*s*] and [*t*] each represented by two different glyphs, for [*s*], the following, 𓋴 and 𓊃; and for [*t*], 𓏏 and

�;? And why three glyphs for the sound [k]: △ ⊠ and ⟳? What is the meaning of the two symbols in the far right of the cartouches of Cleopatra and Berenike ⌒/◯?

Some of these problems are trivial. The inconsistency whereby [k], [t], and [s] are written in various ways is akin to writing the sound [f] differently in the English words "riff," "rough," and "philosophy." That [e] and [y] are both notated with the same glyph here is the converse, and relates to the fact that the words thereby transcribed are foreign. The Egyptians who undertook the transcription found it impossible to write the distinctions a Greek speaker made among eta, epsilon, and iota, just as a modern Japanese finds it impossible to write the difference between [l] and [r] using *katakana*.

The problem with the final pair of glyphs is of a different, more interesting nature, but if not for that problem, the Egyptian in these cartouches would be nothing more than a rather elaborate picture code for the imperfect transcription of Greek names. That final pair of glyphs, however, points to the figural construction of meaning specific to Egyptian.[32] In combination, the two glyphs have no pronunciation and merely serve to indicate that the individual named in the preceding glyphs is a female of high status, a goddess or a queen.[33] Can we call them ideograms then? Yes, perhaps, if all we indicate thereby is some graphic sign that indicates meaning without recourse to pronunciation. In this case, though, the link with any *icon* representing "female" is extremely tenuous, and there is, in fact, a historically traceable phonetic significance as well, so the case is not entirely clear.

This points to the need for greater terminological specificity, and for a more systematic examination of the range of graphic meaning in Egyptian. Consider, then, the following glyphs. Almost anybody can understand something of what they mean.

These glyphs are icons, by which I mean that they rely on a readily perceptible resemblance between the object represented (the signified) and the means of representation, (the signifier). They offer an entry, only minimally conditioned, into the system of signs. They have, of course, been reduced, schematized, and abbreviated, but they nonetheless allow a translucent linkage between the word and the world. They imitate objects that occur in nature, and which might exist anywhere the "natural" environment permitted. They depend only minimally on human fabrication and, consequently, on culturally motivated conventions. We do not need to be ancient Egyptians to have seen them.[34] (It is worth noting here that the notion of the icon need not be limited to the sense of visual resemblance. There is also strong evidence for an aurally iconic element in ancient Egyptian.)[35]

There are, also, many hieroglyphs for objects that do not occur naturally in the world, but are somehow fabricated and implicated in a process of culturally motivated meaning. They may still be readily accessible to our spontaneous understanding, because "culture" in this sense includes both the ancient Egyptians and us. Examples follow:

(First, two ships, one heading downstream and one heading upstream, then, a harp, a balance, and finally—this one may be less immediate—a vine supported between two uprights.)

There are, as well, many glyphs that require greater familiarity with specifically Egyptian culture to be understandable. Some of the glyphs below have meaning in modern popular culture, and others will be more or less familiar to those with an interest in Egyptology.

But what would you say about the following glyphs? In these cases, the degree of iconicity has faded so much that an understanding of them is achieved only with a focused effort to learn Egyptian:

There are, moreover, some glyphs that may well have been icons to the Egyptians, but which have become so opaque that no one seems to know anymore what they, as pictures, represent:

It is quite possible to understand what certain words written with these glyphs mean, but the glyphs themselves are esoteric, geometric abstractions, conventional forms.

We might then consider the capacity for visually motivated meaning on a scale of iconic resemblance. At one pole we would distribute glyphs of readily identifiable objects from the natural world: animals, fish, certain plants, human figures in a variety of activities, body parts, and so on.[36] At the other end of this scale, we might place those glyphs which cannot (or at least, cannot any longer) be identified (but which are not used exclusively for the representation of sound).[37]

Between the two extremes of the spectrum we might arrange those glyphs which are not readily recognizable from the natural world, but which are of a greater or lesser degree of familiarity to those who have studied the material remains of Egyptian culture and the representational conventions of Egyptian art. The spectrum described thereby would be useful in discussing the iconicity of a given glyph, but it would fail to provide for another very important element in the hieroglyphic system, a component which is neither a phonogram nor iconic in any degree, whether to anyone of normal perceptual capacity or to a reader with a competence, even a high competence, in Egyptian representational conventions.

Such a category of glyphs is best represented by the system of mathematical notation understandable from the chart below.

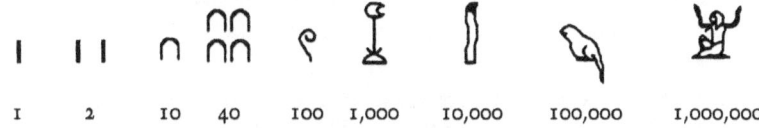

| 1 | 2 | 10 | 40 | 100 | 1,000 | 10,000 | 100,000 | 1,000,000 |

Toward the right, among the large numbers, the glyphs are pictorial. It is indeed hard to resist the idea that the numerals for 100,000 and 1,000,000 in particular operate through an eloquent metonymic transfer: 100,000 tadpoles blanketing the mud; the Nile floods recede. A greater multiplicity astonishes a very god. But at its lower reaches, the system is logical and readily understandable with minimal introduction.[38] It is strictly "symbolic"— that is to say, its means of notation have no relation to the real world of sensible objects, but function, rather, through a combination of abstract symbolic logic and social convention.[39]

It is noteworthy that a far smaller percentage of hieroglyphs is based on abstract symbolic logic than is the case in Chinese, and we would indeed be very shortsighted not to recognize systems of yet more abstract symbolic logic closer to home.[40] Recognizing the hieroglyphs that operate through such a symbolic logic, however, adds another dimension to the overly simple spectrum of iconic/noniconic mentioned earlier, and it exemplifies the diversity of representational strategies in "non-phonetic" writing.

Such a recognition alerts us as well to the need for more technically precise vocabulary in discussion of the glyphs. We have spoken about phonograms, ideograms, and logograms already, and indicated the etymological ground for their meaning. It will be necessary hereafter, however, to go beyond etymology to observe certain conventions of our own in discussing the hieroglyphs. The terms "ideogram" and "logogram" are both etymologically implicated in a complex epistemology that, in the end, refuses to pigeonhole "the word" as exclusively a matter of either sound or sight. Acknowledging this difficulty, we will establish the convention that "ideogram" is to refer to glyphs that retain a high degree of iconicity (resemblance to objects from the real world, whether natural or made), and that "logogram" is to designate written signs that are not used exclusively for the representation of sound. Our discussion, then, will categorize hieroglyphs in three broad groups—phonograms, logograms, and ideograms, moving from the least semantically focused to the most.[41]

Up to this point we have been largely concerned to discuss hieroglyphs in isolation, as single elements notating either individual phonemes or individual words. In their material context, however, Egyptian texts hardly ever (I would indeed like to say "never") isolate individual glyphs for strictly phonetic use. Even the use of individual isolated logograms is rare. There is, nearly always, a broader context including other glyphs and often painting, sculpture, or architectural features to focus the meaning of the hieroglyphic inscription.[42]

Moreover, even the most strongly iconic use of hieroglyphs still usually requires the convention of a single supplementary stroke below or to the side of the glyph in question, which, as it were, points to it and indicates that it is intended to represent the object it appears to be. The hieroglyph of a cobra, for instance, is intended to represent a cobra only if it is accompanied by a small vertical supplementary stroke, as below on the left. Without the stroke it is probably simply the consonant $ḏ$ ("dj"), as on the right.

This supplementarity is expanded in certain other cases. As we have seen, feminine nouns in Egyptian terminate in the consonant t, and the t appears in the writing of such a noun in the form of the phonetic glyph most commonly used for that sound.[43] Thus, in the examples below, the words "eye," "city" (note the crossroads), "mountainous country," and "bee," a phonetic glyph "t" accompanies the supplementary stroke.

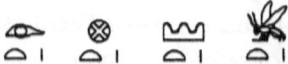

In the cases above, the ideogram is supplemented by a phonogram to make the meaning of the word precise. We might also identify any number of cases where a word spelled out phonetically is supplemented by one or more logograms to focus meaning. Such a logogram is called a determinative.

Determinatives were necessary in part because Egyptian has a large number of homonyms. There are a great many words that, though different in meaning, have the same sound. In such cases, logographic glyphs frequently supplement a phonetic rendering of the word and lessen ambiguity.[44]

When this happens, the iconic or logographic glyph is not itself pronounced, but sets the phonetic structure it accompanies into a semantic category. Consider how such determinatives work in a specific case.

The phonetic structure [tm], for example, can mean a number of things, the name of a god, "close the mouth," "perish," "cease," "be nonexistent." It can mean "be complete" or "make complete" as well. It is used, moreover, to negate certain grammatical structures. Given a plural suffix, it can mean "everyone."[45]

To lessen the ambiguity of the phonetic structure, determinatives may be appended to the phonetic skeleton, thus:

The name of the god is written ⌴ 𓀀,

"close the mouth" is written ⌴ 𓅓 𓀀,

the grammatical negative is written ⌴ 𓅓 ⸺,

"perish" is written ⌴ 𓅓 𓅱,

and "make complete" is written ⌴ 𓅓 𓏤.

The system harbors many complexities. That long horizontal glyph under the phonetic t, for example, is the picture of a sledge such as might be used to haul a block of granite from one place to another (thus the runners, crossbeams, and, perhaps, a rope). Ironically, however, in writing the word "sledge" itself, the picture of the thing may be overdetermined by the addition of a phonetically redundant m, the feminine termination t, and a determinative in the form of a stick of wood. Thus, "sledge" turns out as ⌴ 𓅓 ⌴.

The writing of Egyptian is replete with such redundancies. It is very common to find the duplication of elements of the phonetic structure of a given word, and although in some cases, this may have served a phonetic purpose we have not been able to reconstruct, in many other cases, the repetition seems rather to result from spatial considerations in the composition of a passage for inscription. Sometimes there is, as well, a play between phonetic and iconic glyphs, an expression of wit and source of delight to the Egyptians, with perhaps religious or magical significance as well.

In the earliest writing, especially, the borderline between writing and pictorial representation is very hazy. Complex "pictures" coexist with phonetic strings such that one cannot read the one without reading the other at the same time. On the celebrated Na'rmer Palette, for example, the scene of King Na'rmer's victory over the marsh dwellers of northern Egypt is depicted/written in a composition where several different registers show in different ways the supremacy of the king.[46]

It is probably through the mechanism exemplified by determinatives that the relation between hieroglyphs and Egyptian pictorial and sculptural representations can best be understood. Jan Assmann has pointed to this relationship as we see it in the earliest examples of Egyptian writing:

> Protodynastic pictorial narrative uses picture-signs on two distinctly different physical scales. The large pictures portray a "scene," and the small pictures identify actors and places by including names. The small pictures therefore refer to language (names), the large pictures refer to the world (acts). It would be a mistake, however, to categorize only the small pictures as "writing." The large pictures also act as writing. After all, the entire complex picture "writes" a name, that is, the year named after that particular event. This type of recording is successful only when both types of signs, the small ones with language reference and the large ones with world reference, work together. Neither of the two "media" is self-sufficient in recording the intended or any other meaning. The small signs do not yet make up a writing system but are simply a constituent of a complex recording system.
>
> A new stage is reached when the "large" signs are integrated into the inventory of the "small" ones. This is the origin of determinatives.[47]

As the writing system developed into its mature form, the "small" pictures and "large" pictures came to be integrated into the same formal system, to create the determinative, "originally nothing more than a 'picture' reduced to script size that joins the preceding phonogram as annotation." But the integration of the determinative into the hieroglyphic line does not, of course, eliminate other large pictures from the field of meaning, and, again, as Assmann points out, a complete fluidity is attained between the text with its integrated determinatives and an illustration proper, which stands in a framework of mutual determination with the text proper.[48]

Such mutual determination creates, in Assmann's words, three functions in writing: "The first is to explain the picture.... The second is to identify the persons [therein].... The third is to supplement the rendering of speeches, that is, to record sound, in multiple media."[49] The interaction, then, of picture and writing creates an integral whole that can scarcely be attained in writing systems like the Greek or Roman alphabet, relying as they do on conventional and arbitrary relations between sound and the written word, and insensible, as they are, to the iconic dimension of writing that was so important and so engaging to the Egyptians.[50]

But of course the system created by the Egyptians, with its redundancies, ambiguities, and play, is complicated and rather inflexible for adaptation to other languages, contrasting with the alphabet, whose greatest virtue may well be its flexibility.[51]

Most hieroglyphs are, in themselves, open to reading in several different ways. They may be ideographs when read in a way that emphasizes their iconicity. They may have logographic significance, either in combination with other ideograms or logograms, or with a phonetic supplement, but such a reading will blunt or generalize their iconicity. They may be determinatives, giving a semantic focus to a phonetic structure that is itself ambiguous, or they may serve an exclusively phonetic purpose, representing single consonants or "skeletal" words of several consonants.

The ubiquitous glyph of an eye, for example, can mean "eye" as ideogram, but only with the addition of the feminine termination t and the supplementary stroke mentioned earlier. It performs an exclusively phonetic role in the spelling of the word "milk," jrtt, below on the left; in other words it serves as an unpronounced determinative, as in the words to the right, first m33, "see"; then rs, "be wakeful" or "dream"; dg(j), "look"; and šp, "be blind."

The glyph is used commonly to write the verb jr(j), "do," as well. It may appear alone, or with the supplementary inscription of the phonetic r (sometimes doubled in the emphatic and imperfect participial inflections). In his magisterial Egyptian Grammar, Sir Alan Gardiner takes this usage as phonetically motivated, deriving the phonetic structure jr simply from the word for "eye" (jrt).[52] Gardiner, however, was inclined to favor a phonetic rendering of a given glyph over an ideographic or logographic rendering,[53] and the situation may not be quite so straightforward.

We might well see in it a more interesting logographic extension of the notion of sight as an indication of agency. "Doing" is not the same as "seeing," of course, but the subject's conscious oversight is entailed in the semantic field of performance where *jr(j)* is used in Egyptian, and it is, moreover, evident that the problem of expressing agency with ideograms and logograms taxed Egyptian ingenuity for centuries, leaving its marks in several ways in the hieroglyphic system.⁵⁴

The problems encountered in trying to understand how the glyph of an eye is used in Egyptian—whether simply phonetically, or whether logographically—have a relevance for understanding, not only Egyptian writing, but figural language in a broader sense. They require the alchemy of metaphor, apostrophe, metonymy, and so on, not merely for the construction of a secondary or ornamental sense, but frequently for the construction of any sense whatsoever.

Consider, for example, the glyph below: it consists of a rectangle enclosing two small circles, lined up alongside two fairly abstract shapes, one long and tall and one short and roundish. The whole is looped together with two curvilinear strokes.

The figure is puzzling until you are told it represents a scribe's kit. Then you understand: the rectangle is the palette; the circles, two pads of ink, one black, one red. The long thin object is a holder for reed styli, and the central element, either a water pot or a leather bag to contain the whole. The interlooping of the three may be understood practically (as a leather thong to keep the scribe's tools from becoming separated) or conceptually (so that we may read the reed case, the palette, and the bag together as a unit).

Below are several common contexts for the occurrence of this glyph taken from a standard Middle Egyptian dictionary:

In each case the glyph is accompanied by other glyphs to specify meaning. The determination of meaning depends on the relation between those supplemental glyphs and the glyph of the scribe's kit. Interestingly, the most common words using this glyph, "scribe" and "write," create meaning by undercutting the "literal" sense of the scribe's kit in favor of figural interactions.⁵⁵ Thus, in number 1 above, a man is juxtaposed with a scribe's kit to mean "scribe"; in number 2, a scribe's kit juxtaposed with a rolled and tied papyrus scroll is "writing" or, in a further transference, the verb "write."

To write the word "scribe's kit" itself (thus returning to the "literal" level of meaning) entails a supplementary process; thus, the glyph of the kit is preceded by its full consonantal skeleton written with phonetic glyphs of one or two consonants, as in number 3 above.

To understand why word number 4, n^{cc} ("smooth") is written using the scribe's kit, we must follow a longer logical train: The paints on a scribe's palette must be ground very smooth. If not, the reed pen or brush will simply suck the water out of the granules of pigment and it will be impossible to transfer the paint effectively to another surface. The scribe's kit thus suggests the notion of smoothness, but it is further supplemented by the glyph of a scroll of papyrus, here indicating that the concept in question is in some degree abstract. But this combination alone would be identical with the word "writings" and therefore ambiguous; the problem is thus obviated by the use of the phonetic skeleton (n^{cc}) at the beginning of the word.

The fifth word is an epistolary form, a polite circumlocution for the second person singular that assumes the addressee to have sufficient socioeconomic status to employ a scribe; thus, it says "your scribe" but means "you."[56] Reading such a word requires a complex set of operations. The reader must understand

1. A phonetic structure, which we can now best reconstitute only as far as "$z\check{s}=k$." (And of course, this phonetic structure operates within a sophisticated system of differences that attributes to it meaning based on it being different from "$r\check{s}=k$," "$z\check{s}=j$," "$s\underline{h}=k$," etc.)

2. A system of differences that distinguishes this "$z\check{s}=k$" from a sequence of consonants that is identical in transliteration, but which means, rather, "you write." In speech, various means may have been available to make this difference clear. In writing, it is clear because of the determinative, as mentioned in the next item.[57]

3. The category "man," expressed metaphorically, that is, using a figure based on analogy or resemblance.

4. The category of actions, to mean "who writes." This time, although we are again engaged in a hermeneutic of categories, the figure is metonymic, which is to say, the scribe's palette here is contiguous to, or associated with, rather than analogous to, the person identified under the category "man."

74   LANGUAGE OF THE GODS

5. A syntactic system that allows the expression of person, number, and gender by suffixation, in this case to produce the second person singular masculine possessive suffix.

6. A social system in which status is attached to writing, but more status still to the economic or political position wherein one employs or compels the service of another as a scribe.

7. A strategy of substitution, directly related to 6, which writes "your scribe" but means in practice "you."

One cannot read the word in question without becoming engaged in all these processes at once, and that engagement is phonetic, differential, and figural (and therefore "ideographic") at once. The complex operations required to extract the simple notion "you" from these glyphs were accomplished instantaneously by a competent reader of Ancient Egyptian. It is far less automatic for us, but this can be a theoretical advantage, providing us insights into the problems of expressing various kinds of meaning in a mixed phonetic, logographic, and ideographic system.

FIGURAL AND SPATIAL SYNTAX

We already mentioned the problem of agency in passing, but might return to it here to consider more systematically how abstract notions might be expressed in pictures. The hieroglyphic system reveals an impressive stick-figure semiotics. There are glyphs such as the following which picture people in their labors, at their pleasure, and in the various attitudes and stations of life.

Each of these glyphs can be used to express verbs of various sorts, from the highly specific and uncommon glyph meaning "dig" (second from the right) to the very common and highly generalized figure of a man wielding a stick with both hands, which can mean many things, from "strike," to "take away," to "plunder," to "teach" (as the Egyptian proverb has it, "A boy's ears are on his back"). The comparative rarity of the former glyph and the frequency of the latter reveal a process in the development of hieroglyphs wherein specifically focused and highly iconic glyphs give way to more generalized ones. (One might note, as well, the paucity of glyphs relating to the activities of women compared with those relating to the activities of men.)[58]

A system of ideographs that could accommodate the rich diversity of words for various human actions would have to be enormously complex, and the demands of time and capacity in learning, and then using, such a system would remove it from all practicability. Thus, in addition to favoring glyphs that can indicate a general category of action over a specific action, the Egyptians also found ways to abbreviate complex figures for facility of notation. They often dismembered the stick figures to leave merely legs or arms or the eye, say, as sufficiently explicit expressions of the requisite notion.

Or they combined the body part (usually the arm alone) with a tool or implement of office:

The construction of meaning from glyphs such as these engages various types of figuration. Synecdoche is obviously an element. The part (the arm) is seen to function for the whole (the human agent). But metonymy has a role to play as well; thus, the forearm grasping a scepter can mean "rule" or "control" and that bearing a flagellum can mean "protect." Yet in a broader sense, these figures are also metaphors, operating on the basis of analogy whereby the picture of a human figure or part of the human figure functions to represent a human agent.

These icons of the arm in motion came about only after a process of experimentation which must have begun with the genesis of Egyptian writing. It is still evident on the walls of some Fifth and Sixth Dynasty pyramids where one can sometimes observe how a more complicated glyph evolved into a simpler one, as below (the glyph serves as a logograph for the word "thresh," unaccompanied by any phonetic complement):[59]

There are cases, as well, where a more precise ideogram used as a determinative in the *Pyramid Texts* has been replaced by one or more logographic determinatives of a more general character in later hieroglyphic writing. Below, for example, you may observe the word "reap" (ꜣsḫ) as it appears on the wall of the pyramid of Merenre', on the left, and as it appears more commonly in Middle Egyptian, on the right. In the latter case, the interesting representation of a figure abbreviated to head and arms cutting grain with a scythe, used as a determinative, has been replaced by two logograms, a scythe and a forearm clasping a stick.⁶⁰

The overall trend is toward simplification, producing a system of categories of action and coordinating the diversity and degree of specificity used in the glyphs in a given inscription with the type of utterance in question and the material supports through which it was effected. Thus tomb and temple walls show a far greater diversity of glyphs than do religious papyri in cursive hieroglyphs. Literary narratives and business documents get by with a smaller number of categories as smaller and more specialized glyphs are subsumed under simply the forearm glyph or the glyph of a forearm holding a stick.

There is an evolutionary process in play here. If it is, in general, a process of simplification, it is still important to recognize that there are striking exceptions to this generalization, particularly in the Late Period and the Ptolemaic Era, when the number of glyphs proliferated greatly. (This late proliferation may well represent a move toward exclusivity in the knowledge of hieroglyphs. It coincides with the development of demotic writing for practical documents, on the one hand, and an increasing esotericism in Egyptian religious institutions, on the other.)

Valuable clues about how ideographs and logographs were created to express abstract notions such as agency are to be found among the earliest writing in Egypt. The slate palettes and stone maceheads of the late predynastic period and the First Dynasty reveal attempts to combine elements of individual ideograms and logograms for the representation of more complex notions. On the celebrated Na'rmer Palette, mentioned earlier, a falcon with one human arm perches above a composite sign apparently representing a tribal group that lives on marshland (see Fig. 2.4). The falcon holds a rope tethered to the subjected victim, and the sign as a whole seems clearly to represent the victory of someone associated with the falcon over a people associated with the marshland.⁶¹

Similarly, on the "Towns Palette" (Fig. 2.5), various animals wielding hoes attack fortified encampments and suggest readings such as, "The falcon tribe overwhelms the fortifications of the owl tribe."⁶²

Such complex graphic arrangements as these do not persist in the

Figure 2.4 (left). Detail from the Na'rmer Palette, recto. The composite drawing represents the victory of a falcon king over the inhabitants of the delta. Egyptian Museum, Cairo (CG 14716).

Figure 2.5 (below). Detail from the "Towns" or "Libya" Palette, from Abydos, late fourth millennium B.C.E. Egyptian Museum, Cairo (CG 14238). After Baines, *Fecundity Figures*, p. 43.

Egyptian writing system per se, but find repeated application in painting and sculpture, and exemplify the rich interaction between writing and painting in Egyptian representation systems. Moreover, one pattern observed on some of the early palettes and maceheads does find its way into the standard hieroglyphic writing system of Middle Egyptian. In that type of glyph, a totem animal or object is placed upon a "standard" (by which I mean a high pole with a crossbeam).

On the Battlefield Palette, for example (Fig. 2.6), a falcon perches upon the crossbeam of a standard with a ribbon dangling down the back, and human arms reaching out of the front. The arms clutch a defeated captive with his arms pulled up tightly behind his back just above the elbows.

A similar example can be found on the Bull Palette (Fig. 2.7), but in this case, human arms do not grow out of the sides of the poles, the poles themselves terminate in human hands, which, in turn, grasp a rope, which presumably bound prisoners. John Baines calls these composites "emblematic personifications"; the term is useful for our discussion here.[63]

In the hieroglyphic system, the standard and totem combination persists in several common glyphs. We have already encountered the first of these (from the left) in the cartouche of Pharaoh Thutmose.[64] It is the name of the god Thoth; the others are also the names of gods, Min, Ha, and Wepwawet (moving toward the right).

Figure 2.6. Detail of recto from the Battlefield Palette, late fourth millennium B.C.E. Ashmolean Museum, Oxford (1892.1171), and British Museum, London (20791). After Baines, *Fecundity Figures*, p. 43.

Two further examples below represent, not the names of individual gods, but broader metaphysical categories. The former, on the left, is a falcon perched on a standard, expressing the notion of divinity. It was first used as a determinative for the name of the god Horus, but later transferred to other gods as well. It is also used as a determinative for the word "king" and as the first person singular pronoun, but only for kings and gods. The second example is an alternative writing for that element of the personality called the *ka*.

It is instructive to take note of these glyphs as unusual Egyptian examples of a technical means for the creation of signs which is far more common in Chinese.[65] It is also important to note in passing how such semiotic constructions relate to Egyptian notions of divinity. In targeting Egyptian culture as the other, Western intellectual discourse has at times criticized the Egyptians for being excessively symbolic, at times, for being incapable of abstract thought. The latter prejudice stretches from classical antiquity to the present and leads to characterizations of the Egyptians as primitive fetishists. We will take up this issue in more detail elsewhere, but it is important to see that the process of abstraction, whereby a totem is elevated to a standard, expressing thereby certain abstract notions of divine presence, is in itself a figural process that undoes misconceptions about the putative childish literalism of the Egyptians.

The emblematic representations on the early palettes and maceheads represent the furthest step the Egyptians took toward the expression of a logographic syntax within a single "glyph" (the quotation marks being

Figure 2.7. Detail from the Bull Palette, late fourth millennium B.C.E. Louvre, Paris (E 11255). After Baines, *Fecundity Figures,* p. 43.

necessary because we have no proof that this is a glyph rather than a picture). More extended statements in such form do not appear, maybe because larger syntactic structures cannot be encompassed with enough specificity to allow pictorial expression. On a larger scale, indeed, the integration of syntax into logographic or ideographic expression seems to present intractable problems.

This brings us back again to one of Saussure's insights, and an important issue for our discussion of how a picture can "have meaning":

> The signifier, being by nature auditory, unfolds in time alone and assumes characteristics of time: (1) it represents a span, and (2) this span is measurable in a single dimension; it is a line.
>
> This principle is obvious, but it never seems to be remarked, no doubt because it is too simple. It is, all the same, fundamental, and its consequences are incalculable.... The entire mechanism of language depends upon it. In contrast with visual signifiers (maritime signals and the like), which can offer simultaneous complexities in several dimensions, acoustic signifiers have at their disposal only the dimension of time. Their elements appear one after the other; they form a chain. This characteristic is clear as soon as one represents them in written form, substituting for a succession through time the spatial line of graphic signs.[66]

The temporal span of the utterance is indeed a central element in linguistic expression and must be accounted an organizing principle of the most fundamental sort. In spoken language, time is the dominant mode of organization, and it governs the mechanisms whereby words have meaning relative to other words in a linear hierarchy. The fact that different languages privilege different phases in the linear motion of language—some favoring the end of the utterance for predication, others favoring the beginning, some situating modifiers before the word modified, some after; some favoring prefixes, some infixes, some suffixes (and for manifold purposes)— all this variation suggests that the hierarchical ordering of syntax within time is a matter of linguistic convention. Saussure's point, however—that the dimension of time conduces to a strong role for linearity in linguistic expression—remains important.

His qualification that "the signifier, being by nature auditory, unfolds in time alone," however, seems in its exclusiveness, to go astray. For if time is a fundamental element in linguistic expression, it is not the sole axis, or word order would be the sole grammatical criterion. That syntax plays a role, whether a relatively small one, as in Chinese, or an enormous one, as in Greek or Sanskrit, say, points to another dimension of linguistic expression which Saussure fails to address here adequately.

The artful use of discontinuity in language suggests, moreover, that linearity may be used in its negation, as well as by integration, so that, for example, two conversations going on at the same time may be broken into pieces and shuffled together to create the illusion of simultaneity even while, in point of fact, they are organized in a linear fashion within the utterance. The scene in *Madame Bovary* where Emma and Rodolphe carry on a sympathetic discussion in alternation with the narration of events at a busy livestock auction is a celebrated modern example, but one might find similar deployments of the disjunction of Saussure's purported linearity throughout the history of writing.[67]

This is all the more important when we are speaking of written language. For if time is still an important structural element in reading, in writing it is rivaled by space in a manner that cannot occur in speech. The spatial disposition of written elements also provides means of making meaning, and if we acknowledge this ourselves, even with our heavily phonocentric writing system, by using various typographical conventions, fonts, colors, type sizes, and so forth, then it must be admitted that the hieroglyphic system, with its striking visual potential, had a far greater investment in the spatial deployment of meaning.

A GRAMMAR OF THE FIGURE

The primary tools for this spatial syntax operate within the axes of difference and similarity. When two different signs appear on the same surface, already there is the possibility of a relation between them, a relation which operates across a differential: the two signs are necessarily alike in some ways and different in others. While I would not propose to articulate rules for the calibration of similarity and difference in this context, I believe we can, all the same, deduce certain principles from a consideration of selected examples of hieroglyphic writing.

Our first example is a superb monument now in the Louvre (Louvre E 11007), an artifact of the First Dynasty (see Fig. 2.8). It takes the form of a tall rectangle, its top side slightly curved. Within a raised border on the upper two-fifths of the rectangle, a falcon stands erect upon another tall rectangle. This second rectangle consists of an open space at the top and an elaborately carved sequence of vertical rectangles and stripes at the bottom. The sequence of vertical rectangles and stripes is the conventionalized depiction of a palace fortification with recessed doors and niched or "paneled" walls.

In the open space a snake stretches out, head and neck reared up, facing left. The piece is an early example of the fully established canonical style of representation.[68] In the cobra stretched out inside the enclosure, we read the phonetic structure of the Serpent King's name. The snake is the phonetic $ḏ$ (i.e., "dj"), a unique element in the composition, which otherwise comprises the generic titulary frame of the *serekh*, similar in function to a cartouche, though older and, by virtue of the falcon perched atop it, more iconic.[69]

Much has been said about the sculptural aesthetics of the piece, but that is a separate issue. Our concern is rather with its syntax, which is effected by the juxtaposition of falcon, snake, and palace facade.

The falcon seems to have primacy, given his size and prominence in the relief. The snake is smaller and clearly subordinate to the falcon, but attains a prominence of its own by virtue of its central location in the open space at the top of the rectangle. That rectangle, with palace facade at the bottom, is a rendering of a fortified enclosure, the front elevation below and the aerial view spread above, conforming to Egyptian conventions for the representation of three-dimensional solids.

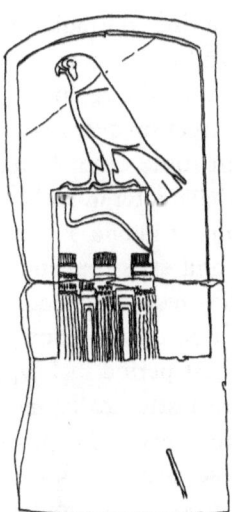

Figure 2.8. Stela of King Djet (or Wadji) of the First Dynasty. The entire stela is just under 4'9" high, including a long base, which would have been sunk into the earth. The portion represented in the line drawing would be roughly 2'6" high. It is carved in fine detail in limestone. Louvre, Paris (E 11007). After Ziegler, *Louvre*, p. 19.

The falcon seems to be standing watch over the snake within the palace. We know from many other examples that the falcon-palace combination is a titulary frame, as I said before. The unique element in the composition, then, is the snake and thus represents a specific individual who has taken on the divinity of the falcon. A certain equation is then effected between the two: the falcon = the serpent, namely, the Serpent King is Pharaoh. This is the syntax of resemblance in the composition, but there is also a syntax of difference as suggested by the imbalance born of the falcon's prominence over the snake.

That difference points to the theocratic nature of the statement made on the stela. The falcon is the Horus King, justified of voice, the unique incarnation of the human and the divine, the Living King for all (Egyptian) time. The Serpent King, however, is a specific human individual who takes on the mantle of pharaoh for a limited time, subject to the circumstances of (human) history.

On the one hand, what the monument means at heart is Hor-Djet; the performative utterance "Horus is Djet" (the copula "is" being our supplement to the visual syntax uniting the two words) is not just the ratification of such a statement but its exemplification in the state. And at the same time, the stela is almost certainly a funerary stela, a signpost perhaps to allow the deceased Serpent King's errant *ka* to find its way back home to the tomb.[70] Thus the realities of human history overtake the ideology of Egyptian time, and the statement "Horus is Djet" is already not true. (Djet is dead and is, thus, Osiris, and the mantle of Horus has long passed on.) And for Egyptians reading the statement, it was already not true, too. The poignancy of the monument resides in this contradiction.

The statement passes more by visual syntax than by grammar proper,[71] but it makes a performative utterance that testifies to the reality of the equation Hor = Djet, even if (whether now, or in its erection over his tomb) that utterance must be taken "historically," or in some other frame of noncontemporaneous reference. This performative character must be considered in each encounter we have with hieroglyphs; it is one of the central knots in reading them and justifies the care and effort expended to write them. It ratifies the permanence for which they seem intended.[72]

The eloquence of the Serpent King's stela can be readily contrasted with much of the written material from this earliest period in Egyptian history. Other writing of the time is less impressive aesthetically and less amenable to a modern reading.[73] There are other funerary stelae (none so fine as the Serpent King's), but the "writing" of these early days known to us tends to consist of labels scratched in ivory or wood for various tomb commodities (oil, in particular). These labels are examples of an earlier stage in the development of hieroglyphs and have yet to attain the formal canonical precision of standard hieroglyphs.

They present many difficulties for readers in that the conventions of spoken Egyptian, with its natural linearity in time, were not yet effectively transferred into a graphic context. Extended utterances are unknown at this early date, and glyphs are disposed over the writing surface without a clear indication of which is to be read first and how they are to relate one to the other. Admittedly, our understanding of archaic Egyptian is limited, which must partly account for the difficulty in reading. It is also evident, however, that conventions of lineation and composition are not yet fully established. The case is paralleled by other examples of very early writing. In Sumeria, too, the earliest writing shows a seemingly random disposition of signs upon the clay tablet, without apparent reference to the grammatical hierarchies of the language.

Gradually, more ordered arrangement of the glyphs and any accompanying pictorial elements are developed, and it becomes easier to extrapolate fully realized and extended utterances from their graphic expression. This offers new challenges to Egyptian artists, because as the possibility to write longer, more fully realized grammatical statements in hieroglyphs increases, parity between the glyph and its pictorial accompaniment disappears, and a clear separation of functions appears between text and picture. The wooden stelae of the Third Dynasty noble Hesire' already show such a division. The portraits of the noble himself are far larger than the glyphs in the written text (even given the exquisite care expended in their carving), and one no longer "reads" the image in the same way one reads the text. Image and text have become, rather, reflections of each other, and inevitably, a supplementary polarity develops between the two.

This separation of the image from the word becomes a constant challenge to the artist's ingenuity. Several groups of reliefs from the Twelfth Dynasty exemplify the success Egyptian artists garnered in their struggle to integrate the image and the word. What these compositions have in common is an emblematic logic in their images and a prominence in size and care of execution in their hieroglyphs. One of the most intriguing examples comes from the Fayum. It was perhaps the architrave of a small door in a temple to the crocodile-headed god, Sobek. (See Fig. 2.9.)

Artists of the Twelfth Dynasty seem to have been particularly concerned with, and particularly skilled at, the integration of written texts and images.[74] Examples can be found from other periods in Egyptian history as well, but less and less often in reliefs and tomb paintings. Among the

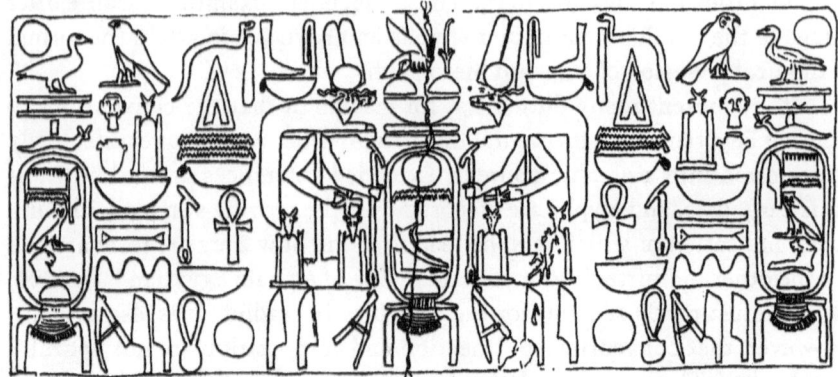

Figure 2.9. Architrave of Amenemhet III of the Twelfth Dynasty from a temple of the god Sobek in the Fayum. Ägyptisches Museum, Berlin (16953). After Schäfer, *Principles of Egyptian Art*, pl. 36.

artifacts in Tut'ankhamun's tomb, for instance, the most impressive deployment of written forms in a pictorial context is not on the tomb walls, but rather on the chairs (especially the wooden chair with the god Heh on the back) and jewelry. Likewise, in the Late Period, this emblematic use of glyphs is exemplified in small articles of great variety and on, or inside, sarcophagi.[75]

The attempt to notate syntax in a closed pictorial space presents a particularly difficult problem if one hopes to make such a notation without the mediation of speech and its various strategies for syntactic structuring (parataxis, hypotaxis, parallelism, morphological marking, and so on), and it is here that the logographic nature of hieroglyphic writing seems to surrender to a certain inadequacy. We can see how certain steps might have been taken toward an independent extended syntax of the logograph and ideograph, particularly in the "underworld books" and "mythological papyri" of the New Kingdom through the Late Period, but there is as yet very little in these texts that we can read and understand. Our inability to understand the lofty cosmological and theological speculations of Egyptian scholasticism found in them stems in part from the inadequacy of the notations in which it has survived.[76]

It is clear enough that these texts describe journeys, in particular the journey of the solar barque through the underworld at night. Their central theme is the agon of light and order, exemplified by the sun god Re' against darkness and chaos, exemplified by the serpent Apep. Stages in the journey are sometimes delineated, hour by hour, and there are, in certain genres, illustrations of cosmological structures known to us from more readily understandable myth cycles. The best examples of these are the weighing of the heart scenes and the anthropomorphic representations of heaven and earth in the papyri called by the Egyptians *Jmy-d3t* and *Prt-m-hrw*, "What Is in the Underworld" and "Going Forth by Day." We have considered these briefly elsewhere.

A unique and extraordinary papyrus in the British Museum[77] suggests the conceptualization of a cinematographic pictorial syntax in Egyptian religious representations (see Fig. 2.10). It is a cosmogonical papyrus, at least in part, but alongside its representation of the genesis of the world, it maintains as well a funerary character. It was written for the lady Henuttawy, a chantress of Amun of the late Twenty-first Dynasty, who is shown at the right end of the papyrus worshiping several stages in the cosmogonic process, from the genesis of the sun at the far left, through the extension of a great primordial serpent (a form of Atum) and a strikingly phallocentric separation of heaven and earth to a relatively familiar representation of the goddess Nut stretched out above a serpent-headed transformation of Geb.

We will discuss the phallocentric separation of heaven and earth elsewhere. Of central importance here, however, is how the four stages of creation flow together as if they were independent cells in an animated sequence. Their precocious ingenuity, however, is highly unusual, and it is only through the awareness of such a potential in this papyrus that one can go on to consider the suitability of other mythological papyri to a similar reading strategy.

More common is the quite baffling juxtaposition of numerous small religious pictures, highly specialized hieroglyphs if you like, within the same pictorial space without a clear guide to how one might construct a hierarchy or sequence through which they might be read. Consider, for example, the following scene from a papyrus in the Egyptian Museum of Turin (Fig. 2.11).[78]

This scene suggests that we should reconsider our assumptions concerning the constraints of time and space as they relate to language and, specifically, to hieroglyphs. If the emblematic expression of syntax is limited, in one regard by space, because it is difficult to express complicated ideas within the limited, well-defined space of a single picture, then the linear unfolding of linguistic expression must also be limited by time, such that the continuous flow of time must be stitched back recursively into patterned form by repetition of previously articulated information, and by morphological markings, whether case endings, grammatical particles,

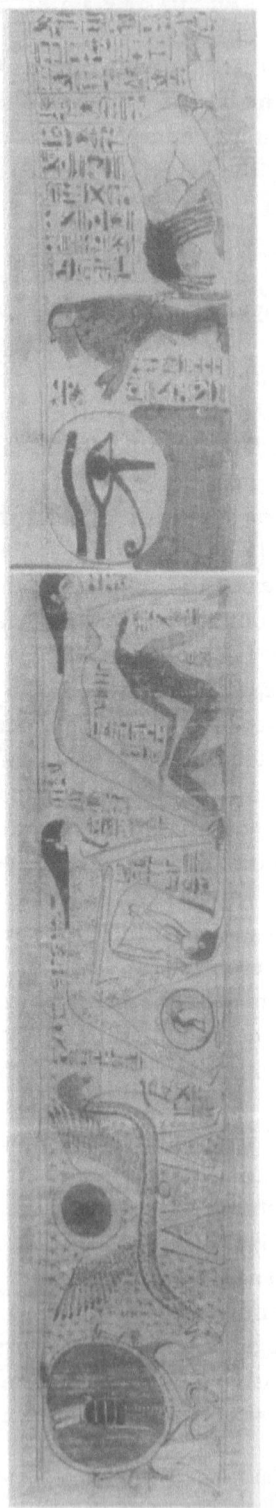

Figure 2.10. The papyrus of the lady Henuttawy, daughter of the High Priest Menkheperre' and chantress of Amun. The scene on the right shows the lady praying before a series of cosmogonic scenes, which progress, in sequence, from the left. The scenes represent a sequence of transformations in a cosmogonic cycle, with a strongly phallocentric emphasis. Late Twenty-first Dynasty. British Museum, London (pBM 10018).

Figure 2.11. Scene from the papyrus of Mesha'redwyseqeb, Twenty-first Dynasty. Museo Eqizio, Turin (pTurin 1769). Redrawn after Niwiński, *Studies of the Illustrated Theban Funerary Papyri*, fig. 76.

tense or aspectual signals, or other linguistic or rhetorical features. Space and time, in this context, provide further registers of meaning always already mutually implicated within the semiotic network.

In hieroglyphic writing the temporal axis must make due allowance for phonetic expression. The expansion of syntax beyond the emblematic personifications to which we just referred must surrender to, or be combined with, linear expression to allow the presentation of complex linguistic utterances. This may seem to work at odds with the pictorial element in the system, thus early European dismay at the combination of human figures, animals, both large and small, body parts, implements, and architectural and landscape features all on the same scale.

In many cases, however, those exigencies of linguistic linearity which might compromise the graphic sense of a written text were complemented by pictures "proper," that is to say, images distinct from the text of the hieroglyphic inscription, but which conveyed similar information in a different way. Thus, on the architrave from the Sobek Temple in the Fayum (Fig. 2.9), the text states that Sobek gives life and dominion to pharaoh, and the emblematic representation of this text says the same thing in a graphic form with a shared set of signs but somewhat different potential for their combination.

So too in the White Chapel at Karnak, there is a rough equality between the pictorial space offered to figural representations of this emblematic sort and to writing proper. The two expressions of the same formula create a mirror effect,[79] and from column to column closely similar representations spread across the monument perform a prayer or mantra, "May God give life, stability, dominion, health and happiness to the Lord of the Two Lands, Kheperkare' Senusert (I)."

The prominence of the glyphs in these inscriptions—their size, their thickness in raised relief, the detail with which they have been articulated—suggests that the relation between the figures and the text is more like that between the phonetic elements of a given word and its ideographic or logographic determinative than like that between a picture and its caption. The glyphs are equivalent to the figures. And if the inscriptions are heavily formulaic and most of the expressions familiar from countless other monuments, then their purpose is not to inform, but rather to perform.

Roland Tefnin has written a series of important articles on the relation between image and writing in Egyptian, demonstrating the integral nature of these two elements, how the word complements the image in a semiotic structure that has all too often baffled modern readers, despite the ubiquity of such reading strategies in popular graphic culture of the contemporary world. (Tefnin's articles are not readily available to English readers, so it will serve our purposes to quote him extensively in the following pages):

> That icon and text constitute the two principal systems of representation by which human societies organize and express their comprehension of the universe—real and imaginary—nothing is more evident. In the Western tradition alone, there is no lack of examples of the simultaneous usage of two languages, the one making precise, completing, or restating the other, for the production of a more comprehensive and complex sense which each functioning on its own would not permit: opera, theater, cinema, advertising, the comic strip would not exist without this conjunction, the main source of their significance. If, in other cases, the connection appears less profound . . . the contribution of a "secondary" language to a "principal" language inevitably provokes the appearance of signifieds of connotation, of supplements of sense.[80]

He goes on to make the point that the visual culture of ancient Egypt spoke with this double language in practically all its manifestations, preserving in hieroglyphs an iconic incarnation that had disappeared from other great writing systems.

> The signs of the hieroglyphic system are maintained through three millennia, in a figurative form perfectly identifiable, with a steadfastness which traditionalism cannot suffice to explain. To speak of a frozen sys-

tem would be to disregard the reality of an evolution manifest by the frequent creation of signs, particularly in the late epochs which experienced in this regard real frenzies. But these new signs were always new images and the creation never brought into question the essentially figurative character of the writing. The explanation of the phenomenon can, no doubt, be found in the very nature of the hieroglyphic sign; using it as a graphic tool designating the phonemes of the language never sufficed to exhaust its complexity. At the same time, graph and symbol putting into operation a double signified, phonological and representative, it finds itself invested, at least potentially, with two distinct functions, linguistic and semiotic. This "double play" of writing appears moreover to be but one manifestation among others of the most characteristic mechanism of Egyptian thought, oscillating between abstract rationality and natural empiricism, nourishing the one by the other in a continual come-and-go across a universe perceived at the same time as signified and signifier, as expression and substance. It seems essential, from this perspective, to emphasize that the ambiguity of the written sign, not constantly realized, but always latent, finds an exact equivalent in the capacity held by the image, of functioning simultaneously in the iconographic and hieroglyphic modes.[81]

The complementary nature of this interaction between word and image is amply demonstrated in numberless examples of Egyptian relief sculpture and painting. In the article I have quoted, Tefnin describes its operation in the tombs of Ra'hotep at Meidum and Ptahhotep at Saqqara, and in another article, he discusses the same relation in the Kadesh reliefs of Ramesses II.[82] My own remarks on the stela of the Serpent King, the architrave of Amenemhet III, and the White Chapel at Karnak make similar points in a modest way.

It is important to note, however, that the "'double play' of writing," its "oscillation between abstract rationality and natural empiricism," can also effect a less harmonious interaction of image and word, a disjunction with profound consequences, not only for Egyptian systems of representation, but for theological and epistemological questions of a more wide-reaching significance. Tefnin himself adumbrates this issue with his reference to "*supplements* of sense" (my emphasis).

Complementarity, the seemingly simple combination of two, otherwise incomplete, elements to produce a whole, can easily shift, under more extended consideration, to supplementarity, where the interaction of the two elements produces not a single unified whole, but rather an emphasized statement of the incompleteness of the parts. For although the combination of parts is essential to the construction of meaning, when the parts are combined, they contradict each other at certain levels and create doubt about any possibility of closure or *stable* meaning.

Such a reading would seem de rigeur in the poststructuralist critical environment from which we are reading, but would it have any "relevance" or cogency for the Egyptians themselves? This is, of course, the sort of question we cannot even ask with full epistemological rigor because it assumes "a way of knowing what the Egyptians themselves thought," when we cannot adequately represent "the Egyptians" without the contamination of our own discursive position entering into the game, "adding some new thread," as Derrida puts it.

And yet we persist in asking the question because, though any text can be shown to be constituted by supplementarity, in certain texts this supplementarity suggests more than simple fascination with the paradoxes of signification. There can be consequences of a more tenacious reach, and the apparent awareness of supplementarity within the discursive consciousness of a culture may persuade us to reconstitute our own awareness of a "self."

Is it that writing per se catalyzes or incites a supplementary fissure in our understanding? We will not attempt to reweave the fabric of Derrida's response to this question, except to note that the synchronic emphasis of his discussion may itself be supplemented by a diachronic double: that the ontogeny of writing is mirrored in its phylogeny and the supplementarity of any of our writings is an echo of the supplementarity of writing at its "historical" origins. This can be seen in a concrete technical sense in the development of writing in Sumer, as tokens come to be enclosed in bulky envelopes of clay, and replicated on the clay surface. In time, the tokens themselves were subsumed into the envelope, which changed to a solid tablet, covered now with our first writing.[83]

In Egypt, the technical process is less transparent, but for that, it reveals a conceptual awareness that is not clear in the almost exclusively economic discourse of the Mesopotamian plain. If economics—the recording of the contents of such and such a jar—is important, so as well is theology—the recording of the contents of such and such a *tomb*. In early Egypt it was impossible to separate what we so readily perceive to be distinct discursive frames.

As always in Egypt, we rely upon funerary sites for the overwhelming majority of our evidence, and the culture of death is where we must make our beginning, but we needn't see there (we are bound, indeed, *not* to see there) only the culture of death, because the implication is mutual: the monument of the dead king is a testimony to the vitality of the signifier. This double bind was already pointed to above in our remarks about the stela of the Serpent King, but here we may go further, both further back and further into the theoretical networks such ancient "writings" imply.

We may go so far back indeed that we must harbor doubts about whether we are in the presence of "writing" at all. The "origins" of writing must, for all that, rouse us to consideration of potmarks, because we would be blind not to see suggestions of writing in these representations on the grave goods of late Neolithic Egyptians, even if it may be going too far to see these marks as "writing" as such. At this stage—that is, at around 3500 B.C.E.—there is no firm evidence that the similarity between these representations and the "words" of later Egyptian is more than fortuitous. Already though, the marking we discern is very plausibly the marking of ownership, thus prefiguring the clear economic function of writing proper in subsequent ages, and the connection with burial foreshadows the funerary and theological connections that are everywhere so important in our grasp of Egypt.

A relatively short step forward brings us into "history," into what we can confidently read as the writing down of language. Consider two characteristic examples from the graveyards of Naqada, the one, an ivory label now in the British Museum (EA 55588), and the other, the impression of a seal in clay, from the School of Archaeology and Oriental Studies of the University of Liverpool (LOI 5245) (see Figs. 2.12 and 2.13).

The seal in clay consists of alternating signs of an offering table and a tall standard with an animal skin and crossed arrows near the top. We know, from more recent evidence, that the standard is that of the goddess Neith and that the table spells out the triliteral consonant skeleton *ḥtp*. In

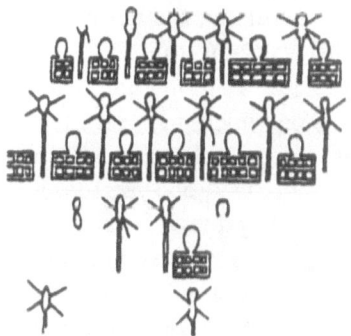 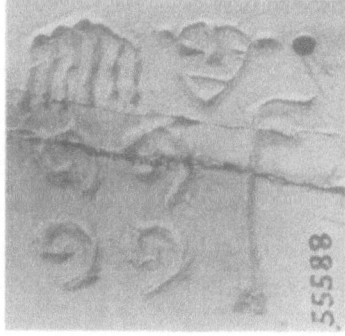

Figure 2.12 (left). After an impression from the seal of Queen Neithhotep, First Dynasty, found at Naqada. Redrawn after Kaplony, *Inschriften*, vol. 3, no. 75, pl. 103.

Figure 2.13 (right). Ivory docket for a necklace of Queen Neithhotep. London, British Museum (EA 55588).

combination these glyphs represent a name, which we shall read "Neithhotep."[84]

The ivory label is an unprepossessing square tablet, scratched, scarred, and broken in half; its inscription more chipped into the surface than properly carved. One of the glyphs on the surface represents a necklace, and there are, as well, four glyphs for the numeral "100." The label serves the mundane purpose of recording the number of beads strung on what must have been one of the queen's necklaces.

By telling us of the existence of the necklace through the ideograph chipped into its face and recording how many beads the necklace held, the label makes readily apparent its economic function: it was a means to protect the commodity, the necklace, from the surreptitious appropriation of a bead here, a bead there. The irony that the label lives on while the necklace has long since disappeared is mundane in the archaeology of the Nile Valley. In the most elementary sense, this is, all the same, the mark of the supplement, one thing which replaces something else, but which is no replacement, even if, in standing for the existence of the necklace, it is (now) our only means of knowing the original. A poor substitute, but a clear index of the use of writing for economic purposes in early Egypt.

More interesting, though, is the presence of "Neithhotep" in the seal impression. "Neithhotep" is a theophoric name; it contains within it, that is, the name of a divinity. The divinity in question is Neith, a fearsome and awe-inspiring Goddess[85] whom one might well wish to mollify and set to rest, as the name Neithhotep, "Neith-is-at-peace" or "Neith-is-satisfied" suggests. The name, then, defers the divine wrath by drawing it to peace in the existence of the woman. And Neithhotep herself becomes a substitute for the Goddess, appropriating and thereby mollifying the divine wrath, while maintaining it, presumably, in the queen's connection to the power of the state. The name is an extension of the queen's power and a marker indicating her ownership of the commodities on which it appears. It is, as well, both apotropaic and mimetic in its discursive implication within the myths and politics of early Egypt, but what is it to us, 5,000 years away?

For us, its supplementarity resides in its emptiness. It is merely a placeholder for someone lost, a label replacing in turn the necklace, a sign testifying to a personal presence, now absent, giving our interest in the most remote and faintest history a point to fix upon. But the point is really no point, in that we know very little of Neithhotep apart from her name.[86]

In combination these two artifacts exemplify the range of the uses of writing in earliest Egypt. They are paralleled many times on wooden, ivory, and ebony labels as well as in the impressions left by seals rolled over the then wet clay of, say, an oil jar. They both indicate possession, but this seemingly simple marking of possession is not simple after all, and the fact that it takes one artifact to describe a tomb offering and another to express ownership is representative of the majority of examples of early writing we find in Egypt. The joint notation of a commodity and a name on the same artifact is rarer, for understandably practical reasons, but it points to a further complication of the work of the supplement.

A FINE AND PRIVATE PLACE

In most early examples, Egyptian writing is a royal prerogative, but the official class of scribes and bureaucrats quickly appropriated its use as well, so that we see, already in the middle of the First Dynasty, seals with the names and titles of the nonroyal dead from their tombs in Naqada, Nekhen, and Abydos (see Fig. 2.14). The use of seals in royal tombs had a clearly practical function, marking possession on jars of commodities provided for the deceased. In the case of the nonroyal tomb owners, however, the seals were very seldom actually used for the sealing of vessels in the burial. If they were made for the tomb *owner*, they also exhibit a supplement pointing out that they were made for him as a *tomb* owner, that is, for someone already deceased. Adelheid Schlott explains,

> Sometime around the middle of the First Dynasty, that is, about 2900 B.C.E., the non-royal dead, too, were given seals to take with them into their tombs, seals that were only very seldom actually used for the sealing of a vessel. They clearly had another function. The name and title of the deceased were inscribed upon them with a supplement [*Zusatz*] that indicated that the seal was made specially for the *dead* proprietor of the tomb. This supplement occurred in two forms, which one can translate as "the transfigured," and "the exalted." "The exalted" was written with the sign of a man sitting upon a stool, from which soon developed the representation of a man who sits before a table and stretches a hand out toward the food lying thereupon. These seals were found near the stores of offerings in the burial chambers. One recognizes therefore what purpose they served: non-royal persons now also used writing for the function which I have

Figure 2.14. First Dynasty seal impression showing the deceased receiving offerings. Redrawn after Kaplony, *Inschriften*, vol. 3, no. 497, pl. 105.

described above in reference to the cosmetic palettes and maceheads of the kings Scorpion and Na'rmer, to record and make eternal. What is most important to man, during his life or after death, is nourishment. And in order that they might have secure access to it even when the natural offerings were no longer adequate, or were robbed, and descendants no longer brought anything, they set them down in hieroglyphs and pictures together with the names (and titles) of those for whom they were intended.[87]

The figure of the beatified tomb owner, seated before an offering table, now serves as a determinative for his name, even as the offering table inscribed before him supplements, represents, and replaces the commodities that, in a royal tomb, would actually have been marked with the seal impression. This is the first clear emergence of the offering scene, which is to become a staple of tomb painting in Egyptian art from here on out. Over the next few centuries, the rudimentary examples scratched into seals are replaced by exquisitely painted and carved examples on tomb walls, among them early masterpieces such as the wooden panels from the tomb of an official of pharaoh Netjerkhet (Djoser) by the name of Hesire'. There are, altogether, five panels, or parts of panels, extant from this remarkable find, but clearly the most important is the offering scene, where Hesire' sits before a table of bread offerings over which are also recorded wine, incense, and small game (see Fig. 2.15). On the other panels, Hesire''s name is accompanied by six of his titles, but here a full thirteen are recorded.[88]

Figure 2.15. Panel from the Third Dynasty tomb of Hesire' at Saqqara. Egyptian Museum, Cairo (88). After Corteggiani, *L'Égypte des pharaons*, p. 36.

It is important to note that in tombs of the kings and highest-ranking officials of the earliest Egyptian state, offerings were not supplemented by written or pictorial representation. Only later, and especially in the tombs of the less well-to-do, does a reliance on pictures and written accounts of tomb offerings become important. There are early burials in which a rough parity exists between the commodities actually included in the tomb and those recorded on the walls, but the provision in writing is far less expensive and allows the less well-to-do to lay claim to handsome stores for the afterlife, even if only in name.[89] Hereafter, the grave goods proper, carefully marked with the owner's name, are duplicated in complex written form in a conventionalized offering list, such and such kinds of oil, such and such kinds of bread, such and such kinds of beer, and so on, so that the eventual disappearance of the material commodities, foreseen even as they are stored laboriously away, can be supplemented by words naming the commodities and standing in juxtaposition to the owner's name, while the owner himself is subject to the same impermanence as his oil, his bread, his cakes of precious incense.

From this economy of substitution, we have come to understand a certain Egyptian belief in the word, in its ability to replace reality, to substitute for the materiality of existence with language. It has often been remarked, indeed, that the Egyptians' genius, and their credulity as well, resided in their faith in the word. It is a commonplace that to the Egyptian, the name had substance.[90] Thus the assertion that the recording of the deceased's name and titles on his tomb walls, not to mention the commodities of the offering list, was a way to give him eternity.

The argument seems plausible enough. The variety of human enterprise and the catalog of nature depicted on the walls of tombs of nobles, from the Old Kingdom mastabas at Saqqara and Giza to the New Kingdom tombs on the West Bank opposite Thebes—even, in fact, in the Ptolemaic tomb of Petosiris—all these depictions suggest not only a delight in life and its multiplicity, but also a conviction that this life is analogous and in certain ways replicable in a world beyond death. The picture and, indeed, the word are simulacra, substitutes for a living world lost or under threat.

The writing and the pictures it accompanies—the two cannot usually be considered separately—are, then, a performance of reality. This same performative nature can be remarked in a great many Egyptian inscriptions, and might be taken a step further in considerations of the programs of decoration found in a wide variety of tombs. Again and again in reading about tombs, one comes upon the assertion that the articles depicted on the walls have a reality that might not merely supplement offerings made by the family or mortuary endowment of the deceased, but that in the case that such offerings should cease to be made, then the words and pictures alone might suffice.

Yet the ways in which Egyptians represented their world are in important ways antimimetic. The conventions of visual portrayal, as studied so intriguingly by Heinrich Schäfer, make no pretense of an illusionary re-presentation of what the individual sees. They are aimed rather at re-presenting in a carefully regulated schematization, an uncovering and spreading out of the relevant information underlying a visual apperception of the phenomenon.[91]

Similarly, the individual objects portrayed in a painting, relief, or sculpture are disposed upon or within the material support as individual and self-integral units with only subordinate concern for their actual disposition in space and time. Roland Tefnin makes the point as follows:

> Fundamental to the understanding of the Egyptian image [is] the recognition of linkage of clearly delimited levels of reading, from the elementary unity of a figure to the global unity of the cosmos, in symbolic coincidence with the architectural unity of the monument.... The figure is not to be confused with the whole person, an image of the king, for example, because the former reveals, under analysis, several unities of sense chosen from the midst of clearly limited paradigmatic series: clothing, crowns, insignia, scepters, flesh colors, and gestures mediate/intervene in a complex combination creating a veritable "phrase," of which a single word suffices to modify the sense, as in the case of what happens in language. It is worth noting that these elementary figures do not necessarily possess any referent in the natural world.[92]

This is an important point because it has been all to easy to set the Egyptians apart as children who really believed that the images in their tombs had the same reality status as actual objects from the real world. As John Baines has pointed out, "A belief that pictures were the same as their subjects would, by any standards, argue a deficient sense of reality."[93] And such a belief would, of course, amount to a failure to understand, at even the most basic level, Egyptian forms of representation, whether written or artistic.

How does this paradox of the supplement in language manifest itself in Egyptian? Although we cannot completely and definitively answer this question, the consideration of the relief in a characteristic, even if very early, tomb from Giza will give us some suggestive insights. And as earlier, we will approach the relief in terms of its construction of differential meanings and figural meanings.

The tomb, located south-southwest of the Sphinx, is that of Wepemnefret, an important official of the Fifth Dynasty, active perhaps under King Neferefre' or his immediate successors (see Fig. 2.16).[94]

Although it should be apparent by now that one cannot speak of the visual and linguistic aspects of Egyptian relief in isolation, in this case, it is the visual figuration of the scene that is most palpable. The relief exemplifies the canonical representational style of Egyptian art and depicts all the figures on its surface in accordance with a very specific system of conventions regarding the planes from which any given object is to be portrayed. This is most obvious in the human figures in the scene, with their heads in profile, but eyes in a frontal view, chest and shoulders in a frontal view, but hips and legs from the side, and so on.[95] This principle applies to all the objects depicted, however, whether in the relief "proper" or in the hieroglyphic text accompanying it. This "aspective" depiction (to borrow Emma Brunner-Traut's term), while it creates a certain semiotic unity throughout the relief, at the same time allows for certain interesting differences that cannot be overlooked. Among, for instance, the figures in the lower right quadrant, notice the scene in which two sculpted figures are

Figure 2.16. Scene from the tomb of the Fifth Dynasty official, Wepemnefret, at Giza. After Hassan, *Excavations at Gîza*, fig. 219. Drawn by I. H. Khalil.

being created, near the middle of the second row. The living sculptors show fully the aspective conventions of Egyptian two-dimensional art; note particularly that their shoulders are depicted in a frontal view. The sculptures they are working on, however, show foreshortened shoulders and indicate, thereby, that they are merely statues.[96] The difference indicated by this rather small detail is of great significance, because it ranges the inanimate statues, on the one hand, against all the other figures in the scene, which are all, in some way or another, animate.

Within this animate group, however, a wide range of differential relations can be observed. We might first consider them in terms of binary oppositions. There are, for instance, forty-nine men and only three women; there are forty-eight "normal-bodied" individuals versus four dwarves. Fifteen figures in the upper right quadrant show identical postures, whereas all the other figures in the relief have some degree of individuality of pose. Those fifteen figures are witnesses to a legal document recorded on the tomb wall, and the pose they have adopted is an outward sign of the testimony they are making.

There is an important similarity between these fifteen figures and the two large figures on the left half of the scene, because the witnesses are present in the service of the large figures, who are the principals in the legal assertion inscribed in the relief. All these figures are parties to the formal legal situation of tomb ownership, and are, consequently, depicted in formal poses with particular conventional associations, a kind of somatic semiotics, whereas the multitude of figures in the lower right quadrant are all depicted in more "naturalistic" poses appropriate to the particular activities they are engaged in.

But the most conspicuous feature of the scene has so far gone unmentioned; it is the differential in size of the figures in question. The two figures on the left tower above all the other figures in the scene, quite significantly so, because the two large figures are the owners of the tomb where the scene is found, and thus the patrons of the craftspeople and workers in the lower right quadrant, as well as the legal principals for whom the witnesses in the upper right quadrant are testifying. To be more precise, it is the largest figure, more than one meter high, who is owner of the tomb. His name is Wepemnefret. The next largest, about fifty centimeters high, is his son Iby. Iby, too, is an important personage here, but he is an owner of part of the tomb only because his father makes that ownership explicit in the legal document that occupies the center of the composition (behind Iby's back, and up to the top of the wall).

In this sense, Wepemnefret and Iby form one-half of an oppositional pair, through their legal right of possession, with all the other figures in the scene, who are supplementary to the ownership of the tomb. But a further opposition must be noted between Wepemnefret on the one hand, and all the other figures in the scene (almost). That opposition is signaled, in part, by headgear. Only Wepemnefret wears a wig. Everyone else has on merely a skull cap—everyone, that is, except for the two statues. The statues also wear wigs, and in this bear a likeness to Wepemnefret; they are, indeed, his likeness, but he is their likeness too, at a certain central point in the creation of the tomb, because if Wepemnefret seems on the one hand to take part of the animate world, he is also inanimate (i.e., dead) as owner proper of the tomb.

Of course, all the individuals pictured in the scene are now dead, but it is only Wepemnefret who is dead in a way essential to the meaning of the scene; the others (with the possible exception of Iby) just happen to be dead, and that does not signify in our reading. This can be seen in the inscriptions in the scene also. Those in solid black are, in the original, incised into the stone (they relate to Wepemnefret and Iby, and the legal situation), whereas the rest, white with a black outline here, are raised relief in the original. They relate to everything else in the scene.

That Wepemnefret's death signifies in a special way is a point we can hardly miss, and it is a point that is central to the received understanding of the representational system here exemplified. To say he is dead is, perhaps, indelicate, a solecism of sorts. For, quite plausibly, it is his intention in commissioning this representation not to be dead, but rather, to memorialize his eternal life.

Now to grapple with this better, we must consider the texts on the wall as well as the pictures (as if the two could be considered separately). Much, indeed, of what we have said already would not have been clear without reference to the texts, but let us make explicit where that evidence resides.

Directly above Wepemnefret, and reading from right to left, in his direction, are his many titles, and finally, in the largest hieroglyphs in the scene, his name. Beginning to the right of the titles, first in horizontal rows, and below, once again in columns, the legal document mentioned earlier is quoted, guaranteeing for Iby, and for him alone, a chamber in the tomb proper and a room in the offering chapel above. In the upper right quadrant of the scene, with the fifteen witnesses to the document, are their names and occupations ("the physician Ni-Ptah-neferhor," "The seal-bearer Tjenti," "the painter Re'-hai," and so on). Such concern for individual identity is apparent throughout the scene, including even the names of several of the craftsmen in the horizontal rows in the lower right quadrant. (Indeed, we suppose Wepemnefret to be a contemporary of King Neferefre' because one of the carpenters is named "Neferefre' Lives," Nfr-f-R'-'nḫ.)

The document inscribed on the tomb wall must now be quoted in full:

> It is Wepemnefret, King's Unique Friend, who says,
> I bequeath in perpetuity to my eldest son, the Lectorpriest
>   Iby, the grant of
> item) this northern burial chamber, in The Gods' Necropolis
> item) this northern offering chamber, in The Gods' Necropolis
> That he should be buried therein and
> Receive offerings continually therein, A Blessed Spirit.
> It is not given to any brother, wife, child, or dependent apart from the
>   Lectorpriest Iby, to whom I have given it.[97]

The understanding of this legal text lays the groundwork for a consideration of one of the most interesting differences in the entire scene, the scene of an intractable supplementarity. For if Wepemnefret's formal pose, wig, ceremonial beard, and formal kilt and the careful listing of his many titles suggest he is herewith installed in eternity, and that his presence there is guaranteed by the texts and representations on the wall, what are we to make of the lively scenes in the lower right quadrant, which, on the other hand, delight in the ephemeral? Many of the activities depicted there might, it is true, serve the eternal provision of the tomb, but the captions above these pictures, in addition to the most matter-of-fact labeling of the activities and identities of the actors, go further to record conversations of the most fleeting and casual nature. One brewer says to another, "What a blabbermouth you are!" Another cautions, "Don't listen to him!" To one sculptor's comment, "I've been at this a whole month now," another shoots back, "Dimwit! how do you figure that!" (See Fig. 2.17.)

The very ephemerality of the comments makes them particularly difficult to translate, and the renderings above are provisional at best, but the comments of the dwarf jewelers on the left side of the bottom row seem relatively clear. "Hurry up and get this collar done," says one, and his com-

Figure 2.17. Brewers and sculptors in a detail from the tomb of Wepemnefret at Giza.

panion answers, "May Ptah love you as [I] do—it'll be done today." One of the two seated behind this first pair has been distracted, and he turns around to say "Look, the metal's there beside you!" His companion, apparently annoyed, shouts out to him, "Pull tight on what you've got hold of! Or do you want to hold things up 'til the break of day!" (See Fig. 2.18.)

The common argument holds that the Egyptians inscribed their tombs and temples with scenes and texts in order to immortalize and maintain in perpetuity what was thereby recorded,[98] that the fixing of the owner's identity and presence on the wall attempt to provide him immortality is plausible when one considers the representation of the owner and his son, especially in the context of the legal document quoted near center top of the wall, properly witnessed by fifteen named individuals in the upper right. But the activities of the craftsmen and brewers and bakers in the lower right quadrant, for all their interest and ingenuousness, undo the fix. Though Wepemnefret may have hoped to claim the gold collars, the statuary, and the coffers they are making, and their bread and beer as well, he cannot seriously have wanted to listen to their bickering and carping for eternity. The representations that provide, then, for his eternal upkeep, hearken back again and again to the quality of a vanished life, vivid in the re-presentation, but subversive of the eternal dignity that, as the argument has it, the "fixing" of writing and image was supposed to accomplish. If the remedy for death is mummification and the laying up of stores (whether in actual substance or through the simulacrum of language), then the remedy is also a threat, which, in compensating through language for the fragility of the body and the unreliability of offerings, points always outside the tomb, and beyond the frame of the individual life, to a broader social context. The charm of the ephemeral seduces the subject away from his claim on immortality.

A final example will illustrate a further complication in the construction of an Egyptian subject. It comes from much later in Egyptian civilization and can be seen in the papyrus of Hunefer, Royal Scribe and Steward of the great king Seti I, and Overseer of Royal Cattle and Scribe of Divine

Figure 2.18. Jewelers and bakers in a detail from the tomb of Wepemnefret at Giza.

Offerings (pBM 9901) (see Fig. 2.19). The setting is the hall of judgment. Hunefer stands alongside Horus before the kiosk of Osiris, who sits enthroned by a lotus pool, his four grandsons emanating from the petals of a lotus. Behind Osiris stand two goddesses, Isis and Nephthys. Each figure under the kiosk is labeled simply with his name, except for the two goddesses. Above them a brief inscription says, *jnk snt.k Jst Nbt-ḥwt*, "I am thy sister Isis Nephthys."

There is no danger of mistaking the first person singular for a reference to a single goddess named *Jst Nbt-ḥwt*; the accompanying illustration clearly shows two female figures, and each carries upon her head, in typical Egyptian fashion, the hieroglyphic representation of her name. Why then, the first person singular pronoun and the singular form of the noun *snt*, sister? You might be tempted to reply, "There is no first person plural independent pronoun attested until very late," as Gardiner informs us.[99]

But if the first singular is intended to replace a plural, then why is this not made clear with the dual of "sister"? At this simple level, then, we have an example of supplementarity operative between the text "I am your sister" and the two female figures which makes possible the "correct" reading of the text even as it contradicts that reading. More significant still is a less obvious form of supplementarity. It is only the two goddesses who are captioned by a full sentence. The other figures seated on the dais are simply named: "Osiris," "Imsety," "Ha'py," "Duamutef," "Qebehsenuf."

Figure 2.19. The royal dais of Osiris as depicted in a vignette accompanying BD 125 from the Nineteenth Dynasty papyrus of Hunefer. London, British Museum (pBM 9901/3). After Faulkner, *Ancient Egyptian Book of the Dead*, p. 35.

LANGUAGE OF THE GODS 103

Not only are the goddesses singled out for fuller grammatical treatment, but the second person suffix pronoun -*k* also appears in the utterance, to be read "I am *thy* sister..." The most orthodox reading of this word would read "thy" to refer to Osiris, seated on his throne before the goddesses. But the characteristic disposition of figures in Egyptian art puts figures in conversation face to face, whereas here, Osiris himself has his back turned on the goddesses (not surprisingly, since the focus of the scene is the interaction between Osiris and the newly vindicated Hunefer).

Could it be then, that "thy" might refer, not to Osiris in this case, but to Hunefer, the deceased for whom the papyrus was painted, Hunefer, who has just passed the test in the hall of judgment to be declared true of voice: the newly transformed Osiris-Hunefer? Perhaps this conjecture reads too much into a simple grammatical infelicity. Then again, it may rather underpin a far more consequential supplementarity, that of Osiris vis-à-vis Osiris-Hunefer, a supplementarity which underlies Egyptian constructions of the human subject in the realm of death, by giving them a divinity to match that of the god, who displayed an all-too-human vulnerability to death. Let us return to Tefnin's analysis of the interaction of image and word on Egyptian monuments for some further discussion of the supplementarity in question.

According to Tefnin, "In the great majority of cases, Egyptian images are organized according to a simple syntactic structure of subject-action-object."[100] In this they resemble the more complex emblematic constructions of ideographs and logographs in the hieroglyphic writing system.

> The inscription indicates, in accordance with a formula very common in the tombs of the Old Kingdom, that "the deceased X contemplates the blessings of the entire land." In his uniqueness, Rahotep is presented to us as the subject of a relation of contemplation, a phenomenon in its own right extremely interesting from the point of view of semiotics and disconcerting for us, accustomed as we are to being the agents of seeing, the unique space for the reading of the work. The image in an Egyptian tomb ignores us. The spectacle plays itself out in a closed circuit for a spectator-image interior to the image. The position of statuary clearly confirms, furthermore, the fact, in as much as it is enclosed (under the Old Kingdom, at least) in an auxiliary compartment, walled and dark (the *serdab*), pierced only by a narrow opening which allows the statues not to be seen, but to see, to be present for the presentation of offerings in the funerary chapel.[101]

Tefnin's insight into the circulation of the Egyptian image, its action upon itself, greatly improves our understanding of the significance of many compositional features that have been puzzling and open to the most drastic misunderstanding. But with the mention of the opening in the *serdab*, and the necessity to receive offerings, Tefnin's insights must admit of a certain blindness, for the image does not ignore us, it is constituted in its very need for a second subject, an entity outside the image who will provide for the upkeep of the spirit of the deceased. It is, moreover, only in our *reading* of the images that they have any "presence" in the world (unless one subscribes to "the beliefs of the ancient Egyptians," which, if they can be known to us at all, can be known only through just such a reading.)

Dead pharaohs during Egypt's heyday could count on magnificent offering banquets provided by the endowments they made while alive. They could not, however, count on them very long. The offering cult of Snefru is known to have persisted for at least four centuries after his death, but it was the exception to the rule.[102] (There is, moreover, ample testimony among the classics of Middle Egyptian of the fragility and impermanence of the tomb and its furnishings, even the tomb of a pharaoh. Thus, in the *Instruction of Merikare'*, one is encouraged to do justice, as a means to immortality.)[103]

If you were not a pharaoh or an exalted member of the nobility, you were well advised to make other provisions for eternity, because the cult of offerings would be fast food compared to that pharaonic banquet. Would your wife and kids carry it on? And after the next generation, who knows? You might however prevail upon a passerby in ages hence to mouth the syllables of your name, particularly if you had an attractive or ingenious stela carved. And that would be your eternity, living on in the word, living on off the word: a thousand jars of beer, a thousand loaves of bread.

Language, then, and the images which stand off, hyperdeterminatives, reach beyond themselves toward a presence, the presence of which can never be guaranteed. Thus the bipolar axes Tefnin so skillfully analyzes—being versus action, denomination versus anonymity, unity versus multiplicity, largeness versus smallness—these must be further deferred in favor of a more pressing phenomenological immediacy. In each case, the binarism Tefnin identifies within the relief must be ranged against an exterior subject, the "second subject," which we become as viewers, to create more complex pairs. (Being versus action) within the relief must be compared and contrasted with our living presence outside. (Denomination versus anonymity) there must stand against our voicing of whatever names are recorded. (Unity versus multiplicity) within the pictorial space must face the differential of interiority/exteriority in our perceptions, while the differential (largeness/smallness) in the largely two-dimensional world of the tomb scene must be confronted with our embodied multi-dimensionality herewithout.

The word and its image, then, for all their mutual self-reference, represent a lack which is to be filled, if not by the provision of real offerings, then by the voicing of name and title, and the cultural memory.

If you take the trouble to learn just a little Egyptian, you will soon be able to read the offering formula, and sound, for yourself, the name of a subject three or five millennia away. Whether this is just a nice museum trick, or an exercise of some further significance depends on how you read, I guess, and it is a topic for another time. Whatever humanistic reassurance may come from such knowledge, however, more pressing questions remain. The word, written, remains to be read, and in being read recalls not just the dead, but the line between, the living body "behind" the letter, the body which the letter has, in naming, (d)effaced: a problem the Egyptians faced themselves.

COMING AND BECOMING 3

The founding of Egyptology as a scientific discipline is frequently credited to Sir W. M. Flinders Petrie (1853–1942). His methodical excavations, and better yet, his careful and timely publications describing his findings, were a great advance over the treasure hunting of most of his predecessors. He was, however, a party to the effacement of the phallus from the Egypt his generation wanted to see. Having found (arguably) the earliest colossal sculptures in the world, three huge and archaic stone statues of the ithyphallic god Min, Petrie chose to describe them as follows (see Fig. 3.1):

> The type is the same in all of these figures. The legs are parallel and joined together, with merely a groove down between them, on front and back. The knees are very roughly indicated. The arms are rudely formed, about half projecting from the surface of the figure. The left hand is in the usual attitude of Min; the right hand is not raised with a whip, as in the figures of historic times, but hangs down the side; the fingers are clenched, and a hole is drilled through the hand, as if for hanging something to it. Down the right thigh hangs a flap of some material in low relief; this is seen to depend from the girdle.[1]

The figures antedate other Egyptian sculpture of similar size by perhaps three centuries, they must weigh about two tons, and they were apparently transported two to three hundred miles.[2] But remarkable as they are, Petrie found it impossible to describe them adequately. That left hand, which he innocuously describes as "in the usual attitude of Min,"

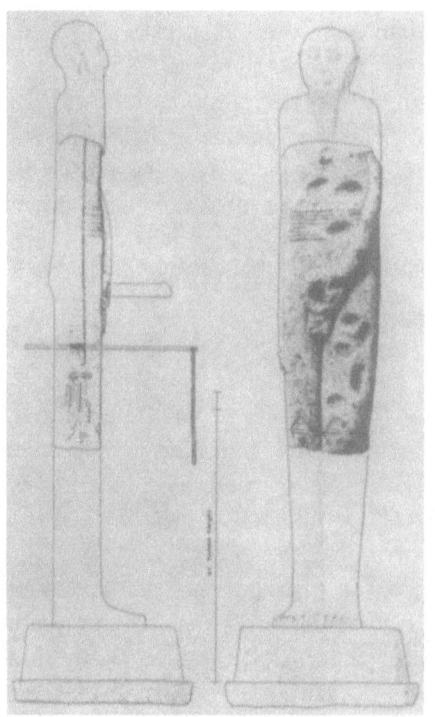

Figure 3.1. Coptos colossus of Min. Ashmolean Museum, Oxford (1894.105e). Adapted from Kemp, *Ancient Egypt*, fig. 28. Used by permission of the publisher.

reaches to a now nonexistent phallus, a separate piece, present in absence by the hole into which it was set. Like many other phalluses on Egyptian sculpture it stands conspicuous in its absence.[3]

Consider the gargantuan columns of the hypostyle hall at Karnak, for example: an army of kings makes offering to an army of the transformations of Amun, many in his ithyphallic form as Amun *kamutef*. And on column after column, someone has taken considerable trouble to chip away at the figures, leaving a gap, where the shaft and glans of Amun's erection are still sharply defined in their absence by a silhouette.

Just over a mile south of Karnak, the Temple of Luxor shows the same defacement, as does Medinet Habu, across the Nile, and Dendera to the north, and Philae to the south, and so on, including even the lovely relief of Osiris-Sokar in his barque in the Ptah-Sokar room of the temple erected by Menma'atre' Seti I at Abydos. Much of this "defacement" must have been perpetrated by priggish Copts or Muslims. Some of it may have come at the hands of ancient Egyptians themselves: the powder scraped carefully off the god's member had powers, aphrodisiac or restorative.[4] But an apothecary would have scraped carefully away at the stone and caught the dust in a vessel of some manner. Most of the damage to these phalluses is violent. The stone was hacked off, the chips left to lie where they had fallen.

The pathology of such vandalism is rooted in more than simple antipathy to polytheism; it has more visceral roots in the figuring of power in the penis, a metonymic smudge we might trace recurrently in "Western" thought, from Plutarch's account of the legend of Osiris down to the 1993 college radio threnody, "Detachable Penis." Petrie, perhaps out of embarrassment, is an accessory to this vandalism after the fact.

WRITING WITH A PEN(IS)

In their incompleteness these legions of mutilated ithyphallic gods give clear testimony of a fear of dismemberment and castration which runs throughout the subsequent history of the West, from the formation of Christian theologies of the body to Freud's psychoanalytic writing and the turgid and hermetic psychological theory of Jacques Lacan.

But this is not exclusively a post-pharaonic queasiness. Look for it and you will find a similar ambivalence over embodiment in the uniquely insightful medium of hieroglyphs. In their iconicity, they exemplify in a highly concentrated and schematic form, the semiotic bind of corporeality. This ambivalence is apparent at a basic level in the semiotic manipulation of the phallus and its seminal trace. Consider its use in the selection of words cited in Figure 3.2.

It should come as no surprise that the phallus glyph is the determinative for words meaning "penis" (1 and 2) and "foreskin" (3), as, indeed, for words meaning "semen" (4) and "urine" (5).[5] It is not difficult, in such a context, to imagine why the Egyptians linked the phallus to a word meaning "the humors of the body" as well (6).

Similarly, one might well expect the glyph to determine words for "male" (7) and "husband" (8). As cause leads to consequence, so the phallus determinative has a logical relation to words meaning "fetus" (9) and "offspring" (10), and there is at least one case where even the word for "mother" is written with the phallus glyph (11b).[6] This is partly because of a phonetic coincidence: the word was vocalized from a consonant skeleton *mwt* and was normally written as in 11a, in part with a homophone meaning "vulture" (11b). The phallus glyph, however, is a common phonogram for the consonant skeleton *mt*. Since the *w* in *mwt*, "mother," is a weak consonant, it is likely to fall out of pronunciation, or at least out of the written form of the word, so the phallus glyph can play a phonetic

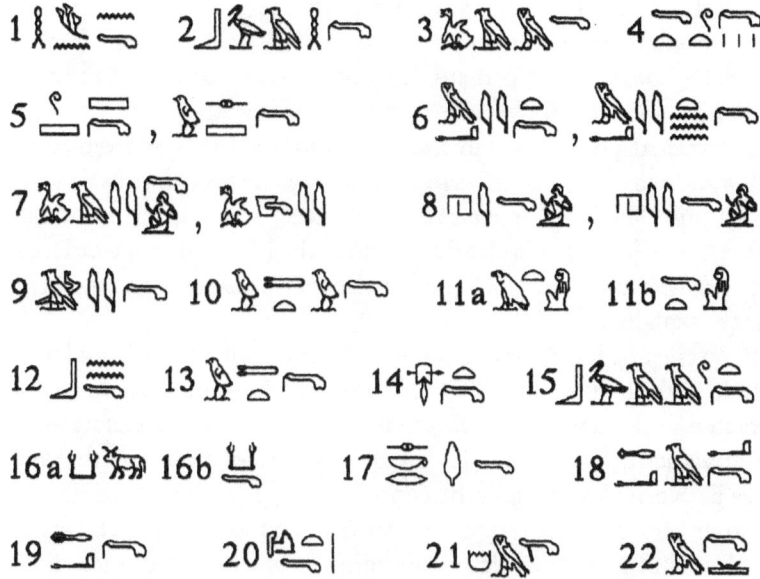

Figure 3.2. Words written in hieroglyphics using the phallus glyphs.

role in the writing. We would be mistaken, however, to overlook the possibility that the use of the phallus glyph here is ironic or playful.

Verbs determined with the phallus include "become erect" (12), "beget" (13), and "impregnate" (14, a derivative of the word "shoot," as in "shoot an arrow"). And it is a short jump to another noun, "virility" (15). Is it metonymy or metaphor in operation when one finds, in two different versions of the word "bull," one having the determinative of the animal itself, as in (16a), and another where the animal is replaced by the phallus (16b)?

Hereafter, the semiotic network of the phallus glyph becomes more complex. On the one hand, it becomes the index of phallocentric pride in serving as the determinative for a verb meaning "adorn" (17). But a phallus glyph also determines a word meaning "an evil influence causing disease" (18), and here our attention must return to the word "semen" quoted earlier, for that very word (4) can also mean "poison."

Violence, as well, becomes one of the connotations of the phallus in a word meaning "rape" (19), and more insidiously in the logograph meaning "men" or "fighters," a pair of arms holding shield and mace followed by an erect phallus (20). On the famous Semna Stela of King Kha'kaure' Senusert III, moreover, the phallus is mutilated (21) as a mark of dishonor characterizing the Nubians, who are proscribed, by the inscribed text, from proceeding north of the position where the stela has been erected.[7]

Finally, consider (22), perhaps the most interesting word of the group. It is either a prepositional phrase for "in the presence of . . ." or "before . . . ," or an adverbial phrase for "in front," "formerly." It is written with the phallus and the scroll determinative, which we noted before as a marker of abstractions. The word is commonly attested, although it is formal and perhaps honorific, and it is clearly related to the less common word for phallus mentioned above (2). The figural quality of this expression remains inadequately explained.[8]

If, on the one hand, associations of poison, pollution, and violence can be made with the phallus, so also is fecundity, both in the common sense associated with engendering children and also in a more generalized and vegetative sense, as we see it depicted countless times in the offering scenes between pharaoh and the conspicuously ithyphallic Amun or Min. So, too, is semen characterized on the one hand as a source of legitimacy, fecundity, and power, while on the other it is associated with violence, illegitimacy, and poison.

Figure 3.3. Detail from the Semna Stela. The stone is carved in fine reddish quartzite. It was erected at a site near the Second Cataract of the Nile to mark the southern border of Egypt under Senusert III. Ägyptisches Museum, Berlin (1157). After the photograph in Forman and Quirke, *Hieroglyphs and the Afterlife,* p. 100.

We just mentioned the Semna Stela of Senusert III (see Fig. 3.3), where the Nubians are characterized as cowardly and treacherous, and where one reference to them is determined by a mutilated phallus. But the pharmakology of the phallus prescribes, on the same stela, a legitimate exercise of power though the transfer of seed from father to son: "If any son of Mine shall hold this border firm, the which My Majesty has made, he is My son and born to Me, the image of a son, his father's champion, who holds potent to this border of the one who begot him!"[9]

The phallus and its seminal trace exist then in a nexus of associations exemplifying, supporting, and extending the power of the father, on the one hand, and promulgating violence, pollution, and danger, on the other. It is, indeed, in this vertiginous pharmakology of the phallus that the Egyptians saw the beginning of time.

THE HAND OF GOD

Atum, the original father, who brought the world into being in Aunu, himself "came" into being in a double sense. Atum is, in fact, defined as "he who became, in coming lengthened, which he did in Aunu.[10] He took his phallus in his fist and made sweet ejaculation from it, and the twins, Shu and Tefnut, were born" (*Pyramid Texts* 1248a–d):[11]

It is remarkable that this text constructs creation as self-presence and figures that presence in "coming." The English pun might almost seem to serve as well in Egyptian. But for all its awkwardness, this is not what could be called a "literal" translation. The semantic field of one phrase in particular, ⟨glyphs⟩ (*jw-s3w*), does not translate quite literally. There is, however, a striking coincidence of figures. The word *jw*, represented merely by the two walking legs in the inscription, is "either a verbal noun or a particle," as James Allen points out.[12] If the former, it may be construed with the phonetic *m* from the preceding owl glyph, to mean "in coming."

The next word has a phonetic skeleton of *s3w*, but is accompanied as well by two ideographic determinatives, the latter clearly a figure grasping his erect penis in one hand while raising the other high in the air. The former determinative, less explicit, activates a broader range of associations: 🦴. It is the glyph of an animal's backbone with the spinal cord extending from both ends. This glyph is often used in Egyptian merely to render the phonetic $3w$, but it would be too hasty to assume that such is the case here. Allen's gloss is helpful syntactically, but the more pressing problem is semantic: what is the lexical range of the term?

At the heart of the word is a root that conveys, among other senses, that of "be long," of space or time. But the English "long" does not convey all of the notions of extension this root implies. It has associations of expansiveness and plenitude which come across only in a kind of translationese, rendering "joyful," for instance, as "long of heart"; "farsighted" as "long of face (or view)"; or "generous" as "long of hand."

In the verbal axis, one finds such figures as "acting with a long reach," which is to say, laying hands upon someone. The determinative of a forearm or a man brandishing a stick specifies senses ranging from, simply, "extend the arm" to "present an offering," "announce someone," and so on.

In the context of Atum's genesis, however, $3w$ is clearly masturbatory. With a causative prefix it means "cause to be long" or "lengthen" with the explicit sense of "make erect," "arouse oneself," or "stiffen." Allen has "growing ithyphallic." And this is, of course, the focus of the text, but it would not be appropriate to restrict it to the masturbatory sense. The lengthening seems also to be figured as a congealing or solidifying of the waters of primeval chaos, as is borne out by another of the most noteworthy Egyptian cosmogonic texts. That second text, though describing the beginning of the cosmos in terms similar to those in *Pyramid Texts* 1248, adopts a different position vis-à-vis those events, addressing the god Atum, rather than describing him:

Words for Recitation: Atum Kheprer, You have uprisen as a hill, you have waxed forth as the Benben in the Phoenix Mansion in Aunu, You have sneezed as Shu, You have spat as Tefnut, You have put your two arms

Figure 3.4. Relief of Senusert I in the embrace of Ptah. Apparently the sole remaining fragment of a festival kiosk in the sacred precincts of Karnak. The calligraphic forms are closely related to those on Senusert's "White Chapel" in Karnak. Egyptian Museum, Cairo (265). After a photograph in Ions, *Egyptian Mythology*, p. 95.

around them, as the arm of the Ka, that your Ka might exist within them. Atum, put your arms around [the king, N].[13]

This text is less explicit than that quoted earlier, and the word I have translated as "waxed forth," *wbn*, has often been taken as the common verb "to rise," as of the sun, but as John Baines has pointed out, there is good reason to associate the word with *bnn*, which relates to expansion or erection in the sexual sense.[14] There is no reason to restrict the meaning to either an exclusively sexual or an exclusively astronomical sense. In neither case, in fact, can a "literal" meaning be discerned, because no description of cosmogenesis can be literal. What is common to the two texts, however, is the figuring of the emergence of being as a form of expansion.[15] The former text, which is apparently the older of the two, is also more remarkable, because in it, the expansion into being is jointly figured as both a process of matter and a process of consciousness.

These two texts belong to the oldest extended body of writing in the world, and already they reflect a basic ambivalence about existence in relation to male sexuality and desire. The first is particularly revealing. Atum's purpose there is pleasure, not parenthood. He acts in complete autonomy of desire, without the need of a partner, and his progeny are accidental, a supplement to the interiority of his autoerotic intent.[16]

It is curious that there has been so little conspicuous comment about the connection between existence and the fulfillment of desire so central to this text. It is tellingly linked to that chapter of the *Book of the Dead* where Osiris, in his commerce with Atum, trades away "sweet ejaculation" (and wind and water) for divinity (175b).

But for some among the old aristocracy of Egyptology, Atum's coming into being caused chagrin and profound embarrassment. E. A. Wallis Budge, the Keeper of Egyptian and Assyrian Antiquities at the British Museum under Edward VII, calls the episode "a brutal example of naturalism." Budge's view is pervaded by theories of race, and to him this account of creation is a vestige of "the coarse habits of the pre-dynastic Egyptians, . . . [of] the indigenous African tribes from which dynastic Egyptians were partly descended."[17]

The American James Henry Breasted avoids Budge's racism, but speaks so tactfully as to be opaque, saying the sun god came into being, "by his own masculine power, self-developed." Breasted's strategy is a familiar one, concealing the autoeroticism of the myth by switching to a different semiotic register, parsing "power" for "penis" and displacing the concrete imagery with a vaguer, "more philosophical," interpretation.

Even Kurt Sethe's magisterial *Altägyptischen Pyramidentexte* betrays the desire to allegorize, and thereby obscure, the masturbatory reference. He reads ⟨glyphs⟩ together with the previous ⟨glyph⟩ (*m*) as *mj-s³w*, "Come-Lengthened," construing the first verb as an imperative, and then binding it with the other members in a hyphenated personification akin to the German "Vergißmeinnicht," that is, "forget-me-not."[18] This grammatical interpretation has not been generally accepted, however, and the masturbatory reference remains clear in any case because of the determinative ⟨glyph⟩, which is as unique as it is explicit.[19]

But such metaphorical projection is not altogether inappropriate; after all, the Egyptians were themselves intimately engaged in the metaphorical recasting of the material imagery of reality, as their writing system amply demonstrates. Yet Breasted makes of metaphor a process of exclusion. The given image is occulted to the advantage of a particular metaphorical interpretation—such "allegory" ("*x really* means *y*") leaves a hole in the weave of Egyptian reality to privilege, after the fact, the metaphysics of Platonic, Christian, and other kinds of Idealism.

Like the rest of the great body of mortuary texts through which we know Egypt, this old inscription requires a caveat: there must, at one time, have been more to the story of Atum's generation of the cosmos than we have been able to piece together. Written references to it are frequent enough, but they are always fragmentary and elliptical, and there are few (if any) representations of it in the visual arts. All the same, the self-intent sexuality of this myth distinguishes it in the body of Egyptian cosmogony and compounds our difficulty in understanding across 45 centuries.

As late as 1992, a prominent Egyptologist, Donald Redford, perpetuated the effacement of this myth by identifying another version of the sun priests' cosmogony as "classic," that in which the first god is conceived as a falcon hatching from an egg.[20] Redford lays claim to the authority of an eminent predecessor, Siegfried Morenz, in his discussion, but "classic" is his own word, and the sleight of hand by which he canonizes the one story to the disadvantage of other, so-called crass versions reveals an embarrassment not too different from the Edwardians' nearly a century ago. (Redford's "classic" version represents, moreover, a classic paradox of origins, "which came first, the chicken or egg?")[21]

Joseph Campbell speaks from a more catholic perspective and regards the myth sympathetically in the broader context of "Oriental" cosmogony, but he still finds there "no developed psychological analogy, . . . simply a primary image of physical creation on the level almost of an unadorned dream symbol." Whatever Campbell may intend by the terms "psychological" and "primary," his contention that the myth contains no developed psychological analogy ignores the psychological thrust of desire, which is, after all, the motivating factor in the episode.[22]

That this very desire should emerge as the motive for the differentiation of existence from chaos is extraordinarily important. The phallocentric iconicity of the scene remains in subsequent formulations of creation and as a "dream symbol." The episode may represent precisely the eruption of the male psyche onto the field of desire, as the autogeny of a nocturnal emission might erupt into the autonomy of masturbation.

There is, however, an odd and telling slippage in many references to this myth, a dislocation that cuts against both the phallocentrism and the autonomy of desire. The slippage occurs in the arousal of multiplicity from the unitary consciousness of the primordial god, for as I said, when Atum comes into existence, he gives birth as well to the next generation of gods. They are siblings, Shu, a god, of the dry air, and Tefnut, a goddess, of moist, corrosive air.[23]

In the text to which we have been referring, the births are not described with any specificity, but elsewhere, Shu and Tefnut are said to have been born from Atum's mouth. This can be explained in part through the opportunism of a pun. A switch of sites has been effected because

"Shu" can be related to *jšš* and "Tefnut" to *tf*. (Both words are synonyms of expectoration.)[24] But deferring the bodily to a lexical figure is only one in a series of refigurations of the myth, and there is more at stake here than merely a pun.

For if, by the convenience of a pun, one manages to preserve the sense of creation via bodily efflux, the transfer of sites, from phallus to mouth, is important, and represents merely the first of a sequence of substitutions whereby the phallic body is displaced in favor of different conceptions of the creation.

The next great corpus of funerary texts we have found, the *Coffin Texts* of the Middle Kingdom, contains a number of important accounts of the birth of Shu. In one, he asserts,

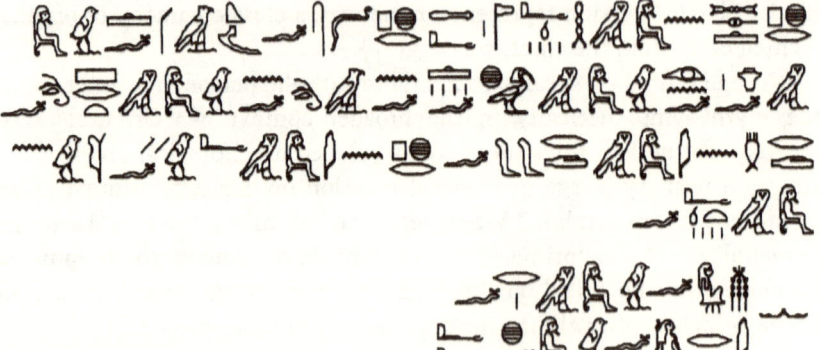

> My being was framed from the flesh of the great god who brought himself into being. He formed me in his heart, he made me through his power, he exhaled me through his nose.... In his feet am I grown, in his two arms am I come to being, in his limbs am I risen.

He goes on, indeed, to repudiate any phallic origin, insisting, "he did not bear me from his mouth, he did not conceive me with his fist."[25] Even here though, while the phallus is repudiated, the bodily is preserved in references to flesh, to the arms, and even to the exhaled breath. And alongside these embodied references already we see a more abstract construction of the creation, through the heart, and the wish, and power.

As Jan Assmann points out, the ancient formulation of creation by self-begetting in bodily efflux is reevoked even as it is disavowed as the process is recast to a more conceptual or intellectual kind of creation.[26] Each recasting, each change of site reveals a deeply ambivalent but seemingly inescapable relation between the phallic body and existence.

And so, in the same corpus of texts where we find Shu denying his origin in the phallus of the father, we find Shu stating the following:

I am this soul of Shu which is in the flame of the fiery blast which Atum kindled with his own hand. He created orgasm [i.e., *ndmmyt*] and fluid fell from his mouth. He spat me out as Shu together with [Tefnut], who came forth after me.[27]

Why should this be? After all, what particular need is there for the body to become involved here? Cosmogonies may well require the separation of discrete elements from some originary state. Indeed, our word "cosmos" derives from a verb meaning to order, arrange, or dispose, and the notion of ordering entails the separation and disposal of multiple elements in some sort of structure. That separation can be figured in many ways, however, as the separation of light from darkness, form from matter, yin from yang, solid from liquid from gas, or indeed, in the fugitive explosion of the "big bang."

Yet the problem of consciousness in relation to the matter of existence leaves one with a limited number of options. Consciousness can be unrelated to matter, "existing" independently and apart, or it can exist in full or partial congruence with the physical substance of the cosmos. Such an understanding has created fundamental paradoxes in the history of Western metaphysics, and even as we must acknowledge a degree of confusion common to both this metaphysical history and to Egyptian constructions of this relation, there are important differences to consider as well. This is where the ingenuity of the cosmogony of Aunu is most apparent.

The origin of the cosmos, as the priests of Aunu imagined it, does not, strictly speaking, entail the *creation* of anything. It is instead a process of transformation, whereby the inchoate materia of preexistence is organized, structured, and fragmented into the discrete phenomena of the world. The world is not fundamentally other from the materia of preexistence, but it is organized differently. Thus Tefnut and Shu are of the same substance as Atum, and Atum is of the same substance as the pre-originary chaos, but the ejaculation into being entails a splitting and reconstitution of preexistence. It is logical that consciousness itself emerge within this continuity, and that the origin of the universe should occur simultaneously with the origin of consciousness. Carried to its full conclusion, such an interrelation would lead to a kind of animism or pantheism, perhaps; something we cannot clearly discern in the extant body of Egyptian philosophical speculation. In terms of the figuring of the person upon creation, however, the cosmogony of Aunu is daring and original. For to figure the simultaneous emergence of consciousness and the material world in terms of sexual pleasure is a particularly trenchant positioning of the subject, self-conscious, conspicuously embodied, and ecstatic (in both the common meaning of "highly pleasurable" and in the etymological context of "standing outside oneself").

And yet the introduction of the body entails complex issues of gender and subject position, and the origin of the cosmos itself is not generally figured in sexual terms. True, there are many accounts of human origin or the origin of families of gods as a result of sexual intercourse, but these take place after the appearance of the cosmos from a primeval other. And even in the cosmogony of Atum, heterosexual embrace takes over to generate the gods once the process of creation has been set in motion, but the originary moment is not figured in such a manner. Indeed, it cannot be. For if the origin of the cosmos itself is to be thought from within, in sexual terms, then it must be ordered in a kind of "first person"[28]—not necessarily in the grammatical sense but in, all the same, a narrative position within the subject.[29] Otherwise, it must necessarily objectify the originary act through narration from outside, and the presence of that outside cannot be explained. For the One must then have become, at least, Two before coupling could begin.

In its interiority, then, Atum's self-generation represents a truer figuring of sexual cosmogenesis within the consciousness of a single subject. But there is, of course, a paradox here as well. The figuring of creation in terms of phallic pleasure already deconstructs itself, injecting a difference, a multiplicity unaccountable from within the interiority of desire. In the context of *Pyramid Text* 1248, this is apparent in the disjunction between intention and result. Atum takes his phallus in his fist for pleasure, but in its achievement, he produces a supplement, the gods Shu and Tefnut.

This differentiation, in paternity, fragments the subject. There is now an outside with a life of its own, which disowns its seminal origins in the chain of displacements we touched upon earlier (recall Shu's insistence, "He did not bear me from his mouth, he did not conceive me with his fist").[30] And Atum, having come into being, fades from the scene. His name appears in various litanies, he attends the magistracy of Osiris in the other world, and his is the name given the sun god late in the aging day, but he figures in no very colorful way in the body of Egyptian myth.[31]

Narrative interest hastens off to the generations after Atum: Shu and Tefnut succeed him and bear Geb and Nut. Nut is disentangled from Geb's procreative embrace, and her star-scattered body is raised high above his, becoming the sky to his earth (see Fig. 3.5). The cosmos at last is come fully to form, and only now do we find a grand narrative, a story of love, murder, death, and paternity: the myth of Osiris.

In one sense, of course, the story that begins with Atum's eruption into being has no ending as long as being continues in Atum's progeny (however diminished and removed). In another sense, though, the story comes to closure with the birth of history, a violent birth which takes place with the murder of Osiris. There is, moreover, an important, and as far as I am aware, unremarked symmetry between Osiris and Atum in this, for once again, at a crucial point in the narrative, it is the most explicitly *male* body that occupies the center of attention, and the persistence of identity is made possible at last only in the deployment of the phallus. Plutarch's version of the story, though late and eclectic in its sources, provides a clear if somewhat too obvious focus on the issue at hand. In his version, as you will recall, Osiris's phallus is lost. As he recounts the story,

> It was thrown right into the river and the Lepitodos and the Phagros and the Oxyrhynkhos gobbled it down, on account of which these among fish

Figure 3.5. Cosmogonic drawing from the Twenty-first Dynasty papyrus of Nespakashuty. Louvre, Paris (E 17401). After Ziegler, *Louvre*, p. 75.

are abhorred, but Isis made a copy in its place and purified this phallus, for which even now, the Egyptians keep festival.[32]

Egyptian sources do not record that the phallus was devoured, but Plutarch's distortion of the story only serves to emphasize a theme common to the Egyptian sources. There as well, the restoration of the body is complete only when the phallus is restored and made miraculously erect. At this point, Isis becomes a small bird, a kite, and flies up to mount the phallus. She thereby receives the semen of the dead god and conceives his son Horus. The seminal trace of Atum has at last been transmitted into god the son, Horus, who, as the instantiation of divine kingship in the human world, enables the beginning of "real" history.

Comparisons of Osiris to Atum are made most explicitly in a pair of reliefs from the Nineteenth Dynasty temple of Menma'atre' Seti I at Abydos, on the north and south walls of the Ptah-Sokar Chapel, apparently a site of profound mystery and holiness (Fig. 3.6). Damaged and mutilated though the scenes are, you can still clearly recognize their significance. On the south wall, the mummiform body of Osiris lies on a bier, ithyphallic. A bird labeled "Isis" perches atop the phallus, receiving his seed for the conception of Horus. Falcons shelter the body at head and foot, and

Figure 3.6. Relief from the south wall of the Ptah-Sokar chapel of Menma'atre' Seti I Temple to Osiris, Abydos. Isis, in the form of a kite, is impregnated by the deceased Osiris, on a bier. Meanwhile, Isis, in human form, and the adult Horus attend at the head and foot of the bier. After Otto, *Osiris and Amon*, pl. 17.

full-sized figures of Isis and Horus stand behind the falcons, stretching out their arms solicitously.

On the north wall, a companion scene pictures Osiris on, apparently, the same bier, but from the other side (Fig. 3.7; note the orientation of the body, and the direction in which the inscriptions are written). Here, however, the god is naked but for armlets and a large collar and pectoral; and whereas in the other scene, he wears the white crown of Upper Egypt, here he is pictured in a wig. He has both arms free in this representation and holds his left hand above his face while with the right he grasps his erect phallus (the phallus is now defaced and chipped away, leaving only its silhouette). The pectoral on the figure reads Sety Menma'atre', but an inscription over the body says, "Sokar Osiris Who Is in His Barque." Again, full-sized figures of Isis and Horus stand at the head and foot of the bier, their arms stretched out toward the corpse.[33]

It is disconcerting to find an adult Horus here assisting at his own conception; in order to explain away the circularity of this construction and the puzzling multiplicity of Horus, both ancient and modern scholars have resorted to variations of the myth.[34] Thus, in some versions, Geb and Nut have not four, but five children, among them one "Horus the elder."

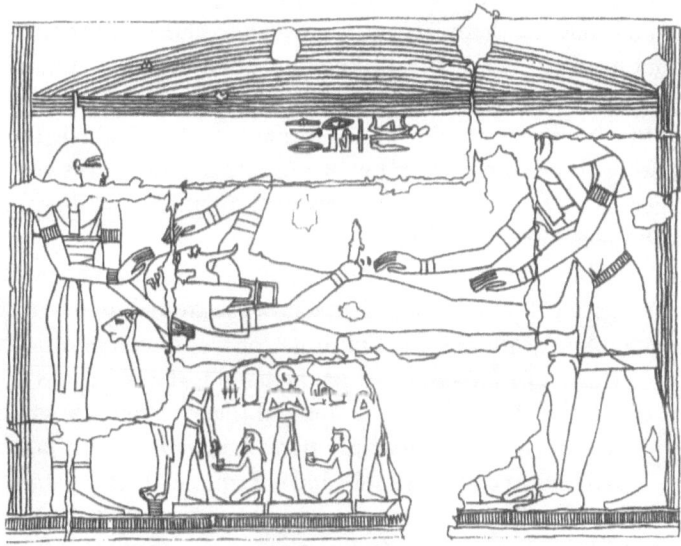

Figure 3.7. Relief from the north wall of the Ptah-Sokar chapel of Menma'atre' Seti I Temple to Osiris, Abydos. The inscription at the top reads "Sokar-Osiris Who Is in His Barque." Isis and Horus attend at the head and foot of the bier. After Otto, *Osiris and Amon*, pl. 16.

Relying on such a supplementary character, then, one can distinguish the Horus who is now being conceived from the Horus who assists at the process. But such an insistence on narrative consistency isolates and trivializes the significance of the myth and needlessly constricts Egyptian constructions of divinity. Such a rationalization underestimates the significance of the scene in several ways.

A historian might first recognize the complexity of thought that the myth represents and discern in contradictions like these the intermingling of different traditions of belief, combined over the millennia for many different purposes. The different Horuses might, thus, represent the calculations of theocrats who assimilated one falcon-headed god from, say, the Delta, with another from Upper Egypt, to support their own claim to legitimacy.

There is, however, a less self-interested accommodation at work here as well, a process of analogy wherein we extend, as it were, epistemological credit to another speaker, believing that the phenomena to which he or she refers might be conceived within our own frame of reference as practically equivalent and valid for appropriation within the same phonetic frame. Thus "Horus" can be less one of the dramatis personae in a drama called Egyptian religion than a region or sphere of religious and secular power, "a name that seeks to delineate an area of reference in a little-known world, in which the area delineated ... may overlap with other areas without replacing them," to borrow Stephen Quirke's apt phrase.[35]

The conception of Horus must, therefore, be taken beyond its anecdotal node in the story of Osiris and read as a central symbol of power and legitimacy in ancient Egypt. The paradox then comes alive. For the adult Horus assisting at his own conception is a timeless figure in his contradictions, conceived now, even as he is acclaimed "justified" and enthroned. The single-dimensioned character of the rationalized narrative disappears with the telling, but the timeless Horus is, indeed, pharaoh, who out of reverence and solicitude for his father, Osiris, lays the ground of his own being as divine king. And similarly, the dominion of Osiris in the other world depends upon the reign of his son in this: the child is the father to the man.

If, in the myth of Osiris, this mutual dependence is somewhat obscured because of the linearity of the narrative, as Helmuth Jakobsohn explains it, it is illustrated more simply and schematically in a parallel construction, from the ideology of royal autonomy, known by the term *kamutef* (more technically, *k3-mwt=f*). *Kamutef* means "bull of his mother" and refers most narrowly to the self-begetting of the god Amun or Min:

> The gods Min and Amun are frequently so named and ithyphallically represented from the Eighteenth Dynasty on. The *kamutef* stands in close

relationship with the monarchy: he is a god who, in the same act, makes a goddess—above all, the queen—into his mate and his mother while she gives (re)birth to the engenderer himself as son. What is of concern here is not the self-origination of the primeval god, but the continual self-renewal of god in the changing manifestation of the at once divine-and-human royal dynasty.... The *kamutef* represents the consubstantiality of a divine father and a divine son, and thus, the sun god and the pharaoh, and therewith as well the consubstantiality of the entire divine-and-human ancestral line with, on the one side, god, and on the other, the then ruling king.[36]

If, on the one hand, the cosmogony of Aunu fragments the one into the many in the emergence of Atum himself as well as his children Shu and Tefnut from the self-begetting accomplished there, the mechanism of the *kamutef*, on the other, starts with the many—father, mother, and son—and, for the purposes of pharaonic ideology, compounds them into one, the bull who begets himself, with the unexplained, but nonetheless acknowledged, passive sexual presence of the female as mother and wife. The *kamutef* does not seem to replace the discourses of royal paternity in the Osiris myth, but merely to instantiate the same nostalgia for phallocentric autonomy on the other bank of the Nile. Thus, while Osirian elements dominate the representational arts of the West Bank in the valleys of the Kings, the Queens, and Nobles, the ring of self-engenderment in *kamutef* is witnessed again and again on the walls and columns of the temples of Karnak and Luxor on the East Bank.

From this distance, it is not possible to construct in detail a specific historical account of how this particular ideological formation took place. We observe, again and again, however, the motif of the transfer of power through fatherhood: the fatherhood of Osiris to Horus, or Geb to Osiris, or Atum to Shu, or Amun to the pharaoh regnant, but it is the link between Osiris and Horus which becomes the longest-lived paradigm of succession in the context of history. Here the disruptions of Setekh, the slaughter and its rectification in primeval violence and judgment, make possible a mimetic stability in the Egyptian myth of the state. The king is dead, long live the king.

Such a transfer of power through the male line is common to many societies, ancient and modern, but despite the seminal trace implicit in such patrilineality, in many cases, a more explicit rationale for such a transfer of power makes appeal through reference to blood. Or indeed, though the transfer extends through the male line, it is framed less in corporeal terms than as a transfer from generation to generation within a certain social class, through the argument that it is the experience of ruling, or a species of political wisdom, or "divine right," which is being transferred. Nor is such testimony absent from ancient Egyptian sources.[37] All the same, it is important to note here the figural concentration on the phallic body. In Egypt, the seminal line and the phallus stand at the heart of the process, and it is in this context that we find the most cogent expressions of power and legitimacy, as well as the most trenchant paradoxes in the Egyptian subject.

FATHERS AND BROTHERS

The texts we have discussed so far express their concern with the power of the phallus and its seminal trace in the highly serious context of theological discourse, and were it to be found only there, it would raise significant doubt about how representative such patterns of discourse could have been. There are, however, other sources that show a strikingly similar construction of sexuality and its relation to power from the very different context of tales in Late Egyptian. Of particular interest to us here are two narratives known as *The Contendings of Horus and Setekh* and *The Tale of Two Brothers*. Both reveal a preeminent concern with the transfer of power through the seminal line and the imposition of power in sexual terms.

The former takes up the age-old theme of the struggle over the kingship between Horus and his uncle Setekh, which can be traced back to the *Pyramid Texts*, and even earlier, but *The Contendings* brings to the stark framework of struggle a wealth of detail and anecdotal elaboration found nowhere else. It comes, moreover, in a unique manuscript from a papyrus datable to the time of Userma'atre'-Skheperenre' Ramesses V, which also contains miscellaneous texts and love poems. It is difficult to say how an Egyptian might have regarded it. It has deep roots in Egyptian religious mythology, but it is so irreverent and so entertaining that it seems a different world altogether from that of the esoteric sobriety of funerary literature such as the *Pyramid Texts*. It was deeply shocking to some of its first modern readers (key passages in the first translations were concealed in Latin), but it may well have been read with a chuckle in the royal court of the Twentieth Dynasty. That should in no way stop us from taking it seriously. Several translations are available,[38] but here, a summary should suffice:

> The story opens in a court of the gods, where a dispute between Horus and Setekh is being judged. For some 80 years, the "two mightiest princes" in the world, Horus and Setekh, have been at battle, and the full company of the gods is completely exhausted with the fighting, but they remain divided on how the conflict should be resolved. The sun god, Pre-Harakhti, takes

Setekh's part because of the daily service Setekh affords him in the cosmic battle against the serpent Apep. The Ennead, however, a company of important gods, side with Horus. The gods are caught in a stalemate, and there are exchanges of letters among the most important of them.

A series of accusations and insults leaves the court stymied, and it is only after Pre-Harakhti's daughter, Hathor, shows herself naked before him, that his good humor returns and he is persuaded to return to the council of gods to pass judgment. Horus and Setekh are asked to speak for themselves.

Setekh makes his claim on the basis of his daily service in slaying the serpent Apep, but Thoth objects, "How can we give the throne to the uncle when the bodily son is present."

With the strong support of his mother, Isis, Horus makes his claim on the basis of the seminal line from his father, Osiris, the previous king, who was acknowledged by all as legitimate.

The court seems persuaded by Isis and Horus, but Setekh is outraged that Isis has intervened and refuses to acquiesce, or even to participate in the legal proceedings as long as Isis is present. This provokes the gods to change the venue of the proceedings, and they move to an island in the Nile, giving strict instructions to the ferryman that he is not to take Isis over to it. Isis, however, changes form and through a combination of trickery and bribery induces the ferryman to take her across. She then transforms herself into a seductive temptress and lures Setekh away from the proceedings.

Impassioned by desire for her, Setekh listens to her tale: She complains that she had been the wife of a cattleherd and had borne him a son. Her husband had died and her son had begun to tend the cattle. A stranger appeared, though, and told the son he would take the cattle and threatened the son with violence. She appeals now to Setekh for protection, and Setekh, in his naïveté, blurts out, "How could the stranger make a claim on the cattle when the son is there!"

This is just what Isis has been after. She transforms herself into a kite and flies to a high tree to proclaim that Setekh has just condemned his claim with his own words. Setekh is enraged and refuses to acquiesce. He reverts to battle with Horus, and they plunge into the Nile to fight on as hippopotami. The struggle goes on and on. (See Fig. 3.8.)

Eventually, the Ennead, utterly exhausted at the battle, implore Setekh and Horus to make up and leave them in peace. They seem to have prevailed. Setekh invites Horus over to his house obligingly and Horus not only accepts, but stays the night. And in the night, Setekh tries to rape Horus, inserting his penis between Horus's thighs, but Horus evades penetration and catches Setekh's semen in his hand. He runs away to his mother, Isis, to report: "Come see what Setekh did to me!" And when he opens his fist to show her, she shrieks, chops off his hand, and tosses it to the waters. Then she replaces his hand magically and lubricates his penis, masturbating him into a jar. The semen of Horus she takes, in turn, to Setekh's garden, to spread on the patch of lettuce from which he makes his salad every day. And when Setekh ate his lettuce that day, he was impregnated by the semen of Horus.

As the tale continues, Setekh insists that Horus appear with him before a court of the gods. He urges the assembly to grant him kingship as successor to his dead brother, Osiris, on the ground that he has, as he says, "done a man's deed" to Horus. The gods begin to jeer and spit and revile Horus, but he only laughs and says that Setekh has lied. And hereupon, the seminal witness is given its own voice.

Thoth, the scribe of the gods calls, "Come out, semen of Setekh!" and the semen of Setekh answers from the marsh where Isis threw it. When Thoth then says, "Come out, semen of Horus," his semen answers, "Where shall I come out?" only to emerge from the crown of Setekh's head as a celestial disk (which Thoth unceremoniously appropriates to set in his own crown).

Further letters are dispatched, this time to Osiris, who reminds the gods that he created barley and wheat and cattle, and that they would be without sustenance were it not for him, adding as well, that Horus is his rightful heir. Eventually Setekh is forced to accept Horus's sovereignty.

Of particular importance to us here is the recognition that the whole world (the world of the gods, no less) is thrown into turmoil over the proper succession to the empty throne of Osiris. The turmoil stimulates a series of struggles, in both word and deed, and all the while, the correct recognition of the seminal line is at issue. A climax is approached when the seminal witness to Setekh's failed attempt to penetrate Horus demonstrates, on the contrary, the successful, if devious, penetration of Setekh by Horus (with the magical connivance of Isis). The deployment of the phallus and the legal recognition of what constitutes its correct deployment show the link between the phallus and power in the sexual semiotics of the ancient Nile. If it stands as a symbol of the legitimate transfer of royal dominion from Osiris to Horus, it can as well be a mark of illegitimate domination. It is particularly noteworthy that sexual penetration is taken to be evidence of the penetrator's superiority to the penetrated. In the case of heterosexual intercourse, this penetration allows the use of the female to perpetuate the seminal line of the male. In the case of the attempted penetration of the male by another male, it is clear that the submissive participant is to be regarded as inferior to the penetrator and unworthy of the inheritance.[39]

Figure 3.8. Series of connected vignettes from the Papyrus Jumilhac (Louvre E.17110). From right to left: Anubis (or "Anup") holds the Bull Bata, who strains to carry away a mummy on his back; a dismembered ram-headed deity; a great phallus; figural representations of Osiris dominant over Setekh (here written *stp*); Horus, son of Isis, dominant over "the Enemy," trussed and speared, and figured as a hippopotamus (cf. the battle of the hippopotami in *The Contendings*). At the end of the series is Osiris on a bier. The accompanying text (not shown here, but located directly above this scene on the papyrus) concerns Setekh's transformation into a panther, which Horus eventually flays, as well as some etymological notes. The vignettes do not read well as illustrations to the text, but seem to be placed with it in a kind of archive of figures of dismemberment and the triumph over Setekh. The scene to the far right, of Anup and Bata, represents another strain of the *Tale of Two Brothers* than the version summarized in this book, but illustrates the longevity of the tale's motifs. Here, we could easily interpret the mummy carried away on the bull as the seminal identity of Bata imprinted onto a bull, as in our version of the tale. The Papyrus Jumilhac dates from the late Ptolemaic or early Roman period. Redrawn after Vandier, *Le Papyrus Jumilhac*, pl. 20. See also pp. 124f, 141, and 257.

That sexual penetration becomes the mark of political dominance and is linked explicitly with violence should provoke no surprise, given our discussion up to this point. The pattern is, moreover, very common in our "Western" heritage.[40] It is also attested in other instances in extant Egyptian texts and suggests an Egyptian distaste for homosexuality,[41] but it speaks as well to the clear hierarchy of gender in Egyptian society. The female, as the passive object of sexual penetration, is unquestionably the subordinate partner in marriage and other structures of power. The exception to the rule in the wonderful magical power of Isis is noteworthy here, and we shall have more to say about it below.

Equally important in this story, however, is the significance of language, both the spoken language of the legal proceedings that recur in the story and the written language of the letters exchanged between the Ennead, Neith, Atum, and Osiris. The story is repeatedly complicated by substitutions of the word for the body, and vice versa, and in this economy of substitution, it draws our attention to a second remarkable tale in Late

Egyptian, *The Tale of Two Brothers*. Again, several translations have been published.⁴² A summary follows:

> The two brothers, Anubis and Bata, and the elder Anubis's wife are all living together at the beginning of the tale, running a farm and maintaining a herd of cattle. Bata is a remarkable fellow and does most of the labor involved in keeping the farm going. Indeed, there is something special about him: "He has a god's strength in him."
>
> One day when Anubis and Bata are out plowing and planting, Bata is sent back home to get a bag of seed. On arriving there he finds Anubis's wife weaving, and when she tells him where to find the seed, he goes off after it without a second thought and loads several bags over his shoulder. Anubis's wife, however, has other ideas and asks Bata to spend an hour lying together with her so that she can "know him as a man." She tempts him with the promise of fine clothes.
>
> Bata, though, is disgusted. He retorts that she and Anubis are like his parents and warns her not to say such a thing to him again, promising, all the same, that he won't let on that she has tried to seduce him. The wife, though, now fearful that she will be betrayed to her husband, makes herself up as if she has been beaten and waits for her husband to return. She then accuses Bata of trying to seduce her and of beating her when she refused, and Anubis, taking her at her word, becomes enraged. He takes up his spear and heads toward the barn, where Bata is, to kill him, but Bata is forewarned by the cattle and escapes.
>
> Anubis chases after him at full speed, and Bata is saved, in the end, only through a prayer to Pre-Harakhti, who places a great body of water infested with crocodiles in Anubis's path. From his safe haven across the water, Bata remonstrates with Anubis and explains what actually happened. At the end of his explanation, with livid resentment, he takes a reed knife in hand and cuts off his penis, throwing it in the water, where a catfish swallows it. Then he grows faint.
>
> Anubis is aghast. He repents, but cannot reach his brother because of the crocodiles. Bata abandons his brother's house, but asks his brother to come for him someday, should he hear news of him. He explains that he will go to the Valley of the *'Ash* (ʿš) Tree to live. Once there, he will remove his heart and put it on a blossom of the tree, and if, on coming to find his brother, Anubis should find the *'ash* tree cut down, he should find the heart and put it in a bowl of cool water. Bata will then revive and go on to avenge himself. Bata's final instruction tells Anubis that he will know something untoward has happened to Bata when a jug of beer goes bad even as he holds it in his hand. Anubis goes home, kills his faithless wife, and goes into mourning for his younger brother.
>
> Bata, meanwhile, does as predicted, setting up for himself a household in the Valley of the *'Ash*. Not long after, the Ennead approach him and, in

apparent sympathy, fashion a wife for him. She is very beautiful, "The fluid of every god is in her," but the Seven Hathors come to see her and predict for her a death by the knife.

Although Bata desires her very much and provides her with every kind of game to eat, he cannot be a husband to her: he is, as he says, a woman like her. With disturbing prescience, he warns her not to go outside, because she will be snatched away by the sea. Predictably, she does go outside one day when Bata is hunting, and the sea rushes up to catch her as she strolls beneath the 'ash tree. She manages to escape into her house, but the sea calls to the 'ash tree to take a lock of her hair. The sea then carries this lock of hair back to Egypt and it permeates the water where the royal wash is done, imparting to Pharaoh's clothes the scent of ointment.

When Pharaoh is given his newly washed clothes, he smells the ointment and quarrels with the washermen, and they, in their alarm scour the riverbank where the wash is done, only to find the tell-tale lock of hair. It is taken to Pharaoh and he becomes so enchanted by its scent that he dispatches messengers to all lands to find its origin.

Bata kills all but one of the first group of messengers who come to the Valley of the 'Ash, but the survivor returns to Egypt to tell of the woman, so Pharaoh sends a squad of charioteers to steal her away. They succeed in doing this, and when Pharaoh urges the wife to tell him about her husband, she reveals that he can be killed by felling the 'ash tree near their house. This is done, and Bata falls dead on the spot.

Anubis, as predicted, finds a new jar of beer overflowing with fermentation in his very hand, and when he takes up a glass of wine, it spoils immediately as well. This is his signal. He goes to the Valley of the 'Ash and discovers Bata dead. Searching for his heart near the felled tree, he finds it and soaks it in a bowl of cool water, in accordance with Bata's instructions. Bata's corpse begins to twitch, and then Anubis helps him swallow the water. Bata's heart finds its seat in his body again, and he is fully revived, even as the brothers are reconciled. Bata now reveals a plan. He intends to go to his wife and exact his revenge, and to do so, he transforms himself into a magnificent bull. Anubis takes him to Egypt, to the palace, and the bull is regarded as a great marvel. (See Fig. 3.8.) Anubis is handsomely rewarded, and Bata comes to live at the palace. A few days later, he encounters his wife in the kitchen and speaks to her, revealing who he is. The wife is horrified, so she exacts from Pharaoh a promise to give her whatever she may desire and then asks for the bull's liver to eat.

Pharaoh is unhappy but agrees, and the next day, the bull is slaughtered. As the carcass is carried into the palace, drops of blood fall by the gateposts and grow miraculously into two great persea trees.

Some while later, the lady finds herself near one of the trees, and it speaks to her, as Bata, alive still despite her betrayal. Now the lady exacts from Pharaoh the promise that he will have the trees cut down and made into furniture. Pharaoh agrees again and calls for carpenters to cut down the trees and make furniture from them. As the lady is watching the felling of the trees, a splinter is chipped away from one of them. It flies into her mouth and impregnates her. A son is born by and by, and when he attains maturity he is so beloved of Pharaoh that he is made viceroy of Kush, and eventually crown prince. When Pharaoh dies, the throne falls to the seminal splinter of Bata become human. This new Bata becomes pharaoh and designates Anubis his heir. When he dies, Anubis becomes pharaoh.

TWO PEAS IN A POD

The profligacy of narrative nodes in *The Tale of Two Brothers* suggests syncretic origins. Although we have no hard proof of it, one can be confident that the story as we have it today represents an intertwining of numerous different narrative and thematic strands, which is not to deny it a sophisticated and accomplished continuity and integration as it exists in the extant manuscript. The tale is very likely related to the myths of Osiris, and it is plausibly one of our earliest extant examples from a store of motifs that recur persistently and widely in folk literature. It is not surprising to find the *Two Brothers* dubbed "Das älteste Märchen," or "the world's oldest fairy tale,"[43] and the lively interest it has begotten among folklorists has generated theories (from the plausible to the fantastic)[44] about its progeny in the folk literature of the West. Clearly the tale is an antecedent to the story of Potiphar's wife in the Bible, and one can cite innumerable similarities between it and other stories, in loci from Homer to Ovid to the Vedas to the Qur'ân. But our interest, however, is not to trace the subsequent lineage of the narrative but to remark on the constellation of themes it engages and the broader net of homosocial perplexities it entails in Egyptian culture.

The tale turns on the themes of death and sexuality and operates under an economy of substitutions whereby the homosocial bond between Anubis and Bata is repeatedly transgressed and reinstated. Even in suggesting a certain parity between Anubis and Bata, from its first extant lines, the tale undercuts that parity, tellingly, by the intrusion of a woman. The first lines read, in Miriam Lichtheim's translation, "It is said, there were two brothers, of the same mother and the same father. Anubis was the name of the elder, and Bata the name of the younger. As for Anubis, he had a house and a wife; and his young brother was with him as if he were a son."[45]

The insistence on the brothers' birth from the same parents, and the fact that they are both named (unlike their parents and the wife of

Anubis), points to a balance, an economy of equality, but this is immediately contradicted by Anubis's seniority and by the fact that he has a wife and a house. And yet because he is the elder, married, and propertied, the identity of Anubis is constituted in a supplementarity which suggests that the inequality between Anubis and Bata puts, rather, the elder brother in the inferior position. This becomes explicit in the assertion that Bata is "an excellent man. There [is] none like him in the whole land, for a god's strength [is] in him."[46]

That Bata should be defamed by the nameless wife, even given his uniqueness, divinity, and moral superiority, incites a series of mutilations and deaths of varying degrees of figurality. Bata's self-mutilation is a kind of death, as is the removal of his heart for safekeeping in the blossom of the 'ash tree. These symbolic deaths lead, then, to a series of (real and not so real) deaths: the 'ash tree which sustains his heart is felled, the bull into which he is transformed is sacrificed, the persea trees that grew up to replace the bull are chopped down and made into furniture. A semiotic equivalence binds the phallus and the heart and the bull, and it is paralleled by a similar equivalence between the 'ash and the persea trees.

The constant engagement on Bata's sexuality and corporeality reveals a hypervirility: Bata's potency cannot be eradicated even when his penis is cut off, his heart removed, and he is slaughtered and hacked down. Sexual generation and vegetative regeneration are fused in the sequential loci of his identity, until eventually his seminal trace comes to penetrate the very heart of the pharaonic state, to allow the replacement of the pharaoh regnant at the beginning of the tale with Bata's heir and reincarnation. The bodily integrity of Bata is constantly transgressed by a series of dismemberments and substitutions, but throughout, the seminal trace persists even if Bata's identity is effaced as he is transposed into his phallus, his heart, a watery infusion, a bull, the blood of the bull, a persea tree, and a persea splinter, finally to emerge, self-engendered, from the womb of his own perfidious mate.

Bata exemplifies the persistence of the self in its very fragmentation, and in this he might be considered a transformation of Osiris. At the same time in (eventually) begetting himself on the wife of the pharaoh, he mimics the operation of the *kamutef*. And through the transmission of self in the seminal witness—even though the semen of Bata is necessarily the substitute semen of a persea splinter—Bata enjoys a victory reminiscent of that of Horus in his contention with Setekh.[47]

But the *Two Brothers* manifests a misogyny not evident in the story of Osiris, the operations of the *kamutef*, or the *Contendings of Horus and*

Setekh. The wife of Anubis is a would-be adulteress and a liar, akin in this to Potiphar's wife. Similarly, the mate fashioned by the gods for Bata betrays him and effects his "murder" on three separate occasions. Yet if the misogyny of the *Two Brothers* is not replicated in the other narratives and homosocial constructions we have considered, in its extremity, it points to a paradox endemic to the Egyptian discourse of male power, sexuality, and autonomy.

This paradox is illustrated most clearly in the *Two Brothers* through the introduction of a mate for the self-emasculated Bata, an intervention that is, on the face of it, pointless. Recall how Bata built a mansion for himself in the Valley of the 'Ash, wanting to set up a household. The Ennead, finding him there, took pity on him and provided him a supremely beautiful companion whom he desired ardently and for whom he provided. Note, though, how Bata cautions her to stay inside his mansion, because he fears that he will be unable to protect her: he says, "I am a woman like you."[48]

The passage is rife with irony. Bata is by now emasculated and exiled, but he sets about building a household like a young groom. The expression "filled with every good thing" (*mḥ m ḫt nbt nfrt*) is reminiscent of the offering formula for the deceased, and indeed, Bata has undergone a kind of death. (The first half of his very name is written with the glyph meaning *b₃*, one of the spiritual components of the individual associated with the ability to come and go from the tomb.) But on going forth from his household (again, the verb "go forth," *pr(j)*, recalls the language of funerary texts), he encounters the Ennead and is awarded a wife to console his loneliness, and at first she seems to be a good match for him, fashioned, as she is with "[the fluid of] every god ... in her" (*jw [mw n] ntr nbt jm st*).[49] The expression recalls the passage at the opening of the tale where Bata himself is described as having a god's strength in him, *js wn pḥty n ntr jm=f*.[50] An ominous note is sounded, though, immediately thereafter, when the Seven Hathors come to see her and predict that she will die a violent death.[51] This particular prediction is never realized in the extant text of the tale, but it adds a chilling note of foreboding to the otherwise seemingly attractive match. In the end, Bata's wife betrays him three times, each betrayal resulting in a kind of death for him. But her treachery is, ironically, the very mechanism whereby it becomes possible for him to undergo that series of transformations which ultimately place him on the throne of Egypt.

The logical deficiencies of the narrative are overcome, then, by a progression of revaluations and transformations which bring Bata to a glorious telos through a kind of Hegelian passion: he is repeatedly destroyed only to be preserved on a different level, eventually to attain the ideological centrality of the pharaonic throne. Yet even this achievement is in the end reversed or transmuted through the designation of his brother Anubis as his successor.

It is not possible to rationalize *The Tale of Two Brothers* completely. The tale does not allow full closure in the triumph of Bata, and in its last lines, it is the defective—and more human—brother, Anubis, who attains the fullest benefit of the process of the narrative. I will not try to explain this, because my interest lies in the constellation of patterns the tale reveals about gender and supplementarity, for in this context, it brings to a heightened clarity some of the problems inherent in the Egyptian constructions of gender we have observed elsewhere.

A conspicuous thread of misogyny is woven through the tale, but that misogyny is inverted in the primacy of place the tale affords female agency. Bata's and Anubis's transformations from peripheral rural figures into the central icons of male authority in Egyptian political ideology are accomplished only because of the betrayals of women. The seminal trace of Bata, staunched by his self-mutilation, is enabled again only by virtue of the receptivity of the mate the gods fashioned for him, and if, being castrated, he is incapable of inseminating her literally, he does so all the more tellingly with a splinter, with blood, and, most important, with language, by demonstrating to her, on two occasions, that he persists despite her efforts to eradicate him.

The series of ironic reversals that allow the persistence of Bata point beyond *The Tale of Two Brothers* to a broader and far more ancient web of supplemental complications in the Egyptian constructions of gender, and we can turn to those now, first, by turning back to the cosmogony of Aunu.

The genesis of the cosmos in Atum's masturbation betrays, in its Sixth Dynasty "origins," a straightforward phallocentric nostalgia. The reach of male interiority toward the autonomous accomplishment of desire in this most direct corporeal moment has an undeniable elegance and simplicity. But that simplicity cannot hold, as we have seen, and it results in displacements to other kinds of bodily efflux, to other bodily sites, and to outright denials of seminal origin as early as the *Coffin Texts*.[52]

More interesting still, it generates a supplemental reformulation such that the originally hypermasculine Atum is bisexualized as "the Great He-She."[53] The phallus and the fist and the force of desire are divided into three parts: a male (the phallus), a female (the fist), and an abstract and detached movement to creation in the primeval, but now inaccessible, mind of Atum. The irony this effects upon the simple phallocentric nostalgia of

Pyramid Text 1248 invests agency in the hands of the female and reduces the male to a tremulous priapic icon. (The genealogy of such a construction reaches far ahead into the West, evidenced, for example in Botticelli's *Venus and Mars*.) Which is not to say that the mythical train of supplements created therewith actually put political agency into the hands of Egyptian women. That is not a conclusion we can draw from the evidence at hand.

It creates, rather, an ambivalence about the range of male authority and autonomy, and in such a preeminently male-dominated sphere of discourse as the inscriptions of Middle Egyptian, it bifurcates agency from the interiority of bodily experience. Thus we find in the myth of Osiris, as well, a "hero," Osiris, who is entirely passive. The exercise of male power and efficacy there is either malevolent, in its association with Setekh, or contingent upon the nurture and protection of Isis: thus, Horus—N.B.: the paradigm of pharaonic authority—is only brought to maturity and to the capability to act through the careful guardianship and shrewd ingenuity of his mother, Isis.[54]

Similarly, in the most blatant attempt to formalize a nostalgia for self-creation in the royal cult, the *kamutef*, we find a god begetting himself, but because of the insistence that this self-generation be analogized to phallic penetration, the autonomy of the operation requires the supplement of woman and hinges, therefore, on an Oedipal unification of mother and mate. History imposes yet another level of irony on this already vertiginous oscillation between male and female in that a new ideology of divine paternity seems to have been central to the efforts of Egypt's most celebrated female pharaoh, Hatshepsut, to legitimize her position on the throne.

Hatshepsut was the queen of a relatively obscure monarch, 'Aakheperenre' Thutmose II, who was also her half-brother.[55] She bore him a daughter named Neferure', but no male heir, so on the death of Thutmose II, his son by another woman (one Aset or "Isis," Eg., *3st*), would normally have been expected to succeed to the throne. This child, Menkheperre' Thutmose III, however, was still very young, so Hatshepsut, following precedent, became his regent. Up until the second or third year of the regency, she identified herself on monuments as such.

Thereafter, however, she abandoned the pretext that she was merely a regent and proclaimed herself pharaoh. At least two other women held the position of pharaoh in the long span of Egyptian history,[56] but in the other known cases, their sovereignty was brief, merely an interlude allowing the successor to come to maturity. Hatshepsut ruled for some fifteen years, by

Figure 3.9. Joint sovereigns Hatshepsut and Thutmose III from the fragments of the former's Red Chapel, now in the open-air museum at Karnak. After Robins, *Women in Ancient Egypt*, p. 45.

contrast, and in the service of her reign, marshaled all the iconographic resources of Egyptian art, even having herself depicted, as often as not, as a male (see Fig. 3.9). In a particularly important innovation, she developed a mythical rationale for her assumption of power, which cast her as the begotten heir of Amun himself. This innovation was, furthermore, adopted into the royal mythology of the New Kingdom, so that other pharaohs after her also made explicit claims to being the children of Amun.

An account of Hatshepsut's conception is given on the walls of her magnificent funerary temple at Deir el-Bahari. It includes a tactful illustration of Amun appearing in the bedchamber of Hatshepsut's mother Queen Ahmes, as well as a more explicitly informative text:

> Amun, Lord of Karnak, . . . transformed himself into the Majesty of this her husband, King of Upper and Lower Egypt 'Aakheperkare' [Thutmose I] and found her asleep deep in the interior of her palace. She awoke at the scent of God and smiled upon His Majesty. He came up to her at once, and He was filled with passion for her, and He gave His heart into her, and He gave unto her His form as god to see. And when He had come before her, she rejoiced at His perfection. The love of Him penetrated her body. The palace was pervaded with the scent of God and every breath was fragrant with Punt.[57]

In Hatshepsut's case, this account is clearly used to legitimize the position she claims as pharaoh, and it is, thus, a remarkable redeployment of the discursive tools of phallocentrism to new and, at least in some

Figure 3.10. The conception of Amenhotep III. His mother, Queen Mutemwi'a, is here visited in her bedchamber by Amun. The ideological construction whereby the pharaoh was seen to have been conceived by Amun was apparently created to support Hatshepsut's claim to the throne, and there is a scene very much like the one above at Hatshepsut's temple at Deir el Bahari. (See Naville, *Deir el-Bahari*, vol. 2 [i.e., *Memoirs of the Egypt Exploration Fund*, vol. 13], pl. 47.) The Deir el Bahari scene, however, is in bad repair, and its accompanying inscription is severely damaged. After Brunner, *Die Geburt des Gottkönigs*, pl. 4, scene 4L.

sense, "feminist" aims. There is a corollary irony in that when later pharaohs, such as Nebma'atre' Amenhotep III, adopt the story for their own ideological purposes, they would seem to undercut the very seminal line they propose to strengthen, depicting their human fathers (unwittingly?) as cuckolded by Amun (see Fig. 3.10). This new construction of divine paternity and filiality, in contrast to that of, say, Osiris and Horus, is exclusive: in an attempt to effect a theocratic closure between Amun and the pharaoh regnant, each pharaoh calls on the myth to effect a special link between himself and Amun, not by identifying his human father, usually the previous pharaoh, with Amun, but by *replacing* his human father with the divine progenitor.

In its circularity, the *kamutef* construction is more exclusive than the other constructions of divine father-and-son which mythically underpin the structure of the pharaonic state. And yet Hatshepsut also made the same claims to being Horus and to being the son of Re' that we find in all the standard pharaonic titularies. The logical contradictions confronting us

COMING AND BECOMING   137

in these constructions of divine paternity must, however, be set aside for the time being, in consideration of a point more relevant to the current line of argument about the discursive manipulation of women in ancient Egypt.

In each of these cases, the supplement of woman underpins and undermines the discourse of a transfer of power through the male line, creating a fascinating and insufficiently studied counterdiscourse of female agency and power. Although it will not be possible to pursue this counterdiscourse in detail here, we cannot ignore certain manifestations of it in Egyptian representational systems.

EXOTIC EROTIC

We begin, once again, by looking at hieroglyphs. We devoted some considerable space to the network of semantic relations in the deployment of the phallus glyphs, so what of the corresponding semiotics of woman and the female body? In this frame of reference, the hieroglyphic system is surprisingly reticent. There are various glyphs depicting, as Gardiner puts it, "the occupations of women." His own font contains only seven of these,[58] and that total can be raised by only three even when one adds three female anthropomorphic deities. His category, "man and his occupations," by contrast, lists some 64 glyphs, and if one adds male anthropomorphic deities to the total, it comes to 72.[59] And what of body parts, then? There are, indeed, glyphs for the female breast and genitalia, but the breast does not occur frequently, and the glyph for the female genitalia ⊔ is usually replaced by a similarly shaped glyph picturing a body of water ⊔. In neither case is there a range of semantic implication comparable to that for the phallus glyphs. Gardiner's formulation is not, of course, formally and genetically rooted in a conscious native Egyptian typology or catalog of glyphs, but in a general, practical way, it is, nonetheless, representative, so the preponderance of male activity and the male body in the glyphic system, even as Gardiner typologizes it, is highly significant.

It seems that certain standards of decorum inhibited explicit reference to female sexuality, and this has led some art historians to observations about reticence vis-à-vis the depiction of human sexuality in Egyptian art.[60] Schäfer, for instance, notes that

> obscene pieces are almost entirely lacking from finds of the earlier periods, while in the racially mixed Late Period they are almost intolerably common. Earlier Egyptians were not immune from such practices, and we can quite often see behind the veil that is drawn over unhealthy excesses

of human behaviour, but they were rarely brought into the open in representational art. Most of the obscene representations that are found have a religious base.[61]

The obnoxious (and all too frequent) racist comment aside, Schäfer points to a significant feature of Egyptian art. Overt sexual activity is depicted only rarely, and references to reproduction, sexuality, and fecundity are generally introduced via some figural alchemy—metaphorical, metonymic, or otherwise. If, in the hieroglyphic system, iconic reference to women is far less common than that to men, so too in painting, relief, and sculpture in the round, figures of men dominate and show a greater differentiation of type, even given the heavy idealization characteristic of Egyptian art. Thus, as Gay Robins points out,

> The ideal form for women is characterised by a youthful beauty in which the figure is always slender; neither pregnancy nor the spreading waistline that many women must have had after years of childbearing is part of the image. There is indeed little distinction between the generations, and man's wife and mother receive what is basically the same treatment. Men too are shown with a slender, youthful image, but they also have a second one with no counterpart among the representation of women, in which the figure is fuller, with enlarged breast or explicit rolls of fat under the chest. This represents a mature and successful official who has achieved a sedentary lifestyle with access to plenty of food. It is not applicable to women, because they could not hold office.[62]

Considered from a slightly different point of view, it is not simply that women could not hold office, but that representations of women overwhelmingly objectify them, by which I mean that the epistemological subject of art in which women are depicted is very rarely a woman herself. There is, obviously, a close relationship here between the economic structure of the funerary industry and the construction of the epistemological subject: tombs and their accoutrements were overwhelmingly created for men, officials in the pharaonic administration. As a consequence, the epistemological position upon which these artifacts are centered is male. The pattern exemplified in the relief of the Fifth Dynasty official, Wepemnefret, discussed near the end of Chapter 2, holds throughout ancient Egyptian history. Thus the subject of the relief, and dominant figure therein, is usually pictured to the viewer's left, and he is characteristically the largest figure in the scene. As subject of the representation in question (and owner of the tomb) he dominates the pictorial space and extends his authority over the other figures in the picture, which are often only a frac-

COMING AND BECOMING   139

tion of his size. The most important exceptions to this general rule entail the joint representation of the tomb owner and various gods. In such cases, the gods enjoy a clear ontological superiority and are usually represented to at least the same scale as the tomb owner. Significantly, though, the owner still generally occupies the "space of the subject." Apposite examples are very frequent; here we might cite scenes from the tomb of Sennedjem (Nineteenth Dynasty) and the weighing of the heart in the papyrus of Ani (Eighteenth Dynasty).

In many cases, the authority in question relates to the fulfillment of the tomb owner's material needs. That is to say, the figures objectified under the tomb owner's gaze are engaged in activities related to his sustenance, the herding and slaughter of cattle, the production and delivery of agricultural products, the pursuit of craft industries, and so on. In other cases, the figures provide a less tangible product, the performance of ritual or entertainment.

To what extent can gender provide an analytical tool here? Most of the enterprises overseen by a tomb owner are carried out predominantly or exclusively by men. Thus cattleherds and butchers are always male, whereas brewers and bakers are of both sexes.

In the case of the provision of entertainment and the performance of ritual, however, there are indications of more significant gender-based differences. Dancing and musical performance are carried out by both men and women, but apparently in separate groups. Sports such as wrestling and stick fighting are the province of men.[63] The objects of erotic attention seem to be exclusively women. Yet how are we to understand what represents an object of erotic attention?[64] This is not an easy question to answer, because we as viewers inevitably bring our own tastes and preconceptions to the appreciation of ancient Egyptian representations, and it is impossible to exclude them from consideration. Certain tentative conclusions are, nevertheless, not only possible, but necessary, and we can make them by noting changes in and divergences from representational canons.

However attractive we may find the painting of a bare-breasted Egyptian woman or goddess, we would be rash to read into this an erotic significance beyond our own personal interest. This is because in formal canonical representation, adult women and goddesses are often depicted barebreasted, with the nipple of the forward breast delineated. This seems to reflect, at least in part, the actual sartorial practices of Egyptian commoners (and perhaps Egyptians of a broader range of classes in the Old Kingdom). It is also, however, related to the representational canon, so that even women wearing tubelike dresses suspended by straps, which would

Figure 3.11. Wooden statuette of a woman from the tomb of Meketre' of the Eleventh Dynasty. Metropolitan Museum of Art, New York (20.3.7).

cover the breasts, are depicted in paintings and relief with the forward breast exposed. We know from sculptural representations in the round, however, that these dresses usually concealed the breasts (see Fig. 3.11).

On the other hand, full female nudity may provide a more confident index of erotic intent, because adult women are rarely depicted nude in Egyptian art. One notable exception to this convention is the sky goddess Nut. Her nudity is closely associated with her role in giving birth to the sun barque each day, so it is less erotic than "motherly" or "theogonic." But the full nudity of certain dancers and musicians depicted in scenes of banqueting and celebration in New Kingdom tombs does plausibly suggest erotic intent.

It appears that fully nude female dancers make their first clear appearance in the tomb paintings of noble (not royal) personages during the middle of the Eighteenth Dynasty. Particularly celebrated is a group that appears in the tomb of the "astronomer" Nakht (see Fig. 3.12). In the catalog to a stunning recent exhibition centering on Amenhotep III, Arielle Kozloff cites the painting and comments:

> Nakht's tomb walls were the first to present a post-pubescent woman—a lutenist, the pivotal figure in a trio of musicians in Nakht's tomb—completely nude (save a few bits of jewelry) with fully frontal breasts. Perhaps

Figure 3.12. Detail of a wall painting in the Eighteenth Dynasty tomb of Nakht (TT 52) in Sheikh Abd'el-Qurna on the West Bank opposite Luxor. Facsimile by Norman de Garis Davies, Metropolitan Museum of Art, New York (15.5.19d).

the artist was inspired by the frankly frontal female fertility goddesses of western Asia which had made their way into Egypt with other eastern art forms from mid Eighteenth Dynasty on. . . . Perhaps the erotic delights of a beautifully formed female body were needed to arouse the male tomb owner's (and perhaps his god's as well) procreative functions in the afterlife.

Nakht's seductive lutenist is compositionally ingenious. To achieve frontal breasts as naturally as possible, the artist swiveled the young woman's supple body into a spiral with right-facing profile legs, frontal torso, and left-facing face, using the rotation of her body and intimacy of her gaze to knit the trio of musicians together.[65]

It is interesting that the breach with canonical convention (through the depiction of the figure frontally rather than in the combination of frontal and lateral views which is typical of Egyptian painting and relief) goes hand in hand with this striking eroticism. As Kozloff points out, the depiction not only is attractively realized, it also exerts an important influence on other contemporary art, as well as that of the subsequent Amarna period. Similar compositions can be found in other Theban tombs, on stelae, and on small articles of the patrician life of Amenhotep III's court. It is, moreover, possible, given this precedent, to take certain steps toward an understanding of eroticism in representations of women who are not entirely naked. Kozloff herself cites the example of the tomb of Menena, where the tomb owner's wife herself appears virtually naked under a gauzy and transparent gown, even as she stands with her husband before the god Osiris.[66]

Although the delicate eroticism apparent here is a departure from earlier Eighteenth Dynasty practice in that it exploits full nudity, even earlier in the dynasty, there seems to have been a rich underlying sensuality, at least in the banquet scenes from the private tombs on the West Bank. The tomb of Rekhmire', vizier to Thutmose III, is considered a consummate example of workmanship, indeed "a culminating point of the classic style,"[67] and it contains in the representation of a banquet one figure that has excited considerable interest. This figure offers an interesting perspective on not only artistic practice and our modern interpretations thereof, but also constructions of gender in New Kingdom Egypt. (See Fig. 3.13.)

Stevenson Smith gives a succinct account of the figure in question:

> The often-cited example of the serving girl viewed from the back splendidly illustrates the quality of line maintained throughout, and is moreover a daring experiment. It was an experiment not carried through logically from our point of view, since the far foot crosses over the one nearest to the observer. It remains, however, one of the most successful of those recurring flashes of observation in which a draughtsman set down a figure as he saw it, and not according to a preconceived idea of how it should be.[68]

Figure 3.13. Detail of a wall painting in the Eighteenth Dynasty tomb of Rekhmire' (TT 100) in Sheikh Abd'el-Qurna on the West Bank opposite Luxor. The text reads, "May your *ka* have a nice day!" a formal way of saying "May you have a nice day." Facsimile by Nina de Garis Davies, Metropolitan Museum of Art, New York (30.4.78).

As in the case of the nude musician from Nakht's tomb, this figure breaks with artistic conventions in its portrayal of the girl's shapely posterior. More conventional depictions would show her hips and legs in straight profile, as is the case with the other standing figures in the scene. For those art historians who took an evolutionary view of Egyptian art, this seemed a step toward the more realistic or naturalistic representational styles they associated with Hellenic and Western art. Thus, in the major published account of the tomb, Norman de Garis Davies, sees the figure as the daring attempt of an artist far ahead of his time to depict things as "we" actually see them, and he chastises that artist's fellows for not being his equal in insight:

> The presentation of a serving maid in three-quarters view from behind . . . was a bold adventure on the part of the draughtsman and one that has few parallels. But his colleagues probably wondered, not at his powers of observation and delineation, but at the admittance of the result into a serious composition. The figure shows indeed much more promise than achievement: the body reveals a wish to render physical structure as well as grace, but the feet have been stupidly kept in accord with the orthodox posture and are crossed like those of a cripple.[69]

Heinrich Schäfer goes some way to correct the Eurocentric myopia Davies exhibits, noting how the figure had been miscopied in several early Egyptologists' enthusiastic quotations of it:

> The central figure . . . , who is seen from the back, was generally considered to be one of the chief "perspective" achievements of Egyptian art, until Balcz discovered that for a century all the artists who reproduced it had "corrected" it according to the standard of their own time. In the original the feet overlap wrongly from a modern point of view. In addition, the line . . . which runs into the nape of the neck to give an expressive shoulder profile, is in the original the rounded neckline of the dress lying on the unforeshortened shoulders. The modern artists' drawings are misleading in other details. It goes without saying that the small toes are not shown and both hands are image-based frontal representations. Thus this justly famous figure has become an instructive example of the real position of such figures in Egyptian art and not a shining example of Egyptian "perspective."[70]

But Schäfer, for his part, fails to explain the radical departure from convention the figure quite clearly exhibits. The depiction of the feet is identical to that of the other standing figures in the scene, and follows Egyptian conventions unremarkably. That the hips should have been moved out of the conventional canon is not, then, an experiment on the trajectory to "true" perspective. It is, rather, a graceful and unobtrusive and, for that, all the more sophisticated departure from convention for the sake of erotic expression. The break in convention, which indeed breaks the viewer's gaze at the conventional ankles and pulls it upward to the curves above might be imagined to precipitate tumescence. The realization of the figure's buttocks and the delicate indication of the top of her pelvic bone just behind the extended arm give her body a fullness that is not as readily apparent in the bodies of her companions and lends the entire scene an elegant concreteness fully consonant with her employment as an object of erotic desire. Indeed, Rekhmire' himself sits to the left, four or more times her size, viewing the entire scene from the dominion of his privileged position as tomb owner and subject.[71] It is surely not insignificant, in this context, that the inscription over Rekhmire' and his wife reads, "The *pleasure inherent in seeing* the beauty of singing, dancing, playing music, and anointing with myrrh" (my emphasis).[72]

In both this case and that cited earlier, from the tomb of Nakht (as well as in other related examples), we find that the female figure is clearly the object of the male subject's gaze.[73] If this represents an "objectification" of the female, it also raises, once again, the curious problem of gender and agency in ancient Egyptian culture. This is particularly so if, as Kozloff argues, the pictures had the pragmatic aim of "arous[ing] the male tomb owner's (and perhaps his god's as well) procreative functions in the afterlife." This would again indicate the dispersion of subjective autonomy onto the sphere of the other, in this case an other of a specifically sexual definition, and would tally with our previous observations about the agency of Isis in the Osiris myth.

The attempt to read anything as "erotic" raises not only questions of cultural familiarity and convention, but also, more important, questions of one's own epistemological stance vis-à-vis the object in question and its relation to personal desire. If our observations on these Eighteenth Dynasty tomb paintings must remain tentative, it is as much because of the problematic status of that word "our" as it is because of the cultural distance between a hypothetical "us" and the Eighteenth Dynasty Egyptians. Indeed, in judging from the absence of antecedents to these paintings in the Middle Kingdom and earlier, and the more obviously religious orientation of Ramesside tomb paintings, one might fairly conclude that our conjectures about the aforementioned qualities of these paintings are not without foundation. But now we turn to a more perplexing intersection of representational conventions and erotic desire, and we must come to ask how it would be possible *not* to interpret the ithyphallic representations of Amun and Min, so common from the Middle Kingdom on (and evidenced as well much earlier), in an erotic, more precisely, *homoerotic*, way.

And our problems here come not so much from a modern homophobia, but from an awareness that the Egyptians themselves apparently had a strong antipathy to homosexuality.[74] But in the face of such an awareness, how do we interpret the legions of representations of the pharaoh making offerings to an unambiguously erect and remarkably endowed god?

One beginning can be made in an attempt to historicize the phenomenon. We thus become quickly aware that a celebration of the phallus is one of the central iconic foci of Egyptian religion from predynastic days through the Roman occupation. On the one hand, we find the three megaliths Petrie described (however inadequately) on their recovery from the earliest levels of the cult sites of the god Min at Coptos. These are, as was pointed out at the beginning of the chapter, among the oldest colossal sculpture in not only Egypt but the whole world, and they are clearly evidence of a cult of the phallus.

At the other end of the ancient Egyptian historical spectrum, we might note the Roman period representations of Min and Min Amun at Karnak, Dendera, and Philae, with an awareness that the age-old cult of Min at Akhmim flourished well into Christian times, and met its end only in the second century C.E. under violent persecution by the Coptic bishop Schenute.[75]

All the same, it is one thing to demonstrate a fertility cult focused on the phallus, and another to demonstrate therein an explicitly homoerotic or homosocial significance, and here, the Coptos megalith and the perdurance of the cult at Coptos into the common era provide only circumstantial evidence. In particular, the Coptos megaliths remain inadequately contextualized. We have no evidence of how they were made objects of worship or subjects of ritual performance. As independent idols, they offer us scant clues to the social and political (much less theological) role they played in the lives of predynastic Egyptians.

Indeed, throughout the Old Kingdom, although there is evidence for the worship of Min and his importance in the pantheon—and this certainly is significant, considering the paucity of evidence for other gods, even gods that later assume overwhelming importance, such as Osiris and Amun—that evidence is for the most part rather abstract. The priapic god so familiar later in Egyptian history is witnessed in the Old Kingdom almost exclusively in his hieroglyphic name: a sort of vajra-like shape lying horizontally over a standard, as we saw in Chapter 2.[76] And we do not have adequate representation of the worship of the god such as became so conspicuous in the Middle Kingdom and New Kingdom.

It is in this contextualized sort of representation that we are confronted with the questions about homoeroticism and homosociality to which I alluded earlier. The preponderance of early representations of the phallus seem closely related to the kings of the Twelfth Dynasty, especially Kheperkare' Senusert I. It is, significantly, at this point that the identity of Min becomes fused with that of the newly important Theban god Amun, and it is also probably important that these representations are in many cases associated with the ritual rejuvenation of pharaoh in the Heb-Sed festival. The festival itself has archaic roots and is represented among the earliest finds of the dynastic period, but in the Middle Kingdom it takes on a particularly phallocentric significance in, for instance, a relief now in the Petrie Museum in the University of London (Fig. 3.14). There, the pharaoh stretches his legs wide as he runs the legendary course of the Heb-Sed ritual while the ithyphallic Min or Amun watches to the right.[77]

More striking still are the many representations of pharaoh before an ithyphallic Amun-Re' or Min on the square pillars of Senusert I's peripteral chapel at Karnak. This is one of the few buildings of Middle Kingdom vintage yet extant, and it is remarkable in its elegance as well as its simplicity. Its sixteen square columns are each covered with cleanly cut religious reliefs in a wonderful symbiosis with large hieroglyphic inscriptions. Most of the reliefs picture the pharaoh before an ithyphallic god, sometimes with another party as well. A characteristic scene is reproduced at Figure 3.15, in which the god Atum leads Senusert to Amun *kamutef*. Above the king are a shortened form of his titulary and predictable formulas of immortality and eternal power.

Atum, preceding the king, is saying, "Come in peace, Senusert, and see your father Amun-Re'. It is because he loves you that he gives you the kingship of the Two Lands."

Amun himself is saying, "Welcome, welcome, Kheperkare', son of my body, beloved one, thou whose flesh I endow with life, dominion, and happiness eternally."

Figure 3.14. Senusert I running the Heb-Sed course before the "Great God," Min or Min-Amun. Now in the Petrie Museum, University of London (14786).

Figure 3.15. Atum leading Kheperkareʾ Senusert I before Amun-Reʾ, relief from a column of the "White Chapel" of Senusert at Karnak. The chapel, almost entire, has been reconstructed on the grounds of the open-air museum at Karnak.

As Figure 3.15 shows, Amun is shrouded rather than naked. Thus the only exposed part of his body, apart from his head and right arm, is his erect penis. This is the case as well on most of the forty-eight carved column faces in the monument, so that we might come to the best understanding of the piece by *mis*reading some of its inscriptions. Consider, for instance, the inscription accompanying one of the scenes of pharaoh making an offering to the ithyphallic Amun.[78] Conventionally, it would be read, "I have given all life, stability, and dominion to my son Kheperkareʾ in the presence of the Ennead." But the last phrase, m bȝḥ psḏt, "in the presence of the Ennead," could also be read as m ḥnn psḏt to mean "with the phallus of the gods." It might be that such misprision is not so mistaken after all, for given the preponderance of similar scenes henceforth in Egyptian history, one might not be going too far to say that they represent the figural center of a web of relations that suggest fecundity and fertility, love, dominion, and stability through the conspicuous physical spectacle of the erect phallus of god.[79]

One might well wonder how public this was. (As we will see later, such a priapic spectacle holds explosive potential.) With the case of the masturbatory cosmogony of Aunu, and the scene of Horus's conception at Seti's temple at Abydos, we have good reason to conclude that the scenes before us are privileged, and were available only to an exclusive class of priests and officials connected with the temple cult and the funerary ritual, but the erection of Amun is everywhere apparent in the great Hypostyle Hall of Karnak, a site apparently accessible to a broader group of commoners.[80]

What, moreover, is the relation between the ithyphallic Amun and the other men (or gods) in the picture? A characterization of these scenes as homosexual would assume too much, perhaps, since there is rarely any physical contact between the figures in question, but we must then come to ask how it would be possible *not* to interpret them homoerotically, as an explicit celebration of the phallus among males. Although the figurality of Egyptian representational systems smudges the overt sexuality of these reliefs into other areas of organic (re)production, it cannot eliminate that sexuality, and the fact that it is exclusively a sexuality *between men* points to a paradox vis-à-vis the overtly antihomosexual manifestations of Egyptian culture, which are unambiguous, if not numerous.

Most significant, such homoeroticism cannot be dismissed as "just a symbol," and as we will see, its consequences beyond Egyptian culture are as hard to dismiss as to understand clearly. And even in acknowledging them, we must come back to them to note a lack, the lack of the female, not for the enforcement of a normative heterosexuality, but as a condition of the phallocentric celebrations which we have now seen so consistently in Egyptian culture. It might be well to make perforce another misreading here before moving to a final, strikingly opposed vision of the relation between power, gender, and sexuality in ancient Egypt. That misreading calls us back to the *kamutef*. The accepted and perfectly justifiable reading of this phrase consists of a set of simple genitive juxtapositions, $k\dot{z}$-mwt=f means "bull of the mother of him." But juxtaposition in Middle Egyptian is not exclusively an indication of genitive relation. It can also indicate equivalence. In this context, upsetting and deconstructing the entire phallocentric hierarchy of the *kamutef*, is the reading of not "bull of his mother, but "the bull *is* his (own) mother"; incompetent philology, perhaps, but an encapsulation of the conundrum of gender in ancient Egypt.

ANTITYPE

In the middle of the fourteenth century B.C.E., arguably the most prosperous and cosmopolitan era in Egypt's history, a radical upset befell the royal house, the reverberations of which were felt in a broad way throughout the country. This so-called Amarna period[81] makes its most incisive impression for us in the visual arts and in the speculations we are led to when reading its religious texts. It is in the former area that Amarna provides the most apposite stimulus for our current engagement upon phallocentrism, and in that context it is no less striking in the oppositions and complexities it presents than in its famous monotheism, which we will discuss elsewhere.

Amarna centers upon the pharaoh Akhenaten, the erstwhile Neferkheperure' Amenhotep IV. A junior son of Nebma'atre' Amenhotep III, he was apparently not groomed for the throne, but on the death of an elder brother, the designated crown prince, became the royal heir and came to the throne as coregent in the last years of his celebrated father's reign.

Akhenaten's image in Egyptian relief and sculpture is so striking and unexpected that it has been widely suspected he was afflicted by some kind of disease or congenital abnormality that led to conspicuous physical deformation. His body is shown, almost without exception, with a protruding belly and broad hips on enormous thighs and spindly lower legs. Although his shoulders are sometimes relatively broad, his chest is not. His breasts are large, as are his buttocks, so that without such indications of gender as the crowns he wears and his royal titles and names, one would have every reason to assume the figure depicted to be female.

The face is no less striking: there are large, pendulous lips, high cheekbones, and long sunken cheeks, which lead by way of an oversized jaw to a long protruding chin. The eyes are narrow and almond-shaped, and they are placed high and close to the brow. The physical eccentricities of Akhenaten's image and the fact that he is not depicted in the art of his father's reign have led to speculation that physical deformity caused his seclusion through most of the reign of Amenhotep III, and that he was chosen as pharaoh only as a last resort after his elder brother's demise.

Such an extraordinary departure from the representational norms of Egyptian sculpture has spawned a lively brood of conjectures over motivation. Predictably, some have seen these physical manifestations as evidence of "inversion" of various sorts: thus, there has been speculation that Akhenaten was a woman masquerading as a man, or was homosexual or hermaphrodite, or that he was a pantywaist who allowed his wife Nefertiti to institute a kind of petticoat government. More plausibly, pathologists such as Elliot Smith have conjectured that he suffered from some kind of endocrine disorder, perhaps Frölich's syndrome, arguing from the characteristically feminine distribution of fat in Frölich's sufferers.[82] It is, after all, undeniable that the figure of Akhenaten makes a stark contrast with the broad-shouldered, narrow-hipped idealizations of the male form found in portrayals of other pharaohs, from King Den of the First

Dynasty,[83] to Snedjemibre' Nakhthorheb (also called Nectanebo II) of the Thirtieth,[84] to the rulers of the Ptolemaic and Roman periods.

Art historians, after the first shock of seeing the extraordinary and in some ways rather grotesque way in which Akhenaten is depicted, have generally moved on to praise the new naturalism of the Amarna period, on the assumption that Akhenaten actually looked as depicted. That is something we will probably never know, but there are two important complications that must be taken into account in considering the figure of Akhenaten, and they both make it more difficult to accept the "new naturalism" hypothesis.

The first problem is Akhenaten's apparent virility. He was the spouse of perhaps the most beautiful (or at least most beautifully depicted) queen in Egyptian history, and he is pictured with her in moments of striking intimacy, with as many as six daughters. But Frölich's syndrome inhibits the development of the genitals beyond an infantile stage, and would preclude Akhenaten's ever having become a father, as would many of the other endocrine problems that produce similar effects on body shape.

More interesting still is the fact that the eccentricities of Akhenaten's physique appear, from the earliest days, in the portrayal of his family and subjects as well. This is not without precedent. In other periods in Egyptian art as well—importantly, in the period immediately preceding the Amarnan—high officials' and courtiers' appearances are to some degree assimilated to that of the pharaoh.[85] But in these other cases, the assimilation is a part of the general idealization of patricians in Egyptian art, whereas in the case of Amarnan art, especially early Amarnan art, the distortions and eccentricities of portrayal can hardly be characterized as idealizations. Clearly, we have here a style of portrayal that, whatever its origins, pathological or otherwise, quickly assumes a rhetorical or ideological significance ranging far beyond its grounding (or not) in some heightened "naturalism."

And there is good reason to assume that such a representational contagion, as it were, corresponds with the abrupt change in trajectory in thought and political structure the Amarna period represents. This change is most pointed in the reevaluation of the cult of Amun, which, as we have seen above, is intimately caught up with the phallocentrism of earlier Egyptian religion, even as it develops its own hyperphallic manifestations.

We might, then, look to Amarnan art not as some species of psychosexual inversion, but rather as a normative inversion[86] of the hypermasculine representation of power and divinity that had become so common in the cult of Amun *kamutef* during the Middle Kingdom and early New

Kingdom. In particular, one colossal representation of Akhenaten unearthed at Karnak strongly suggests such a possibility. The statue (reproduced here as Figure 3.16) is of sandstone, one of a series that seems to have fronted an enormous temple known as the Gempaaten (*Gm-pꜣ-jtn*), built in Karnak before Akhenaten abandoned Thebes for his new capital at Amarna. Parts of three of these colossi are now in the Egyptian Museum in Cairo, and while the other two show Akhenaten in a pleated kilt and sash, this representation would appear to be naked, with skinny arms, large breasts, heavy thighs and buttocks, a pendulous belly, and large navel, and most tellingly, no indication at all of genitals. One could hardly imagine a more consistent semiotic inversion of the figure of Amun *kamutef*, the god Akhenaten worked so hard to discredit and dispossess.

The colossus is, indeed, so feminine in appearance that it has been suggested that it is not intended to represent Akhenaten at all, but rather Nefertiti.[87] Donald Redford has another explanation for the mysterious colossus. He asks,

> Is this really [Nefertiti]? Is [Akhenaten] depicted as hermaphroditic? Was it an expression of a deep theological doctrine? For my own part, I can imagine that this image might have been clothed with some sort of applied garment. In any case, it need not be pointed out how ill-advised it is to read profound meaning into such a flimsy piece of evidence.[88]

Figure 3.16. Colossus of Akhenaten found in eastern Karnak on the site of his Gempaaten temple. Photograph by the author.

One might reply, however, that a piece of sculpture of several tons, in such a fine state of preservation, hardly qualifies as "flimsy," following, then, with the question, why its creators might have chosen to carve this statue naked, only to have gone on later to augment it with some sort of applied garment.

It seems rather that this figure is merely one in a series of examples in which Akhenaten is depicted with physical features that had, in more conventional Egyptian art, applied to the feminine figure alone. The naked colossus is not different in kind, but merely in degree, from other sculptures of Akhenaten, exemplifying the extreme limit of Amarnan figural representation of the king. And this is, indeed, where the significance of this colossus resides for our current purpose: not in its reflection of Akhenaten's physical body, but rather in its extension of the discursive practices of Amarna religion into the figural realm of the visual arts, to the inversion of those hypermasculine representational conventions applied to Amun, the god Akhenaten took every effort to dethrone, deface, and destroy.[89]

If, on the one hand, the depictions of Akhenaten in Amarna art have feminized him, leading to conjecture about hermaphroditism, homosexuality, congenital barrenness, and so on, then it should, perhaps, be no surprise that a similar discourse has tried to make a man of Akhenaten's queen Nefertiti. It is, all the same, shocking to find her so characterized on the basis of the exquisite portrait bust now in the Ägyptisches Museum in Charlottenburg, Berlin. The bust is one of the most celebrated objects in the entire corpus of Egyptian art, surpassed in fame only by Tut'ankhamun's golden mask. It is the portrait of a woman with a high crown. It is made of limestone with a highly polished and richly painted surface, easily one of the great masterpieces of portraiture in all history. Yet this is what Camille Paglia has found it possible to say about the portrait:

> The bust of Nefertiti is artistically and ritualistically complete, exalted, harsh, and alien. It fuses the naturalism of the Amarna period with the hieratic formalism of Egyptian tradition. But Amarna expressiveness ends in the grotesque. This is the least consoling of great art works. Its popularity is based on misunderstanding and suppression of its unique features. The proper response to the Nefertiti bust is fear. The queen is an android, a manufactured being. She is a new gorgoneion, a "bodiless head of fright." She is paralyzed and paralyzing. Like enthroned Chephren, Nefertiti is suave, urbane. She gazes toward the far distance, seeing what is best for her people. But her eyes, with their catlike rim of kohl, are cold. She is self-divinized authority. Art shows Akhenaten half-feminine, his limbs shrunken and belly bulging, possibly from birth defect or disease.

This portrait shows his queen half-masculine, a vampire of political will. Her seductive force both lures in and warns away. She is western personality barricaded behind its aching, icy line of Apollonian identity.[90]

Paglia is a master of the sweeping and ill-supported generalization,[91] but she outdoes herself here. One can only suspect that her argument owes much less than it should to a serious consideration of the object. But what is worthy of note here is her extravagant orientalizing gesture taking Nefertiti as butch, which is possible only in a discussion oblivious of the context in which Amarna art develops, and the serious challenge it presents to the traditional Egyptian canon.

The iconography of the subject in Amarnan art exists in a tangle of possibilities we cannot reorder fully and unequivocally, partly, of course, because of the depredations of Akhenaten's restorationist successors, partly because of the mirages that deform our view of such a remote time, partly because of the operations of our own desires upon the object of view, and partly, as well, because the discursive tools whereby any such constructions might be made are always already entangled and implicated in *différance* and polyvalency. The appeal of that subject persists, nonetheless, and perhaps nowhere more seductively than in the enigmas of Amarnan representation of gender.

One of the most important insights of the current reevaluation of the ancient world has come from the study of gender, and it has confronted us, once again, with the delusion that "our" values are the progeny of Greek values, carried through the long darkness of the Middle Ages, to be revivified in Renaissance humanism and modern American democracy. We have been forced to reconsider our debt to the ancient Eastern Mediterranean, particularly in view of the clear evidence that women had far greater rights and freedoms in the supposedly despotic Orient that was ancient Egypt, than in the supposedly democratic Occident that was classical Athens. But we must hasten to add that for all the difference between Egypt and Greece in the living standards and personal freedoms afforded women, ancient Egypt remained a society controlled by men and represented to us, almost exclusively, in the voices of men. And it is important to add that this androcentrism is not merely an abstract preference for male power in government, economy, and the various modes of written discourse. It was, rather, a figurally concentrated and corporealized phallocentrism, which sees the site of male identity and power in the phallus and marks the discourses of theology, royal legitimacy, and social cohesiveness with the seminal trace. The point in noticing this focus of attention is not primarily salacious or puerile or comically ribald (although it can be amusing, and improper and erotically entertaining). In a more significant sense, however, it calls our attention to the broader and more wide-ranging constraints of our bodily epistemology, to questions of whether it is, indeed, possible for us to think and make representation as, "simply," people, rather than as specifically "men" and/not "women." Can we, in fact, gain some epistemological perspective that does not depend on our necessarily gendered embodiment? And given that embodiment, how are we to face the problem of multiplicity in Being? Note well: by that multiplicity in Being, I do not intend to say "multiplicity of beings," but to point to the fragmentation or dissemination of the subject upon a multiplicity of sites, which is one of the entailments of our corporeality. This leads to a problem that has bedeviled modern reconsiderations of Egyptian culture as well as, apparently, Egyptian culture "itself." We will soon move on to that field of contention, but in the construction of a polarity between an "us," monotheistic individuals living in polities where self-determination is the form of government, and "the Egyptians," polytheistic multitudes under the yoke of pharaonic despotism, we have failed to understand the Egyptians and ourselves as well, and at the root of our misunderstanding lies, or stands, the phallus.

4
... THREE, TWO, ONE, ZERO

Among the offerings depicted on the walls of Egyptian tombs, you can find all sorts of food and drink, wine, milk, and so on, but it's the bread and the beer I remember. A matter of personal taste, perhaps. But there's a good deal more to it than taste, as these, with onions, were the staples of the Egyptian diet. It wasn't, however, solely a matter of nutrition. No need, then, for the many varieties of bread, some quite aptly "cakes." And the beer was not drunk solely for nutritional reasons.

The types of bread listed in a class of Egyptian texts called "onomastica" run to the forties. There is dry bread, there's good bread, there's white bread, *kershet* bread.[1] Great loaf, sparrow rolls, date cookies, milk biscuits, and tables full of cakes which we know only through Egyptian proper nouns, the most and least descriptive of words.

As for the beer, it was called something like "henket" and sounds something like a thick stout perhaps, a fermented mixture of half-baked bread and Nile water. It must have tasted best, wouldn't you think, taken from a terra-cotta cooling pot strategically placed in a shaded and breezy corridor. And there were other things to drink besides this ordinary beer, of course. Triple-strength beer, for one thing, and a special beer for festivals, but wine as well, appreciated by vintage and region, from "new wine" (a nouveau beaujolais à l'égyptien, no doubt) to the dregs of a cheap old wine "such as the servants might drink."[2]

The diversity betrays an Egyptian delight in consumption and one comes to feel sorry for Osiris, forced to trade his bread and beer for peace of mind. The diversity reveals many other things as well, about material culture and economic development as well as the organization of knowledge.

LISTS

Consider, for instance, the fowling scene in Khnumhotep's tomb at Beni Hasan (Fig. 4.1). The composition is hardly naturalistic. Master of the Tomb Khnumhotep sits resolutely upon a cat-footed stool, behind him stands his son at half scale. They are hidden in a reed blind that cuts the composition roughly into half. A marsh spreads over the full height of the wall in a broad oval, painted in with blue zigzag patterns like the hieroglyph for "water." In its center rests another geometric construction, a flattened hexagram bisected by a line. The whole is a net, and in it—what fowler ever had such a good day?—are nearly twenty braces of ducks, arranged by species. Pains were taken to identify each species and within each species, the individual birds are unique. Outside the net, flocks of ducks begin to alight, and in the lower corners, birds crowd the branches of two trees.

The two human figures are handsomely canonical, but the hieroglyphic caption is still finer, and the marsh scene here is a real tour de force. It would be anachronistic to call it Aristotelian, but the concern for type and typing is as analytical as Aristotle's, though far more vivid. The individual fowl are stretched into poses one could never actually effect upon a living duck. They would, all the same, prove better guides to identifying the birds in question than a photo you might chance to take. Each could be

Figure 4.1. Khnumhotep netting fowl. From his tomb at Beni Hasan. Here, from the facsimile by Nina de Garis Davies, now in the Metropolitan Museum of Art in New York (33.8.18).

named, and you, the namer, would thereby gain a certain knowledge, and thus power, over them.[3]

But you may recall, there is disagreement about how the Egyptians regarded the names and images of things, conspicuous in their mutual implication in Egyptian culture. The frequent contention is that the name had an essential link with the thing and could, if necessary, replace the thing, should that thing be lost or irremediably damaged. And even in less extreme circumstances, the name or image of the thing could represent it or stand in for it for a range of practical and aesthetic reasons. As Kemp points out, for instance,

> Within [the] rearrangement of entities to illustrate the concept of harmony through the balancing of pairs we can glimpse a simple example of one form of the Egyptians' thought processes: the manipulation of words, especially names, as if they were discrete units of knowledge. Ancient knowledge, when not of a practical nature (such as how to build a pyramid and how to behave at table), was essentially the accumulation of names of things, beings, and places, together with their associations. "Research" lay in extending the range of associations in areas which we would now term "theology." Meaning or significance was left in the mind and remained largely unformulated.[4]

In our world today, the notion that a particular word has an essential relationship with the thing it names seems childish or primitive. "A rose by any other name," and so forth.[5] Thus, we might be inclined to dismiss the Egyptians as fundamentally flawed in their understanding of reality, as entirely different from ourselves. As Kemp goes on to explain,

> The esteem in which names of things were held is nicely brought out by a class of text which scholars call "onomastica." The best known, compiled in the late New Kingdom ... by a "Scribe of Sacred Books" named Amenemope, and much copied in ancient schools, has the promising heading: "Beginning of the teaching for clearing the mind, for the instruction of the ignorant, and for learning all things that exist." But without a single word of commentary or explanation it runs on as a list of names of things: the elements of the universe, types of human beings, the towns and villages of Egypt ..., [the] parts of an ox, and so on. To the modern mind this form of learning appears like the most stifling kind of pedagogy.[6]

The onomastica do, indeed, seem stifling in extended recitation, as would, for instance, a dictionary, but Kemp begins to concede to a kinship between this type of knowledge and our own systems of understanding the world. "We can," he says, still recognize some validity in this: the study of the natural world, whether bird watching or classifying plants, begins with knowing names, and with arranging the names in groups (the science of taxonomy), just as was done intuitively in the onomastica, which served as memory aids for the range of knowledge which was absorbed simply as a result of being a reasonably well-educated Egyptian.[7]

But Kemp's own conjecture that a reasonably well-educated Egyptian would probably have used these onomastica merely as memory aids suggests that his criticism of them as "the most stifling kind of pedagogy" may be too hasty. We don't share the educated Egyptian's memories, and we ourselves would indeed do better with these lists of nouns if they came with predicates too. How much more vivid it would be if, instead of merely the name "*kershet* bread," we were to read, "to make *kershet* bread, do the following..." With such a recipe we would be able to reproduce more concretely an Egyptian experience of life.

We should not, however, conclude from the fact that the *Onomasticon of Amenemope* doesn't give us a recipe for *kershet* bread that Amenemope himself didn't know how it was made, or what it tasted like or what its cultural context was. So also, the presumption that "ancient knowledge was... essentially an accumulation of names" cannot be supported on the basis of this evidence. (The existence, moreover, of ancient Egyptian medical texts which give us not only names for ailments but also procedures for treating them demonstrates the direct written linkage of nouns with predicates to the end of instruction in a practical art.)

The opening of the onomasticon does sound grandiose, given its ambitions toward "learning all things that exist," but we should not forget that it also claims merely to be the *beginning* of such a teaching. Now it could be that the word "beginning" here ($ḥ3t$-^{c}) is intended to refer merely to the physical object that is the text. We cannot say so, definitively, however, because the very existence of the text is always already the beginning of a kind of knowledge once it engages the reader's attention. So, in this claim on the beginning of knowledge, we come back to the importance of the name and to the particularly Egyptian intersection of the name with a picture.

The fact that Egyptian representational systems have an iconic significance that is impossible to replicate in our dry alphabets brings to the onomasticon a potential that it could not have otherwise. If, as John Baines points out, "a belief that pictures were the same as their subjects would, by any standards, argue a deficient sense of reality,"[8] so also, the belief that the name is the same as the thing named would argue a fundamental flaw in Egyptian perceptual capabilities. But the combination of the name with the picture, even though it does not reconstitute the object, enables a far more sophisticated knowledge than either alone might. Knowledge of this particular type is indeed a kind of power or capability. Knowing the name of that thing in your car that mixes fuel and air and knowing what it looks like are the first steps necessary to repairing a carburetor. In countless other contexts, it is upon the combination of the name and a set of figural (whether visual, aural, olfactory, or tactile) associations that we found more complex, technical, and analytical kinds of knowledge. Such image-based regimes of knowledge are the ground upon which more sophisticated understandings of the interactions of things are built, and we must be careful not to mistake the obvious presence of these building blocks in the Egyptian cultural record for the absence of more analytical and theoretical understandings in their view of the world.[9]

The context of offering scenes in tombs gives us, moreover, evidence that the Egyptians were themselves cognizant of the difference between the name and the thing, on the one hand, and the image and the thing, on the other. The donation of offerings, for example, was not in itself sufficient for the creation of the special powers and strengths that the offering formula promises to the deceased. The objects donated were invested with such powers only through the performance of the requisite rituals.[10] Such rituals are of course supplementary, both in the conventional sense, in that they are "added to" the material content of the offering, and in the Derridean sense, in that they, even as additions, are what makes the contents of the offerings what they *are* in magical or religious terms.

It is in this context that one can understand how the images and words so apparent in Egyptian material remains might be considered adequate replacements for the objects they represent. If it takes ritual performance and pronouncements to turn donations into offerings in the strong, magical sense, then ritual performance and recitation might likewise be able to transform pictures of donations into offerings in that strong sense.[11] At the heart of this operation, however, is the economy of replacement. We touched on this subject before. Now, though, it is time to consider this economy of replacement from a somewhat different angle, that of multiplicity.

There is clearly a fascination with number and multiplicity in ancient Egyptian culture, and certain specific numbers have well-attested associations that are manifest in textual as well as visual representation. There is also, however, a well-evidenced impetus toward the one, unity, or oneness, which surfaced at least once in a paroxysm of intellectual crisis, the

Amarna revolution, as well as in more benign and speculative contexts. One might, indeed, at least heuristically, erect a polarity between oneness and multiplicity in the attempt to better define the subjective field in ancient Egyptian thought. In doing so, we uncover abundant testimony to the richness and diversity of life in the ancient Nile Valley. We also strike upon more perplexing and provocative manifestations of the one versus the many. The supplementarity of writing is one of these; the related cognitive process of categorization is another: difference and *différance* in the scrape of individual case against type and class.

More germane to our present concern, however, is the problem of G/god/s. No problem is, perhaps, more obvious or controversial in our coming to terms with Egypt. The vilification of Egypt in the Bible is above all a vilification of polytheism, and the derogation of Egyptians as primitives in thrall to cat-headed idols, among both the classical Greeks and Romans, as well as in more modern times, is at heart a problem of multiplicity.

Subtler and better-informed observers have noticed, however, that the very representations which, in literal terms, suggest a world of freakish combinations of animal and human, might, when understood in figural terms, allow the transposition of the many onto the one. Some have gone further, to imagine that the very possibility of the one is entangled in the reality of the many.

THE NATURE OF */ˈNE-TJER/

"Polytheism" is a word born of ignorance. None of the so-called polytheists among the religious of this world has created a comparable term in self-description. It is only as the antithesis of "monotheism," and therefore only from the parochial view of monotheists, that "polytheism" has meaning. The meaning ascribed to the word, then, cannot but be derogatory and dismissive. And so, even if we have talked of Egyptian polytheism along the way, it is time now to reconsider this classification to come to a better understanding of the range and diversity of religious experience to which the material and written remains of ancient Egypt bear witness.

Our discussion here must be circumscribed and general. There are already excellent and detailed discussions elsewhere, particularly in Erik Hornung's *Conceptions of God in Ancient Egypt: The One and the Many*,[12] but taking our cue from Hornung, we will be well advised in the first place to consider the Egyptian word most commonly translated as "god" in order to gain some idea of how it expresses the aforementioned diversity of religious experience.

𓊵 The word is romanized to the consonant skeleton *nṯr* and may have been pronounced something like "*netjer" or "*natjir."[13] The glyph itself is a picture of a pole wrapped with a cloth, the end of which blows freely in the wind at the top of the pole, rather like a flag. The glyph is attested early in the Old Kingdom and found commonly throughout all periods of Egyptian civilization thereafter. It is the most typical graphic rendering of "god."

There is apparently a direct link to the material culture of ancient Egypt here. Egyptian temples were first identifiable from a distance thanks to tall poles from which banners had been unfurled, and in the figural economy by which a banner moving in the unseen wind could be analogized to represent the class of unseen forces came the notion of "god" or "gods." There may have been a fetishistic edge to this economy, such that the flag and flagpole themselves were sacred objects, which would, as Hornung suggests, tie this ancient symbolism in with the fetishism sometimes excited by modern national flags.[14] One would, however, seriously underread the figural potential of such a transfer from the material world to religion by restricting its significance to fetishism. We can see this, in part, because of other ways in which "netjer" is written.

𓊸 Another common rendering is found mostly in hieratic rather than hieroglyphic texts. It pictures a hawk on a standard and, again, enables a figural economy whereby the power and majesty of the hawk are made abstract, through the standard, so that the glyph as a whole means something more than merely "hawk" (which is, indeed, written differently. See p. 262).

𓀭 Still another common rendering of "god" is to be found in the determinative for god found at the ends of the names of individual gods. It also occurs in isolation (although rarely) to render *nṯr*. The anthropomorphism of this third glyph bears witness to an intersection between the divine world and the human. It first appears, in fact, in early texts, associated with Osiris or a spirit of the transfigured dead, an *akh* (i.e., *ȝḫ*).[15]

But if the anthropomorphism of this glyph bears witness to the intersection of the divine world with the human, but it also brings us face to face with one of the most controversial aspects of Egyptian religion, for like as not, you will find among the handsome gods and goddesses in a given Egyptian relief, some others who have human bodies, to be sure, but the heads of birds and animals. Some Greeks and Romans recoiled in horror before these composite beings: they were offended by such transgression of category boundaries and exasperated by a people who might bow down and worship bulls and cats and snakes and the like. And it would be rash to assume that Egyptians didn't, in certain cases, worship specific animals. Indeed, the cults of Apis, Mnevis, and Buchis in, respectively, Memphis, Aunu, and Armant[16] invested great religious importance in specific specially marked living bulls; when those bulls died, they were mummified with extraordinary care and ceremony.

Some Egyptologists have sought to explain this type of animal worship as the decadence of a late and morally debilitated Egypt after the more philosophical religion of ancient times had been corrupted and misconstrued. Others have seen this as merely a superstitious popular manifestation of what was, at heart, a more philosophical belief on the part of the wiser and better educated. But to restrict Egyptian religious experience in any of these ways is shortsighted. There must certainly have been, throughout Egyptian history, individuals who chose to invest living beings, whether animal or human, with divine power; and there must as well have been those who saw the significance of such manifestations of divinity in a much more abstract way. It is not, in any case, within our reach to know these things definitively. We are left only the options of interpretation and criticism, basing our constructions on what we have of the material and discursive remains of Egypt. But perhaps the distance this imposes on our labors is merely a difference of degree and not of kind from the more proximate tasks of understanding in our commoner experience.

The fact that certain Greeks and Romans, and some of their successors, were offended by the hybrid nature of many Egyptian gods in itself points to the figural nature of such constructions. The combination of attributes in the representation of the figure of divinity no more implies the phenomenal existence of that particular figure than does the fact that Isis is often depicted with the hieroglyph for a throne on her head mean that there is, in some divine sphere of existence, a beautiful goddess named Isis who goes through the day with a throne on her head. This is, rather, a part of the figural economy of Egyptian representational systems, not a snapshot of reality.

The issue of idolatry raises similar problems, but only the most narrow-minded literalism can rest in the belief that Egyptians, in ministering to images of gold and silver and stone, were worshiping those objects in themselves. As Siegfried Morenz has explained, the ritual context in which such images are employed, and the fact that they must be ritually animated (through the ceremony of the "Opening of the Mouth," or something similar),

> entitles us to exempt the Egyptians from the charges hurled at them by Old Testament writers for pagan idol-worship.... The ancient Egyptians

would have agreed that the material and the sculpture fashioned from it were inanimate; this was why they were given vitality by the ritual.... An Egyptian might have argued, ... "We believe that in what appear to be statues not endowed with life we do in fact worship the power of the gods present in them, who are endowed with life."[17]

Putting words in the mouths of the dead is perilous, but Morenz is persuasive here, and we might buttress his imaginative reconstruction with the observation that the cult image is not the object of worship *in isolation*. There is always a context, the physical setting of the temple, the performative sphere of ritual, and so on, so we must credit Egyptians with (more or less) sincere attitudes of worship analogous to those one might find in a contemporary church or synagogue on a typical Saturday or Sunday.[18]

We are handicapped, even as we are enabled (as always) by our sources of knowledge: most of what we see comes from the context of royal patronage and the cult of pharaonic authority. We must acknowledge a fissure here in the discernible roots of some ancient Egyptian religious experience in the local community, on the one hand, and the overarching interests of the state and its religion(s) on the other.

Clearly, certain Egyptian religious traditions grew out of local belief and reflected the particular interests of particular communities. Gods like Ptah, for instance, had a special meaning in Memphis before they had national meaning. Other gods, such as Ha'py, the Nile as god, had a national significance, undoubtedly, but it was a significance born of the importance of the river to Egypt as a whole and had a direct link thereto which could only secondarily be brought under the sway of the theology of the state. Here, "polytheism" was a manifestation of geographical and social diversity, a way of relating the local community to intangible forces important to that community, such as the change of the seasons, the cycle of the river, the processes of growth and decay, human life and death.

There was, obviously, another "polytheism" which held sway by virtue of the regime of classification, intellectualization, and legitimation employed by the state for its own purposes. This range of beliefs co-opted local religions and local autonomy in the promotion of pharaonic centralism. The process is not transparent from this remove, but it must certainly have gone hand in hand with the development of a figural economy in writing. The same economy of individual scraping against class and genre can be observed in a fragmentary way in, for example, the semiotic implication of numerous falcon gods into the figure of Horus, who as we have seen, betrays his multiple origins in a startling diversity and in an important dynamic paradox.

The persistence of such logical paradoxes as this implication entails has long irritated modern students of Egyptian religion. Inconsistency and contradiction have been cited as evidence of primitiveness or inadequate understanding on the part of the Egyptians, in putative contrast with Greeks or Jews or Christians (ironic as that may seem!). But what may appear to some as contradictory or illogical, or at best, indeterminate, is, as Morenz explains, one of the most important virtues of the system of Egyptian beliefs.

> This formlessness is but the necessary counterpart to an attitude of mind that is of the utmost importance; it explains why the Egyptian gods merged in the way they did, and—again in contrast to Greece—called into being a great system of theology. This theology accentuated the existing tendency to strengthen the local gods by fusing them with higher ones, for it led to earnest theoretical speculations about the problem of how the numerous deities in the pantheon could be reconciled with a single God. In their efforts to this end thinkers took the course we have indicated above: namely, they avoided liquidating individual gods but did not remain content with building up a hierarchical pantheon; they boldly went on to advance the theory that behind the plurality of gods there was a basic unity. The pantheon was classified in two ways: according to families of kindred deities and according to the specialized functions which particular gods performed.[19]

This is an interesting and important insight, but the uppercase letter by which Morenz singles out the word "God" provides a hint of his own controversial stance vis-à-vis Egyptian religion. He implies that Egyptian religion at its best was actually monotheistic, so if we must recognize, as he says, that "behind the plurality of gods there was a basic unity," we must offer a corrective and turn the tables on him, to understand that behind the unity there is also a basic plurality. The figural transfer of Egyptian thought enables such recontextualization and reclassification in ways that the more rigid categories of Greek and Christian thought do not.

Thus it has often puzzled readers of Egyptian religious texts to find references to "god" (or "God"), that is to say, to *netjer*, unspecified as to number or identity. Such references, being grammatically singular, have opened up the possibility, in some views, that the Egyptians were thereby indicating their belief in ("the single, true") God, but such a conclusion is hasty and sentimental. Hornung explains,

> As a rule, Egyptian officials did not need to have contact in their work or in private with the totality of the pantheon, but with a particular single deity, who might change from situation to situation. Therefore the wis-

dom teachers seldom use the plural "gods," and use a divine proper name, such as Khnum, only when a specific characteristic or activity of that deity is meant—in the case of Khnum; his forming mankind on the potter's wheel [depicted here at Figure 4.2].[20]

A given reference to *netjer*, therefore, should likely as not be interpreted pragmatically: the speaker is not advocating monotheism, necessarily, but is rather making appeal to the god most appropriate for his personal circumstances, a religious orientation sometimes termed "henotheism."

Such henotheism may have enabled local understandings of religion to maintain their particular integrity alongside other understandings of different geographical origin or social circumstance or, indeed, within a far-reaching if remote pantheon that mirrored the political hierarchy of the state.

Yet another type of henotheism is apparent in Egyptian history as well. In this type, which has been studied in great detail by Jan Assmann, the plurality of gods is not denied, but is subordinated and contextualized vis-à-vis a distant and hidden, yet omnipresent and absolute deity who was identified with Amun-Re'.[21]

Figure 4.2. Khnum, the Great Potter of Mankind. Khnum is a creator god in a different sense from Atum or Ptah; he is credited with the creation of individual human beings on his potter's wheel. Here he is shown creating Queen Hatshepsut and her *ka*. Note that both of the figures on the potter's wheel are male. This is one example of the manipulation of representations of gender during Hatshepsut's reign. Redrawn with restorations after Naville, *Deir el-Bahari*, vol. 2 [i.e., *Memoirs of the Egypt Exploration Fund*, vol. 13], pl. 48.

Amun has obvious political and geographical significance, and it is readily apparent that his emergence as leader of the Egyptian pantheon was intimately linked with the political supremacy of the Theban royal house from the Middle Kingdom on, but he was not the first of Egypt's gods to come to prominence because of friends at court. Horus, too, seems to have benefited from such connections, yet the prominence of Horus immediately deconstructs itself into a multiplicity of identities and a constellation of relations, which illuminates the idea of henotheism even as it vitiates any attempt to regard *him* monotheistically: there is a Horus associated with Hierakonpolis in Upper Egypt, but there are Lower Egyptian cult sites of great antiquity as well. It may be more relevant to think of Horus not as a local god risen to national prominence so much as one figure of a pair, the embodiment of pharaonic authority, legitimacy, and order who exists in tandem with his counterpart, Setekh, a figure of disorder and wildness.

If Horus and Setekh represent a divine binarism as an expression of royal authority, there are as well other numbers which play an important part in the figuration of power and authority relating the political with the religious world. The cosmogony of Khemenu (i.e., *Hmnw*, Hermopolis, el-Ashmunein) is structured around the number eight. Indeed, the modern Arabic name of the site has a dual termination, revealing even today an underlying binarism in the cosmogony. The cosmogony of Khemenu, in fact, is formed in the interdependence of male and female growing out of the personification of four abstract characteristics of the preexistent chaos. If those characteristics as abstract nouns were *huh* ("endlessness"), *nun* ("watery chaos"), *kuk* ("darkness"), and *amun* ("hiddenness"), they could be personified and paired with grammatically female counterparts, Hauhet, Naunet, Kauket, and Amaunet, and therefrom the creation of the universe could proceed.[22] As Donald Redford acknowledges, this cosmogony remains opaque in many ways to modern scholars.[23] Perhaps this is because of its very simplicity. The categories of grammatical gender offer an expedient mechanism for overcoming the chaos of preexistence and allow personification and sexual generation without further ado. But if this is the simplest of Egyptian cosmogonies, it is also the least satisfying; it is known to us only because it is mentioned in passing in discussions centered on other issues. It is important, though, in highlighting the significance of gender difference in Egyptian religion, a problem which plays itself out in several different ways. We have already discussed this issue in the context of Atum's cosmogony, but there is evidence throughout Egyptian texts of the great significance with which gender difference was invested. Gardiner styles one section of the *Onomasticon of Amenemope* "Persons, Court, Offices, and Occupations."[24] The beginning runs "*nṯr, nṯrt, 3ḫ, 3ḫt, nsw, nsyt* . . ." (god, goddess, male spirit, female spirit, king, queen, . . . etc.) Although the list fails to specify individual gods, spirits, and the like, it is careful to note gender difference as a criterion for separate categorization, with the female secondary to the male.

This is apparent as well in the divine family triads common in Egyptian religion. We have seen Osiris-Isis-Horus already, but there are also nuclear families for Amun-Mut-Khonsu, Ptah-Sekhmet-Nefertem, Horus-Hathor-Ihy, and so on. The inconsistencies in some of these groups point to an after-the-fact imposition of normative family values upon originally independent and unrelated deities which seems at times sentimental and theologically irrelevant. That is certainly not the case with Osiris-Isis-Horus, as we have seen, but consider the fact that according to the Cosmogony of Khemenu, Amun's consort is one otherwise unknown "Amaunet." In the highly articulated theology of the Theban gods, she is, on the other hand, consistently identified as "Mut." Horus, similarly, is sometimes characterized as the husband of Hathor, other times as her son—her name, Ḥwt-Ḥr, "The Household of Horus," could indicate either, as could the iconographic similarities of Hathor and Isis (they are sometimes indistinguishable). Likewise, Thoth is sometimes matched with a wife named Seshat and son named Hornub; at other times the wife is one Nehmauit and the son, Nefer-Hor. In none of these triads is the child a daughter, and in many cases the wife and son have only the sketchiest identity in comparison with the father/husband.

Other triads with a more highly articulated theological significance can be found. These triads do not mix genders, but indicate, rather, a syncretism among important gods. In one text, in fact, such triads, or trinities, are described as universal: "All gods are three: Amon, Re', and Ptah, and there is no second to them. 'Hidden' is his name as Amon, he is Re' in face, and his body is Ptah."[25] Morenz notes other similar trinities, Ptah-Sokar-Osiris, Ptah-Pre'-Horsiese, and so on. It is significant, in this connection to note that the Egyptians characteristically indicated plurality by the use of the number three. We have already seen this in connection with the writing system, but here, in addition to specifically articulated identifications of three named gods, we may see the workings of henotheism.

One of the most important triads in Egyptian religion represents an inversion of the husband-wife-son pattern just discussed. That is the triad Atum-Shu-Tefnut, which we have already mentioned several times. It is worth returning to it for a moment, however, because this inversion is deeply implicated in one of the fundamental problems of Egyptian religion, the *différance* of creation. This *différance* is not bridged in a single act moving from nonexistence to existence, but rather through the interposition of a liminal stage, an Urzeit, or Ur Time, known in Egyptian as *zep-tepy* (i.e., *zp-tpy*), "the first time," allowing for the self-engenderment of Atum. In a beautiful and important account thereof in the *Coffin Texts*, for example, we find the following passage:

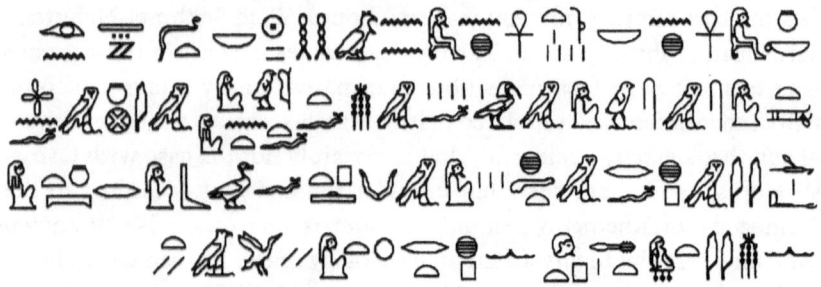

Life am I and Lord of Years,
   I live for all the cycles of Time,
   the stretch of Perpetuity is Mine;
Ancient Atum fashioned me in his mastery,
   when he bore Shu and Tefnut in Aunu,
   when he was One alone,
   when he came into being as the Three,
   and when he parted Geb from Nut;
This, before the first generation was born
   and before the primeval Ennead came to be.[26]

Jan Assmann elaborates that

in the *Coffin Texts* (to be precise, in the sequence of utterances from 75 to 83 which relate to the god Shu) this theology has already appeared in a considerably elaborated form. The primordial state is described in four categories: the primordial water, endlessness, pathlessness, and darkness. Atum "swims" ... "sleeps" ... or "is indolent" ... in Nun, [then] masters the passage from preexistence to existence in an act of self-genesis ... and at the same time to a triad as well: in the same "breath" arise Shu and Tefnut from the self-generating Urgod. The ancient idea of representations of self-begetting and secretion are taken up and at the same time disavowed for the benefit of a conscious and "intellectual" creation.

Particularly significant for Utterance 80 is the constellation of the one "become three" with his children, described in *Pyr.* 1653 as the *ka*-embrace; as embodiments of cosmogonic principles, these are named as

"Life" and "Maat," as well as "Neheh" and "Djet." According to other traditions the god of magic, Heka, and the pair Hu and Sia ("Command" and "Memory") arise by the same disposition of cosmogonic principles in this first cosmogonical phase.[27]

(The mention of the pair Hu [ḥw] and Sia [sj3] here is worth noting. They are important personifications, as gods, of what we might specify further as "generative command" and "penetrating cognition" or "awareness," and we will have occasion to refer to them again.)

By this point any simplistic notion of Egyptian "polytheism" as a concatenation of superstitions should have dissolved to reveal a profoundly sophisticated and complex engagement upon the conundrum of number. The break from nonbeing to existence is not at heart a question of *how* many, but rather a question of how *into* many. The One swims inert, and Being is attained only in the overcoming of the One by bridging the *différance* that constitutes stasis-and-movement, body-and-thought, self-and-other, cognition-and-utterance.

Erik Hornung has pointed to an interesting consequence of this paradox of the one and the many in noticing how the time before creation is referred to as a time when there were "not yet two things" (*Coffin Texts* 2.396b; 3.383a). The jump from nothing to two things this formulation implies suggests an underlying ambivalence about the possibility of presence as a single undifferentiated whole.[28] Existence is, in such a context, the extension of a spectrum from "two things" to "millions" (cf. the frequent reference to the creator as "he who made himself into millions"), but such a range, two to millions, calls into question the very existence of the one and engages the same supplementarity of Atum we discussed in Chapter 3. His own coming into being is simultaneous with the birth of his children Shu and Tefnut. The binarism of the latter two is paradigmatic for a multitude of pairs in Egyptian thought, and the way this binarism steals the limelight of cosmic history may also help explain why Atum faded from the scene of the narrative once creation was set in motion.

MIND AND BODY IN MEMPHIS

It may be that our discussion so far has raised more questions than answers, but we can, all the same, proceed by turning to a century's work on one particular document, asking just two questions, When was it written, and How do we read it? The "document" is written in stone, the stone now resides in the British Museum, and these two questions about it have occupied some of the preeminent Egyptologists of the twentieth century.

Our answers here will be different from theirs; and if on the one hand, we relinquish from the beginning any hope of finding a definitive answer to either question, our responses, on the other hand, may at times verge on a kind of precision that to some may seem altogether obtuse. "When was it written?" for instance:

It was written in 1909, when Adolf Erman first put the word "Memphite" and "theology" (or more correctly, "memphitischer" and "Theologie") together in his "Ein Denkmal memphitischer Theologie" for the Prussian Academy.[29] For to assume that there was specifically a Memphite theology in pharaonic Egypt is already to assume too much. Yet the precision of "1909" is also misleading, because the impetus for Erman and the other scholars who devoted their energies to this remarkable text came earlier, most visibly in 1901, in James Henry Breasted's brief article, "Philosophy of a Memphite Priest."[30]

Breasted, however, actually "wrote" his rendition of the Memphite Theology earlier, copying out the inscription by hand from a badly damaged and unprepossessing block of stone for his contributions to "the great Berlin dictionary" (the *Wörterbuch der ägyptischen Sprache*). Amid the masterworks of the superb collection in the British Museum, this particular inscription had gone little noticed for close to a century. The stone had been given to the British Museum in 1805 by Earl Spenser, but it remained something of a wallflower. What we see today is a heavy, nearly black block of basalt roughly four and one-half feet wide by two and one-quarter feet tall; an inscription once covered the face, but now it is worn faint throughout and has vanished altogether within the circumference of a large irregular circle in the middle of the top surface. A squarish hole is cut deep into the stone in the center of this circle, and there are ten rough channels radiating out from the hole in an irregular starburst, evidence of ignorant disregard in post-pharaonic Egypt, when the stone was used as a nether millstone.

The full or partial erasure of some thirty-six lines in the center of the inscription divides the text into two relatively discrete parts. Indeed, it would be fascinating to know just how the first part of the text, which concerns the justification of Horus's claim to his father's throne, is related to the last part, which contains a difficult cosmogonical treatise. But that we will likely never know, given the destruction the stone has suffered. Even in this regrettable state, however, it is still one of the most important texts in the history of Egyptian thought. Indeed, Breasted was so excited by the inscription that he rushed to print with it, abandoning the thought of a fuller study incorporating relevant supplementary material in Egyptian and

Greek. It was, to him, a document of such importance that "it seemed imperative to immediately put as full a text as possible before students of Egyptian thought and religion."[31] He declares, in fact, that the work is "the oldest known formulation of a philosophical *Weltanschauung*."[32]

Weltanschauung is a vague and dated term, but it points to a series of subsequent "writings" of the "Memphite Theology" that are firmly grounded in the German philological tradition. I already mentioned Erman's 1909 article. This was followed in 1928 by Kurt Sethe's *"Denkmal memphitischer Theologie," der Schabako-Stein.* Then, in 1939 and 1941, Hermann Junker published two long monographs on the text, the first on its theological and the second on its political significance.[33]

None of these "answers" to the question of when it was written is satisfactory, though, because it is, of course, the ancient Egyptian writing of the text that draws our attention. It will be useful in this context to draw a distinction between the particular inscription on that black basalt block in the British Museum and something else called "the Memphite Theology" (which must first be historicized to the early twentieth century C.E., even if we should eventually come to conclude that it represents a coherent religious doctrine of pharaonic vintage). We will take our lead from Sethe here and call that inscription the Shabaka Stone and ask ourselves, now, when *it* was written.

And here we must adjust somewhat our understanding of the word "written." For of course to carve something into an obstinate stone block with copper chisels is a very different matter from writing it out on paper in the gentle shadows of the British Museum, as Breasted had. The writing, or more properly, carving, of a text on stone is an elaborate and painstaking gesture joining past and future through a memorial link in the present. All the same, there remains some similarity between Breasted's effort and the inscription on the Shabaka Stone in that both "writings" are, in effect, *publications*. If the inscription on stone cannot achieve a contemporary circulation of the text comparable to that in (even) an academic journal, it can still serve to fix and preserve a text that would, otherwise, be threatened with extinction. And this is just what King Shabaka claims to have done in the second line of his text:

> His Majesty had this writing copied out anew in the house of His Father, Ptah-South-of-His-Wall. For he had discovered it to be the work of those who came before, but it was worm-eaten and could not be understood from beginning to end. Thereupon he [had it copied] anew, better than it had been before.

And now our eye is drawn to a defacement more surgical and self-aware than the barbarous abuse of the block as a millstone. The top line of the inscription is larger than any other on the stone and it is written in an almost symmetrical mirror image, centered on the single hieroglyph "life" (*'nḫ*) and reading out therefrom, to both the left and right. It shows the now familiar hallmarks of the fivefold royal titulary, but for an erasure of the final name, the "nomen" in the last cartouche. Why should the pharaoh's fifth official name, Shebek (*Šbk* or *Šbk-t3wj*), have been erased, while his prenomen, Neferkare' (*Nfr-k3-Rʿ*), remained intact?

One answer suggests itself in the identity of Shabaka's dynasty, the Twenty-fifth, a dynasty of kings who wore upon their brow not only the cobra of pharaonic dominion in Egypt, but another cobra as well, for their dominion, and origin, in Nubia, or "Kush," the land south of Egypt (present-day Sudan). Whatever may be said about the Egyptians themselves, it is abundantly clear that the Nubians were black Africans. They had long been under Egyptian influence, but in the disorder of the Third Intermediate Period, when pharaonic rule broke down and Egypt was dismembered into petty states, the Nubians threw off Egyptian rule and built up their own heavily Egyptianized kingdom around the area of Napata, more than 300 miles south of Aswan.

By the latter half of the eighth century B.C.E., the Nubians had grown strong enough to advance north of Thebes to claim control of Upper Egypt, and we know them in this context as the Twenty-fifth Dynasty. Shabaka's brother, Pi'ankhy (or Piye), is recognized as the founder of the dynasty, but in the latter years of his reign he apparently exercised only limited authority in Lower Egypt. Coming to the throne in 716 B.C.E., Shabaka reinvigorated dynastic power by marching north into Memphis and making it the new seat of government.

Now we come once again to the writing, and "unwriting," of the Shabaka Stone, for the preservation and memorialization of an ancient and neglected document is clearly within the archaizing and antiquarian nature of this Twenty-fifth Dynasty. Like the Mongol and Manchu rulers of China, the Nubian pharaohs made it their aim to be more "native" than the natives they had conquered. And resentment of such an "alien" intrusion might well be behind the erasure of Shabaka's fifth title, for if the fourth, "Neferkare'," is classically Egyptian (and recycled, in fact, from the titles of several pharaohs dating back as far as the Second Dynasty), the fifth, "Shebek," is unique, an Egyptianized form of the Nubian "Shabaka" (or "Shabaqo"). Was this surgical defacement of the Shabaka Stone, then, the revenge of a latter-day and xenophobic Egyptian? That is as far as our speculation can lead in this direction now, for we are called back once again by a seemingly innocent word in Shabaka's colophon on the stone to ask again, "When was it written?"

In claiming to fix for all time a text that had been "worm-eaten and could not be understood from beginning to end," the inscription speaks of, simply, "this writing" (zš pn, see above, pp. 72–73, for zš), but from the reference to worm damage, we must conclude that the writing in question had been on papyrus, or perhaps leather, in a scroll of some significant dimensions. When might this "original" writing of the text have taken place?

Breasted states judiciously that the colophon "proves that the remarkable ideas in our inscription are as old as the 8th century B.C., with a strong presumption that they are older."[34] He goes on then to speculate that it was probably written in the Eighteenth Dynasty. His evidence for such an assertion lies in the way the inscription is disposed upon the stone, something we will come back to.

Erman, Sethe, and Junker abandon all such caution and argue for an origin of the Memphite Theology in very early Egypt. For Erman, it dates to the founding of Memphis; for Sethe, it reaches back into the first half of the First Dynasty (i.e., ca. 3000 B.C.E.); and for Junker, it must be no later than the Fifth Dynasty (2465–2323 B.C.E.). Sethe, indeed, seems to feel that the most important thing about the text is its age; "Das Alter des Textes" is, literally, his first concern.

Although in detail Erman, Sethe, and Junker all differ, in general they ascribe the Memphite Theology to early Egypt because of a perceived archaism in linguistic usage and because they regard the heavy emphasis on Memphis and its god Ptah as evidence for an early Memphite attempt to assert supremacy over the priests of Aunu (Heliopolis). This, of course, might lead us directly back to the cosmogony of Atum and the issues it raises about subject position and the body, but we will not entertain those issues again just yet, because the early dating of the Memphite Theology opens up a new area of concern about when it was written that must be addressed here.

This early dating is highly controversial, but even in the 1990s not all noted Egyptologists have abandoned it,[35] despite an important article by Friedrich Junge which demolishes the philological grounds for ascribing the text to the Old Kingdom or earlier.[36]

For Junge, the colophon's claim that the inscription preserves an older text that had grown illegible and worm-eaten is a remarkable piece of propaganda. It brings to mind, as he says,

> the personal position of King Shabaka. It had been necessary for him to subjugate [his rival in the delta] Bocchoris and newly rebellious Lower

Egypt (and its rulers, admittedly Libyan, but securely established as "Egyptian"). He had to find a way to "liberate" the land. As a gesture toward tradition-conscious elements [in the north] who were still, in all likelihood, opposed to the Nubians, there could have been no more effective measure than to erect a stele which conserved an ancient text treating on a mythical level the unification of ... Upper and Lower Egypt under a single ruler, the legitimate heir to the entire kingdom. [This text], moreover, placed ancient Memphis, "The Balance Scales of the Two Lands," in the foreground once again, in connection with Horus and Setekh in a conciliatory way; the ruler in question was now Shabaka, and he would not merely respect the tradition in question, but, indeed, openly promote it once again. And all this would happen under the eyes of all-powerful Ptah, whose good will he could lay claim to, and to whom already his brother and predecessor Pi'ankhy had shown great respect, as had indeed Shabaka himself through the enlargement of the Temple of Ptah at Karnak.[37]

Shabaka's position was delicate indeed. He was himself clearly a foreign ruler, but had to maintain a credible position as the supreme ruler over not just his Upper Egyptian stronghold, but also over the many competing princelings in the Delta, both native and foreign, all the while guarding against the persistent threat of Assyria, which was brutally expanding into Palestine and Syria just across the Sinai Peninsula. If, as Junge suggests, Shabaka saw in the Memphite Theology a powerful propaganda tool, then we must bow to his perspicacity and resourcefulness. One might go on to suggest, in fact, that he actually had it written, for the most cynical motives, and ascribed, purely for political purposes, to an ancient tradition.

Junge does not take such an entirely jaundiced view of Shabaka and his text, arguing instead that Shabaka's claim might well be true, but true in a different sense than we might first expect.

To wit, that quite ancient texts, which were perhaps to be found, worm-eaten, in the library, whether in complete form, or as compendia, were, as sources of the most disparate import, folded into a [single] text; the actual compilation thereby should have played a less significant role than the adaptation and free transformation in the sense of a more complex and more advanced new configuration, so that the text now was truly "better than it had been before."[38]

Such considerations have led many scholars to conclude that the "original" Memphite Theology might date back as far as the Ramesside period, and if, in fact, we consider the "writing" of the Memphite Theology to consist of the laying out of a text in particular words and phrasings on a papyrus or leather scroll, or scrolls, which then were extracted and edited and recombined for inscription onto the Shabaka Stone, then, indeed, our question "when was it written" might well lead plausibly to the answer "sometime in the late New Kingdom, likely in the Ramesside period, which was, after all, a time of profound and exceptional religious speculation."

We might go further, however, thinking of "writing" in yet another way still, to formulate a still more significant answer to that question "when was the Memphite Theology written?" But to do so, we must first make some attempt to answer the other question I mentioned before: how do we read it?

How *do* we read it? That is a big question, and I cannot attempt the kind of classic philological commentary you might expect, so I must apologize in advance for the small answers I have. The philological commentary has already been done, in the work of Sethe and Junker, and there are very helpful philological notes on portions of the text more readily available in English, by James Allen,[39] and in French, by Serge Sauneron and Jean Yoyotte.[40] My considerations here will be limited mostly to the order in which the text is written and read, its visual syntax and spatial disposition.

I mentioned earlier that Breasted was led to consider an early Eighteenth Dynasty origin for the Memphite Theology because of the way the text was laid out upon the stone.[41] It was he who first figured out how to proceed from line to line in reading this inscription, because it does not read in the standard way, from right to left.

As we have seen elsewhere, hieroglyphs can be read either horizontally from right to left or left to right or, as in the titulary of Shabaka, in a mirror reading from the center out both left and right. If in vertical columns, as is the case with most of the Shabaka Stone inscription, they are generally read from top to bottom, proceeding from right to left, and as indicated earlier, those individual glyphs which are not vertically symmetrical, "face" into the direction from which they are meant to be read.

The Shabaka Stone cannot be read this way, however. In several details, it displays a highly eccentric disposition over the stone. The 62 vertical lines of text which covered more than 80 percent of the inscribed surface are to be read in "retrograde" form, a characteristic of certain religious texts on papyrus.[42] This means that the order in which the columns are to be read is reversed, even though the arrangement of individual glyphs within those columns remains normal, namely, facing to the right.[43] As for the two horizontal lines at the top of the inscription, the first, Shabaka's titulary, reads as indicated before, from the center out to the right and left. The second line (the "colophon" referring to a worm-eaten scroll) reads, unusually, from left to right.

Overall, then, the text is to be read as indicated in the schematic diagram shown in Figure 4.3. This diagram, however, provides us with only the most general guidelines. It is important to specify more carefully how a reading is to be accomplished, and in this case, we recall the full title of Sethe's important article on the text, "Dramatische Texte zu altägyptischen Mysterienspielen I." The term "dramatic" is applied because in Sethe's view, the first part of this text was intended to be delivered as a "mystery play." So lines 10 to 12 and 13 to 18 are, indeed, arranged responsively.

Here we come to a fine detail in the arrangement of speeches, which is indicated on the surface of the stone by the disposition of certain specific glyphs, creating an exception to the general rule that individual glyphs "face" into the direction from which they are to be read. In these specific cases, the reading of the glyphs is wholly dependent upon a spatial syntax where characters who are speaking to each other in the text are arranged visually face to face (see Fig. 4.4).

Thus, as Figure 4.4 shows, when (a) Geb is speaking to Horus or (b) to Setekh or (c) to both of them at the same time, the glyphs indicating their names are disposed visually on the stone to indicate this situation, as above. The same is true for lines (d) Horus speaks to Isis and Nephthys, and (e) Isis and Nephthys speak to Osiris.

Such a disposition of the glyphs on the surface of the stone is reminiscent of Egyptian pictorial composition, which generally places the more

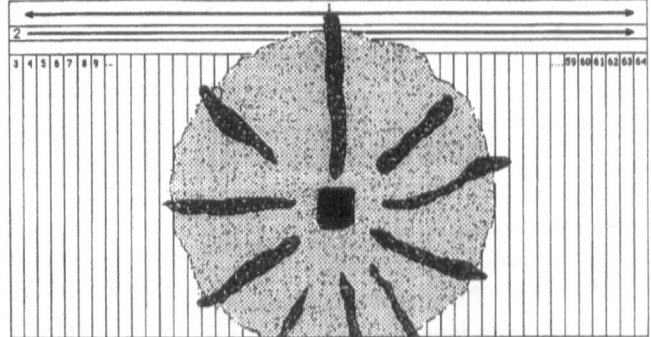

Figure 4.3. Diagram of the disposition of text on the Shabaka Stone. British Museum, London (498). The center of the stone was ground away when it was used as a nether millstone.

Figure 4.4. Shabaka Stone, examples from lines 10a–21a: (a) Geb to Horus; (b) Geb to Setekh; (c) Geb to Horus and Setekh; (d) Horus to Isis and Nyphthys; (e) Isis to Nyphthys and Osiris.

important character on the left and subordinate characters on the right, but such a spatial syntax within a single line of hieroglyphic text is rare. In the cases mentioned so far, it is also of relatively little consequence beyond its immediate practical significance. Later on in the text, however, the spatial disposition of the lines of the inscription assumes a much more important role in the construing of its meaning. This section of the text contains the cosmogonical discussion I mentioned before, the part that Breasted, and many Egyptologists since, have found so important. (Figure 4.5 reproduces the crucial section.)

It takes but a glance to see some of the irregularities here. Line 48, for instance, is written retrogressively and horizontally; such a spatial disposition is unique on the stone, coordinating this brief horizontal text with the vertical text directly beneath it. This is because it is a heading for the text below. Line 48 reads, "The gods which are come into being in Ptah"; and underneath, in lines 49a through 52a, then, one reads "Ptah-upon-the-Great-Throne," "Ptah-Nun," "Ptah-Naunet," and "Ptah-the-Great," each followed by a determinative showing the iconographic form of Ptah (mummiform, with a skull cap and w_3s-scepter) standing in a shrine. Below these determinatives, the inscription becomes difficult to read because of the millstone's abrasion, but it is clear enough to show further specifications: Ptah-Nun is "the father [who engendered] Atum"; Ptah-Naunet is "the mother who bore Atum"; and after Ptah-the-Great comes the description: "He is the heart and tongue of the En[nead]." (Lines 49 to 52 continue beyond the limits of the abrasion to the stone, but the remaining text is too scant to provide us any useful information.)

More important still, lines 53 through 55 are each, in sections, doubled into two lines within the space of one. To translate these lines means not only rendering them into English, but also arranging their disposition on the page into something like the following:

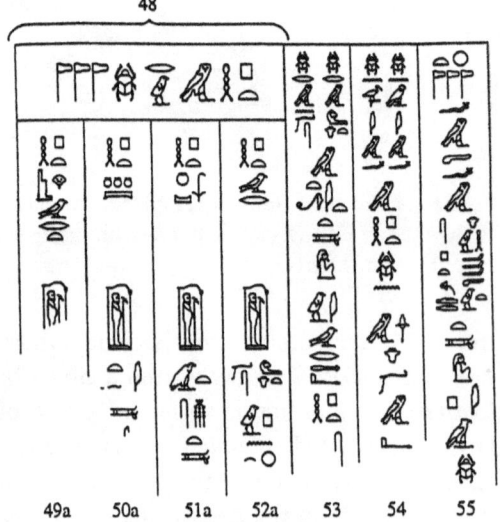

Figure 4.5. Shabaka Stone, from lines 48–55.

53 It is as the image of Atum that something is come into being in the heart ...
that something is come into being on the tongue

54 It is as Ptah that Horus came into being in him ...
that Thoth came into being in him

55 His Ennead is before him as the teeth and semen of Atum ...
the lips and hands

And here we come to the center of what is of interest in the Memphite Theology, what makes it for Breasted, "the most remarkable monument of Egyptian thought which we possess."[44] For Sauneron and Yoyotte, this is "one of the rare Egyptian texts which analyzes the genesis of the created universe methodically, and not without remarkable refinements with regard to experimental psychology."[45] Donald Redford, contrasting this version of the creation with other cosmogonies, states the following:

> As in most cultures the most fundamental spiritual tenets took their rise in remote antiquity, if not prehistory, and the intelligentsia of a later, more polished society found themselves saddled with an embarrassingly primitive baggage. Without discarding anything, however, the Egyptian wiseman [who wrote the Memphite Theology] reinterpreted and shaped his crass traditions into something at once both sophisticated and imponderable.[46]

The Memphite Theology is, undeniably, a remarkable document, and it clearly ascribes an intellectual and volitional motive to creation, with a focus on the heart or mind of the creator and the manifestation of thought in language and material reality. For this reason the theology has been cited as an antecedent to the first verses of both the Book of Genesis and the Gospel of John, a connection to which we will return later. We should be careful, however, in our consideration of the text along these lines, because the heavily "intellectual" or "spiritual" prejudices of the Western philosophical tradition, in their opposition to the body and to bodily experience, have played a large role in the high estimation of the Memphite Theology in contrast to the other Egyptian cosmogonies. Redford's remark above about "crass traditions" is signal in this regard.

The problem becomes more complicated still when we return to the question of when the Memphite Theology (as distinct from the Shabaka Stone) was actually written, because it entangles us in considerations about the origin of religious thought in ancient Egypt and whether the Memphite Theology represents a primordial religion of wise men that became corrupt in historical times, as is putatively demonstrated by the plentiful evidence of polytheism in dynastic Egypt, or whether the Memphite Theology is, rather, the culmination of an evolutionary "refinement" or "sophistication" rising out of the "crass" and "embarrassing" popular religious beliefs of remote antiquity. Yet these problems must be held in abeyance for the time being in favor of our more concrete engagement with the spatial disposition of the text, for in the very way the text is presented on the Shabaka Stone, we can draw certain important conclusions about the relation between the "intellectual" or "spiritual" motives for creation and their concrete instantiation.

Consider another quotation from Breasted's seminal article,

> It is clearly stated that everything first exists in the mind as thought, of which the "heart" is the seat; this thought becomes real and objective by finding expression, and of this the tongue is the channel. "Heart" is thus by meton[y]my, the concrete term for "mind", while in the same way "tongue" is the concrete term for "word" or "command," the *expression* of thought. Thus, *mind* and the *expression* of its content are denoted by "heart" and "tongue."⁴⁷

"Heart" and "tongue" in Egyptian (*jb* or *ḥȝtj*, and *nś*) are plausibly reconfigured to the English "mind" and "expression," as Breasted points out, but he proceeds to the following dubious conclusion:

> I am not inclined to credit the Egyptian of that age with any clear metaphysical conception of mind; it is not mind as the capability of thought, with which Ptah is here identified; but assuming mind as already existent,

Ptah is here the source of the ideas, notions and plans which the mind entertains. He is to be sure, called the ⟨heart⟩ "heart" or "mind" of the gods without qualification and ⟨heart⟩ is clearly explained as the seat and source of ⟨thought⟩ "thought". Nevertheless when we examine the development of the idea, we find that it is not *mind* pure and simple, but the *content* of mind or better the *source* of that content, with which Ptah is identified.[48]

The problem with Breasted's characterization is not that "the Egyptian of that age [had no] clear metaphysical conception of mind," but rather the assumption that we *do* have such a clear metaphysical conception. And note the blithe separation of "mind pure and simple" from "the content of mind." How can such a distinction be plausible?

There is, moreover, a problem in the assumption of priority of the metaphysical impetus to creation over the physical instantiation thereof, and this is where the spatial disposition of the text on the stone is so telling. In Middle Egyptian, the language of the text, the relation of sequential clauses is extremely important even though we do not yet understand it adequately. Without delving into grammatical subtleties, suffice it to say that when clauses or sentences come in *spatial* sequence, there is some likelihood of *temporal* or *causal* sequence as well. Thus it is possible, given the Egyptian equivalent of "I sailed upstream to Thebes. I had an audience with His Majesty" to understand "I sailed upstream to Thebes and I had an audience with His Majesty," "When I sailed upstream to Thebes, I might have an audience with His Majesty," "I sailed upstream to Thebes because I had an audience with His Majesty," "I sailed upstream. Then, I had an audience with His Majesty," and so on. There are, indeed, more precise ways to specify the relation between the former clause and the latter, but these options are not always exercised.[49] Clearly, though, writing clauses in sequence may suggest that the first element of the sequence has some priority over the others.

Note, then, in this context, that the writer of the Memphite Theology (or at least the redactor of the Shabaka Stone) has gone to considerable trouble to avoid this suggestion. Why else would we see the doubling up of text in lines 53: "It is as the image of Atum [that something is come into being in the heart / that something is come into being on the tongue]"? There, particular trouble has been taken to place the in-formation of the heart and the in-formation of the tongue in parallel relation. An anomaly in spatial disposition serves to prevent the dissociation of the bodily from the intellectual. Indeed, although I have followed most of the commentators in translating the Egyptian *m ḥ3tj / m nś* as "in the heart / on the tongue," one could protest that the preposition *m* here is not in fact a locative, but rather a predicative particle, and that a more apt translation should give us "something is come into being *as* the heart / something is come into being *as* the tongue."

Although the writer of the Memphite Theology is obviously concerned to express the primacy of Ptah in the creation, he is not willing to dissociate Ptah from the physical manifestation of that creation, here expressed by the phrase "image of Atum." He operates, instead, from the ubiquitous Egyptian economy of analogy, comparing the Ennead of Ptah with the Ennead of Atum, not to dissociate an intellective and metaphysical creation from the physical and explicitly sexual, but rather to analogize the one to the other in mutual implication. This becomes even more apparent in line 55 both through the "standard" reading of the text and through some interesting puns. As you will recall, the text reads, "His Ennead is before him as [the teeth and semen / the lips and hands] of Atum." This follows on the bottom of the previous line, where all life is described as pervaded with the heart and tongue of Ptah. "His" Ennead, therefore, is Ptah's Ennead, but the presence of this Ennead before Ptah is explicitly and visually physical and corporeal. The word "teeth," *jbḥw* in Egyptian, is written to include the word "heart," *jb* within it visually (as well as, we assume, aurally).[50] The words "lips" and "hands" are both written with clearly iconic hieroglyphs and the word "semen," *mtwt*, contains (as we have seen before) a picture of the phallus, as well as another word, *mtw*, which signifies, in the Egyptians' understanding of human anatomy, afferent vessels linking the heart with all other parts of the body. On top of all this, the preposition we have rendered "before" is *m b3ḥ*; as mentioned in the preceding chapter, this word is written with the phallus glyph, and not, apparently, simply for phonetic reasons.[51] Thus one might extract from "His Ennead is before him as [the teeth and semen / the lips and hands] of Atum" a secondary reading of "His Ennead is the phallus, the teeth, the heart, the ribs, the phallus [again!], the semen, the vascular system, the lips and the hands of Atum." Far from distancing a metaphysical conception of creation from the corporeality of the process, this text is written with special care to emphasize the intimacy, indeed the simultaneity and mutual implication of the intellective and the corporeal.

It comes as no surprise to find that many commentators on this text have resisted such a mutual implication of mind and body. Junker, for example, although he points out correctly that it is not a question of two Enneads being created here, goes on to say,

> According to the teaching of Aunu, Atum engendered [the Ennead] in an unnatural manner; according to the teaching of Memphis, on the contrary, Ptah fashioned it through his word. If we render the succinctly composed text in a more fully detailed idiomatic way, it runs, "His Ennead is before him, fashioned through his word = his teeth and lips, which correspond to the phallus and fingers of Atum. They may indeed say in Aunu, that the Ennead is supposed to have come into being through the phallus and fingers of Atum. In reality, however, the divine Ennead is come into being through the word = teeth and lips in this mouth, which named all things, etc."[52]

Junker second-guesses the original Egyptian text in his "more fully detailed idiomatic way" by creating a "reality" that excludes the material, corporeal images of the cosmogony of Aunu in favor of a more metaphysical "reality" in the Word, but of course his denial of the figural / literal engagement of the phallus and fingers in itself depends upon the figural and literal engagement of the heart as equivalent to thought, and the teeth and lips as equivalent to words. His insistence on a separation of the body and the word is misleading, but it is not uncharacteristic. He is clearly uneasy with the interpenetration of "symbol" and reality, as he admits, shortly after the passage quoted above:

> There is, admittedly, something curious about the propensity to symbolism in Egyptian religion, and the boundary between image and reality is here so very easily blurred, one depends so heavily on the symbol, that its symbolic character falls entirely into the background. Such is, above all, the case here, where cosmic powers are personified and likened to regional pantheons, as with Shu and Tefnut.[53]

Given the positivistic context of early-twentieth-century Egyptology, such reluctance to accept the interpenetration of symbol and reality in Egyptian thought led to rash conclusions about the Egyptians' intellectual capabilities. Thus, for all his admiration and sensitivity to the subtleties of Egyptian philosophy, we find even James Henry Breasted unable to take the Egyptian genius for the figural fully seriously:

> In estimating the above exposition of the main ideas of this stela, it must be remembered that these ideas are in a language little suited to the conveyance of philosophical notions; I have therefore tried to employ only the most unequivocal passages, leaving aside all the many passages, of which

several different, but all grammatically admissible versions might be made. It must be remembered also, that the thinker using this language was as little skilled in such thought as his language was ill-suited to its expression. And finally it is to be noted that modern study of the language has given us but slight acquaintance with Egyptian of this kind. I have tried to express in English the thoughts of the Egyptian in all their crudity, as he thought and expressed them. That they thus exhibit numerous paradoxes, is only in harmony with what we know is everywhere common in Egyptian religious thought, thus illustrating again what is almost an axiom in modern anthropology, that the mind of early man unconsciously and therefore without the slightest difficulty, entertains numerous glaring paradoxes. But in spite of this, we have here, at an astonishingly early date, a philosophical conception of the world, which is to some extent valid even at the present day.[54]

Junge has noticed a similar prejudice in the work of Junker and Erman,[55] but this is especially disappointing in Breasted, for his voice was one of the few in his day which was not the mere mouthpiece of a pervasive Hellenocentrism.[56]

The dilemma here is how to free the figural and analogic nature of Egyptian thought from the logical binarism of the narrower Western philosophical tradition. (Nietzsche's devastating critiques of this aspect of Western philosophy had yet to penetrate the academic mainstream of Egyptology.)

John Wilson, writing nearly fifty years later, has partially freed himself from the binarist traps that ensnared Breasted:

To our modern prejudice, this makes the Ptah creation a nobler activity; but it is not certain that the ancient meant to belittle the more physical story. Perhaps he was simply expressing the correspondence of alternative myths when he said: "Now the Ennead of Atum came into being from his seed and by his fingers; but the Ennead (of Ptah) is the teeth and the lips in this mouth which uttered the name of everything and (thus) Shū and Tefnūt came forth from it."[57]

All the same, Wilson betrays an essentialist, metaphysical prejudice that cannot be supported in the Egyptian context. He concludes his discussion of the Memphite Theology as follows:

The creation stories of the ancient Egyptian were . . . in terms of his own experience, although they bear loose general similarity to other creation stories. The most interesting advance lies in a very early attempt to relate creation to the processes of thought and speech rather than to mere physical activity. Even this "higher" philosophy is given in pictorial terms arising out of Egyptian experience.[58]

The assurance that with the Memphite Theology the Egyptians had made intellectual or spiritual progress over the "crasser" traditions of earlier times must be reexamined. Consider once again the spatial disposition of lines 53 through 56 of the Shabaka Stone, where because of the significance of linear juxtaposition in Egyptian grammar, elements of the text have been doubled up within a single line, to emphasize a simultaneity of various actions and phenomena. This visual syntax is one manifestation of a far-reaching dilemma of Egyptian religion, the dilemma of immanence versus transcendence. On the Shabaka Stone, despite the obvious interest in promoting Ptah as preeminent god in the Egyptian pantheon, the text insists on the simultaneity of thought and its manifestation in language, and underlying this is a similar, but implicit, recognition of the mutual implication and interdependence of form and matter.

ON THE TIP OF YOUR TONGUE

Much of the excitement generated by the Memphite Theology among the first generation of scholars to take it seriously stemmed from an interested concern to find intellectual or "spiritual" dimensions of cosmogenesis there. Finding such a prioritization of mind over matter, they could relegate the more explicitly corporeal versions of the creation, especially the "unnatural" cosmogony of Atum, to the margins of Egyptian religion, either as outmoded and embarrassing reminders of the not-yet-civilized denizens of the Nile Valley, or as popular corruptions and deformations of an elite primordial religion. But to make such arguments persuasively, the antiquity of the Memphite Theology was crucial, and with Junge's incisive criticism of the grounds upon which such dating had been established, it became necessary to reconsider the significance of the Memphite Theology.

Together with this change in perspective on an ancient Egyptian document, however, we must as well make a change in our perspective on the relation of mind and body, and in this context, the Memphite Theology reveals neither the supremacy of Ptah at the head of all divinity, nor the priority and superiority of the mind in creating the cosmos by verbal fiat. It engages, rather, a deeply ambivalent and conflicted experience of mind and body that teeters between an authoritative and centered subject, on the one hand, and the supplementarity of language, multiplicity, and, inevitably, death, on the other.

We can return, then, to the question of when the Memphite Theology was written because, so contextualized, *a* Memphite theology can arguably be said to have been "written" into Egyptian thought very early. If the document itself cannot be dated much before the Ramesside period, there are, all the same, other early texts that show a similar ambivalence and comparable psychological subtlety and penetration. Among the *Coffin Texts* of the Middle Kingdom, for example, is a majestic and terrible spell for "Becoming Magic":

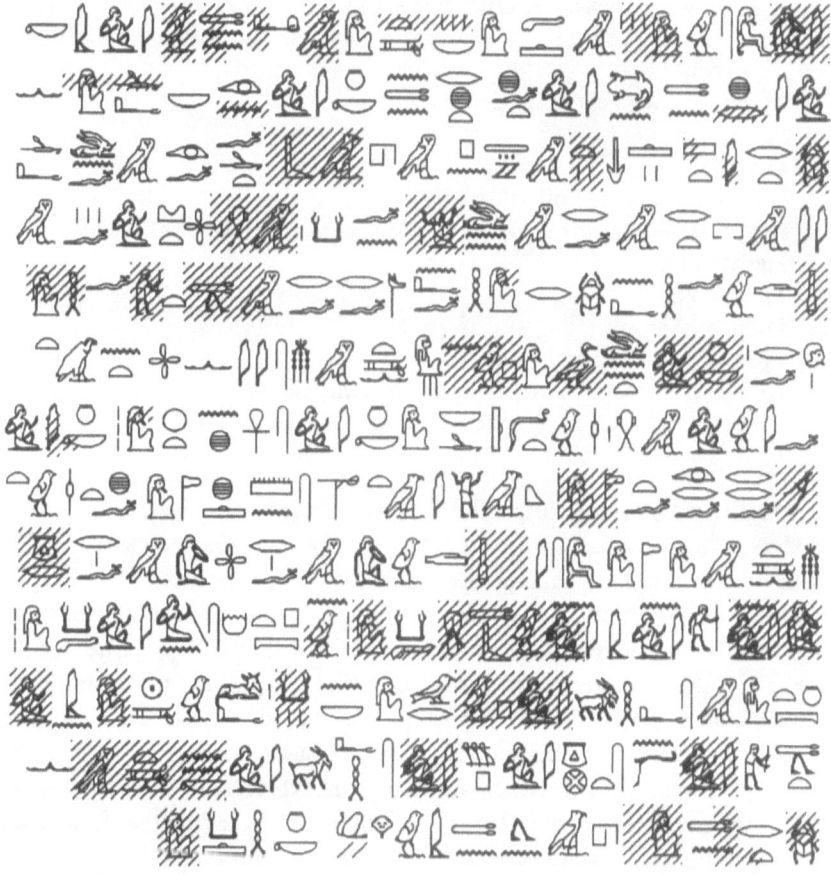

O noble ones in the presence of Lord Atum,
Here am I, come before you,
Fear me, in accordance with what you know.
It is I whom the Sole Lord created before there were yet two things in this land,
When he sent forth his sole eye,
When he was alone, going forth from his own mouth,

When his million *ka* were there, protection for his retinue,
When he spoke with one who comes to being with him, over whom he rules,
When he took *Hu* upon his speech.
It is I who am the very son of Who-Bore-All, born before he had a mother,
And I am under the protection of the command of the Sole Lord,
It is I who give life to the Ennead,
It is I who act howsoever I like, father of gods, lofty of standard,
who make the gods effective in accordance with the charge of Who-Bore-All,
August god who eats and speaks with his mouth.
I am fallen silent,
I have bowed down,
I am come shod, O Bulls of the Sky,
I am seated, O Bulls of Nut, in this my dignity, Greatest of Lord of *Kas*,
Heritor of Atum,
I have come.
I take my throne.
I gather unto me my dignity.
All is mine, since before you came to being, Gods.
Go down upon your haunches.
I am Magic.[59]

The text has a startling sublimity, but conceals, as well, a persistent anxiety. The deceased, confronted here by myriad gods and threatened by their number, mystery, and power, counters with a response framed in the language of dominion. He claims preeminence over the multitudes, ordering them to be fearful (line 3) and to go down before him (line 24). He speaks on the authority of the Sole Lord (line 4) by virtue of, tellingly, his position as the son. For all the speaker's bravado, there is a persistent ambivalence in his claims on the authority of the father. The act of creation, proceeding from the paradoxical context of unity ("when he was alone") in the presence of millions ("when his million *ka* were there"), has now left the speaker alone before the threat of the many. His claims of authority rest on the magical efficacy of the word, and it is through the word most explicitly that the father is said to have brought forth the world. (*Hu*, indeed, is the word made flesh, i.e., substantialized as a god, the hypostasis of a command so powerful that it engenders the entities of which it speaks.) So also, it is language, specifically the language of command, in which the speaker's authority resides.

But the word is also alien. The creator, in his cosmogenesis, goes forth from his own mouth and speaks with one who comes into being with him, a doppelgänger whose threat must be neutralized immediately with the claim of continued dominion ("over whom he rules").

The generative word coming forth from the mouth is twinned, moreover, with its opposite in reference to the appetite of the "august god who *eats*" as well as speaks with his mouth. And so, the antidote for the word and the mark of the subject's authority as the heritor of Atum is silence, and silence is the first of the sequence of dignities he manifests on coming to the throne.

The "Son of the Sole Lord," then, claims paternity of the Ennead and full autonomy in the exercise of his desire. The "I" of the subject is prominent and forceful, but the source of the subject's authority, the One Lord, is absent and in his absence exemplifies a supplementarity and proliferation of sites of Being mirroring the threatening multiplicity of the many gods confronting the subject. There is clearly a strong sense of self-awareness and presence, but beyond that center lies darkness and an unarticulated threat. The authority of generative command personified as *Hu* echoes back uncannily from the empty space of supplementarity, because its presence here occurs through a kind of name-dropping, even as the source of his authority, "the One Who Bore All," is nowhere to be seen.

This problem recurs throughout the creation myths. The supplementarity of progeny—whether the expectorated entities Shu and Tefnut, or the bodily sites heart and tongue, abstracted to Mind and Word, or for that matter, the Generative Command or *"Hu"* mentioned here—inevitably disrupts the unity of being upon which the figure of a Creator depends. The resulting multiplicity is rich and exciting, but it presents a persistent challenge to the idealizations of authority upon which Egyptian civilization is dependent: pharaoh, Ma'at, Amun, Ptah, and so on.

The paradox leads to a fundamental problem in Egyptian thought, the relation of the creator god to what he creates. We have already seen how this is engaged on the Shabaka Stone through the unorthodox lineation of key passages where the word and the body are mutually implicated. A similar example can be found in a series of puns on the word *kheper* in religious papyri.

The term *kheper* (i.e., *ḫpr*, written with the glyph of the scarab beetle; see Fig. 4.6) expands figurally from the facility with which, as the Egyptians saw it, this beetle transformed itself into being out of a ball of dung buried in the sand. They borrowed the image of the beetle to represent notions of transformation and coming into being. The verb "become" or "come into being" is, moreover, homophonous with the word "dung beetle."[60]

Thus, in the *Bremner-Rhind Papyrus*, a long and important papyrus of the fourth century B.C.E. (pBM 10188), we find the following statement: *ḫpr.j ḫpr ḫprw pw* (28, 21), "My coming into being, this is the coming into being of what is come into being."[61] In *pTurin* 54065, one finds a somewhat expanded version:

ḫpr.n=j ḫpr.n ḫprt
ḫpr.n ḫpr.t nb.t m ḫt ḫpr=j

No sooner had I come into being than Being came into
  being.
Each being came into being once I was come into being.[62]

It is the sequence of events that is at issue here, and there is some controversy about precisely this, because of the aforementioned ambiguities of the orthographic representation of the Egyptian system of verbal inflection. But the problems here are not solely the result of our imperfect understanding of the Egyptian writing system. The dilemma goes deeper than that, because it is related to the imponderables of Being and matter, and because the Egyptians themselves do not seem to have come to a stable consensus. Indeed, from early attempts to figure and describe the process of creation in the *Pyramid Texts*, through the sophisticated discussion of the *Bremner-Rhind Papyrus*, there runs a continual ambivalence about the relation between intent and material reality. I have schematized this ambivalence at Figure 4.7.

The *Coffin Text* quoted above, in its mention of *Hu*, or "Generative Command," gestures toward yet a further elaboration, as diagrammed at Figure 4.8.

In each case we find that the sovereignty of the unified subject, as creator, is undermined by the fissioning multiplicity of creation, resulting as it does in divisions between thought and language, mind and body, male and female, desire and agency, and so on. The place of the subject is called

Figure 4.6. The glyph *kheper* upon a standard. Part of a vignette to accompany BD 30 from a text of the *Book of the Dead* owned by one Mutirdais. From Thebes, Ptolemaic period. British Museum, London (pBM 9951, vignette 4). After Faulkner, *Ancient Egyptian Book of the Dead*, p. 57.

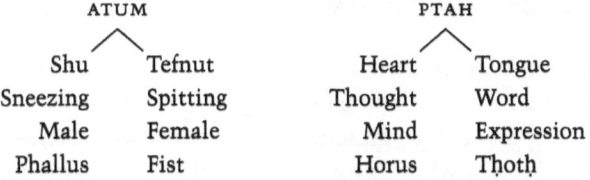

Figure 4.7. Binary structures in Egyptian cosmogony, I.

Figure 4.8. Binary structures in Egyptian cosmogony, II.

to question: is it in the thinking heart or the speaking tongue? is it in the abandon of orgasm or the conscious exercise and application of the hand? Perhaps the sharpest questioning of the subject's place comes in the third triad above, for there, if the primordial god (called Re' in most citations of this particular version of the fissioning) is invested with the power of *Hu* such that his commands materialize into reality, his companion power of *Sia* raises doubts about his autonomy as an epistemological subject. *Sia* does not mean "will" or "intent," but rather "perception," "recognition," or "awareness." The mind perceives and understands and proceeds immediately to creation in generative command, but where is the intention of the subject in this process?

Might it be that divine perception is in itself a sufficient cause, that awareness at such an absolute level needs no complement of intentionality? If so, then where does the need for generative command come from? It would seem to introduce something external to the absoluteness of such an awareness, something we might recognize, yet again, as the supplementarity of the word.

We have hit upon a central conundrum of Egyptian thought here, the edge of a difficult transition between Being and beings, One and many; and the very fact that one might proceed to a list of different loci of subjectivity demonstrates how successfully multiplicity undermines the authority of the One. It is, indeed, only in the Amarna period that a short-term defense against the many was devised.

PATHOLOGIES OF MONOTHEISM, I

The discovery of Amarna—and I will use this word as a shorthand designation for the broad range of changes in Egyptian culture that came to the fore under Nebkheperure' Amenhotep IV, or Akhenaten—seemed for some while to be just what Egyptologists had been looking for ever since there had been such a thing as Egyptology. (One can argue, after all, that the discipline itself began out of an attempt to bolster accounts of "the spiritual history of mankind" in the Bible with hard tangible evidence from the ancient Near East.)

Here, at last, was a glorious interlude during the most romantic of Egypt's great dynasties, the Eighteenth. At the height of Egyptian power and cultural sway, a new voice was heard, that of "the first individual in history" proclaiming the love and benevolence of the One God, thereby turning the tide against centuries of paganism and Oriental cruelty. He ruled from a sparkling new capital at the side of his exquisitely beautiful wife, dandling on his knee, as often as not, a darling daughter or two. Here, at last, was a philosopher king who had abandoned the despotic ambitions of empire in Palestine and Nubia for the bliss of family and the advancement of spiritual life. If, after a short seventeen years, Egypt returned to its idols and its empire building, then that was all the more proof that ignominious paganism was a false religion, and that once the mantle of monotheism had passed from Egypt to the Hebrews, the True God would triumph.

Indeed, when evidence was found for an Israelite community among the ethnicities of the broadly cosmopolitan New Kingdom, the legend of Akhenaten was readily married to the biblical story of Joseph, and it seemed that perhaps the roots of biblical monotheism may first have imbibed the waters of the Nile.[63]

If in the popular culture Egypt found a new alter ego to contrast with the kitsch of mummies and curses, it also found advocates among the intellectual elite, such as Sigmund Freud, who saw in Akhenaten a precursor to the patriarch Moses. And, in fact, the plenteous material evidence of Amarnan culture and its immediate surroundings point unmistakably to high drama and brilliant intellectual and cultural change directly linked with a single individual, Akhenaten. Not only has his city Akhetaten left us the best preserved and most extensive ruins of a city of the *living* in all Egypt (by the irony that it was abandoned after his reign), but the art of his reign as well offers abundant evidence of a radical departure from the traditional representational conventions. Some 300 cuneiform tablets discovered in the ruins of Akhetaten give us, moreover, a picture of Egypt's international position that is unrivaled for its intimacy. Reading the plaints of client princes in Palestine and Syria, one might indeed conclude that Akhenaten had given up Egyptian imperial ambitions there.

The fact that Akhenaten's regime came to an abrupt and definitive end only a few years after his death has added further drama to Amarna and given it a clear sense of closure such as one is hard pressed to find anywhere else in the three millennia of ancient Egyptian history. On top of all this, the fact that the magnificent treasure of Tut'ankhamun dates to the period of restoration immediately following Akhenaten's reign and shows many examples of not only the artistic style of the Amarna period, but also its religious doctrines, adds further splendor and pathos to the age of Akhenaten, even though it was, officially, Tut'ankhamun who restored the traditional religion and reinstated the priests of Amun.

This has all enclosed the Amarna period in a kind of romance surpassed in Egyptian history only by the Cleopatra legend and has led even sober historians like James Breasted to fantasies such as the following:

> In the midst of a whole land . . . darkened by clouds of smouldering discontent, this marvellous young king, and the group of sympathizers who surrounded him, set up their tabernacle to the daily light, in serene unconsciousness of the fatal darkness that enveloped all around and grew daily darker and more threatening.
>
> In placing the movement of [Akhenaten] against a background of popular discontent like this, and adding to the picture also the far more immediately dangerous secret opposition of the ancient priesthoods, the still unconquered party of Amon, and the powerful military group, who were disaffected by the king's peace policy in Asia and his lack of interest in imperial administration and maintenance, we begin to discern something of the powerful individuality of this first intellectual leader in history. His reign was the earliest age of the rule of ideas, irrespective of the condition and willingness of the people upon whom they were to be forced. As Matthew Arnold has so well said, in commenting on the French Revolution: "But the mania for giving an immediate political application to all these fine ideas of the reason was fatal. . . . Ideas cannot be too much prized in and for themselves, cannot be too much lived with; but to transfer them abruptly into the world of politics and practice, violently to revolutionize the world at their bidding—that is quite another thing.". . . And so the fair city of the Amarna plain arose, a fatuous island of the blest in a sea of discontent, a vision of fond hopes, born in a mind fatally forgetful that the past cannot be annihilated. The marvel is that such a man should have first arisen in the East, and especially in Egypt, where no man except [Akhenaten] possessed the ability to forget.[64]

Breasted is wrong in his view of Akhenaten and his Amarna enclave in several interesting ways, as we shall see, but most tellingly in his insistence that Akhenaten was the first individual in history and that as a denizen of "the East," he was anomalous in such a role.

Akhenaten was clearly an individual (but not the first), and his rule was clearly rooted in a range of ideas about life, power, energy, and divinity, but the disruptions he caused were not merely the result of too fervent a commitment to ideas. He made a concerted effort to eradicate the name of Amun, and one can imagine great socioeconomic disruptions in both the intentional derogation of the Theban priesthood as well as the less intentional effects of abandoning the old capital for the new city of Akhetaten on the Amarna plain.

Modern evidence of the destruction Akhenaten left in his wake comes mostly in the form of defacements to the names of gods, especially Amun, and theophoric pharaohs' names, throughout Egypt.[65] Even though Akhenaten and his queen Nefertiti were to suffer the same indignity themselves in subsequent generations, one reason we know so much about them is because their monuments were less often defaced than fully dismantled and concealed, or abandoned altogether.[66] Much of what was hidden from view as fill for subsequent pharaohs' monuments or covered over by sand and silt has now been recovered, and the Amarna period has become one of the better attested in the whole course of Egyptian history. Among the most important remains in this capacious body is a group of hymns and reliefs from the tomb walls of Akhenaten's courtiers. They provide an index of what is different about Amarna and why it has attracted so much attention.

It is plausible that Akhenaten may have conceived and composed these hymns himself, and it is probably this distinction that separates him most eloquently from all the other pharaohs in Egyptian history. There is certainly evidence of other "individuals" in Egypt long before Akhenaten —certain pharaohs emerge as individual personalities from under the heavy concealment of theocratic absolutism, and some private individuals also peer out from between the lines of formulaic (auto)biographies or wisdom literature—but the link between the name of Akhenaten, these texts, and dramatic cultural change cannot be paralleled elsewhere in the three millennia of Egyptian history.

Although general discussions of Akhenaten's religion often show enthusiasm for a putative personal concern on the part of the sole god, when those discussions turn to specific detail, it is largely the naturalism and vividness of certain passages that are singled out for praise. We find references to a broad natural vision such as the following, extolling the vivacity which the sun's presence, in light, brings to the world:

The two lands are in festival,
The sunfolk have awakened and they rise to their feet,
   You have roused them,
They wash their limbs and don their clothes,
   their arms in praise of Your splendor.
The whole land goes about its work,
The herds all graze in satisfaction on their fields,
Trees and pastures shine bright green.
Fowl fly from their coveys,
   their wings raised in praise of Your *ka*.
The herds prance on their hooves,
All that take to wing, all that alight—
   they live because You rise for them.
Ships fare north, and south as well,
The roads lie open when You shine.
Fish in the river leap up before You,
Your rays stream deep into the green sea.[67]

The sun is seen as the vital force that maintains the multitude of natural phenomena; it is as well the originary motive for life in all animate beings. The sun shapes the infant in its mother's womb, the sun creates semen in the father. In a particularly observant and artful passage, the sun is depicted as breathing life into an egg, to enliven the chick before it breaks forth from the shell:

[hieroglyphic text]

> The chick in the egg speaks forth from a stone:
> because You give him breath therein, to bring him to life,
> You've brought it about for him
> > that he fulfill his term to break forth, from the egg;
> > and he goes forth
> > from the egg, to speak, his term fulfilled.[68]

Such minute observation is charming and immediate, and the literary care expended—the symmetry of the three indented lines, for instance (classical rhetoricians term this an epanodos)—is engaging on a more formal level. The devotional link between this vividly articulated world and the creator and sustainer god symbolized by the sun disk has suggested biblical parallels in Psalm 104, and the apparent personalism of the Amarna hymns, because it is monotheistic, has been readily appreciated, overshadowing the widespread personalism of the "polytheistic" sun hymns of the New Kingdom and Osirian hymns from as early as the Middle Kingdom.[69] Grimal, for instance, asserts:

> The originality of Akhenaten was to turn the rays of the Disc into a physical reality, the tangible manifestation of the creator within the range of the common man. He therein provided an image that was easy to understand and avoided the need to rely on a specialized clergy as sole intermediaries between men and an impenetrable god. The Aten literally provided mortals with immediate perception of the divine, in complete contrast to Amun, who was the "hidden" god.[70]

But this seeming personalism is deceptive. A more careful investigation of Amarna theology reveals a tight bottleneck between "The Living Aten" and humanity: only Akhenaten (and perhaps the members of his immediate family) stood in a direct relationship to the god of Amarna, and Akhenaten himself was the unique intercessor between the god and humanity at large.

A subsequent section of the hymn is also extraordinary for its focus on the different races (literally "skin colors") and languages of people, for whom the sun god provides means of sustenance in accordance with their different geographical circumstances. In particular, the hymnist praises the ingenuity of a god who created a Nile on the ground for the Egyptians and a Nile from the heavens (in the form of rain) for foreigners. Such universalism held broad appeal in an age of seemingly triumphant Western imperialism, intellectual and cultural as well as political and military; thus, it is not surprising to find Breasted extolling it in the following terms:

> In these hymns there is an inspiring universalism not found before in the religion of Egypt. It is world wide in its sweep. The king claims that the recognition of the Sun-god's universal supremacy is also universal, and that all men acknowledge his dominion.[71]

But in the late twentieth century, claims of universalism must be considered in an entirely different light. Here, one begins to see another side of Amarnan religion. There is an obvious awareness of empire in these lines. The Egyptian empire in Palestine-Syria, Libya, and Nubia may have provided a temporal example for what is, in the hymn, a greater, all-inclusive dominion the one god holds over all men, all women, all animate creatures, all lands. As we saw earlier, certain other gods were conceived as omnipresent, or at least widely present, in earlier Egyptian religion, but the presence of the sun god here is yet more comprehensive, because he has no rivals. The ambitions of the hymnist become yet more apparent in the statement, *nn wn ky rḫ tw wp ḥr z³=k (Nfrḫprwrʿ Wʿnrʿ)|*, "There is no one who knows you apart from your son (Neferekheperure' Wa'enre')|" (who is, of course, Akhenaten).

The enlightened philosopher king whom some early Egyptologists wanted to see in Akhenaten must give way to a totalitarian with exclusive access to god. Akhenaten displays unshakable self-assurance regarding his god, so that even in extolling the god's benevolent life-giving energy, Akhenaten turns the praise around to mark his own perceptual and interpretive authority; the originator of the discourse is the hearkening subject, so that when the hymnist exclaims, *smnḫ.wy sy sḫr=k*, "How wondrous Your counsel in its efficacy!" we must accept the epistemological authority of the speaker, who is (solely) in a position to evaluate the efficacy of this "counsel." Indeed, the very word *sḫr*, "counsel," already defines the relation of Akhenaten with the god; and with the statement quoted earlier, "There is no one who knows you apart from your son [Akhenaten]," the exclusion of the rest of us is assured. This brings one to a series of questions about the god whose praise the hymnist so eloquently sings. What sort of god is this?

The hymn we have examined and the rest of the corpus of Amarna hymns address him as "You" or, in the biblical tone of earlier translators, "Thou." The Egyptian words used are all masculine singular pronouns.[72] But the god is "distant" and "alone" in many descriptions. The latter adjective is related, of course, to his uniqueness, but the word seems more than simply a description of his unique ontological character as "god." It also speaks to a degree of isolation and unknowability. There is no there there, not merely because of the religious antifiguralism of Amarnan culture, but also because the god has no subject position. There is no getting into his point of view. It is impossible, in fact, to discern intentionality in his benevolence, which has led James Allen, for one, to conclude that the Amarna ideology was not a religion at all, but a natural theology akin to that of Theocritus.

Putting aside the strengths and weaknesses of Allen's view for the time being, it will serve us well to consider the problem of naming this god of Akhenaten's. It has become conventional to refer to him as "Aton" or "Aten," from the Egyptian word *jtn*, "sun's disk." The association follows naturally enough from the apparent iconography of the god: it is depicted as a solar disk whose descending rays of light terminate in small hands. Jan Assmann points out, however, that the association of the god with the word "Aten" is erroneous for two reasons. In Egyptian usage, if the deity is referred to as *jtn* or Aten, it is only in names, such as Akhen*aten*, Baket*aten*, and Ankhesenpa*aten*.

The god's formal name is actually an elaborate title, like the title of the king, in two parts, written properly in cartouches. After year nine of the reign, this title was modified, apparently to remove all possible trace of anthropo- or zoomorphism. But the tendency toward abstraction and antifiguralism is evident even in the earlier name, and it reveals to us a god that is remarkably insubstantial and distant—more an abstraction than a god.[73] The names usually appear in a rigid pattern, in symmetrical pairs arranged on each side of the sun disk (which is, notably, pictured with a uraeus facing the viewer). In the earlier name one still finds the figure of the falcon god, [Re'-]Horakhty, and mention of Shu as well, as the essence of light, as below:

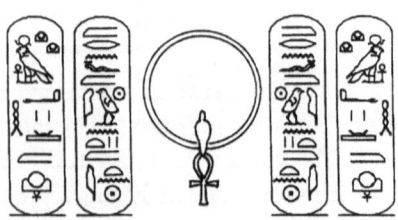

"Horus of the Two Horizons lives, Who Rejoices in Lightland,"

"In His Name of the Light [Shu], Which is in the Disk"

The full reading and interpretation of the later version remain obscure in certain points, but are not far off from the following:

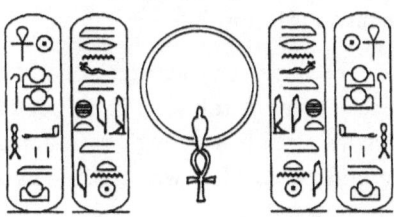

"The Ruler of the Two Horizons lives, Who Rejoices in Lightland,"

"In His Name of . . . , Which Comes Forth from the Disk"

It is remarkable that the name has been placed in cartouches and interesting that, unlike the general practice in the royal titulary, the second name is not an independent appellation but rather a further definition and description of the first. The second set of cartouches omits Horus and Shu and has a more dynamic sense in the phrase "Which Comes Forth from the Disk." Otherwise, however, the two versions are equally indefinite, which supports Assmann's contention that the god of Amarna is god as light, which is to say that beyond the assertion that it is experienced as all-encompassing light nothing more concrete can be said of it. Thus, indeed, the iconic representation of the god is derived from a glyph meaning not "sun" or "sundisk" but "light."[74]

A simpler way to refer to the god exists, however, and that particular appellation may lead us to some deeper observations about what this god might have represented to the believers of Amarna. That name is $p3$-jtn-$ˁnḫ$, or, in Egyptological parlance, "pa-aten'ankh." Distinguishing this from the simpler "Aten" is the epithet $ˁankh$, "living," which is in accord with Akhenaten's antifiguralist insistence that the traditional images of Egyptian gods were dead, whereas this god, the "living sundisk," was alive and impossible to capture in stone or paint.

The god of Amarna is, indeed, so impersonal that it was difficult to characterize correctly or appropriately in figural terms; thus, it is incorrect not only to *call* the god "Aten," as we just pointed out, but also to *conceive* of it as the sun disk, even though one draws such a conclusion readily from the reliefs of the Amarna period.[75] As Assmann notes,

> The cosmic god is life itself, in light and time, and personal devotion to it is just as unthinkable as the opposite. The piety of the individual can make itself manifest and differentiate itself, then, only with regard to the king. . . .
>
> Whereas god *quite simply* is life, flourishing, growth, continued existence, and passing away, the King is life for him who reveres him, and death for him who disregards him.[76]

Concomitant with the depersonalization of god in Amarnan thought comes a greatly increased role for the king in religious affairs, and this is striking because there was already a strong centralizing tendency to focus religious significance and political power tightly upon the pharaoh. As James Allen points out, however,

> For the earlier theology, the reality as well as the manifestation of the divine can be appreciated by human beings: an individual can claim to "know his god" (*rḫ nṯr.f*). In Amarna, this is a privilege reserved to the king alone, and is the final theme of the "Great Hymn". . . . The reservation of knowledge of the true nature of reality to the king alone explains the emphasis on Akhenaten's "teaching" in the Amarna texts. It also underlies the unique role that Akhenaten envisioned for himself.[77]

Thus one of the consequences of Akhenaten's monotheism was a tight monopoly on religious meaning in the hands of pharaoh himself, to the exclusion of everyone else. This leads Allen to the conclusion that The Living Sundisk is not, in fact, a god, but rather a natural principle, and that the only god in Amarnan religion is Akhenaten himself. This requires a rather eccentric reinterpretation of what "god" means, ignoring direct references in the religious literature of Amarna to *pa-aten'ankh* as "god" (i.e., *nṯr*), but the point about a religious monopoly is well taken, and it is echoed elsewhere, in, for example, the work of Barry Kemp:

> It has proved impossible to write a history of Akhenaten's reign which does not embrace an element of historical fiction. It is as if one has to decide which actor would best play the part: an effete, limp-wristed dreamer, or a fearsome, despotic madman. If the religious idealism points to the former, his approach to his own position and the simple fact that he achieved what he did takes one to the opposite pole. For Akhenaten's escape from the past had its limits. Kingship in Egypt was embedded within theology, and it was not Akehnaten's intention to diminish the power of Pharaoh. Quite the reverse. Between the simple vision of a life-giving sun on the one hand, and humanity and nature on the other, stood the king and his family as sole intermediaries.[78]

In the Amarna period royal favor thus was the key to individual success not only in the administrative and military hierarchies of the empire (as it had traditionally been), but also in matters of religious thought, where there was now an impassable barrier between the individual and direct religious experience, in the form of pharaoh:[79]

> The king is not the cosmic source of these gifts [of the sun, of light, of the Nile, etc.] but the social authority who decides their individual allocation as, precisely, barter for individual authentication in the totality of social communication: "[One's] lifetime is in Your hand, You give to those whom You love, they live because of Your allocation." The chief concept in this exchange, whereby the life of the individual is governed entirely by the king and determined and shaped internally [by the king] is ḥzwt, "favor." This word represented, in any case, one of the central concepts of Egyptian culture and thereby ties Amarna theology in with the ancient tradition in part, but nothing really distinguishes the special position of the king in Amarna and its polemical contrast with the general trend of the New Kingdom more sharply than the monopoly of this ḥzwt in the hand of the king. A sharp and forceful separation of the cosmic-natural level and social-personal level of the divine is thereby produced here (and only here in the intellectual history of Egypt). On the cosmic level šȝy, "fate," is the portion which is afforded all the living over time, the development of the creature in the dimension of time; on the social level, on the horizon of favor, which is governed by the king, šȝy is individual welfare as the reward for individual proof and "personal piety."[80]

Any question of personal religious devotion during the Amarna period thus takes on a particular character. Individual religious experience is banned, and the apparent informality, intimacy, and charm one sees in depictions of the royal family must be reassessed:

> The shape of the Aten held no mystery. The divine force that passes understanding was revealed to mankind through the Aten's earthly agent: the king. Hence the paired cartouches: large ones for the Aten, small ones for the king—god and the son of god, ruling together. . . .
>
> In two dimensional art—wall reliefs and stelae—the royal family group was portrayed in scenes of relaxed informality, but these scenes were themselves the object of devotion by courtiers and officials. This warm family life of the king seems not to have been intended as an example or as an encouragement for greater contact between the royal family and the rest of society. It was used, one might think perversely, to set them apart as a loving group so perfect as to warrant veneration. In the prayers of courtiers Akhenaten and Nefertiti were invoked as gods alongside the

Aten. The new cult offered no channel for personal piety amongst the people. For them it was not a democratic cult, only a revised and eccentric focus for loyalty. We can match his place in the history of thought as an early rationalizer with an equally precocious niche in the history of rule: that of the glorious dictator.[81]

There is an important and far-reaching irony in this to which we can make only passing reference here, but it is the crux of the (mis)constructions of an ancient Egypt in subsequent Western consciousness. The "oriental" despotism of the pharaohs is therein regarded as consistently and logically parallel with Egypt's idolatrous polytheism. In such a context the Amarna interlude appears as the transitory effulgence of the "one true God," which sputtered only briefly before being extinguished under the oppression of the disgruntled generals and hierophants of wicked Thebes.

A more thoughtful consideration of the evidence, however, reveals a much more complicated situation. Akhenaten's monotheism was certainly not a period of increased political or intellectual freedom for New Kingdom Egyptians. If anything, it was rather a tightening and constriction of possible constructions of the divine that went hand in hand with a strict cult of personality centered on Akhenaten. How successful this cult was in redirecting the piety and allegiance of Egyptians living outside Amarna is debatable, but within the bounds of Amarna, at least, the experience of monotheism represented a narrowing of intellectual life and a tightening of pharaoh's political and economic control over the lives of his subjects.

This was not to last. The final years of Akhenaten's reign already show signs of political, and perhaps ideological, malaise. Nefertiti, who was so prominent early in the reign, seems to have suffered a reversal of some, not well understood, sort. Another royal consort, one Kiya, clearly gained Akhenaten's favor. Yet another shadowy figure named Smenekhkare' ascended to the throne for a brief time, perhaps as Akhenaten's coregent, perhaps as his successor, perhaps, even, as his lover.[82] Smenekhkare' undertook some building projects in Thebes, but where he held court is uncertain, and his connection to the throne was brief. He died young and was succeeded by Tut'ankhamun.

BEING AND NOTHINGNESS

The boy pharaoh who became a household name in 1922 when Howard Carter discovered his tomb has generally been considered a political cipher. He assumed the throne at, roughly, age nine, and seems to have died at about age eighteen. The common assumption has been that he was the puppet of others, such as the elderly priest Ay or the general Horemheb—a not unlikely possibility. Certainly, on his ascension to the throne, he cannot have exercised significant personal power. His reign, however, represents a watershed in Egyptian history because it clearly enabled a return to the traditional religion and traditional ideology of the state. Thebes became, once again, the religious capital, and the royal residence was returned to Memphis. Amarnan representational styles exercised a continuing, although gradually diminishing, influence on Egyptian art, and there is some similarity between the solar religion of the mid to late New Kingdom and that of Akhenaten's reign, as Assmann points out in his magisterial study, *Re und Amun*.[83] Nevertheless, the religious strains in question were already a part of solar religious ideology earlier in the Eighteenth Dynasty, so any commonality between Amarna religion and subsequent Egyptian religion is best seen as the result of their having a common origin. Clearly, with the accession of Tut'ankhamun, the cult of The Living Sundisk comes to an end, and the primacy of Amun is restored. This is apparent from a stela erected in Tut'ankhamun's name that was unearthed at Karnak. It is called the "Restoration Stela" and has been the focus of much interest for its veiled description of the depredations of the Amarna period:

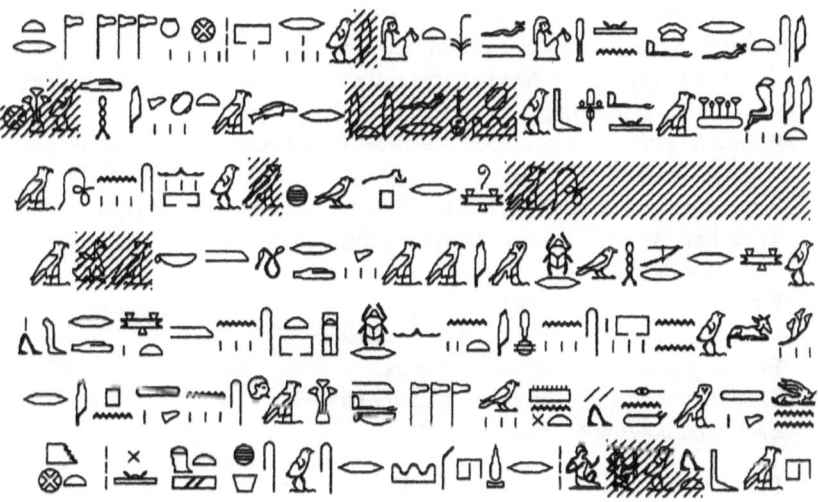

For when His Majesty rose sovereign,
the Sees of God and Goddess,
from Elephantine in the south to the marshlands of the Delta ...
... [lacuna] fallen down to ruin,
The temples fallen to decay, gone to vacant tracts, overrank with katcha'
weed
———the sanctuaries, as if never there, and sacred halls given up to foot
paths.
The land struggled on in calamity,
because the gods had turned their heads away.
If an army was sent to Nubia to extend the borders of Egypt, their efforts
came to nothing.
If someone called on god upon his knees to put things in His hands, no
god came forth to answer.
If someone called upon a goddess, likewise, she made no response:
Their hearts were turned in on themselves, their eyes were white with
wroth.
But after many days passed by, [?]
His Majesty rose to the throne of His Father,
Reigning over the demesnes of Horus,
Black Egypt and the Desert Red, under His sway,
Each land bowing to His powers.[84]

I would, however, draw your attention to a section of the stela far less often quoted, from the beginning of the inscription, because there, in conjunction with Tut'ankhamun's titulary, we see important evidence for the return to the classic ideology of pharaonic divinity with all its splendid claims and with, as well, one of its most pervasive and complex intellectual dilemmas:

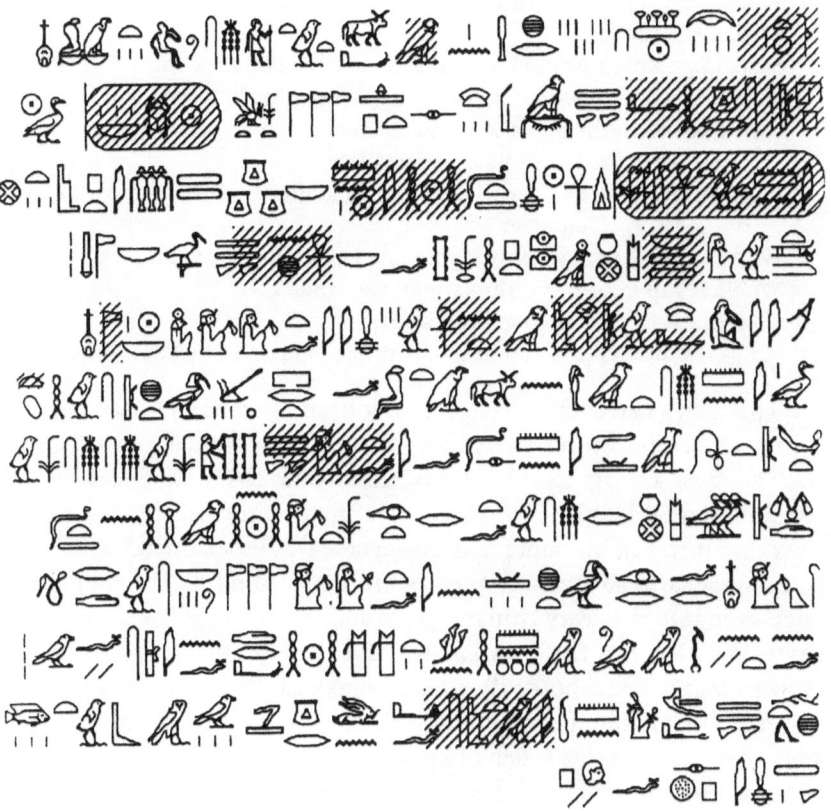

Regnal year [lacuna], month 4 of the Inundation, day 19 under His Majesty,
Horus: Strong Bull, Epitome of the Generation;
of the Two Ladies: Well-ordered in Laws, Who Pacifies the Two Lands;
Horus of Gold: Who Elevates the Crowns and Satisfies the Gods;
He-of-the-Sedge-and-the-Bee: (Nebkheperure')|;
Son of Re': (Tut'ankhamun, Ruler in Thebes)|, Given Life Like Re' Forever and All Time;
Beloved of:
  Amun-Re', Lord of the Thrones of the Two Lands, Foremost in Karnak,
  Atum, Lord of the Two Lands at Aunu,
  Re'-Horakhty,
  Ptah, To-The-South-of-His-Wall, Lord of 'Ankhtawy
  and Thoth, Lord of the Language of God.
Ascending to the Horus Throne of the Living, like his father Re', each day,

> The Good God, son of Amun, child of the Kamutef,
> Seed of Beneficence,
> Sacred Egg which Amun Himself sustains, his Father of the Two Lands,
> Who fashions him who fashioned him, Who bears him who bore him,
> For whose birth the Souls of Aunu convened that he be made the King for all time, the Horus who endures forever,
> Beautiful Ruler, who does what is beneficial for His Father, and for all the Gods,
> Who has made firm what was corrupted as a monument for all time,
> Who has suppressed evil throughout the land;
> That Ma'at be secure upon her throne,
> And show up lies as abominations [in] the land, as in its First Time.[85]

The king's cartouches have actually been usurped by those of a successor, Djeserkheperure' Horemheb, but Tut'ankhamun's full titulary is well attested on articles from his tomb and elsewhere, and on this "Restoration Stela," his first three royal names are still legible, so it is clear that it was in his name that this decree was proclaimed.[86] One might be tempted to read hints of the restorationist aims of Tut'ankhamun's reign even into that very titulary, given such phrasing as "Well-ordered in Laws, Who Pacifies the Two Lands." But this formulaic epithet is very close to that of Amenhotep III, whose reign was apparently untroubled by insurrection or significant domestic disorder, so we might be better advised to avoid resting much of a case on it alone. There is eloquent testimony to the reassertion of Amun's supremacy in sculpture from the boy king's reign, both in a physical likeness between the god's visage and Tut'ankhamun's and in the gestural language exemplified by the fragment illustrated in Figure 4.9.

We find, moreover, the repeated assertion of Tut'ankhamun's lineage in the phallocentric line of Amun Kamutef. The pharaoh was traditionally thought of as the incarnation of god, as we have seen earlier, but the fact that that point is made repeatedly here bears particular significance after the rupture in the traditional ideology that Akhenaten's reign produced. Also significant is the triad of biological figurations of the pharaoh's origins: he is "child of the Kamutef," "Seed of Beneficence," and "Sacred Egg which Amun Himself sustains." The phrase "child of the Kamutef" engages Tut'ankhamun in that phallocentric cycle central to the cult of Amun, but in addition to this, he is termed the "Seed of Beneficence," and here the seed in question is specifically the seed of grain or some other plant (the word is determined with a plow and a small circle, the picture of a seed).

Figure 4.9. Tut'ankhamun under the hand of Amun (?), statue fragment now in the Metropolitan Museum of Art, New York (50.6).

The next reference, "Sacred Egg which Amun himself sustains," recalls the embryology of Akhenaten's Great Hymn to the Sundisk, but the circle returns to the phallus of god with the phrase *tw3 Jmn ds=f*. The word *tw3* is the source of perplexity. It has a range of meaning extending through the lexical fields of the English words "sustain," "maintain," "hold aloft," "support," and so forth, with homonyms meaning "appeal to" and "to crown [a king, etc.]." With the former words it is usually determined with glyphs of a man standing with a staff or holding something, (even heaven itself) up above his head: [glyphs], or [glyph]. In this case, however, the word is determined with a phallus and a papyrus scroll: [glyphs]. It has presented translators with some difficulty. Bennett, thus, glosses it as "scion of Amun himself," and Hermann Schlögl reads the phrase as "den Amun selbst zeugte" (whom Amun himself engendered).[87] Clearly, there is a claim of divine paternity involved here, but in addition to that, we see the collusion of paternity and power in the establishment of Tut'ankhamun as king by virtue of his seminal link to Amun. We have seen such claims several times before, but if they have come to seem predictable at this point, it is all the same worth noting that here, in the context of the restoration of the traditional religion, the phallocentric ideology of power is reinvoked.

There is another element in this passage, however, which has more direct bearing on the theme of the current chapter. That is the element of time and eternity, exemplified in the repeated use of the words *nḥḥ* and *ḏt*, as well as the final line I quoted.

Nḥḥ and *ḏt* have been extensively studied as terms referring to different ways of looking at eternity in time and space. According to Assmann,

> It turns out [from an examination of the use of the words in religious texts] that *nḥḥ* denotes time in its discontinuous aspect, as an (unending) number of cycles, whereas *ḏt* represents the continuous aspect of time as extent in a more spatially conceived dimension. *Nḥḥ* is cyclical perpetuity and *ḏt* is linear permanence. Both concepts relate to the future: *nḥḥ* as the actualization of an unbounded future as it streams into the present in virtually cyclical courses, and *ḏt* as the duration, stretching into the unbounded future, of a perfectedness in time. This distinction presumably derives from the aspect opposition which Egyptian, at least originally, had in common with the Afro-Asiatic language family.[88]

The ideology of pharaonic power was perennially concerned with the stability of the pharaoh's identity and preeminence into eternity, and now more than ever, one might imagine, at this crucial time in the return to orthodoxy after the Amarna interlude. Thus, both *nḥḥ* and *ḏt* figure prominently (and, from our perspective, how ironically!) in the claims made for Tut'ankhamun's reign. But since both concepts relate to temporal stability and regularity and recall to us a problem raised earlier: how Egyptian religion is not so much a question of "polytheism," but rather a question of how the break from nonbeing into Being was—or can be—accomplished, that is to say, not a question of "how many," but rather a question of "how *into* many." We can find a partial answer in the last line I quoted from the Restoration Stela: "And [that Ma'at] shows up lies as abominations [in] the land as in its First Time [*zp-tpy*]."

The restoration was not merely the reinstitution of a traditional orthodoxy as the state ideology; it was the restoration of truth and the primeval order exemplified by the goddess Ma'at and reaching back to the beginning of time, the *zp-tpy*, or "First Time," mentioned in the quotation. This "First Time" is the first moment of creation, when the primeval hillock arose from the ocean of Nun and the origin of the universe was accomplished. There are adequate textual references to this First Time to lead us to believe that it represented a kind of Golden Age for the Egyptians, and it is fitting and readily understandable that Tut'ankhamun's spokesmen would hearken back to this time as an ideal for emulation in their own unsteady and anxious transition period. This, however, is not of central concern for us. The answer to the question of how *into* many lies in what happened "before" that First Time, and *that* is a point of dispute between two of the most distinguished Egyptologists of the current generation, Erik Hornung and Jan Assmann.

Hornung made his first sally into the field in the epoch-making book, *Der Eine und die Vielen* (1971, translated into English by John Baines as *Conceptions of God in Ancient Egypt* in 1982). The book has become one of the classics of Egyptology, and its discussions have caused a fundamental rethinking of a number of questions on the question of number in Egyptian religion.

The problem of nothingness is important because it is here that the question of Existence comes to aporia at a profoundly complicated, though utterly basic, level. How is the nonexistent to be grasped? Is it, say, a category of potential being which, for various reasons, does not attain being? Or is it simply one of several contingencies which does not happen to be realized? Or is it a mirror of Being in the negative, either the excluded, or the complementary pole against which Being is defined? Or is nonbeing the fundamental (non)ground within which the possibility of Being is attained? It is not for us to determine the nature of nonbeing; our task is to try to uncover what the Egyptians imagined in their construction of nonbeing.

They certainly had an understanding of the simply and contingently nonexistent, but they knew they had not therewith exhausted the field. Hornung is worth quoting at length on this problem:

> When the deceased is accepted at the judgment as one of the justified and blessed, and is allowed to proceed to the pastures of the hereafter, his way passes by many dangerous places, among which is a gate called "swallower of those who do not exist."
>
> Finally he reaches Osiris, the ruler of the dead; he is then before a god who is characterized by one among many epithets as one "to whom comes that which is and that which is not (*ntt jwtt*)."
>
> These are [two] examples chosen almost at random from the large number of passages in which the Egyptians speak of non-existent entities. What do they mean? Up till now the problems in interpreting these statements have been avoided by translating as simply "nonexistence" (or "the nonexistent"), and then at most remarking in a footnote that what is meant is that which does not yet exist, which could potentially exist—and that is the end of the matter. But the "nonexistent ones" mentioned above, who are to be swallowed by the gate in the hereafter, are deprived

of all potential to exist; they constitute something that is definitively and irrevocably nonexistent. In many other cases, as, for example, when the king renders his enemies "nonexistent," the interpretation as not yet existing is not appropriate, even though it may be valid for one of the many aspects of Egyptian nonexistence.[89]

When the king renders the enemies of Egypt "nonexistent," the sense intended is clearly the commonplace inversion of the not yet existent, that which no longer exists. And were we to restrict our investigations within the course of history, the pair, that which no longer exists and that which does not yet exist, would exhaust the category of nonbeing, but the Egyptians reached beyond the boundaries of history in their most cogent adversions to the nonexistent, and we must follow their lead. Think, for instance, about one of the forty-two negative avowals that the dead were imagined to make in their confession before Osiris. There, cheek by jowl with "I have not blasphemed," "I have not committed adultery," "I have not stolen," "I have not borne false-witness," and so on, is to be found the statement,

"I have not known the Non-existent."[90]

This statement is deeply puzzling. What we can say about it, however, is that self-consciously denying knowledge of the Nonexistent implies that the Nonexistent can be known and might therefore attain to some kind of existence.[91] Knowledge of this Nonexistent is, however, to be abhorred: it represents a threat related to the threat posed by the Apep serpent, the perennial enemy of the sun god, who must be defeated daily to ensure the continued existence of the cosmos. As Erik Hornung understands the situation,

> Since the created world is bounded and ordered in time and space, it follows that it has an end and must disappear; it is an island or an "episode" . . . "between nothingness and nothingness." It has duration, but there is no such thing as eternal existence, which would be a contradiction in terms. The pair of Egyptian words we translate "eternity" (*nḥḥ* and *ḏt*) in fact means "time"; for this reason the only preserved explicit statement about the existent defines it as *nḥḥ* and *ḏt*.[92]

In visual terms, Hornung relates this to the Ouroboros snake, a serpent that arches around in a circle to grab its own tail in its jaws. The symbol survived the demise of ancient Egypt and found its way into medieval European alchemy. "The complete circle of the snake's body," says Hornung,

> illustrates ... the nonexistent, which encompasses the world continually on all sides. In late Antiquity this image remained so powerful as a symbol that Gnostic writings and magical gems influenced by Gnosticism used it freely; in them the Ouroboros still signifies the "outer darkness" that encircles the world, that is, ultimately, the nonexistent or the extreme circumference of the world—the two amount to the same.[93]

Here is where Hornung parts company with Assmann. For the latter, nonexistence as a negative threat is only infrequently evoked in Egyptian thought, and the movement from Being to what Hornung calls nonexistence is, rather, a movement of the many back into the one.

The question needs to be asked not at the existential level of an individual's existence, for there, clearly, the coming and going of life and death exemplify impermanence, but not nonexistence, and the most obvious aim of Egyptian religion is to defeat this impermanence in order to attain an existence beyond this life. It is rather at the cosmological or ontological level that the question has its greatest relevance, for the question is not significantly the survival of one individual's being, but rather the survival of the world or the cosmos as a whole:

> *Nḥḥ* and *ḏt*, the two lexemes which describe the Egyptian idea of eternity in a still more closely analytical double aspect, unambiguously appertain in his understanding to this side of the eschatological horizon, which time describes, and which is given to Being altogether. This "world-time" would then also be of the sort which the Egyptian designates as ʿḥʿw, except that it here marks not the stretch between birth and death, but that between creation and the end of the world. The endlessness and unboundedness of this time would be only apparent, arising out of a sort of optical illusion from the standpoint of the transitory individual existence; from onto- or cosmological viewpoint out, *nḥḥ* and *ḏt* also prove to be terminable and interior to the world.[94]

For Assmann, then, the here and now, on the one hand, and the beyond, on the other, are both elements of a single world. The threat of nothingness that appears (infrequently, at that) in certain religious texts is not a threat of nonbeing, but rather a threat of disorder and corruption:

> The negation of *nḥḥ* and *ḏt* is apparent not in absolute unboundedness, but in what is bounded in another way. The beyond which we showed in the preceding section to be the realm determined through *nḥḥ* and *ḏt* is an

absolutely innerworldly category. The boundary which in Egyptian thought serves for the conceptual distinction between time and eternity runs within Being, that is, the cosmos.⁹⁵

Thus physical death is not a negation of life, but rather a transformation, which Hornung himself amply demonstrates. And because Assmann tries to understand the polarities within the dimension of time as transformations rather than mutual negations, he is dissatisfied with the exclusive binarism Hornung erects:

> Hornung's ontological understanding of time as "Being" and eternity as "Nonbeing" does not, in my opinion, adequately exclude a dualistic conception of time (which would, in many ways, remind one of ancient Iranian motifs). In his interpretation, time (= nḥḥ and ḏt), which is likened to Being, appears as an episode between nothing and nothing.⁹⁶

Consequently, the notion that being is an island or episode between nothingness and nothingness must also be called into question. For Jan Assmann, the one and the many, time and eternity, are based on a model of a single undifferentiated ground beyond existence and nonexistence out of which the latter two are born with creation, so that there is not, as Hornung sees it, an island of existence between states of nonexistence, but rather a phase of being comprehensive of existence and nonexistence, both of which come about with the first differentiation of the one: "World and time don't form so much an 'island between nothing and nothing,' but more precisely an interval of multiplicity, diversity and differentiation between oneness and oneness."⁹⁷

Nonbeing, then, for Assmann, would seem to be a nonpossibility, even in the apocalyptic extremes of the cosmos, its origin from the one, and its destruction into the one. This represents a significant difference with Hornung, for whom nonexistence remains the supplement of being, neither eliminated nor transformed:

> Egyptian ontology is based on the insight that the nonexistent is not simply transformed into the existent and thus eliminated. Creation does not remove what was there before it; as well as the sum total of existence there is a remainder which is endless and which is never transformed into existence.⁹⁸

Whatever the difference between these two eminent Egyptologists, they both, in the end, hold the view that the Egyptian world is a matter of presence, and that this presence is exemplified in manifold forms throughout the world of the living, in what they term the existential dimension, and also in the broader cosmological dimension, as an aspect of the world's being in time (whether that being is itself bounded by nothingness or bounded within the *différance* of one as opposed to many).

Without intending to decide between the two, or to presume upon the penetrating erudition of either, one cannot but be drawn back to a seemingly simpler aspect of the entire problem which entails the grammatical construction of the negative and the identity of great-grandfather Atum. For Atum, whom we have had so many occasions to refer to, is homophonous with one of the Egyptian negatives, *tm*, and, as we pointed out long ago, is differentiated in writing only by the addition of a determinative, in the former case, a seated god, in the latter, two arms in a gesture of negation. But negation is, in this formulation, completion as well, and we must go on to notice two other similar correlations between terms of fulfillment and finality. The god Kematef, for his part, is "the god who has fulfilled [i.e., completed] his time," and his name is related to the verb *km*, "complete," "bring to an end." Similarly "Wenennofru," an epithet of Osiris, is translatable as "the good / good things is/are in a permanent state of existence," but it can as well mean "nothing is in a permanent state of existence," because *nfr* can mean "fully ripened, at an end," or indeed, as a numeral, "zero."

POST-ANCIENT ÆGYPTIANS   5

Our legacy in Egypt is deeper and of weightier consequence than has been broadly acknowledged for at least two centuries, which is ironic, since we now know more about Egypt than anyone since late antiquity. We can see things meant for the eyes of god, we can read the words of Egyptians in their own hand, we know a range of details about Egyptian life that the pharaohs themselves would never have dreamt of. The sancta sanctorum of Karnak, Saqqara, and Abydos lie open to our hiking boots. The doors of workshops at Amarna and Deir el-Medina are ajar, we can survey in our living rooms the plans of an entire city on the ancient Nile. We know which of Ramesses' teeth ached and the size of Seti's nose.[1]

But what difference does all that knowledge make anyway? We aren't Egyptians, after all.

Perhaps the line of that difference is drawn categorically at death, as a single individual's awareness and experience go dark, but the exclusivities of an individual awareness do not engage the first person plural. If solipsism is possible, it's not within earshot of language, and so the "we" must come again (whether articulated grammatically or not), and "we" must come to ask, what is at stake in constructing a past. "Our" past.

The question is not merely, or even most pertinently, a question of the past. It is more crucially engaged with that presumptuous "our": how the lines of inclusion and exclusion drawn by that small word circumscribe our present and constrain our future. In other words, to what degree *are* we actually what we *say* we are? to what degree are the imagined pasts we construct relevant accounts of who we are in the present?

The construction of a "relevant" past is frequently stated in terms of a *legacy*, especially if that past is distant and intangible, and there is a magnetic temptation to attribute such a legacy to a certain time, a certain place, a certain culture, a certain people. A word like "legacy," moreover, presumes a positive and beneficial link between the past and present. But more honestly, we must examine the link between ourselves and our putative ancestors to discover all the consequences—positive, negative, and otherwise—of being (in whatever fashion) descended from them.

And what are the parameters of such an examination to be, how are we to decide what is held to be common beyond the borderline of individual death? Geography, genetics, the persistence of political and socioeconomic structures—who would be so rash that they would deny the relevance of these to our lives over the shorter term? But if the "legacy" of which we speak lies hundreds or thousands of years away, how can we overstep our most immediate circumstances to claim some relevance beyond?

Nationalism remains a potent force in the world, but most of the cruder equations between modern national identity and specific ancient antecedents have been shown to be unsustainable and largely romantic. Notions of the "East" and the "West," however, persist (even alongside and contradicting the more recent, and more overtly materialistic, designations "North" and "South").

The thirst to identify an origin of some description drives a preponderance of our inquiries about the past: "They were the first . . . , and we are . . . in their footsteps." All too easily, however, this enterprise is compromised from the start by unconscious, or at least unacknowledged, assumptions about who we are.[2] Our desire to locate in time and space the first instance of a given technological achievement is also strong; we claim as putative ancestors, therefore, the inventors of important or familiar objects in our material world. But the link is a tenuous one. I can say "They invented X." Can you not say in reply, "So what? Knowing the origin of X does not make X any more or less important in our lives. The wheel, for instance, is no less important to us because we don't know who 'invented' it."

Perhaps the origins of our more abstract legacy in thought have a stronger claim to significance. That we think in such and such a way, as did "our ancestors" from such and such a time and place, may indeed reveal certain things about us. Our best chance of learning something new from such a comparison comes when the *problems* or *mistakes* of a past cultural moment, well understood, illuminate a current dilemma. Many of our claims of legacy, however, lack this specificity or candor or critical awareness. We make them rather to stake a broad claim upon some great human achievement, which we hold up as evidence that we enjoy or have attained thereby a higher degree of humanness, a greater human plenitude. This can be misleading in several ways, but none more damaging than when we claim the achievement in question as the particular legacy of a certain ethnic, religious, racial, or political group. The other groups didn't catch on, and consequently, their descendants aren't quite as good, quite as human, as "we" are.

Thinking like this can range from the coarsest and most obviously fallacious to the extraordinarily subtle and complex. If the most blatant examples of racism and chauvinism along these lines may be waning in the modern world—and that is by no means certain—the subtler, more complex, and more deeply rooted delusions of cultural superiority by virtue of a cultural legacy remain, stubborn and recalcitrant. There are still legions of otherwise intelligent and well-meaning people who see in "Western Culture" the fullest flowering of the human spirit and the *telos* toward which other "less advanced civilizations" will eventually, if belatedly, make their hapless way.

Technical problems abound for those who make such an assumption; for while it may well be possible to trace the history of the elements of a material culture through time and across space, it is a far more daunting task to trace the course of an idea over a like expanse. The concatenation of ideas into institutions and the interaction of ideas with the material world create such complexity that explanations for their movement through history and over and across the world are likely, always, to be controversial.

The technical difficulties of explaining history are, however, not my primary concern. It seems to me, rather, that the most truculent problems we encounter in making a claim to a given cultural legacy are not problems relating to how and when such and such an idea or thing came from Northumberland to London, or from Shanghai to Tokyo, or from Nevada City to Sacramento, but rather questions of an ethical and epistemological nature. In claiming a particular legacy in the past, are we defining ourselves as the result of historical processes, or are we instead expressing the ambition toward a fullness yet to be (perhaps never to be) attained? All along we have problematized the "we" in these constructions of who we are, but perhaps it is even more a question of "are," a question of being, and how we exist in relation to the past. Are we, in other words, a plenitude of being as the consequence of history, or are we the as yet unrealized potential of our actions in the present toward the future, the (always incomplete) movement toward the fulfillment of our best intentions?

If the latter is the case—and I contend it is—then lines of historical influence and transmission between ourselves and those cultures in which we claim a legacy, even if plausibly discernible, are less important than how we intend to use that legacy. These are the claims that matter because they describe and project the possibilities of our thought toward the future.

GIFT

Since the late eighteenth century, most of "our" claims to a cultural legacy have invoked classical Greece. In particular, it has been widely accepted that our intellectual, aesthetic, and ethical roots are to be found in fifth-century Athens. Representative of the most enthusiastic assertions about the Greeks are the works of Edith Hamilton, especially in her popularizing book of 1930, *The Greek Way*:

> Five hundred years before Christ in a little town on the far western border of the settled and civilized world, a strange new power was at work. Something had awakened in the minds and spirits of the men there which was so to influence the world that the slow passage of long time, of century upon century and the shattering changes they brought, would be powerless to wear away that deep impress. Athens had entered upon her brief and magnificent flowering of genius which so molded the world of mind and of spirit that our mind and spirit to-day are different. We think and feel differently because of what a little Greek town did during a century or two, twenty-four hundred years ago. What was then produced of art and of thought has never been surpassed and very rarely equalled, and the stamp of it is upon all the art and all the thought of the Western world.[3]

Hamilton's deepest admiration for classical Greece comes not exclusively from an objective consideration of its civilization, but from a personal sense of anxiety about the present (her present) world, and she sees in Greek thought and art the potential for salvation from the unpleasant complexities of modern life:

> What the Greeks discovered, or rather how they made their discoveries and how they brought a new world to birth out of the dark confusions of an old world that had crumbled away, is full of meaning for us to-day who have seen an old world swept away in the space of a decade or two. It is worth our while in the confusions and bewilderments of the present to

consider the way by which the Greeks arrived at the clarity of their thought and the affirmation of their art.⁴

Hamilton's adoration here is, as well, a homogenization replacing the striking intellectual diversity and vigorous contentiousness of Greek thought with a pabulum of bourgeois affirmation and five-and-dime positivism—how are we to identify the "affirmation" of Euripides' *Medea* or the "clarity of thought" in Aristotle's defense of slavery? Such an apotheosis of the Greeks, moreover, goes hand in hand with her crude reduction of non-Hellenic culture to a single, inchoate mass:

> The Greeks belong to the ancient world.... But they are in it as a matter of centuries only; they have not the hall-marks that give title to a place there. The ancient world, in so far as we can reconstruct it, bears everywhere the same stamp. In Egypt, in Crete, in Mesopotamia, wherever we can read bits of the story, we find the same conditions: a despot enthroned, whose whims and passions are the determining factor in the state; a wretched, subjugated populace; a great priestly organization to which is handed over the domain of the intellect. This is what we know of the Oriental state to-day. It has persisted down from the ancient world through thousands of years, never changing in any essential. Only in the last hundred years—less than that—it has shown a semblance of change, made a gesture of outward conformity with the demands of the modern world. But the spirit that informs it is the spirit of the East that never changes. It has remained the same through all the ages down from the antique world, forever aloof from all that is modern. This state and this spirit were alien to the Greeks. None of the great civilizations that preceded them and surrounded them served them as model. With them something completely new came into the world. They were the first Westerners; the spirit of the West, the modern spirit, is a Greek discovery and the place of the Greeks is in the modern world.⁵

It may seem unfair to draw Hamilton into the argument at this point. No modern classicist is as extreme or naïve. The view she expresses was, however, common and broadly popular just a few decades ago, and it is useful to consider this Hellenocentric model in its crudest form as a kind of baseline to understand how far the current debate has progressed.⁶

That current debate might be understood in outline by brief reference to the positions of Martin Bernal and Mary Lefkowitz. A storm broke in 1987 with the publication of Bernal's *Fabrication of Ancient Greece, 1785–1985*, the first volume of a grandly ambitious project entitled *Black Athena*. *The Fabrication of Ancient Greece* laid out Bernal's overall plan before arguing in extensive and persuasive detail about the modern (mostly eighteenth- through twentieth-century) intellectual tide that replaced Egypt with Greece as the foundation of Western civilization.

Bernal contends that in broad terms, there are "two models of Greek history: one viewing Greece as essentially European or Aryan, and the other seeing it as Levantine, on the periphery of the Egyptian and Semitic cultural area."[7] He calls these models the Aryan and the Ancient and argues that although the Aryan model is the one most of us have been brought up to believe, the Ancient model is to be preferred, and was only displaced from its preeminent position (from the time of the Greeks themselves through the Enlightenment in the eighteenth century) by the rise of theories of race and Indo-European linguistics in the late eighteenth century. He proposes a return to the Ancient model, with some revisions, contending "that there is a real basis to the stories of Egyptian and Phoenician colonization of Greece set out in the Ancient Model." His "Revised Ancient Model" posits that the Egyptian and Phoenician colonization began somewhat earlier than the original Ancient model suggests, "in the first half of the 2nd millennium B.C.," and that

> Greek civilization is the result of the cultural mixtures created by these colonizations and later borrowings from across the East Mediterranean. On the other hand, it tentatively accepts the Aryan Model's hypothesis of invasions—or infiltrations—from the north by Indo-European speakers sometime during the 4th or 3rd millennium B.C.[8]

Among Bernal's most vocal critics is Mary Lefkowitz, the author of the book *Not Out of Africa: How Afrocentrism Became an Excuse to Teach Myth as History*, and editor of a volume of essays responding to *Black Athena* called *Black Athena Revisited*.[9] Lefkowitz disagrees with Bernal's claims about Egyptian cultural influence on Greece, doubting even the Greek claims of dependence on Egypt, which Bernal takes seriously, and relying instead on more conventional explanations for the etymologies of Greek words Bernal tries to link to Egyptian. She minimizes demonstrable cultural links Bernal stresses and rejects completely any notion of Egyptian colonization near the Black Sea, the Aegean islands, or the Greek mainland.

What is difficult to imagine here is how a controversy like this could have garnered so much public attention and how it could have reached the level of intensity and acrimony it has exhibited, when the dispute is seemingly over such small potatoes as the etymology of *hiketis* or the question of whether Euripides had visited Egypt. There is, of course, much more at stake, but in a curious way, neither Bernal nor Lefkowitz seems willing to acknowledge the fact outright.

Lefkowitz accepts as indisputable that "the ancient Greeks were the inventors of democracy, philosophy, and science"[10] and makes no attempt in her book to persuade us of these debatable claims. She takes aim instead at obvious canards such as that Cleopatra and Socrates were black and that Aristotle stole books from the great library at Alexandria (claims which, incidentally, do not appear in *Black Athena*). And Bernal, for all his laudable intention to reduce European cultural arrogance, seems quite ready to accept claims of the preeminence of the Greek legacy in the West, as long as Greece itself can be shown to have been strongly influenced by Egypt (and Semitic western Asia). In the beginning of the (already) quite technical introduction to his first volume, he breaks off—all of the sudden —into a single emotional paragraph that points toward the greater issues at stake. (Note the rhetorical use of italics, and the appeal to "Western Civilization"):

> The Revised Ancient Model maintains that the earlier population was speaking a related Indo-Hittite language which left little trace in Greek. In any event, it cannot be used to explain the many non-European elements in the later language.
>
> *If I am right in urging the overthrow of the Aryan Model and its replacement by the Revised Ancient one, it will be necessary not only to rethink the fundamental bases of "Western Civilization" but also to recognize the penetration of racism and "continental chauvinism" into all our historiography, or philosophy of writing history.*[11]

Both Bernal and Lefkowitz seem to leave unstated the most contentious point of all, and, indeed, to agree in vesting Greece with enormous influence on subsequent "Western civilization," but when pressed toward the argument on those grounds, each tends to retreat to less controversial detail.

What then of "Greece" in "the West?"

The reductionism of the question must, already, raise eyebrows. What are we to understand by "Greece"? Hamilton mentions "a little Greek town" during the span of "a century or two." She seems to mean, roughly, fifth- and part of fourth-century Athens chronologically, but the geographical suggestion of Athens is bathed in the glow of a sentimental "small town" figuration. The claims Lefkowitz echoes (but does not support) for "democracy, philosophy, and science" cannot be adequately addressed, even by ardent philhellenes, within that limited scope (either geographically or chronologically). The claims are both too broad and too narrow. Greek philosophy is more than Plato and Aristotle, and Greek science made few of its celebrated "discoveries" in Athens.[12] Claims limited to "democracy, philosophy, and science," moreover, ignore the readily demonstrable influence of Greek architecture and representational styles (especially sculpture) on Renaissance and subsequent Western art. And as for "democracy," there we find ourselves facing an extremely complicated set of problems, all the more difficult for having been debased in popular political rhetoric for, already, centuries.[13]

Clearly, meaningful arguments about the Greek (or for that matter, the Egyptian) legacy in the West must be made on more precise and rigorous grounds than these. How you might construct such arguments will depend, of course, upon who you are, what you believe, where and how you live, and many other contingencies. In the interest of clarifying my own perspective, I would (in addition to the remarks already made about Greek representational styles) further characterize Greek influence on the West in the following ways. There is, certainly, a strong correspondence and a highly plausible line of influence between Western rhetoric and that of classical Greece, in large part because of the self-consciously classical education of the elites of Western Europe and, to a lesser extent, North America in the eighteenth through early twentieth centuries. The "West" owes a "debt" to "Greece," as well, as I see it, in defining "reason" to mean an intellectual discourse of empirical evidence, logical binarisms, and the syllogism, with a strong orientation toward teleological closure. Argument, public debate, and litigiousness, as well, characterize both ancient Athens and the modern West, and there may well be such a thing as a "legacy" here.[14]

My topic is not, however, the Greek legacy to the West, but rather who "we" are vis-à-vis the ancient civilization of the Nile, so what I have just argued may seem out of place or even altogether wrongheaded. I think we might agree, though, that while there is a legacy of classical Greece in the "West,"[15] we must recognize that the "West" amounts to a great deal more than this Greek legacy can be made to account for.

Surely even the most conventional philhellenes would consent to the proposition that in addition to this Greek legacy, there is also, at least, the Judeo-Christian tradition.[16] Because of monotheism, because of a common body of mytho-historical narrative taken from scriptures accepted by both Jews and Christians, because of certain ethical codes exemplified by the Ten Commandments, because of a history in common in Europe and the Americas and (to a lesser extent, perhaps, in the Near East), people speak of a Judeo-Christian tradition and distinguish it from the putative Greek heritage in the West. It is probably not necessary to point out that this "history in common" is hardly the history of common endeavor, that the common mytho-historical narrative is subjected to radically different hermeneutic ends by Jews and Christians. Even the notion of a common "monotheism" must be thrown open to question, for both its inclusiveness and exclusiveness.[17] Still, it is defensible to speak in some terms of a Judeo-Christian tradition; most defensible, it seems to me, in terms of its phallocentrism and its paternalist authoritarianism. Yet these very characteristics could also be argued to be relevant to the Greek legacy in the West, so what was proposed as a distinction between a Hellenic legacy and a Judeo-Christian one, may on further consideration be considered a similarity.

But still this begs the question of an Egyptian legacy. How—in combination with and/or contradistinction from the Hellenic and Judeo-Christian—might we construct such a legacy? There are many basic links between our civilization and that of ancient Egypt that we might adduce: the use of base 10, for example, or our solar calendar.[18] If we are to acknowledge a Greek legacy in the representational arts of the "West," then we must be willing to acknowledge more ancient roots still, in the art of ancient Egypt.[19] There are many examples of the persistence of Egyptian material culture in ours,[20] and even some of the most frequently cited examples of difference turn out, in the end, to delineate not difference in itself so much as similarity on a grander scale.[21]

Paradoxically, however, a listing of elements such as these, rather than expanding our sense of the Egyptian legacy in our civilization, seems to limit and confine it. For more penetrating examples, we must look deeper and at the same time more abstractly into who we are.

We have focused on three areas of interest within the representational networks of the ancient Egyptians: writing and the word, multiplicity, and the phallic body. As these are mutually implicated in ancient Egyptian thought in many complex ways; so too, in the subsequent history of the West, these three discursive strains are interwoven—or tangled—into a complex web of relations that provide one perspective on the range of our Egyptian heritage. Although it is not possible to disentangle these threads entirely while discussing their consequences in Western thought, one may well see more of one particular color than of another in the pattern formed at any given point along the way.

HABEAS Φ?

Let us recount, then, a mythical narrative of Osiris in his central role of "us"; which would be to imagine a history centered upon a figure plausibly called "Osiris"—Osiris, that is, in the role of the subject we "read" from.

This Osiris is father, engenderer, and king. This Osiris is also the son, the sacrificed son of Geb who rose once again, like Christ. This Osiris is the sovereign subject as well. But the position you read him from is removed and resurrected, the subject of a senseless passion.

In our account, we will begin near the end and work backward. There can be no claim to comprehensiveness in this endeavor; we will simply pick up a few stitches in the cloth of our history, as exemplary, and open the way for a fuller discussion later. Where, though, can we find Osiris in the modern world?

One response would be taken from the postmodern psychoanalytical theorist Jacques Lacan. For Lacan,[22] the myth of Osiris is central to a psychological paradigm triangulated among the phallus, the subject, and the signifier:

> What is most striking in the [myth of Osiris] is its transparency, its immediacy, its clearness, in contrast to the laborious attempts of psychoanalysis to decipher, even to formalize. It seems as if this myth needs no interpretation. On the contrary, it is the myth itself which interprets, as if we had reached a core beyond which deciphering cannot go, a center which drives all deciphering. This myth, which exposes the fate of the divine initiate, presents and displays the dramatic relationship between the "real penis" threatened by castration and the "phallus" now a symbol, a simulacrum, the signifier of rejuvenation and sexual pleasure. One cannot help [but] recognize here what Lacan formulated as the passage from that which he designates φ to that which he designates Φ, "the symbolic phallus impossible to negate, signifier of jouissance." What is more, the "fragmented body" of Osiris, mentioned by Lacan, becomes in his words, "the fragmentation of the signifier"—the phallus being that "signifier of the very loss which the subject endures by the fragmentation of the signifier." (*Écrits* 715)[23]

In Lacan's view, the modern subject comes to self-knowledge by discovering or recovering or uncovering something he terms the phallus and designates with the Greek capital Φ, "For the phallus is a signifier, a signifier whose function, in the intra-subjective economy of the analysis, lifts the veil perhaps from the function it performed in the mysteries."[24] It is crucial to Lacan's argument that the phallus come as a replacement, a simulacrum that stands in place of the real phallus (i.e., the penis), thereby

> rendering it sacred and larger than life to make it a cult object.... If the phallus fills in for the absent, destroyed, and lost penis (due to a savage and sub-human aggression), this supplement is also valorized, but on a higher plane (it is elevation itself) in exchange for the sacrifice and the loss.[25]

It is in this context that Lacan can assert "the function of the phallic signifier touches here on its profound relation: that in which the Ancients embodied the νοῦς (nous) and λόγος (logos)."[26] With an almost invisible sleight of hand, Lacan draws on the late classical link between Osiris and Hermes, which allows him to move from the penis of the supposedly castrated Osiris to the phallus as symbol of *nous*, the Idea resident in the material body of the human subject.

This is the indispensable grounding for a separation of the body from language and cognition, a move Lacan makes idiosyncratically. That idiosyncrasy should not, however, blind us to the broader generality with which this move has been made over the course of the "Western" tradition. Lacan, for his part, follows Plotinus and has a kinship with the latter's identification of the male with the One, the Spirit, and the formative principle in the universe, a move that, of course, relegates the female to a secondary and derivative materialism of the body "in-formed" by the male.[27]

The dialectic whereby the phallus is lost, only to return symbolically as the *nous*, provides a telling link to Hegel's *Phenomenology of Spirit* as well as to Plotinus and classical Idealism. Jean-Joseph Goux has recognized this link and noted the curious omission, in Hegel's references to the myth, of any mention whatsoever of the penis or the phallus:

> The principal figure, called Osiris, has opposed to him (as his enemy) the negation as external other, as Typhon. But the negation does not remain thus external to him . . . ; instead, the negation enters into the subject itself. The subject is killed. Osiris dies; but he is perpetually restored, and thus posited as one born a second time, as a representation—he is not something natural but something set apart from the natural and the sensible. Thereby he is defined and posited as belonging not to the natural but to the realm of representing, the soil of the spiritual, which endures beyond the finite. According to his own inner definition, Osiris is the god of representation, the represented god. The fact that he dies, but is also restored to life expresses explicitly the point that he is present in the realm of representation as opposed to sheerly natural being.[28]

Goux's critique of the passage is insightful and pointed, and he raises an important problem in the Hegelian use of the myth which has broader ramifications in the history of Western thought, ramifications that bear directly on our Egyptian legacy:

> When Hegel tells and interprets the myth of Osiris . . . he never mentions a decisive component of the myth: the missing penis, and Isis's fabrication of the phallic simulacrum. In the myth, as it is reviewed and interpreted by Hegel, the phallus is conspicuous by its absence. If Hegel analyzes in

great depth the process of death followed by resurrection, this movement of the negation of life and its restoration that so interests him, he remains silent on the phallic simulacrum, an issue that Plutarch, the canonical source, nonetheless chooses to expose.[29]

Goux's focus is philosophical and psychoanalytical, and he does not touch on the religious context in which the same operations take place. In countering Hegel's version of the myth, Goux points out three problems that, for him, betray "what the myth is explicitly about." He argues—and I will quote him here at length—that

(a) First, the representational level to which Osiris has access, after his death to the sensible and the natural, is the fabrication of the phallic simulacrum which is of central importance. The other parts of the fragmented body are brought back to life, but this one, in contrast to the others, is not recovered, and must be fabricated, constructed; and it constitutes the object of a cult. . . .

(b) This same movement initiates the movement between the mind (immortal) and the body (perishable), and also between the intelligible and the sensible, the signified and the signifier. Death must intervene, dissolving the sensible, immediate naturalness in order for the unnatural spiritual element to distinguish and disengage itself. But it appears in this scission that death is also—or first of all—the loss of the penis (as a natural or immediate member) and that the phallus (become simulacrum, representation) comes down on the side of the spiritual, the side of affirmation, of the sublation by the spirit as opposed to the deadly materiality which is the negative element.

(c) It must also be noted that Osiris is for Hegel the moment when god becomes a subject—and consequently the moment when man himself becomes a subject, since the principle according to which God is determined for men is also the principle that determines man in his essence. God becomes a subject: this means that there is a transition from "unconscious life" or "general vitality" to "ipseity," to the self. But it is death/rebirth (the second initiatory birth) that advances this subjectivity. God "is a subject that estranges itself from itself and is held fast in its own negativity, yet within and out of this estrangement it restores itself" (*Lectures* 622). Here, too, the link between castration, phallus, and subject, such as it is articulated by Lacanian theory . . . corroborates the Hegelian analysis of the Osiric moment, provided that this analysis is rewritten so as to restore the myth from which the lacuna left by Hegel amputates an essential element.[30]

Be reminded here that the "essential element" which Hegel effaces,[31] which Lacan and Goux see as central to the myth, is itself a Greek accretion, as we saw earlier. We will return to the consequences of this accretion below, but we must first consider another lacuna Hegel leaves in the genealogy of Western thought.

HIDE THE SAUSAGE

If the phallus is indeed as important as Goux sees it, for Plutarch and Plotinus as well as for Hegel and Lacan, then we must raise the question of what happened between the late classical world of the former and the modern and postmodern world of the latter. There are, plausibly, important similarities between the Idealism of the One in Plotinus and the Idealism of Spirit in Hegel, as indeed in the dialectical transformations Lacan brings to "spirit" (as psyche) in the intrusion of the phallus (as Φ). But how was the thread lost between the death of Plotinus in 270 C.E. and the development of Hegel's philosophy of Spirit at the end of the eighteenth century?

In the doctrine of the Word, early Christianity found common ground with influential strains of Platonic and Neoplatonic Idealism (and, we might add, with the Memphite Theology), but in its formulation of the relationship between the Word and the world (especially in the bodily life of men and women), it insisted on paradoxes that could not be accommodated in the classical formulation. As Peter Brown explains,

> Pagan Platonists regarded the Christian myth of redemption—an Incarnation, a Crucifixion and a Resurrection of the body—as a barbarous innovation on the authentic teachings of their master. To them, it was as if some vandal had set up a vulgar and histrionic piece of Baroque sculpture beneath the ethereal dome of a Byzantine church. The more "liberal" pagan Platonists had hoped to "civilize" the Christian churches by writing *"In the beginning was the Word"* in golden letters on their walls; but they would not tolerate even St. John when he said that *"The Word was made flesh."*[32]

The Idealism of the pagan philosophers imagined a total separation between the world of the Logos and the material existences within which our human perceptions of it were imprisoned, but in accommodating classical philosophy to Christian doctrine, Augustine of Hippo found it necessary to reject this radical dualism to allow for the possibility of moral and spiritual growth within the confines of bodily existence. The interrelation of the divine Word and fleshly existence becomes the crucial nexus for him, as for other Christians, between the human world and God, and as such, it reflects the characteristic Christian assertion of the dual nature (human and divine) of Christ.

It is crucial to the "difference" of Christianity, that is, to its unique consideration of the relationship between the human and the divine, that the figure of Christ partake of both the human and the divine, and that he therefore suffer death upon the cross, and it is no less crucial that the Christian believer gain access to the divine through the "incorporation" of the body and blood of Christ. In an important essay on this enfleshment of the Word, Henry Staten demonstrates some of the complexity and difficulty this doctrine entails, particularly in the Gospel of John:

> John's Logos does not take on flesh only as a disguise of His divinity (this is the Gnostic or "docetic" interpretation); rather, the Incarnation is the very essence of the process of cosmic redemption. But the real descent of the divine Logos into the flesh sets off a general deconstruction of all the oppositions that belong to the system of the original distinction between Logos and flesh. After it is asserted that the Logos became flesh, in the very act of assertion, neither Logos nor flesh can any longer mean what it meant before, nor can the transformation be elucidated by means of the other concepts that are themselves placed under erasure by the transformation that they would be called on to explain.[33]

Staten is particularly insightful in unpacking the metaphor of the "dying" grain, falling to the ground to provide the possibility of renewed life (a theme common to the myth of Osiris, of course), and his discussion of the significance of Christ's death is supported by countless representations, in words and otherwise, of the Passion. In concluding his essay, however, he asserts:

> There is only one Son because there is only one death, this unique death that is the seal of individuated being or telos of individuation; God's love and God's sacrifice must equal the force of my love for my own only, precious life and the autoaffection set off by the thought of giving up this life.[34]

But this view is too sympathetic and too "humanistic" in the end. As significant as the death of Christ must be in Christian theology, the act of fathering by the Father, the supreme agent, in a unique expression of power and authority, is a prerogative jealously guarded. It overcomes and mutilates the humanity of Christ in the interest of preserving absolute autonomy. It is no accident that this autonomy is figured in explicitly sexual, indeed phallocentric, terms.

The embodiment of God was, as Staten argues, dramatically exemplified through the death of Christ in the Crucifixion, in the all-too-human suffering so excruciatingly depicted in numberless representations of Christ's Passion. If one proof of his humanity was his human death, however, another must be seen in his birth. He did not spring fully formed from the mind of God, like Athena, but entered the world in the normal human way, the days of his gestation accomplished, inconveniently, while his mother and earthly father were away from home, in Bethlehem to pay their taxes (Luke 2:1–7).

The Christian myth insists upon the fatherhood of God and the seminal trace of the Father in the divine Son. Christ is, in the words of the Nicene Creed, "the only begotten son of God," and the details of the conception of Christ are well known to anyone familiar with the Christmas story. That story is so long naturalized in our culture that it may almost pass the ear without being heard, but the succinct description of Mary's pregnancy was, in the foundation of the Church, the sign of a daring and, to some minds, utterly outlandish transgression of categories. The Gospel of John takes an abstract tack on the issue, but develops the problem of Christ's being, as Henry Staten points out, in the single phrase *ho logos sarx egeneto*, "the Logos became flesh."[35]

> The orthodox insistence on the actual consubstantiality of the divine and human natures of Christ is a genuinely daring innovation, one that goes hand in hand with the insistence (derived from Judaism) on the resurrection of the body. Both of these doctrines contradict the "pneumaticism" of the Gnostics and the pre-Christian transcendentalism, which can conceive of the realm of the spirit (*pneuma*) only as completely severed from the body.[36]

Staten makes incisive criticisms of the refusal to follow through the incarnation of God in man, but if he argues persuasively about the corporeality of God in Christian theology, he does so gingerly, sidestepping the question of the sexuality of Christ. Here we come to a hidden chapter in the history of Christian theology, a betrayal of the Incarnation.

Christian theology explains the appearance of Christ in the world as the sacrifice of God, of "His only begotten Son," in expiation of the original sin of mankind. This appearance makes eternal life possible for the Christian believer and establishes a crucial and indispensable link between the material world of human life and the eternal world of God. The capacity of God to take on a human body marks the potential of the human individual to attain salvation in eternal life: "The Incarnation is the very essence," as Staten explains it, "of the process of cosmic redemption."[37]

This potential and its fulfillment in the story of Christ is usually illustrated with the stories of the Nativity and/or the Crucifixion and Resurrection. The innocence of the Christ child and the Passion of Christ in death obscure, however, the underlying sexuality of the notion of incarnation and leave unanswered some of the most basic questions about the nature of sexuality and divinity in Christianity. It is here, then, not surprisingly, that we begin to see the significance of Egyptian religion in Western thought, not through speculations about the genesis of Greek philosophy in Egypt, but rather in the dilemmas posed by the phallic body in the minds of Egyptian theologians, as in the doctrines of the Church Fathers. These dilemmas lie at the very heart of the heavily freighted notion of sin in early Christianity. That sin is traceable in the mythochronology of the Bible to Original Sin, the eating of forbidden fruit by Eve and then Adam.

When Augustine of Hippo treats of sin, he acknowledges the special nature of this Original Sin of Eve and Adam, but it is of central importance that in discussing the lives of men and women within the course of human history, he replaces Original Sin with the sin of lust. The mention of lust here is signal, for if the Original Sin seems eccentric, even difficult to take seriously,[38] the sin Augustine treats as paradigmatic for all other sin is much more concrete, and he is unambiguous about its sexual manifestations.[39] Underlying such speculation is a deep anxiety, for

> even those who delight in this pleasure are not moved to it at their own will, whether they confine themselves to lawful or transgress to unlawful pleasures; but sometimes this lust importunes them in spite of themselves, and sometimes fails them when they desire to feel it, so that though lust rages in the mind, it stirs not in the body. Thus, strangely enough, this emotion not only fails to obey the legitimate desire to beget offspring, but also refuses to serve lascivious lust; and though it often opposes its whole combined energy to the soul that resists it, sometimes also it is divided against itself, and while it moves the soul, leaves the body unmoved.[40]

For Augustine, lust demonstrates the propensity of the will to be overcome by the body. The erectile capacity of the penis is not a manifestation of the desiring will (which might somehow, therefore, be satisfied), but rather a manifestation of lust, which is entirely separate from the will. In this capacity for revolt against the commands of the will—coming to arousal in inappropriate situations as well as failing to be aroused when the subject desires it—Augustine identifies the exemplary failure in human morality, the inability to subject the desires of the individual subject to the will, which, properly ordered, can be none other than the will of

God. Thus the penis figures the individual subject's propensity to fragmentation, the revolt of the body against the sovereign authority of God, here bearing an important similarity to the Lacanian phallus (which must be sublated in order to attain its full representational capability, i.e., which must be somehow overcome if the subject is to achieve psychological maturity).

It would have been possible, one imagines, to let the issue drop at this: lust would be merely exemplary of a multitude of sins precipitated by the subordination of will to the inclinations of the body and the material world. Augustine, however, cannot let the matter rest. There is, here, as Peter Brown has noted,

> an unmistakeable sign of what will become distinctive in Augustine's religious attitude—a sharp note of unrelieved anxiety about himself and a dependence on his God, expressed more woodenly than in the language of the *Confessions*, but nevertheless, quite recognizable: "I shall apply myself," says Soul, "with diligence and close attention—that is, if no shadows creep in upon me, or, *what I fear most deeply of all*, if those shadows stir my pleasure."[41]

PATHOLOGIES OF MONOTHEISM, II

In the enormously influential pathology constructed by Augustine, human sexuality is the site of a self-alienation, an accommodation to the bestial in human nature, and a necessary humiliation for the race of Adam after the Fall. Can the particular sexual pathology that bedevils Augustine be contained within his loquacious and eccentric theology, or is it merely one transformation of a phallocentric and at the same time sexually dismembered tradition of religious thought with roots in Egypt? The very question will, no doubt, seem out of place or even offensive to some, but it is an important question, all the same, because Christianity places such a heavy burden on the interpenetration of the body and the Logos and leaves the Logos, thereby, implicated in the status of the body and, in particular, in its sexuality. This difficult point in Christian theology is part of a knot of problems relating the world of the spirit with that of the body in traditional Christianity.

That the Christian God enters the world as a child is so central a feature of Christian doctrine, it hardly needs mentioning, but it is often forgotten how clearly this embodiment is also an engenderment. The explicit paternity of God, so succinctly stated in the Nicene Creed, is set forth no less clearly in the New Testament (Matthew 1:16–20 and Luke 1:26–35).

The specifically sexual nature of the conception of Jesus cannot be doubted, given the vocabulary both Matthew and Luke choose in their accounts. The Christ child must, as human, be either male or female; and given the ideological context from which the religion emerges, it can hardly be surprising that the former alternative wins out. Written reference to Christ's maleness, however, serves primarily to situate his identity within the cultural patterns of his society. He is circumcised, he is raised as a carpenter, he performs the tasks appropriate to a Jewish boy in his upbringing, and so on. His sexuality is passed over altogether. Pictorial reference is, however, more specific, and in certain rare cases, surprisingly sexual.

Leo Steinberg has made a fascinating study of the problem in his book *The Sexuality of Christ in Renaissance Art and in Modern Oblivion*. He notes a great number of Renaissance representations where the sex of Christ is emphasized to such a degree that one might consider them a category of *ostentatio genitalium*, or "display of the genitals," comparable to the common medieval motif, *ostentatio vulnerum*, "the display of the wound." He illustrates his argument with numerous representative paintings of the Christ child in which the Virgin holds the child in a way that emphasizes his maleness. These do indeed seem to be aimed, as Steinberg argues, at verifying the humanity of the baby Jesus.

He shows as well a somewhat smaller number of paintings of the body of Christ crucified and after its deposition from the cross, again demonstrating persuasively that the positioning of articles of clothing and the hands and arms serve to draw attention to the maleness of the dead savior.

The most surprising references in the book, however, are to a handful of paintings and etchings that depict an ithyphallic Christ (see, for example, Fig. 5.1).[42] Steinberg explains the problems these works create:

> Is it conceivable that Christian artists would assign the erection motif to the figure of the dead Christ? The loins of these figures are, of course, draped; but it had long been the special pride of Renaissance painters to make drapery report subjacent anatomic events. Even the infant erection was sometimes betrayed only by the heave of the loincloth. . . . Could a like signal emanate from the dead Christ? What, for instance, are we to make of the *Pietà* by Willem Key . . . ? Shall we construe the turbulence of the loincloth as an inflation of vacant folds, or are we bound to interpret these surfaces as reactive to forms beneath, insinuating a phallic tumescence? The latter . . . seems an unholy notion. Yet the problem is posed again in the famous Pietà etching by Jacques Bellange . . . , and again in a late 16th-century anonymous Flemish *Christ as Victor over Sin and Death*. . . . Finally, a positive answer becomes compelling when we compare certain images of the mystical Man of Sorrows, dating from 1520–32,

230 POST-ANCIENT ÆGYPTIANS

where phallic erection is unmistakable.... There are three paintings of the subject by the young Maerten van Heemskerck.⁴³

Steinberg is frank about his ambivalence, but his conscientious investigation leads him to conclude that the erection motif is actually there, and not merely a personal interpretive idiosyncrasy. So he is led to consider whether the paintings are sincere expressions of religious thought or blasphemies:

> I do believe that Heemskerck's images of the Man of Sorrows were conceived with a Christian will and de profundis.... Nevertheless, they remain deeply shocking. Their vision of a settled Christ, alone in sterile, self-centering masculinity, seems to us—and must have seemed to most artists—a miscarried symbol. And it miscarries on more counts than one.

Figure 5.1. Willem Key, *Pietà*, after 1530. Staatliche Kunsthalle, Karlsruhe (replica of a painting in the Alte Pinakothek, Munich).

Not only because Heemskerck's sense of human anatomy as a jerked mechanism is here especially chilling; and not only because the precision of the physiological datum, favored by utmost proximity, overwhelms the symbolic purpose.[44]

Steinberg mentions two problems of particular importance for us in the consideration of these images of the Christ. He is disturbed by the "vision of a settled Christ, alone in sterile, self-centering masculinity." He then goes on to suggest that a symbolic reading of these pictures fails because the symbol is "miscarried." This brings us to some of the central issues at stake in a comparison of Osiris with Christ, such a comparison as I argue speaks for a far more important Egyptian legacy in Western thought, specifically in Christianity, than has ever been acknowledged.

First, regarding the apparent sterility and self-centered masculinity of the renderings: the ithyphallic Christ is not seen impregnating anyone, woman, angel, or kite (like Isis). What is the purpose of his erection, in that case? To what object would Christ's desire be directed? These paintings and etchings leave the question entirely open. There is an old tradition figuring the Church as the bride of Christ, but it begs credulity to imagine the Church personified with such sexual explicitness.

Can, then, the ithyphallic Christ be made to bear any relation to ithyphallic Egyptian deities? If so, He would bear a far closer resemblance to the Osiris figure who lies alone with an erection or, indeed, to the masturbating Atum. If we imagine, on the contrary, that van Heemskerck's ithyphallic Christ is in pursuit of procreation, then we face the problem of a continuing chain of Sons of God, a chain of insemination, not unlike the chain of Osirises and Horuses in Egyptian religion. The already strained "monotheism" of Christian Trinitarianism could not sustain such a proliferation. (This might be one reason the motif has been suppressed.) If, as Augustine says, it is only lust that can excite erection, then the erect Christ would suggest a too-human incarnation, a lustful Jesus. In a broader context, it brings us to a further consideration of the supplementarity of Christ's maleness, a daunting problem to anyone who would make Christianity gender-neutral, or at least gender-egalitarian.

One might suggest that the formulations of Augustine and his fellows, in their condemnation of all sexual desire as "lust," could not allow Christ to come to ejaculation (not consciously, at least).[45] The stark equation of sexuality with evil throws a formidable obstacle into any construction of the sex life of Christ, but how then should we understand the numerous explicit references to the begetting of Christ upon Mary by God the Father? In one sense, yes, these demonstrate a particular intimacy of relation

Figure 5.2. Maerten van Heemskerck, *The Man of Sorrows*, ca. 1532. Museum of Fine Arts, Ghent, Belgium.

between Christ and God which no humanly begotten subject could possibly claim, even as they prove that Christ is the Son of God.

Yet once the agency of sexuality is admitted for God the Father, how can it so summarily be denied God the Son? The central problem here is not one of sexuality per se, but of authority symbolized in the phallus. God the Father begets a son, who is called God as well, but the chain ends there. If God the Son were in turn to beget a child, would that child be human or divine? What would the consequences be for monotheistic exclusivism?

There is the hint of an Oedipal rivalry here, between God the Father and God the Son, but the Father prevails, Christ dies on the cross as the sacrifice of God for an otherwise irredeemable humanity, and the interior subjectivity of this God, the Father, as a sexed being, remains utterly opaque. And here we are drawn beyond the Christian world, further back in the history of thought, and closer to home (?) in Egypt.

But before that, let us consider Steinberg's assertion that the ithyphallic Christ is a miscarried symbol. He identifies the trope of the resurrected flesh in the erect phallus and even mentions the Osirian antecedent:

> Let me assume that the ithyphallic motif in these images of the mystical Man of Sorrows was mysteriously meant. One might conjecture that Heemskerck's symbol simply inverts the archaic biblical euphemism of "flesh" for penis.... Heemskerck's paintings would reverse that trope by representing the risen flesh in the roused sexual member. It is no far cry from one to the other—no straining leap of imagination to equate penile erection, reciprocally, with flesh vivified.
>
> As a symbol of postmortem revival, the erection-resurrection equation has roots in pre-Christian antiquity; it characterized Osiris, the Egyptian god of the afterlife, represented with his restored member out like a leveled lance.[46]

But in the consistent and comprehensive incarnation of Christ, we come up against the problem discussed earlier in connection with Henry Staten's article on the Word and the body. Here the complications are, if anything, even greater because the danger of a supplemental chain of divine or semidivine beings must be brought into consideration, and because the notion of sexual pleasure on the part of Christ has to be imagined. The paradoxes cannot be resolved. In the monopoly of paternal authority mandated to God the Father in traditional Christian theology, there is already an imbalance and an erasure that leave indelible scars on the religion thereafter. But it is important to consider as well what relation problems of this character may pose in a genealogy that posits Judaism too as a response (dialectical in important ways) to Egyptian religion. The ground has been prepared for us by Howard Eilberg-Schwartz.

FULL-FRONTAL DEITY

Christian exegetes in the Middle Ages saw the Old Testament as a kind of foreshadowing of the New, interpreting the events recounted there as prefigurations of the major events in the life of Christ. Jewish readings of the Torah do not, of course, take this view, but there is, nonetheless, a figuring of the sexual paradoxes of doctrinal Christianity in the early history of Judaism which reflects yet further on the question of Egyptian patterns underlying the cultural legacy of the Abrahamic religions.

The religion of the early Israelites is not beset with the problems inherent in the incarnation of divinity, which as we have seen, are so intractable in Christianity, but God is, all the same, a male, unequivocally, and His gendered identity has created a related set of paradoxes and complications.

The Israelites, though originally not monotheists, in the course of developing an identity distinct from their neighbors in Palestine (and farther afield in Egypt, Mesopotamia, Syria, and what is modern-day Turkey), developed an exclusivistic monotheistic orthodoxy that figured Israel as the bride of Yahweh. Early injunctions against the worship of more than one god and idolatry are couched in the same terms as injunctions against adultery. It is not the case that other gods do not exist (as Christian and later Jewish doctrines maintain), but rather, that Israel is under an exclusive covenant with a single god and cannot justifiably worship any other.[47]

This figurative construction of the relation between the human and the divine was highly successful in maintaining a distinct identity among the Israelites, even as they were militarily and economically threatened repeatedly throughout their early history. It created, however, difficult contradictions in Israelite culture because the priesthood was exclusively male. In his insightful book, *God's Phallus*, Howard Eilberg-Schwartz has demonstrated how the underlying homoeroticism of a male priesthood ministering (as central agent for a nation or people figured as female) to an explicitly male God has created unresolved tensions and deep ambivalence about the corporeal nature of divinity. As he summarizes the argument,

> The idea of a divine phallus and of divine maleness in general became more and more incoherent as Israelite religion tended toward an exclusive relationship with one God.[48] In ancient Israel, the very idea of a penis presupposed the existence of an other, an other of the opposite sex, with whom some sort of satisfaction could be achieved and reproduction assured. The idea of divine genitals was therefore potentially disruptive unless God was imagined with a lover, and the biblical writers never conceptualized God as sexually active with anyone but Israel. As we have seen, the solution of imagining Israel as a metaphorical woman generated other dilemmas: as part of this collectivity, Israelite men were placed in a potentially homoerotic relationship with God. The phallus of God thus represented a scandal in this religious mythology. By diverting the gaze from bodily parts of the deity, particularly from the front and genitals, the myths skirted the conceptual problem that lay at the heart of a system which did not imagine its God in sexual relations with other gods. This avoidance eventually made the entire body of the deity a problem.[49]

Although we cannot do justice here to Eilberg-Schwartz's argument as it relates to a broader Judaism, we can see the ground for an important link between the phallocentrisms we examined earlier in ancient Egyptian thought and those we have just discussed with relation to Lacan, Augustine, and so on. It is particularly worth quoting Eilberg-Schwartz on the similarity between the religious constructions of phallocentrism and influential strains of psychoanalytical discourse:

> Feminist criticism has not been alone in focusing on the connection between masculinity and religion. The nature of this relationship has also been central to psychoanalytic theories of religion. Despite important tensions and differences between feminist and psychoanalytic discourses, both regard masculinity and religion as deeply entangled symbolic domains. Both are interested in exploring how male experience and ideas about masculinity shape and are in turn shaped by religious symbols, particularly images of divinity.
>
> The precise nature of male projection, however, is typically understood differently within psychoanalytic and feminist criticism. For Freud and his followers, religion reflects and repeats the experience of having a father.[50]

One might, indeed, go a bit further, in pointing out that in both Freudian (and Lacanian) psychology on the one hand, and in the monotheisms we have considered on the other, the question of the father's phallus becomes a central concern. Paternity is characterized as the most potent evidence of authority, and the presence of the phallus, as instrument and symbol of that paternity, is an obsessive concern. Such is also the case in various Egyptian constructions of phallocentrism. The ideology of Amun Kamutef, the self-engendered god, provides perhaps the most straightforward naked exaltation of god's phallus and autonomous paternity (linked as it is with the unadulterated phallocentrism of the god Min), but we have seen repeatedly, and in considerable detail, how similar constructions of phallocentric authority inform a wide range of Egyptian religious experiences.

So too, in the insistent maleness of Yahweh, the insistent paternity of God the Father, the insistent threat of phallic lust in Augustine, and the insistent, though sublated, male sexuality of Lacan's constructions of representationality, we come again and again to the phallic body. (Even Hegel, in failing to mention the phallus at all, might be said to preserve it in its pointed erasure—the Hegelian intellectual strategy par excellence.)

In so many of these constructions, however, the motifs of hiddenness, censorship, even outright castration strike us as well. As Eilberg-Schwartz points out, the Hebrew prophets cannot see the phallus of Yahweh: when they attain a vision of God, the middle of His body is always clothed by a blinding light. The phallus of God the Father in Christianity is likewise invisible to the prophets, disciples, and so on, but His sexuality in begetting Jesus is unmistakable. The phallus of Jesus, however, presents a very different problem, and although it is apparent in the Christ child in a broad historical range of representations, when Christ is come to maturity it is nearly always hidden.[51] Christ is as good as castrated, because His phallus cannot come to generative use under the exclusive paternal authority of God the Father, but of course, Christ is never spoken of as castrated or emasculated in the Bible. There is, however, in the erasure of His sexuality, a telling similarity to the motif of emasculation in Lacanian psychomythology. There, too, the penis becomes an embarrassment and it must be displaced in order that the subject attain the Phallus.

Lacan, moreover, read this displacement into the myth of Osiris as well, straining thereby toward a universal psychopathology of emasculation. His Osiris, though, is the Osiris of Plutarch, not the Osiris of Egyptian myth, and so even in seeing the legacy of Egypt in his work as in the other examples we have cited, we must make finer discriminations.

There is no more loss of the phallus, or castration, in the Egyptian myth than there is loss of mind, body, sight, or anything else. The fragmentation of the subject on death is clearly a penetrating concern in Egyptian thought, but when it comes to the phallus, it is not the site of loss or emasculation, nor is it "the possession of the woman" as Lacan has it. It is a site of pleasure, supplementarity, agency, sovereignty, paternity, dominion. Even presence itself[52] . . . but not loss.

Return then, again, to Atum. We have mentioned the startling supplementarity of the episode before: Atum's intention is pleasure, but he attains paternity as well with his action, setting up a chain of succession that was read by the Egyptians to represent the natural order of theocratic power in the universe.

The economy of succession in the male line defuses the supplementarity of paternity in the myth of Osiris,[53] but this was not, apparently, fully sufficient to defuse the supplementarity of the Cosmogony of Aunu. Thus, as you will recall, an ambivalence about divine genesis through masturbation is reflected even as early as the *Coffin Texts* (remember Shu's insistence, "He did not bear me from his mouth, he did not conceive me with his fist").[54] More significant in the longer term, as we have seen, is the displacement of that particular figuration of genesis onto an oral or verbal act: thus the ancient references to Shu and Tefnut coming into being in sneezing or spitting or, more significantly still, the figuration of creation through divine utterance (*Hu*) or the word of Ptah—in other words, through the *Logos*.

Such a transformation of the relation of father and child has profound relevance in Christian theology, and it is one of the routes used to soften the blow of Word into flesh. There is, here as well, however, a supplementarity that cannot be fully erased. Thus, in the renowned passage with which the Johannine Gospel opens, "en arkhē ēn ho logos kai ho logos ēn pros ton theon, kai theos ēn ho logos" ("In the beginning was the Word, and the Word was with God, and the Word was God"), even though the third clause creates an equivalence between the Word and God, the second undercuts this equivalence in that supplementarity where the Word is posited in opposition (as much as apposition) to God. (The Greek preposition *pros* is commonly used of objects conceived in opposition, aggressively even, in a way that the English "and the Word was *with* God" fails to convey.)[55]

The supplementarity involved in this configuration raises troubling questions about intentionality. In the Cosmogony of Aunu, we have no clear sense of Atum's intention beyond his desire for pleasure.[56] It is in Christianity, however, that we see the consequences of this paternal supplementarity carried to a particular extreme. Divinity is given explicit embodiment in Christ, and God eventually sacrifices His only begotten Son in expiation for Original Sin or for the sins of mankind in a more general sense. God the Father thereby insinuates His presence among humankind, but as I have argued, the threat of a regression into a lineage of divine beings (the succeeding generations of the first divine insemination) must be truncated by the effective castration of God the Son.

If traditional Christian doctrine understands the sacrifice of Christ on the cross as expiation for human sinfulness, we might rethink this construction as a strategy to preserve the absolute authority of God the Father against the threat of supplementarity.[57]

We may, indeed, even characterize the roots of Abrahamic monotheism as an attempt to counteract the supplementarity of being that results when the sole god is constructed as a male. In Israelite religion, a degree of stability is established by making God's partner the female community of Israel, as Eilberg-Schwartz has shown. In Christianity, similarly, the Church is sometimes seen as the bride of Christ, but more tellingly, Christ is left without a bride, and God the Father maintains his monopoly on divine authority by denying His Son any reproductive capacity.[58]

These discrepancies in the treatment of supplementarity may illuminate a signal difference between Egyptian and "Western" culture. Monotheism in the latter was highly productive intellectually, in large part because it encouraged new forms of expression and new distinctions between the monotheistic "hosts" and their far older and more civilized "polytheistic" rivals, distinctions that were perhaps necessary to maintain a cohesive identity in the face of the greater power and technological sophistication of those rivals.

It is of the utmost importance to note, however, that the difference on which this discrimination between the monotheists and their rivals is based is a difference created through dialectic. The authoritarian centralism of Israelite and early Christian monotheisms stands, indeed, in stark contrast to the multiplicity of Egyptian religion (as well as, one imagines, other eastern Mediterranean and Near Eastern "polytheisms"), but in constituting the antithesis to this "polytheistic" thesis, Judaic and Christian monotheisms preserve a metaphysics of presence that leaves them deeply indebted to Egyptian ideologies of being. This may, in fact, be where the greatest Western legacy in Egypt is to be found, in the notion that the individual maintains a distinct integrity beyond the boundaries of life and that this persistence has great ethical significance.

LIFE IN THE WEST

The Egyptians' belief in the persistence of individual identity and their rigorous interrogation of the materiality of being led them to extraordinary labors aimed at the preservation of the subject. We have surveyed these processes and their philosophical and religious ramifications only briefly, but you will agree, I believe, that Egyptian efforts toward preserving the flesh were extraordinary, and concur as well that the alternatives they prepared toward preservation of the name, provision of a substitute body, and so forth, in case the body should be lost, reveal a profound attachment to the conviction that the individual identity must be preserved at all cost. We can certainly make a distinction, in this case, between what the Egyptians did in this regard and what "we" ourselves do. James Henry Breasted proposes to do just that when he discusses the Egyptian concept of the *"ba,"* but even as he does so, he adopts a position of condescension and presumes to a superior knowledge in both himself and his reader regarding an immaterial reality that, by his lights, the Egyptians had not grasped:

> Ba has commonly been translated as "soul," and the translation does indeed roughly correspond to the Egyptian idea. It is necessary to remember, however, in dealing with such terms as these among so early a people, that they had no clearly defined notion of the exact nature of such an element of personality. It is evident that the Egyptian never wholly dissociated a person from the body as an instrument or vehicle of sensation, and they

resorted to elaborate devices to restore to the body its various channels of sensibility, after the ba, which comprehended these very things, had detached itself from the body.[59]

Breasted, in admitting that *ba* is only roughly translatable, nonetheless translates the word as "soul," then goes on directly to say that the Egyptians, by virtue of being such an early people, had no exact understanding of the soul.

The elaborate measures they undertook in mummification came from the assumption, common enough in our own day, that the departed could never be wholly dissociated from his body. In granting that we too, "if we attempt to picture our departed friend at all," still think of that friend "as existing in the body," Breasted engages the contradictions inherent in the situation of remembering the dead. Does his "at all" suggest that there is some other possibility for re-membering the deceased friend ("if we attempt *to picture* our departed friend at all"), or rather, does he suggest that such a memory is always in some way or other a picturing ("*if* we attempt to picture our departed friend at all")? Even in straddling the paradox of re-membering the dead, he makes the extraordinary presumption that "we" have a knowledge in this area which they lacked: "[The Egyptians] had no clearly defined notion of the exact nature of [the soul]." In the same breath, he presumes the existence of a transcendental realm of "the soul" as if it were within the same category of knowledge as how to build a steam engine or perform an appendectomy. "We" can build steam engines and perform appendectomies, and the Egyptians could not, but that does not mean we are any closer to understanding the nature of the soul than the Egyptians were. Or, indeed, to understanding whether such an entity exists at all.

Although Breasted seems bent on demonstrating a difference between the Egyptians and "us," his demonstration points as well to a similarity—a similarity of far greater significance than the difference he proposes to illustrate: the notion that a discrete personal identity should survive all time was the bedrock of Egyptian religion, as it is bedrock of Christianity.[60] In this insistence, and indeed in the long-standing assumptions that have been made that even the body itself might survive in some manner (an idea that has had some considerable currency throughout the history of Western culture), "we" bear more similarity to the Egyptians than we do, for example, to the Greeks.

But even in acknowledging such a similarity (whether legacy or no), we are at the same time articulating a difference, as we can see by a further reference to G. W. F. Hegel. For all his prejudice and spiritual positivism,

Hegel was extraordinarily prescient in his characterization of Egyptian thought in this particular regard, even as he shares some of Breasted's presumption. In his study, "The Oriental World," he discusses Egyptian strategies of figural meaning, disapprovingly, but with surprising insight:

> The comparison of the course of human life with the Nile, the sun, and Osiris is probably not to be taken as a simile, as if birth, the increase in strength, the height of strength and fruitfulness, decline and weakness, were to make themselves manifest in these different phenomena equally or in a similar way; rather, the imagination saw in this variety one subject, one vitality. This unity is however altogether abstract; the heterogeneous shows itself therein as urgent and driven and in an unclarity which stands out in sharp contrast to Greek clarity. Osiris represents the sun and the Nile, and just the same might we say, the sun and Nile are symbols of human life and spirit; each is the symbol of the other. Figure and significance are mixed, the one with the other; each one is the figure, each one is the significance. Osiris is the god who instructs humankind, which finds its happiness through his institutions; the symbol is the Nile or the sun, but likewise, spiritual content is a symbol of the Nile and the course of the sun. These different representations are interknotted, so that the one can be explained by the other. The symbol is turned over into the significance, and this is a symbol of the symbol, which in turn becomes the significance. No designation is a figure without being as well a signification; each one is every other, the one is explained by the other. But each is also the essential content, the essential definition. We are to regard this idea as the center of Egyptian material perception, which is so rich and so self-contradictory that its instances crowd into one another. It results thus in a concrete representation which is knotted together with many other representations wherein the individuality of each basic nodus remains and is unresolved into a generality.[61]

It is, indeed, quite plausible that the Egyptians regarded diverse phenomena in the world as reflecting ("symbolizing") one another, their meaning(s) analogous or figurally interchangeable. Transformations, metaphors, anthropomorphisms, iconography in writing: all these point to a vividly constructivist understanding of "reality," which might take the complex form of the philosophy of the Memphite Theology, or might be concretely figured in a scarab (*kheper*) with a human head, demonstrating "transformation" (*kheper*), as in Figure 5.3. There is explicit evidence of the interchangeability of certain deities in special contexts; certain constructions of creation can be understood as interchangeable; even the "substantialist" attitudes we perceive in Egyptian writing might be construed as examples of the interchangeability of material reality and language. The testimony of Egyptian material culture persuades us that such figurality encouraged the creation of abundant images for which there are no material counterparts in the world: ibis-headed men, cattle with solar disks rising from their foreheads, and such.

Even if one sets aside Hegel's Eurocentrist prejudices and Idealism, there are important reservations we must voice before acquiescing to Hegel's reading: What are the limits of transferability in Egyptian figural systems? Where do the analogies or transformations stop? (For we cannot assume that Egyptians were willing to see any figural structure as analogous to any other.) Where, moreover, did the authority lie for determining which analogies were permissible and which were not?

The contrast Hegel draws between the Egyptians and the Greeks can be instructive here, for if the Egyptians in their figurality are "rich and ... self-contradictory," with one "concrete representation ... knotted together with many other representations ... unresolved into a generality," then the Greeks, for Hegel, exemplify a "clarity" in their figural practice.

What is this "Greek clarity"? The immediate context suggests it is a figural strategy where the symbol cannot be turned over into the significance, where every designation is either figure or signification, not both. Hegel is arguing for a clear distinction not only among phenomena, but also between signifier and signified. Figural language does not in itself have any reality status. It is forever directed beyond itself to a "real" significance.

Reading a bit further in the *Philosophie der Weltgeschichte*, we come to realize that the clarity in question is not merely a matter of the deployment of figures in language, but that it is tied to the emergence of consciousness itself. As he explains,

> Plato recounts that an Egyptian priest said the Greeks remained eternally but children; on the contrary, we can pronounce the Egyptians to be sturdy and driven boys who are only to become young men through ideal form, through clarity about themselves.[62]

In Hegel's view, it is only with the Greeks that the human spirit attains its first maturity, finding a clear ontological directionality which frees it from "Nature," allowing the human spirit to attain the universality of "Spirit." "Nature" is, among other things, the materiality of existence, whereas the universality of "Spirit," which purportedly allows self-understanding, is an abstract and idealized state of being, dominated by mentalist or intellectual experience and divorced from the corporeal.

Hegel's particular view of the emancipation of Spirit from Nature is of less moment to us here than the underlying dualism upon which it is founded. In that context, it has much in common with long-standing ideologies of being in the West. Although to Hegel, this represents an evolutionary stage indispensable to the progress of civilization, without his positivistic orientation, we might see such a contention as symptomatic of an attempt to dissociate human value from the materiality of lived experience.[63] Indeed, in exemplifying the Greek grasp on a clarity of human self-consciousness with the story of Oedipus solving the riddle of the sphinx, he finds himself in the embarrassing position of having to undercut his own example, awarding Oedipus the prize, only to take it away from him (on account of the abominations of the Theban royal house), in order to bestow it upon a generalized abstraction of Greek identity:

> We already find this transition articulated in the story of Oedipus. A sphinx, the very image of the Egyptian riddle, appeared in Thebes and posed a riddle with the words, "What is it which goes on four legs in the morning, on two in midday, and in the evening on three?" The Greek Oedipus solved the riddle and overthrew the sphinx from its perch through the answer, it is man. This is correct. The riddle of the sphinx is the Spirit, man, the one who is conscious of his own being. But paired with the solution to this riddle by Oedipus, who thus reveals himself as one who knows, is the most atrocious ignorance about himself and what he does. The ascent of spiritual clarity in the ancient royal house is bound up with abomination out of ignorance. This is ancient patriarchal rule, which is imperfectly compatible with knowledge and which is thereby broken up. This knowledge will first be purified through political principles, it is disastrous when unmediated. Self-consciousness must still be formed through civil principles and political freedom and harmonized with the Spirit of the beautiful in order to become true knowledge and moral clarity.[64]

This passage is exemplary of Hegel's propensity for slighting the individual lived experience in favor of an ideal spirit, an apotheosis of freedom. Personal experience, the texture of the individual life, is made supplementary to what Hegel terms the universal, the self-conscious spirit of freedom. One could go into far greater detail, of course, with regard to this particular Orientalist pathology and the system of supplementarity on which it is founded,[65] but our interest in Hegel here stems from his exemplary place in the history of Western subjectivity and the similarity he bears on the one hand to a figure such as Lacan (who is much more forthright about the body and its significance for the individual psyche, but who makes symbolic emasculation a necessary element in maturation), or on the other hand, to a figure such as Augustine (who subordinates indi-

Figure 5.3. A human-headed scarab beetle of steatite carved for a woman named Aset. *BD* 30b appears on the underside. Amulets in the shape of the scarab beetle (or *kheper*) were common from the First Intermediate Period through the Graeco-Roman era. Since *kheper* (*ḫpr*) also means "become" or "transform," these objects were invested with great symbolic meaning and sometimes show transformations themselves. British Museum, London (EA 38073).

vidual perception of the world to the domination of divine will, utterly denigrating the corporeality of human existence).

Can we say, in our ping-pong course through Lacan and Augustine, Hegel, Plotinus, and so on, that there is something we can characterize as "Western." Can we go on to mark this in significant ways vis-à-vis an Egyptian legacy? The answer to this question is to be found in the pervasive supplementarity of the Western tradition.

We have seen repeatedly how displacement and supplementarity function in Egyptian representational systems: how the progeny born of Atum's masturbation are supplementary to his object, pleasure; how the sexually explicit nature of this cosmogony is displaced to expectoration and sneezing; how the physicality of this is in turn displaced to a mental and verbal creation. In a parallel construction of gender, we have seen how woman is made the supplement to the heavily phallocentric male identity of god and pharaoh. Supplementarity pervades Egyptian representational systems, and in its oscillations between phallocentrism and logocentrism, it underlies the subsequent history of the Western subject.

But we must allow for a multitude of differences as well (even in acknowledging the significance of these Egyptian differences in the dialectical afterplay of Western metaphysics). And we can see the backbone of difference in this regard by coming back to the question of interpretive authority within the figurality of Egyptian culture. Where, we asked earlier, did the authority lie for determining which analogies were permissible and which were not?

This is not a question we are likely to answer, given the scarcity of metacritical discourse in extant Egyptian texts. We do, however, have some sense of how the boundaries were drawn under Akhenaten, because it was done with some ruthlessness. Pa-aten'ankh, the solar disk of the

Aten, is radically different from previous expressions of the divine among the Egyptians because of its antifigurality. The entire Atenist experiment, as has often been pointed out, represents a strict limitation on the uses of figurality, which is controlled by Akhenaten's authority.[66]

Apart from the Amarna period, though, it seems that there was a broad liberality—in the view of Hegel and the like-minded, indeed, a flagrant promiscuity—in the way Egyptians could analogize and figure "reality." It is not coincidental that constraints on the deployment of figures in conceiving reality go hand in hand with Atenist monotheism. And we must acknowledge a crucial similarity here between Akhenaten's monotheism and the Abrahamic tradition in the West. The three strains of monotheism that developed in the Middle East long after Akhenaten's ill-fated experiment show a like insistence on ecclesiastical control over the deployment of figurality, and they bear, moreover, a heavy resemblance in this regard to long-standing and broadly influential strains of Western philosophical thought.[67]

Furthermore, in the common Idealist insistence that the material world, so often characterized as a world of appearances, points to another, separate world, a world of noumenal Reality apart, eternal, and indestructible (whether the world of God, the world of the Word, the world of the *Idea*, or the world of the Spirit), we perceive how the supplementarity of Egyptian representational systems underlies the subsequent Western fabrication of a supplementarity of Being itself.

This alienation of lived experience from absolute meaning might in its own right be seen as a central component of Western thought. Where then, would that put the Egyptians? For all their supposed otherworldliness and "obsession" with death, they might be regarded as more practical and lucidly mindful of the present than later thinkers, who imagine the Real to exist in a realm apart from the world of everyday material experience. Such an argument is counterintuitive, given the animal-headed deities, the highly centralized theocracy, and the prodigious expense and effort devoted to religious and funerary establishments in ancient Egypt, but regarded from a different perspective, it is an argument that offers valuable insights upon "our" own otherworldliness.[68]

There is a fine irony in the fact that the symbol of subjective identity should so often, in ancient Egypt, be asserted through the phallus. In a sense, we come, thereby, full circle. For if the phallus is the site of the suborning of divine will in Augustine, if it is the replacement for a castrated penis in Lacan, if it is indeed sublated into oblivion in Hegel, it remains, in Egyptian thought and representation, a linchpin holding the present reality to the world of the spirit.

Thus, following Hegel's contention, we can see the phallus of Osiris as both actual phallus and symbol of resurrection; the resurrection of Osiris is then a figure of his virility, and his virility is a symbol, in turn, of the vitality of the natural world. Each symbol maintains its center on a phenomenal reality while at the same time reflecting figurally the meaning of a multitude of other phenomenal realities, which are themselves symbolic, and so on and so forth. But while the Egyptians seem, as we read them, to have maintained a firm grounding in material reality even as they relished a proliferous engagement upon the world of imagination, they remained bound to existence. The sine qua non of their funerary practice (and consequently, the center of our perspective on them) remains the persistence of individual identity; in this insistence on the ground of being lies the absolute basis of reality for the Egyptians. And in this they are our fathers and mothers in the West.

Yet wait. We must remain mindful that as Barry Kemp put it, "Egyptian thought cannot . . . be recreated as a living intellectual system" and that even in referring to the Egyptian, we are "creating in [our] own mind images [we] hope correspond to the way things were in ancient Egypt."[69] We cannot, of course, be assured that the construction we make of Egyptian materials is the same construction an Egyptian would have made of these materials.

So return yet again to Atum, for his presence remains an embarrassment, a banana in our pocket. For now we must imagine him as the god of emptiness, the avatar of nothing, the end of being and its fullness in the "not." For "Atum" (i.e., *tm*) as you recall, means "not" and "perish," "cease," and "be nonexistent." It means "be complete" or "make complete" as well.[70] If negation is, in this formulation, completion as well, we are brought to a striking possibility. Can the Egyptian West be as well the Egyptian East? Can the plenitude of nonexistence which is, apparently, comprehended by the word "Atum" be lined up against the plenitude of emptiness that is *śūnyatā*, the Buddhist absolute?

Such a question can be asked only in a context of rarefied conjecture, and even in such a context, it can hardly support a plausible history of transmission or genealogical connection. More important, though: the very fact that such a question can be asked brings us back to the fundamental inquiry of our enterprise, the question of who "we" are and how the "we" that we construct can be related to a world of breathtaking remoteness and daunting alterity. And we must concede that even if the essence of emptiness was resident in the palace of Atum, Egyptians looked upon its face with terror and abhorrence. The justification of Osiris-Ani, standing before the tribunal of Ma'at, comes in a voice which swears, "I have not known nonexistence." It is, even now, the figuring of this voice, in hieroglyphs, which speaks to us, presenting us a range of the possible. Its speaking presence confronts us with the challenge of *différance* and the ever proliferating richness of intellectual choice. It opens our minds to the unaccustomed and resurrects our bodies from the sepulcher of Idealism. In its antiquity it invites us to be something new.

REFERENCE MATTER

NOTES

For full authors' names, titles, and publication data on works cited in short form in these Notes, and for abbreviations, see the Bibliography, pp. 297–310.

Exergue

1. Kemp, *Ancient Egypt*, p. 3.
2. Ibid., pp. 2–5 passim.
3. Derrida, "La pharmacie de Platon," pp. 71–197. In this instance, I have used the translation by Barbara Johnson, "Plato's Pharmacy," pp. 63–64.
4. *Book of the Dead* 175b. The text is extant in the Eighteenth or Nineteenth Dynasty *Papyrus of ꜣny* (pBM 10470) and the Nineteenth Dynasty *Papyrus of Rꜥ* (pLeyden T 5). I have used the former, reproduced in *Book of the Dead, Facsimile of the Papyrus of Ani in the British Museum*, pl. 29; reprinted (with an unreliable translation) in Budge, *Book of the Dead* (Ani), pp. 185–86. For a translation of the entire utterance, see T. G. Allen, *Book of the Dead*, pp. 183–85.
5. Thus, the full titulary (i.e., list of titles) of Ani. See Faulkner, *Ancient Egyptian Book of the Dead*, p. 9.

CHAPTER 1 *The Reverential Slaughter*

1. Consider, for instance, Frazer's discussion, in chapter 37 of *The Golden Bough*, of the similarity between the myths surrounding the birth and death of several "oriental" gods on the one hand, and the birth and death of Christ on

the other, in terms of both nature and history. It is clear, however, that he considers Christianity a definite step forward in human history, as in the following passage (p. 419): "It appears from the testimony of an anonymous Christian, who wrote in the fourth century of our era, that Christians and pagans alike were struck by the remarkable coincidence between the death and resurrection of their respective deities, and that the coincidence formed a theme of bitter controversy between the adherents of the rival religions, the pagans contending that the resurrection of Christ was a spurious imitation of the resurrection of Attis, and the Christians asserting with equal warmth that the resurrection of Attis was a diabolical counterfeit of the resurrection of Christ. In these unseemly bickerings the heathen took what to a superficial observer might seem strong ground by arguing that their god was the older and therefore presumably the original, not the counterfeit, since as a general rule an original is older than its copy. This feeble argument the Christians easily rebutted. They admitted, indeed, that in point of time Christ was the junior deity, but they triumphantly demonstrated his real seniority by falling back on the subtlety of Satan, who on so important an occasion had surpassed himself by inverting the usual order of nature.

"Taken altogether, the coincidences of the Christian with the heathen festivals are too close and too numerous to be accidental. They mark the compromise which the Church in the hour of its triumph was compelled to make with its vanquished yet still dangerous rivals. The inflexible Protestantism of the primitive missionaries, with their fiery denunciations of heathendom, had been exchanged for the supple policy, the easy tolerance, the comprehensive charity of shrewd ecclesiastics, who clearly perceived that if Christianity was to conquer the world it could do so only by relaxing the too rigid principles of its Founder, by widening a little the narrow gate which leads to salvation."

2. See, in particular, Plutarch, *Peri Isidos kai Osiridos* 20–38.

3. The *Pyramid Texts* are a body of texts inscribed within the tombs of several Fifth and Sixth Dynasty pharaohs, first, in the tomb of Unas around 2300 B.C.E. The language shows variations that seem to reflect linguistic change over time, which suggests that at least some of the *Pyramid Texts* had a long previous history in spoken form.

4. "Prince Abbas Hilmi [i.e., Abbas II] has collected the monuments of a former time in this place." The inscription memorializes the laying of the foundation stone by Prince Abbas Hilmi II, on April 1, 1897.

5. Redford, *Egypt, Canaan, and Israel*, pp. 8f.

6. Sometimes termed the "Great Hymn to Osiris," this rather long prayer comes from an Eighteenth Dynasty stela of one Amenemope, now in the Paris (Stele Louvre C 286), published by Moret in "La Légende d'Osiris." The text is also transcribed in De Buck's *Egyptian Readingbook*, pp. 110–13. An English translation can be found in Lichtheim, *Ancient Egyptian Literature*, 2: 81–86. The quotation is taken from lines 10 and 11 on the stela.

7. "Nedyet" (i.e., *Ndjt*) is readily linked to *ndj*, "to fall to the ground." Among the numerous citations of the place in the *Pyramid Texts*, the following are clearly important: "Isis comes and Nephthys comes, one of them from the west and one of them from the east, one of them as a 'screecher,' one of them as a kite; they have found Osiris, his brother Seth having laid him low in Nedit; when Osiris said 'Get away from me,' when his name became Sokar" (*Pyramid Texts* 1256a–bPN). "Osiris was laid low by his brother Seth, but He who is in Nedit moves, his head is raised by Rēʿ; he detests sleep and hates inertness, so the King will not putrefy, he will not rot, this King will not be cursed by your anger, you gods" (1500f.). "The Great One has fallen in Nedit, the throne is released by its occupant" (2188). Here I quote Faulkner's translations from *Ancient Egyptian Pyramid Texts*.

8. See, for example, Otto, *Ancient Egyptian Art*, pp. 61–62: "In the course of this worship of the relics of Osiris, unrelated ancient cult symbols are often reinterpreted as relics. This happens, for example, in Letopolis (the second Lower Egyptian nome), where the unintelligible nome sign is interpreted as the god's shoulder blade. In Busiris, the djed pillar, probably a kind of sheaf of grain, is said to be the backbone of Osiris; and finally Abydos itself claims to possess his head in the form of its beehive-like nome symbol. But this doctrine applies not only to parts of his mutilated body; the god himself is supposed to be present in many forms in various parts of the country."

Horst Beinlich points out that some of the identifications in question were made on the basis of puns. Thus Amun (i.e., *Jmn*) in his association with Thebes, suggested that the skin (*jnm*) of Osiris had been deposited in Thebes. He also shows in tabular form how the body parts of Osiris were identified, one by one, with each of the nomes in Lower Egypt and Upper Egypt. Sometimes this results in an excess of body parts. The lower jaw, for instance, was said to have been left in both the third Upper Egyptian nome and the ninth Lower Egyptian nome. See Beinlich, "Reliquie," pp. 230f.

9. "Great Hymn to Osiris," ll. 1–3. See note 6.

10. This version is from the stela of Sobek-iry (Louvre C 30). The hymn dates from the Middle Kingdom and was very popular, occurring in numerous versions from the Middle Kingdom into the New Kingdom. The original text is most readily available in Sethe's *Ägyptische Lesestücke*, p. 64.

11. From the Papyrus of *Nwnw* (pBM 10477), printed in Budge, *Book of the Dead* (Nu). More readily available is T. G. Allen's translation, pp. 118–20.

12. Erik Hornung has suggested that all the Egyptian gods are subject in some degree to death, which he characterizes not as an end but as the mark of a transformation. See Hornung, *Conceptions of God*, pp. 151–65.

13. A young Alan Gardiner wrote the classic article on the formula as an excursus in his edition, with Nina de Garis Davies, of *The Tomb of Amenemhēt*, pp. 79–93. A briefer account can be found in Gardiner, *Egyptian Grammar*, pp. 170–73.

14. *Pyramid Texts* 535–36 (from Utterance 327). I follow the grammatical analysis of James Allen, *The Inflection of the Verb in the Pyramid Texts*, 65c, p. 45.

15. Hornung, *Conceptions of God*, p. 176. Hornung makes a persuasive argument about "the negation of all positive struggle," but in doing so hits as well upon a fundamental problem of Egyptian ontology, for even as struggle may not be positive, it is also at the very heart of being, from that primeval time when "two things" came forth in the land. See the discussion of *Coffin Texts* (Utterance 261), below, pp. 168–69.

16. The Smaller Hierakonpolis, or Two Dog Palette, reverse side. Illustrated in Kemp, *Ancient Egypt*, fig. 14.

17. *Pyramid Texts* 590–92.

18. Photographs are rare, but there are excellent ones by Max Hirmer in Otto's *Ancient Egyptian Art*, pls. 16 and 17, with brief commentary on p. 69.

19. In the cult of Amun kamutef, the center of voice is the son, who claims to have engendered himself as bull of his mother (i.e., $k\jmath$ $mwt=f$), an important construction of royal autonomy (see Chapter 3). In the cult of Min, there is little trace of a narrative of even the simplest sort. The focus is rather a figural construction in which male virility is mirrored in agricultural fertility: raw phallic energy equals, somehow, the rank abundance of vegetable life. The figure must be extended as well to the cosmogony of Atum, great-grandfather (and father) of Osiris, but that is for later.

20. The *ka* (i.e., $k\jmath$) is represented in hieroglyphs by two arms bent at the elbow with the hands outstretched. The arms are arranged so that the entire glyph takes roughly the shape of the letter *U*. Some have proposed that the arms are outstretched to embrace or support, and indeed, in tomb paintings one sometimes finds the *ka* of the king accompanying the king himself as if to support him in his encounters with various gods. Another suggestion, however, may be more accurate: that the arms are outstretched to receive offerings, for the *ka* clearly maintains a specifically physical role in the afterlife of the subject. It receives offerings and serves as a channel for the physical sustenance and enjoyment of the deceased. See, for example, the wonderfully concrete representation emerging from the false door of Idu in his mastaba at Giza (G 7102). A photograph is to be seen in Forman and Quirke, *Hieroglyphs and the Afterlife*, p. 30. Homonyms mean "food" or "offerings" (obviously relating to the deceased's capacity to consume), as well as "bull" (perhaps relating to the deceased's sexual potency—"bull" in this context is sometimes written with the glyph of the phallus; given a feminine termination *-t*, the word *kat*, i.e., $k\jmath t$, means "vagina").

The *ba* (i.e., $b\jmath$) is represented in hieroglyphs either by the glyph of a jabiru bird (*Ephippiorhynchus senegalensis*) or by a human-headed bird preceded by an incense pot. The latter is used in painting and relief as well as hieroglyphic writing. The avian character of this aspect of posthumous existence symbolizes the ability to move, specifically to come forth from and return to the tomb. The word also represents spiritual power (especially that of a king or god), and one occasionally finds that one god is described as the *ba* of another. Gods and pharaohs may have multiple *bas*.

21. Compare Freud's notion that the consciousness of specific body parts in the maturing child comes as a result of awareness of pain in such-and-such a body part. As Judith Butler explains, "In 1923, in *The Ego and the Id*, Freud [states] quite clearly that bodily pain is the precondition of bodily self-discovery. He asks there how one can account for the *formation* of the ego, that bounded sense of self, and concludes that it is differentiated from the id partially through pain: 'Pain seems to play a part in the process, and the way in which we gain new knowledge of our organs during painful illnesses is perhaps a model of the way by which in general we arrive at the idea of our own body.'" See Butler, "Lesbian Phallus," p. 134.

22. Diodorus Siculus, *Bibliothecae Historicae Quae Supersunt* 1.91.

23. Quirke, *Ancient Egyptian Religion*, p. 152.

24. It may be, however, that such disjointing of the deceased was not part of the original process of mummification, but rather the remummification by survivors of a body that had been disturbed by animals or looters after the original burial.

25. Theoretically, according to Spencer, *Death in Ancient Egypt*, pp. 36, 158, human-headed Imsety overlooks the liver, falcon-headed Qebehsenuf the intestines, jackal-headed Duamutef the stomach, and baboon-headed Ha'py the lungs. In actual practice, however, according to Brier, *Egyptian Mummies*, pp. 84–85, it seems that this division of labor was rarely accurately realized.

26. Various theorists have posited a link between writing and violence because the writing surface, of stone or metal or parchment, is "penetrated" and "disfigured" as the written characters are there "inscribed." In considering the Egyptian use of papyrus, or the East Asian use of paper, at least, such a link is inappropriate because the writing in question is less inscribed through the force of the pen, than transferred by the tip of the reed stylus or brush.

27. Diodorus Siculus, *Bibliothecae Historicae Quae Supersunt* 1.91.

28. See the discussion by Pascal Vernus in "Name," pp. 320–26.

29. Sauneron, *Priests of Ancient Egypt*, p. 126.

30. Vernus, "Name," pp. 320f.: "Point d'arbitraire du signe chez les Egyptiens, mais, au contraire, la croyance en un lien essentiel entre le signifiant et le signifié, entre le N[om](*rn*) et ce qu'il désigne. Cela vaut pour toute réalité, objets, institutions, plantes, animaux, hommes, rois et divinités. Jusqu'en Copte, *rn* peut se construire avec le suffixe possessif, comme les noms désignant ce qui est inné et qu'on ne peut acquérir. . . . Corrélativement, le N[om] d'un homme participe de son être, et en constitue une manifestation, parallèlement à son corps, à la manière du *ka* avec lequel il s'identifie parfois."

31. "The God and His Unknown Name of Power," in Prichard, *Ancient Near Eastern Texts*, pp. 12–14.

32. David P. Silverman, "Divinity and Deities in Ancient Egypt," in Shafer, *Religion in Ancient Egypt: Gods, Myths, and Personal Practice*, p. 28.

33. The *Sayings of Kha'kheperre'seneb* has been translated numerous times, first by Alan H. Gardiner in his *Admonitions*, pp. 109f., with a commentary, pp. 95–109 and 110–12. Lichtheim's translation can be found as "The Complaints of Khakhepperre-Sonb," in *Ancient Egyptian Literature*, 1: 145–49.

34. The formula occurs as early as the Eighteenth Dynasty on, for example, the heart scarab of an official named Neb'ankh (i.e., *Nbʿnḫ*) of around 1710 B.C.E. (see Andrews, *Amulets of Ancient Egypt*, pp. 56f.). I refer to the practice as one of the New Kingdom because that is when it becomes widespread, and that is when the preponderance of textual evidence for it appears, on scarabs as well as in funerary papyri. The formula in question is chapter 30B of the so-called *Book of the Dead*, here quoted in the former of two occurrences in the *Papyrus of Ani* (pBM 10470), reprinted in Budge, *Book of the Dead* (Ani), p. 11 (my translation).

I here adopt a variant in the last line in the formula that is not adopted by many translators. The issue in question is whether to read a word in the final line as *ḥnm* or *ḥnmw*. In the former case, it could be taken as a participial form of a verb meaning "join," "unite with," "enter," etc. In the latter, it would be understood as the proper name of the god Khnum, who was reputed to have created humans on his potter's wheel, and it would be constructed as an appositive to "you." This latter version is the version chosen by Lichtheim, Gardiner, and others in their translations, and it must be admitted that most versions of the formula insert a determinative of the ram-headed god along with the phonetic *ḥnm(w)*. In the *Papyrus of Ani*, however, only the phonetics are written, with no determinative at all. Though a minority version, this reading seems preferable to me.

35. John Baines points out that it was "freedom to act [that] led to wrongdoing," even as that very freedom, "to follow the heart (which also means to have a good time) was a positive value." Baines, "Society, Morality, and Religious Practice," in Shafer, *Religion in Ancient Egypt*, p. 164.

36. Assmann, *Maât*, pp. 11f.: "Mais si on cherche à élargir les limites de notre mémoire culturelle et à regagner une partie de ce continent intellectuel submergé, c'est la notion de la Maât d'où un abord herméneutique doit procéder. C'est l'analyse des textes et images dans lesquels cette notion est développée qui peut nous donner une 'vue de l'intérieur' du monde pharaonique et qui peut nous apprendre la façon dans laquelle les anciens Égyptiens eux-mêmes ont vécus et interprété leur vision du monde."

37. Ibid., p. 17: "La difficulté réside dans l'étendue singulière de l'acception de ce concept, qui englobe des notions comme vérité, authenticité, justice, justesse, droiture, ordre, sacrifice, etc."

38. Ibid., p. 26.

39. Ibid., p. 26: "Le but de l'éducation égyptienne est l'homme qui sait écouter, homo auditor, l'homme qui entend, qui obéit, l'homme attentif, bien-

veillant, docile, qui s'incline devant celui qui parle et accepte le conseil qu'on lui donne. Toute la civilisation égyptienne semble être fondée sur, et animée par, cette faculté de s'écouter l'un l'autre. Toute la vie sociale dépend de la faculté de s'entendre."

40. Ibid., p. 57.

41. Ibid., pp. 25f.: "Sous l'Ancien Empire, ce sont toujours ces deux chemins qui mènent à l'état d'jm3ḫw et par là à la survie: La Maât et la carrière. Chacun est indispensable. Par l'un, on obtient l'intégration affective dans la mémoire sociale; par l'autre, on obtient la distinction d'un homme important. Pour perdurer, il faut les deux: l'intégration et la distinction, la conformité à la Maât et l'importance de la position sociale.

"Nous avons dit que sous l'Ancient Empire la Maât était identifiée à la volonté du roi. Or, il semble paradoxal que ce ne soit pas la carrière, c'est-à-dire le service du roi où la Maât s'accomplit, mais le service des hommes. En fait, ce n'est pas une contradiction. A cette époque, on ne distingue pas entre l'état et la société; le roi veut que l'on serve les hommes, il aime la solidarité, parce que la solidarité est le fondement de l'état. Pour le service du roi, il n'est pas besoin d'une éthique prescriptive. Ce n'est pas une exigence, mais un privilège. Les avantages sont trop évidents pour qu'il soit nécessaire de faire appel à la solidarité. Ce n'est pas une question d'altruisme, mais d'ambition, laquelle, contrairement à l'altruisme, est naturelle et n'a pas besoin d'être suscitée. C'est d'ailleurs précisément ce qui change avec le Moyen Empire, où la dynastie . . . a alors un évident besoin de propagande."

42. Ibid., p. 67: "Cette nouvelle vision est à la base de ce qu'on pourrait appeler "l'invention de la vertu" . . . un moyen de s'intégrer et de se distinguer.

"L'avènement de la vertu, comme succédané des deux chemins anciens, la Maât et le mérite, se révèle par un vocabulaire nouveau. Le terme le plus général est nfrw, "beauté, bonté", qui correspond à—et sera traduit plus tard par—le grec a[r]etê. D'autres termes sont plus spéciaux, tels jwn nfr "bonne nature", qdjt "qualité", bj3 "caractère", j3mt "grâce, gentillesse", w3[ḫ-]jb "patience, bienveillance", etc."

43. Ibid., p. 85.

44. Ibid., p. 89: "L'individu n'est plus confronté, devant le tribunal divin, à un adversaire, mais à la Maât elle-même. La confrontation revêt de ce fait une signification tout à fait différente, qui se traduit par l'image de la balance et l'action de la pesée du cœur."

45. Rudolph Anthes, "Note Concerning the Great Corporation of Heliopolis," *JNES* 13 (1954): 191.

46. Quirke, *Ancient Egyptian Religion*, pp. 66–67.

47. The text is well known because it is included in Sethe's important chrestomathy, *Ägyptische Lesestücke*, pp. 70–72. A detailed philological account can be found in Schäfer's *Mysterien des Osiris*.

48. In the text of the king's command, he is identified by, presumably, his most practical and important titles. Most of these are repeated in the other

direct references to Iykhernofret on the stela, but additional titles appear uniquely in the lists given above small determinatives of him in the lower left and right corners of the stela, on the raised border. Epithets vary as well. On the left raised border he is identified as "Iykhernofret, Justified of Voice," whereas on the right raised border, he is identified as "Iykhernofret, son of Sat-Khonsu." Finally, above the seated figure of Iykhernofret before his offering table, we find simply jmy-r sd³yt, Jyḫrnfrt, nb-jm³ḫ, jr n St-Ḥnsw, "Master of the Royal Seal, Iykhernofret, the Revered, son of Sat-Khonsu." Schäfer discusses the titles individually, with reference to the particular responsibilities they seem to confer, in his *Mysterien des Osiris*, pp. 35–41. Questions remain, however, concerning the significance of the use of particular titles and epithets in particular places on the stone.

49. He uses the form jr.kw, the so-called Old Perfective of the verb "to do," to announce that he has completed the tasks assigned to him.

50. Although more detailed accounts of the festivals and rituals associated with the cult of Osiris are inscribed on the walls of the Temple of Hathor at Dendera (extensively studied by Chassinat in *Mystère d'Osiris*), these inscriptions are not precisely datable and in any case are not earlier than very late in Pharaonic Egypt, or perhaps from sometime in Ptolemaic Egypt.

51. For instance, by Lichtheim in *Ancient Egyptian Literature*, 1: 123–25, and by John A. Wilson in Prichard, *Ancient Near Eastern Texts*, pp. 329–30.

52. Much of the discussion of Egyptian art tends to regard it as an intermediate form that would eventually give way to illusionism using perspective and foreshortening, representational strategies attributed first to the Greeks. What this discourse usually fails to acknowledge is the different purposes of representation to which the Egyptians put their art and the consequently different goals achieved. If Egyptian art shows only relatively modest interest in creating the illusion of the real, it also leaves the eye freer to move over the surface of the representation without constraining it to a fixed point of observation. See Bryson, *Vision and Painting*, esp. chap. 5, "The Gaze and the Glance," pp. 87–132.

CHAPTER 2 *The Language of the Gods*

1. Derrida, *Marges de la philosophie*, p. 4: "Cette discrète intervention graphique, qui n'est pas faite d'abord ni simplement pour le scandale ... cette différence marqueé entre deux notations apparemment vocales, entre deux voyelles, reste purement graphique: elle s'écrit ou se lit, mais elle ne s'entend pas. On ne peut l'entendre et nous verrons en quoi elle passe aussi l'ordre de l'entendement. Elle se propose par une marque muette, par un monument tacite, je dirai même par une pyramide, songeant ainsi non seulement à la forme de la lettre lorsqu'elle s'imprime en majeur ou en majuscule, mais à la texte de l'Encyclopédie de Hegel où le corps du signe est comparé à la

Pyramide égyptienne. Le a de la différence, donc, ne s'entend pas, il demeure silencieux, secret et discret comme un tombeau: oikesis. Marquons ainsi, par anticipation, ce lieu, résidence familiale et tombeau du propre où se produit en différance l'économie de la mort. Cette pierre n'est pas loin, pourvu qu'on en sache déchiffrer la légende, de signaler la mort du dynaste."

"That passage in Hegel's *Encyclopedia*" refers to *Enzyklopädie der philosophischen Wissenschaften im Grundrisse* (1827), 458, which can be found in Hegel, *Gessamelte Werke*, 19: 335.

2. Plutarch, *Lives* 27.5 (in the life of Marc Antony).

3. Bowman, *Egypt After the Pharaohs*, pp. 158f.

4. Diodorus Siculus, *Bibliothecae Historicae Quae Supersunt* 3.4.1–4. I am indebted to Haun Saussy for the translation.

5. Compare Jan Assmann, "Ancient Egypt," pp. 29f.: "The thing, here the crocodile, does not simply represent the word or the concept 'crocodile' but a concept of 'crocodilicity' as an aggregate of the behavioral qualities of the crocodile transferred to humankind."

6. In, for instance, the exquisitely carved glyphs characteristic of the Old Kingdom, as well as in the wild proliferation of chubby glyphs from the Ptolemaic period.

7. *Ammianus Marcellinus* 17.4.10–11. The bee is, in fact, used in the pharaonic titulary, but it would seem that the meaning "king" in this case is derivative of the association of the bee with Lower Egypt. So also is the "sedge" associated with Upper Egypt. The phrase in the titulary is typically, then, "He *of* the sedge and the bee," rather than "He who is sweet, but with a sting."

Napoléon had a cartouche designed for himself, like many a Nile traveler since. His employs the bee as well, combining it with a star (more accurately Akkado-Sumerian) to create the name *Divus Rex*, "divine king." See, for example, the plaques in the lower corners of the wonderful frontispiece to the *Déscription de l'Égypte*.

8. V.-David, *Le Débat*, pp. 110–12.

9. Martin Bernal's account is fascinating in *Black Athena*, vol. 1, esp. pp. 224–33.

10. The question is whether the mode of the visible really is, in the Joycean phrase, ineluctible. That is to say, is the difference between "ideogram" and "logogram" merely a "différantial" convention of Greek, or is it a feature of some broader human or sentient prejudice or predisposition in the manipulation of signs? Clearly the ideogram, though fitted out with the metaphysical appurtenances of Idealism, might just as well be conceived in a sense more strongly sensory. There is, after all, the strongly visual pedigree of the word "idea" from "see" (*idein*). The relatively straightforward polarity of see/hear this invokes was, however, distorted to suggest a false (or in any case, eccentric) polarity of (pure) intelligibility / speech in the reaction against Leibniz and Pound by the camp of Hegel, Rousseau, and Saussure.

11. "De l'alphabet des hiéroglyphes phonétiques employés par les Égyptiens pour inscrire sur leurs monumens [sic] les titres, les noms et les surnoms des souverains grecs et romains."

12. Compare Derrida's silent intruder in "différance."

In Egyptian, the sign for the cartouche is derived from a glyph composed of a circle tangent to a short line either under it or to one side (depending on the direction in which it is to be read). This glyph conveys ideographically the notions "encirclement," "eternity," and "protection." In one view, then, the cartouche proper is a protective enclosure, "the device which excludes all inimical elements from the royal name." See Wilkinson, *Reading Egyptian Art*, p. 193. It marks, as well, with an ironic complementarity, the dominion of the king, his control of all the bounded regions of the Two Lands.

13. Cook, *Reading the Past*, pp. 8f.

14. See Christiane Ziegler's excellent account of the decipherment "Des Signes sans secret," in *Mémoire d'Égypte*, pp. 80–109; she discusses the Dendera zodiac on p. 104. Peter France discusses the theft of the zodiac in *The Rape of Egypt*, pp. 106f.

15. Manetho, *Ægyptiaca (Epitome)*, frag. 50, from Josephus, reads "Tethmōsis", whereas frag. 51, from Theophilus, reads "Tuthmōsēs"; in frag. 52, Syncellus gives us "Touthmōsis." The Latin of Eusebius reads "Tuthmosis." See *Loeb Classical Library: Manetho*, pp. 100–116 and passim.

16. In addition to hieroglyphics, Egyptian was written in hieratic, demotic, and, much later, Coptic. Hieratic began as merely the reed-pen and ink version of carved or painted hieroglyphs. Hieratic is attested very early, but even near the beginning of Egyptian writing, it was more abbreviated and less iconic than hieroglyphic writing, and in time, it became more and more cursive in form and distinct from hieroglyphic script.

Demotic (from the Greek *dēmos*, "people") represents a further cursivization, but doesn't make its appearance until the seventh century B.C.E. The chain of transformations that enabled the emergence of demotic from hieroglyphic through hieratic script was so radical that no one-to-one correspondence can be effected between demotic and hieroglyphics. Hieratic (from the Greek *hieros*, "sacred, holy") was so named because by the time the Greeks encountered it, it was used almost exclusively for religious documents, having been supplanted in secular life by demotic.

Coptic appears in the fourth century C.E. as the final written expression of Egyptian. It is closely associated with the Egyptian Christian ("Coptic") Church and is written in the Greek alphabet with the addition of six additional letters derived from demotic.

17. The work, in full title, *Grammaire égyptienne ou principes généraux de l'écriture sacrée égyptienne* . . . was republished in 1984 by the Institut d'Orient, in Paris. A fascinating document, and monumental tribute to Champollion's genius, *Grammaire égyptienne* is, nonetheless, a far from ade-

quate *grammar* of Egyptian. It is devoted for the most part to a painstaking examination of Egyptian orthography.

18. Champollion's work, in this area too, was outstanding, and significant advances came only after decades in the work of successors such as Emmanuel de Rougé and Heinrich Brugsch. Major advances were made in the last decades of the nineteenth century by the Berlin school of Adolf Erman, Georg Steindorff, and Kurt Sethe, and in this century by Battiscombe Gunn, Alan Gardiner, and Hans Polotsky, but there are many questions yet unanswered, especially in the areas of verbal inflection and interclausal relationships.

19. For a further refinement of Saussure's division between signifier and signified, see Gumbrecht's "Farewell to Interpretation," pp. 389–402, esp. 397: "Complexifying Saussure's sign concept, Hjelmslev not only distinguished between 'content' (the signified) and 'expression' (the signifier), but also projected a second distinction—between 'substance' and 'form'—onto this binarism. The four concepts and the four fields of linguistic phenomena that he thus established ... can be related to the main concerns of contemporary theory-positions."

20. Saussure, *Cours de linguistique générale*, p. 166: "Dans la langue il n'y a que des *différences*. Bien plus: une différence suppose en général des termes positifs entre lesquels elle s'établit; mais dans la langue il n'y a que des différences *sans termes positifs*" (emphases in the original).

21. Ibid., p. 164: "Toute les valeurs conventionnelles présentent ce caractère de ne pas se confondre avec l'élément tangible qui leur sert de support. Ainsi ce n'est pas le métal d'une pièce de monnaie qui en fixe la valeur; un écu qui vaut nominalement cinq francs ne contient que la moitié de cette somme en argent; il vaudra plus ou moins en deçà ou delà d'une frontière politique. Cela est plus vrai encore du signifiant linguistique; dans son essence, il n'est aucunement phonique, il est incorporel, constitué, non par sa substance matérielle, mais uniquement par les différences qui séparent son image acoustique de toutes les autres."

22. Ibid.: "[Or ce qui les caractérise, ce] n'est pas, comme on pourrait le croire, leur qualité propre et positive, mais simplement le fait qu'ils ne se confondent pas entre eux. Les phonèmes son avant tout des entités oppositives, relatives et négatives."

23. Ibid., p. 31: "Toute définition faite à propos d'un mot est vaine; c'est une mauvaise méthode que de partir des mots pour définir les choses."

24. Ibid., p. 28: "Il est en effet capital de remarquer que l'image verbale ne se confond pas avec le son lui-même et qu'elle est psychique au même titre que le concept qui lui est associé."

25. Ibid., p. 32: "C'est un système de signes où il n'y a d'essentiel que l'union du sens et de l'image acoustique, et où les deux parties du signe son également psychiques.... Dans la langue, ... il n'y a plus que l'image acoustique, et celle-ci peut se traduire en une image visuelle constante.... Chaque image

acoustique n'est, comme nous le verrons, que la somme d'un nombre limité d'éléments ou phonèmes, susceptibles à leur tour d'être évoqués par un nombre correspondant de signes dans l'écriture."

26. My discussion is based primarily on the Micro Gallery CD-ROM catalog of the collection of the National Gallery, London. This has recently been made commercially available as The National Gallery, Complete Illustrated Catalogue, with CD-ROM, compiled by Christopher Baker and Tom Henry (London: National Gallery Publications, 1995). I have also referred to Gombrich, "Botticelli's Mythologies," and L. D. and Helen S. Ettlinger, *Botticelli*. As the Ettlingers point out, the association with the Vespucci comes from the depiction of wasps emerging from the tree trunk near Mars's head. The Italian *vespe* means "wasps," and they appear just where a coat of arms might be expected on cassone paintings (p. 138).

27. There is, however, no classical or Renaissance text describing Venus and Mars as depicted in this painting. Gombrich, "Botticelli's Mythologies," p. 139.

28. The original impetus for the depiction of Venus as triumphant over Mars through the power of love may reflect astrological lore, but as Gombrich points out, the astrological interpretation in no way excludes a moral application (ibid., p. 67). It has been argued that the painting is intended as a reconstruction of a lost classical painting of the wedding of Alexander and Roxanne by Lucian, especially in its depiction of the cherubs toying with Mars's armor (pp. 139f.).

29. It will now be necessary to point out that allegory is one of the most restrictive types of figurative meaning, often appealing to an authority over the narrative that has been appropriated and manipulated by political authorities (e.g., the Church, the Confucian state). Perhaps it needn't be so, but there are, in any case, other types of figural meaning that must come into play in reading a picture: metaphor, metonymy, prosopopoeia, apostrophe, and so on.

30. The satyrs, moreover, either occupy the right side of the canvas with Mars, or appear to be moving toward it.

31. Indeed, the sleeping Mars accompanied by a wakeful Venus bears an important visual and conceptual resemblance to the scenes of Osiris's resurrection in Seti I's temple at Abydos. While it may be impossible to trace a lineage of influence over the three millennia separating the two works, such a line of influence is of less significance than the conceptual homology posed by juxtaposing the two. In both, the female, modestly clothed and wakeful, stands watch, as it were, over a naked, or nearly naked, male (ithyphallic in the Seti reliefs). Both sets of representations make a deft association of the male with the body. In both, the female is dissociated from the body in some degree, in *Venus and Mars* by the modesty of her clothing and the way the lines of the composition (in the ribbons on her gown and the braids and strands of hair with which they coalesce) direct the gaze from the body to a resting point in her face; in the Osirian reliefs by the relegation of the anthropomor-

phic Isis to the edge of the composition. In one of them she appears twice, anthropomorphically, as stated, and as a kite (bird) hovering over Osiris's erect phallus to receive his seed. Her sexuality is so obscured that she no longer finds representation as a human in the intercourse scene, whereas the erection of Osiris is the center of the composition in both of the temple reliefs.

32. Young had correctly surmised that this was a "female termination." The upper element derives from the phonetic termination -*t*, a marker of female nouns in Egyptian, but in a Greek name, like Cleopatra or Berenike, such a *phonetic* marker is extraneous, and the burden of meaning has shifted.

The lower element has a complicated history relating to filiation and corporeality. For conjectures about its meaning, see Gardiner, *Egyptian Grammar*, p. 467, glyph F51, and p. 474, glyph H8.

33. The Egyptian female termination -*t* had probably gone unpronounced for a very long while already. Fecht conjectures that it had disappeared already in the Early Dynastic period. See his *Wortakzent und Silbenstruktur*, sec. 268.

34. I use "icon" here to designate a representation dependent upon resemblance to the represented. Although aware of objections to considering such resemblances "natural," I believe that even if we insist that they are not natural, but rather culturally conditioned, then we must still admit that they are thus conditioned in so broad a cultural context that the distinction between nature and culture becomes merely academic.

35. The phonetic structure of Egyptian is a puzzle that requires us to imagine the sounds of words for which we have only a phonetic skeleton. The writing system was efficient enough with only this skeleton, but to us, the voice of Egyptian is silent. All the same, there is a tantalizing sense, to judge from the phonetic readings of certain glyphs, that Egyptian had a kind of aural iconicity as well. The word for "cat," transcribed by Egyptologists as *mjw*, cannot be far off from *meow* (or the *mão* of Mandarin, for that matter), and there is a high degree of iconic consistency in moving from the hieroglyph for "cat" to such a phonetic representation. A similar aural iconicity may be conjectured for the Egyptian word for "donkey" or "ass" , transcribed ꜥꜣ, to represent two guttural consonants unknown in English. (The sound ꜥ has some kinship to Arabic *'ain* and Hebrew *'ayin*. It may represent a voiced *'alif* / *'āleph*. The sound ꜣ seems to be related to the Arabic *'alif* and Hebrew *'āleph*, and may represent a glottal stop of some sort.) The combination of a voiced glottal stop and an unvoiced glottal stop may express what we in English aim for with the onomatopoetic "heehaw," although it is important to note that in English, "meow" and "heehaw" are both merely representations for the sounds cats and asses make, not words for "cat" and "ass" as is the case in Egyptian. (Jan Assmann has pointed out to me, as well, the possibility of aural iconicity in one of the Egyptian words for "dog," *jw*, even more apparent in an alternative reduplicated form *jwjw*.)

Other examples suggest themselves as well: "Lion" 🝊 is *rw* (a growl?), and "hawk" 🝋 is *bjk*. The glyph for "cormorant" 🝌, used more commonly as a biliteral phoneme in the word "enter," is transcribed ʿ*q* (the *q* representing an emphatic "k" sound related to the Arabic sound *kāf* and the Hebrew *qōph*). This may be an Egyptian rendering similar to our English "quack." Do cormorants "quack" or "whoop" or "caw" or what?

36. It may be worth recalling Diodorus Siculus's notice of iconicity in Egyptian. See p. 46.

37. In the absence of a knowledge of what the glyph in question represents, it may seem impossible to make the determination that it is not used, completely and arbitrarily, for the representation of sound. The characteristic ordering of glyphs in the hieroglyphic word, with phonetic glyphs preceding ideographic or logographic glyphs, however, often gives persuasive evidence of the nature of the glyph in question.

38. Haun Saussy brings to my attention Schmandt-Besserat's argument in *Before Writing*, especially pp. 157–98. Schmandt-Besserat regards the step from "one sheep, two sheep, three sheep, four sheep" to "one, two, three, four sheep" as a necessary step on the way to writing.

39. "Symbol" and "symbolic" are terms fraught with contradiction, in some usages suggesting a high degree of iconicity and in others requiring a divorce from any iconicity whatsoever. I intend the latter meaning here. See V.-David, *Le Débat*, esp. pp. 17–26. I am grateful to Haun Saussy, once again, for bringing this book to my attention.

40. In our culture, mathematical and musical notation provide examples of abstract sign systems that are not phonetic. The numeral 5, for example, has nothing to do with the concept "five" apart from our having agreed that it is to represent "five." In this case, the "our" of which we speak is a very inclusive community, worldwide today, and very ancient as well in its Hindo-Buddhist origins. This sign can, of course, be identified phonetically, but that identification would be accepted by a smaller group of individuals than the group represented by "our" in the previous two sentences. For this "our" of which we speak would all understand "5" even if their phonetic representations of it ranged from *wu* to *fünf* to *cinco* to *itsutsu* to *pañca*, and on and on.

41. The range of strategies for the logographic construction of meaning is quite broad and includes direct representation of objects from the real world, figural constructions of meaning relying on metaphor, metonymy, and other figural constructions, as well as constructions that operate through symbolic logic, and combinations or juxtapositions of the aforementioned possibilities. It would be interesting to compare and contrast the various logographic writing systems known to us today in terms of their respective degree of reliance on each of the above strategies. I suggest that Egyptian is among the most heavily iconic, while Chinese is particularly adept at juxtapositions of different strategies.

42. See Assmann, "Ancient Egypt," esp. pp. 24–26.
43. See above, p. 65; and p.261n33.
44. It may well be the case that words which appear to us to have identical phonetic structures ("homonyms") were, in spoken Egyptian, distinct. As noted before, however, the writing systems—all three, hieroglyphic, hieratic, and demotic—fail to notate vowels, so to the eye, at least, there are a great many "homonyms."
45. Other unusual meanings for the word as well as further specification and examples of usage can be found in Erman and Grapow, *Wörterbuch der ägyptischen Sprache*, 5: 300–306.
46. The Na'rmer Palette is a large ceremonial palette of late Predynastic or early Dynastic origins, found by J. E. Quibell in 1897 in excavations at Nekhen (Gk., Hierakonpolis).
47. Assmann, "Ancient Egypt," pp. 19f. (Assmann's emphases).
48. Ibid., pp. 20–24.
49. Ibid. p. 24.
50. The inadequacy of phonetic writing systems is apparent in the efforts of those who use such systems to go beyond the limits of phonetic representation. In this age of computerized communications, one sees one example of such an attempt to escape the boundaries of phoneticism in the as yet primitive system of "pictographs" created with colons, dashes, parentheses, and the like to make faces in the line of type, which to be read, require the reader to reorient the line vertically rather than horizontally. Thus ":-)" produces a smiling face, ":-(" a glum one.

A far more sophisticated reemergence of iconicity from the constraints of the alphabet is observable in the Graphical User Interface (GUI) computing environment pioneered by Apple and subsequently copied by Microsoft.

51. Thus the Greek alphabet became the prolific ancestor not only of the Roman, Cyrillic, Coptic, Etruscan, Lydian, Lycian, Phrygian, and Glagolytic alphabets, to which it maintains a close resemblance, but also of superficially rather more distant descendants in the Georgian, Armenian, and perhaps Runic alphabets. And it goes on to be applied, with more or less copious diacritical specification, to the writing of various languages far removed from its East Mediterranean roots, such as Vietnamese and some languages of the Khoisan family.

A contrasting situation occurs with Chinese, which, though far more logographic than Egyptian, was nonetheless widely imitated and adapted in East Asia, giving rise to the hybrid system of Japanese as well as a number of less well known writing systems such as Xixia (Hsi-Hsia), for the notation of Tangut. The adaptation of Chinese to the notation of other languages in East Asia provides an excellent counter to arguments about the evolution of simplicity and phoneticism in writing, but the complex reasons for its success over a vast and extraordinarily diverse cultural and geographical area are intimately related to the place of Han culture relative to other East Asian cultures and differ in important ways from the reasons for the success of the alphabet.

52. Gardiner, *Egyptian Grammar*, p. 450, D4.

53. As the following observation reveals: "The student may be puzzled at finding ⌬ in *sḏm* here treated as a triliteral sign, while in §22 it was described as an ideogram. This contradiction must be explained. In the case of the triliterals the distinction between phonograms and ideograms becomes particularly precarious. Thus probably all words containing the consonants *ḥ + t + p* are etymologically connected with the verb-stem *ḥtp* 'rest,' 'be propitiated,' they are, moreover, all written with the sign ⌬ representing a loaf placed on a reed-mat—a sign taken over from a word meaning 'altar,' perhaps literally 'place of propitiation.' The sign ⌬ in any given word may be described as ideographic in so far as any connexion of meaning is discernible between that word and the word for 'altar,' 'place of propitiation'; it may be described as phonetic, on the other hand, in so far as the sound-value outweighs, or throws into the shade, such similarity of meaning" (ibid., p. 45).

54. A common Late Egyptian variant writes *jr(j)* as follows: ⌬. This further complicates the issue, in that the consonantal structure is accounted for by a first glyph (the reed leaf used phonetically). A following glyph, a seated man with hand to mouth, occurs in numerous readings indicating agency related to consumption, utterance, or cognitive process. Is the prothetic, then, merely an elaborate phonetic representation, or does it reinforce the notion of agency in its occurrences?

55. Even the figurality of such a construction as ⌬ is rather complex. On the one hand, the palette would seem to bear a metonymic relation to the word "scribe," whereas on the other, the figure of a seated man is an icon analogous to the idea "scribe." The icon is, however, defective, in that the seated man is not shown in the characteristic pose of a scribe, writing. On this basis, one could say that the palette too is iconic and that it is only more defective than the icon "seated man" in so much as we, with our humanistic biases, might see a stronger analogy in man (*man* who writes) than we see in tools to write (man who *writes*). Can we not just as well say that the man is a metonymic figure and that humanness is merely associated with or adjacent to "scribe" just as the palette is associated with or adjacent to "scribe"?

56. See Smither, "An Old Kingdom Letter," pp. 16–19, especially 18, note c. The modern equivalent is "Have your people talk to my people," as Andrew Lewis suggested.

57. If the words "your scribe" (i.e., "you") and "you write" (i.e., the second person singular of the verb "write") were phonetically identical in spoken Egyptian, context would very likely have clarified the distinction between the two homophones. It is also quite possible that accent or vocalization would have distinguished one form, say, *zoshek, from the other, say, *zeshek.

58. Gardiner's *Egyptian Grammar*, on pp. 442–48, lists 59 separate glyphs

under the heading "Man and his Occupations," whereas only seven are listed under "Woman and her Occupations."

59. *Pyramid Texts* 657a. The glyph on the right is from the pyramid of Teti, whereas that on the left is found in the pyramids of Merenre' and Neferkare' (Pepi II).

60. The glyph on the left is from *Pyramid Texts* 657a in the pyramid of Merenre'. That on the right is the form found in Faulkner's *Concise Dictionary of Middle Egyptian*, p. 6, cited from *Urkunden des ägyptischen Altertums*, vol. 5, p. 161, line 16.

61. A recent discussion of the "reading" of the Na'rmer Palette can be found in Fairservis, "Naʿrmer Palette." See especially pp. 10f.

62. See John Baines's discussion in *Fecundity Figures*, pp. 42–45.

63. Ibid., p. 42.

64. See above, pp. 54–55.

65. In Chinese there is a greater number of "symbolic" or, more precisely, "self-referential" graphs wherein noniconic written elements are placed in visual relation to one another for the logical expression of some notion. Examples include the archaic graphs for "above" and "below." The former is a longer line (curved in some cases) with a shorter line above it, the latter a longer line with a shorter line below. These have evolved into the following graphs: 上 and 下 .

66. Saussure, *Cours de linguistique générale*, p. 103: "Le signifiant, étant de nature auditive, se déroule dans le temps seul et a les caractères qu'il emprunt au temps; a) il represente une étendue, et b) cette étendue est mesurable dans une seule dimension: c'est une ligne.

"Ce principe est évident, mais il semble qu'on ait toujours négligé de l'énoncer, sans doute parce qu'on l'a trouvé trop simple; cependant il est fondamental et les conséquences en sont incalculables; . . . Tout le mécanisme de la langue en dépend. Par opposition aux signifiants visuels (signaux maritimes, etc.), qui peuvent offrir des complications simultanées sur plusieurs dimensions, les signifiants acoustiques ne disposent que de la ligne de temps; leurs éléments se présentent l'un après l'autre; ils forment une chaîne. Ce caractère apparaît immédiatement dès qu'on les représente par l'écriture et qu'on substitue la ligne spatiale des signes graphiques à la succession dans le temps."

67. Gustave Flaubert, *Madame Bovary*, part 2, chap. 8.

68. In addition to criteria of balance and proportion, one might cite the simple fact that the falcon stands upright, its gaze directed straight forward rather than hunched over as in precanonical versions (such as that on the glyph from the Na'rmer Palette mentioned on p. 76 and Fig. 2.4).

69. There is disagreement about how to read the name in question. Some take it as "Djet," some as "Uadji," and others read into it an iconicity, calling the sovereign in question "the Serpent King."

70. The assumption that the king's *ka* needed a sign to return to his tomb is simply speculation based on what we know of religious and cosmological beliefs centuries more recent.

71. The syntax so pictured is, however, a common occurrence in Egyptian grammar, nicely exemplified in the pharaonic titulary, but evident as well in ubiquitous nominal compounds, patronymics, and appositives. It is not, however, unambiguous, since the direct genitive can take the same morphological structure (the simple juxtaposition of two substantives), and cases where juxtaposition is used to express the independent notion $x = y$ are unusual in literature (here taken in the broadest possible sense of "extended writing about something"). Thus, independent statements where the work of the copula is accomplished by juxtaposition alone are rare.

72. Hieroglyphic inscriptions are true to their name in that they belong overwhelmingly to the category of "sacred inscriptions." Here, in speaking of the sacred, we are not talking about religion in an isolated sense, but about an ideology of divine power that comprehends many aspects of the pharaonic state. This sacred character of the content of hieroglyphic texts goes hand in hand with their inscriptional character. There is a direct link between the writing and the material support in which and upon which it is effected. Hieroglyphs have proved easier to learn to read than the other forms of Egyptian, hieratic and demotic, so, as a practical expedient, modern Egyptologists transcribe hieratic texts into hieroglyphics for publication. But we must not because of this lose sight of the difference in inscriptional context between the hieroglyphic and the hieratic.

73. See Westendorf, "Die Anfänge der altägyptischen Hieroglyphen," pp. 57–87.

74. Similarly successful examples can be found in the lintel of Kha'kaure' Senusert III from Medamud (now in the Cairo museum, illustrated in Lamy, *New Light*, p. 77), the relief of the same pharaoh running before the god Min (now in University College, London, illustrated in Baines and Málek, *Atlas of Ancient Egypt*, p. 111; see Fig. 3.14), and on the lovely "White Chapel" (again, of Senusert III) in the "open-air museum" at Karnak.

75. The sarcophagus of Amenemonet in the Louvre (E 5334) is a fine example. Photographs are to be found in Ziegler, *Louvre*, pp. 72–73.

76. This inadequacy is not, of course, the only reason that these religious doctrines remain so inaccessible. One must be ever aware of prejudices of monotheism and Hellenocentrism, which have obscured our understanding, and it is also important to imagine an "original purpose" for these mysterious texts wherein "explanation" is a low priority. They were probably in large part mnemonic and certainly must have been augmented in a living Egyptian culture by discursive traditions now lost. Priestly training, pietistic discussion, participation in ritual, a far fuller cultural understanding of myth than we can piece together today—all these discursive contexts would have helped to clarify

or more strategically focus the mysteries in these texts. Erik Hornung's fascinating and beautifully illustrated *Valley of the Kings* goes some considerable distance in explaining these difficult texts, but they remain opaque in many important ways.

77. *The Papyrus of Henuttawy* (i.e., Ḥnwt-t3wj, pBM 10018). This papyrus is, as far as I am aware, illustrated in full only in Lanzone's *Dizionario di mitologia egizia* (1884), plate 159.

78. From Drovetti's collection, the papyrus of the Mistress of the Household and Chantress of Amun Mesha'redwyseqeb (i.e., Mšʿ-rdwj-sqb, pTurin 1769), again, of the late Twenty-first Dynasty.

79. The so-called White Chapel was found in pieces as the filler for a pylon erected in the New Kingdom, but was recovered, almost complete, and reconstructed in a courtyard off the main axis of the vast temple complex at Karnak by the French architect Chevrier in 1938. The Egyptian name of the "White Chapel" would translate as "She who elevates Horus, the Beloved of the Double Crown." Parkinson, *Voices from Ancient Egypt*, p. 123.

Structurally rather simple, the building consists of a platform with central ramps leading up from ground level in front and back. Sixteen square columns, arranged in four rows of four, elevate a flat roof with cavetto cornice. The flat surfaces of the building provide excellent space for inscriptions.

80. Tefnin, "Discours et iconicité," pp. 55–56: "Que l'icône et le texte constituent les deux systèmes principaux de représentation par lesquels les société humaines organisent et expriment leur compréhension de l'Univers—réel et imaginaire—, rien n'est plus évident. Dans la seule tradition occidentale, les exemples ne manquent pas d'usage simultané des deux langages, l'un précisant, complétant ou redisant l'autre, pour la production d'un sens plus vaste et plus complexe que ne le permettrait chacun fonctionnant par lui seul: opéra, théâtre, cinéma, image publicitaire, bande dessinée . . . [Tefnin's ellipsis] n'existeraient pas sans cette conjugaison, source essentielle de leur significance. Si, dans d'autres cas, l'intimité paraît moins profonde . . . [my ellipsis] l'apport du langage "secondaire" au langage "principal" provoque inévitablement le surgissement de signifiés de connotation, de suppléments de sens."

81. Ibid., p. 6: "Les signes du système hiéroglyphique se sont maintenus, durant trois millénaires, dans une forme figurative parfaitement identifiable, avec une fermeté que le traditionalisme ne peut suffire à expliquer. Parler de système figé serait méconnaître la réalite d'une évolution manifesteé par de fréquentes créations de signes, particulièrement aux époques tardives qui connurent à cet égard de véritables frénésies. Mais ces signes nouveaux furent toujours de nouvelles images et la création ne mit jamais en cause le caractère essentiellement figuratif de l'écriture. L'explication du phénomène est à chercher sans doute dans la nature même du signe hiéroglyphique dont l'usage comme outil graphique désignant les phonèmes de la langue ne suffit pas à épuiser la complexité. A la fois graphe et symbole, mettant en œuvre un double

signifié, phonologique et représentatif, il se trouve investi, au moins potentiellement, de deux fonctions distinctes, linguistique et sémiotique. Ce "double jeu" de l'écriture paraît bien d'ailleurs n'être qu'une manifestation parmi d'autres du mécanisme le plus caractéristique de la pensée égyptienne, oscillant entre rationalité abstraite et empirisme naturaliste, nourissante l'un par l'autre en un continuel va-et-vient à travers un univers perçu tout à la fois comme signifié et comme signifiant, comme expression et comme substance. Il paraît essentiel, dans cette perspective, de souligner que l'ambiguïté du signe d'écriture, non constamment réaliseé mais toujours latente, trouve un exact équivalent dans la capacité détenue par l'image de fonctionner simultanément sur les modes iconique et hiéroglyphique."

82. Tefnin, "Image, écriture, récit," pp. 7–24.

83. See, for example, Schmandt-Besserat, *Before Writing*, or for a summary presentation, Roaf, *Cultural Atlas*, pp. 70–71.

84. More precisely, *Nt-ḥtp*. There is some controversy about which glyph to read first, and whether the glyph *ḥtp* should be read simply as *ḥtp*, or whether it represents an inflected form of the verbal *ḥtp*, either *ḥtp(tj)* or *ḥtp(wj)*. These subtleties are not of immediate relevance to our argument, but those with further interest may see Kaplony's magisterial *Inschriften*, pp. 590–92, for detailed treatment.

85. I use the uppercase *G* because of Neith's relation to the lineage of a less individuated hypostasis of female divinity, which was, evidently, widespread in the late Neolithic east Mediterranean.

86. She was connected to the early king, 'Aha, either his mother or his consort, perhaps.

87. Schlott, *Schrift und Schreiber im alten Ägypten*, pp. 125f.: "Etwa von der Mitte der 1. Dynastie, das heißt von ca. 2900 v. Chr. an, wurden nichtköniglichen Toten auch Rollsiegel mit ins Grab gegeben, von denen jedoch nur ganz selten eines tatsächlich zum Versiegeln eines Gefäßes benutzt wurde; sie hatten offensichtlich eine andere Funktion. Auf sie sind der Name und Titel des Verstorbenen geschrieben und ein Zusatz, der zeigt, daß das Siegel speziell für den *toten* Grabinhaber hergestellt wurde. Dieser Zusatz kam in zwei Formen vor, die man mit 'Verklärter' und 'Erhabener' übersetzen kann. 'Erhabener' wurde mit dem Zeichen eines auf einem Stuhl sitzenden Mannes geschrieben; daraus entwickelte sich bald das Bild eines Mannes, der vor einem Tisch sitzt und eine Hand nach den darauf liegenden Speisen ausstreckt. Diese Siegel wurden neben den Opfervorräten in den Grabkammern gefunden. Dadurch wird erkennbar, welchem Zweck sie dienten: Nun verwendeten auch nichtkönigliche Personen die Schrift in der Funktion, die ich oben in Bezug auf die Schminkpalette und Keulenköpfe der Könige Skorpion und Narmer beschrieben habe: Um festzuhalten und zu verewigen. Das Wichtigste, was man zum Leben vor und nach dem Tod braucht, sind Nahrungsmittel. Und um sie mit Sicherheit ewig zur Verfügung zu haben, auch

dann, wenn die Naturalbeigaben nicht ausreichten, geraubt waren und die Nachkommen keine mehr brachten, hielt man sie in Hieroglyphenschrift und Bild fest zusammen mit Namen (und Titel) dessen, dem sie zugedacht waren."

88. Ibid., pp. 134–35.

89. Ibid., p. 127.

90. See Chapter 1, pp. 26–27.

91. The discussion in Schäfer's *Principles of Egyptian Art* represents the most detailed and technically precise analysis of this representational system. Consider in this context as well the article on the aspective, by Emma Brunner-Traudt in the same volume, pp. 421–48.

92. Tefnin, "Discours et iconicité," p. 9: "Fondamentale pour la compréhension de l'image égyptienne [est] la reconnaissance de l'enchaînement de niveaux de lecture clairement délimités, depuis l'unité élémentaire de la figure jusqu'à l'unité globale du cosmos, en coïncidence symbolique avec l'unité architecturale du monument. . . . La figure ne saurait être confondue avec un personnage entier, une image de roi par exemple, car celle-ci révèle, à l'analyse, plusieurs unités de sens choisies au sein de séries paradigmatiques nettement délimitées: vêtements, couronnes, insignes, sceptres, couleurs de chairs, gestes interviennent dans une combinatoire complexe créant une véritable "phrase" dont, à l'instar de ce qui se passe dans le langage, le remplacement d'un mot suffit à modifier le sense. Il est à noter que ces figures élémentaires ne possèdent pas nécessairement de référent dans le monde naturel."

93. Baines, *Fecundity Figures*, p. 70.

94. The conjecture comes from the fact that one of the carpenters pictured on the tomb wall is named Neferefre'-'ankh, "Neferefre' lives." See Hassan, *Excavations at Gîza*, 2: 200.

95. This is but the most cursory characterization of a highly sophisticated visual language. It is discussed in magisterial detail in Schäfer's *Principles of Egyptian Art*, esp. chap. 4.

96. This is one of various examples one could cite to show that the Egyptians consciously chose the formal conventions of their art and did not simply blunder into them because of a "primitive" or "childish" technical or perceptual handicap.

97. Cf. Hassan, *Excavations at Gîza*, 2: 190. See also Schlott, *Schrift und Schreiber im alten Ägypten*, pp. 156–62.

98. Thus, for example, Schlott, *Schrift und Schreiber im alten Ägypten*, p. 111: "Man benützte Bild und Schrift, insbesondere die hieroglyphische, auch dazu, etwas buchstäblich 'festzuhalten,' zu 'verewigen.' Dazu genügte es, daß sie vorhanden waren; ob sie auch gesehen werden konnten, war zweitrangig."

99. Gardiner, *Egyptian Grammar*, p. 53, par. 64.

100. Tefnin, "Discours et iconicité, p. 10.

101. Ibid., pp. 10–12: "L'inscription indique, selon une formulation très courante dans les tombes de l'Ancien Empire, que 'le défunt X contemple (m33

au duratif, littéralement: "est contemplant") les félicités de la terre entière'. Dans son unicité, Rahotep nous est ainsi donné pour le sujet d'une relation de contemplation, phénomène déjà par lui-même extrêmement intéressant du point de vue sémiotique et déroutant pour nous, accoutumés comme nous le sommes à être l'émetteur du regard, le lieu unique de la lecture de l'œuvre. L'image de la tombe égyptienne nous ignore. Le spectacle se joue en circuit fermé pour un spectateur-image intérieur à l'image. La position de la statuaire confirme d'ailleurs très clairement le fait, puisqu'elle s'enferme (sous l'Ancien Empire au mains) dans une pièce annexe, murée, obscure (le serdab), percée seulement d'une mince fente qui doit permettre aux statues non d'être vues mais de voir, d'assister à la présentation des offrandes dans la chappelle funéraire."

102. Snefru was a particularly popular pharaoh, and there are even records of a cult of his memory in the Middle Kingdom, but by that time he had been recognized as a member of the pantheon. Trigger, Kemp, O'Connor, and Lloyd, *Ancient Egypt*, p. 95.

103. See, for example, Lichtheim's translation in *Ancient Egyptian Literature*, 1: 99–107, esp. p. 100.

CHAPTER 3 *Coming and Becoming*

1. Petrie, *Koptos*, p. 73. See also the article by Bruce Williams, "Narmer and the Coptos Colossi."

2. Kemp, *Ancient Egypt*, p. 82 and p. 328, n. 24.

3. Stevenson Smith is even more evasive in his account of the images in *Art and Architecture*, pp. 29f.: "Three badly battered standing figures of the fertility god Min were found in the early strata of his temple at Coptos. They were about 13 feet high and are more remarkable for their size than for skill in handling the human figure. The body is in the form of a long cylinder and the stone is worked as little as possible. Only a portion of one bearded head was recovered, with its surface badly damaged. The drawings of shells and animals which are roughly cut on the strip which hangs down from the girdle show a better delineation of form than do the few summary details of the figures themselves."

4. See Lacau and Chevrier, *Une Chapelle*, p. 166, par. 465. The colossi of Min, similarly, reveal concave depressions on the torso and legs where the stone was rubbed away, presumably for some medical or magical purpose.

5. Though note now the sexual significance of the organ overtakes its urinary significance in the latter case: the phallus is always drawn erect, even though many men are apparently incapable of urinating with an erection.

6. See Faulkner, *Concise Dictionary of Middle Egyptian*, p. 106. The citation in question is from the Prisse Papyrus, which contains the important wisdom texts, *The Teaching of Kagemni* and *The Teaching of Ptahhotep*.

7. In his drawing of the stela in *The Egyptian Sudan*, Budge gets this wrong, showing an ejaculating phallus, but Sethe records the glyph more carefully in *Ägyptische Lesestücke*, p. 84, l. 4, noting, moreover, in his *Erläuterungen zu den ägyptischen Lesestücken*, "The word ḥm is determined with a defaced phallus: 'unmanned,' 'unmanly' (apparently, 'womanly'?}" (pp. 137f.). A photograph of the relevant passage from the Semna Stela has appeared in Forman and Quirke, *Hieroglyphs and the Afterlife*, p. 100. See Fig. 3.3, l. 4.

8. Could it, perhaps, mean (rather grandiosely) "in (your) presence" through a hyperbole relating to the cosmogony of Aunu as "generated by (you)" or "existing by (your) grace"?

9. The Semna Stela of Senusert III (Berlin 1157), in Sethe, *Ägyptische Lesestücke*, p. 84.

10. The syntactic structure *Tm(w) pw ḫpr* . . . is precisely that of a definition, establishing an equivalence between Atum on the one hand, and the rest of the sentence through the mechanism of the copular particle, *pw*.

11. *Pyramid Texts* 1248a–d (from Utterance 527). The text is found in slightly variant forms in the pyramids of Meryre' Pepi I, Merenre' Nemtiemzaf, and Neferkare' Pepi II. The version quoted here is from the first, on the basis of the transcription in Sethe, *Die altägyptischen Pyramidentexte*.

12. James Allen, *Genesis*, p. 78.

13. *Pyramid Texts* 1652–1653b (from Utterance 600). The version found in the pyramid of Merenre' Nemtiemzaf I has been partially effaced. The version reproduced here is from the pyramid of Neferkare' Pepi II. It is based on the transcription in Sethe, *Die altägyptischen Pyramidentexte*.

14. Baines, "Bnbn," pp. 390–93.

15. There may be some significance to the choice of *ꜣw* here because of a relation between this sense of expansion and the inception of eternity as "*ḏt* time," or "*djet* eternity," as Assmann puts it. This may suggest a complementarity with the Osiris of the pharaonic cult, who, in begetting the new Horus-king, instantiates the cyclicality of "*nḥḥ* eternity," in contrast to the eternal continuity which proceeds from Atum's masturbation. See Assmann, *Zeit und Ewigkeit*, p. 43.

16. There may be a basic difference in male and female responses to masturbation caused by the biology of orgasm. If male masturbation produces the supplement of semen (or other kinds of supplement), as well as the loss of erection, female masturbation may, as Maria Torok suggests, be the foundation of a female sense of autonomy and power. See her "Meaning of 'Penis Envy,'" esp. pp. 10–15.

17. Budge, *Gods of the Egyptians*, 1: 297.

18. Sethe, *Übersetzung und Kommentar*, 5: 147: "ḫpr wohl nicht Pseud., sondern echtes Part. nach dem 𓂺 bei P. zuschließen. Da das folgende Wort für 'onanieren' nicht, wie man meist angenommen hat . . . mit *iw* 'kommen'

beginnt, das nicht ohne 🕊 und womöglich auch ⟨𓏺𓂻𓅬⟩ geschrieben wäre, sondern mit 🕊 𓂻 'komm,' also ein Ausdruck wie Vergißmeinnicht, Noli me tangere ist und das 🕊 nicht als die Präp. davon abzulösen ist, so wird das *ḫpr* wohl absolut als 'entstehen' zu verstehen sein (nicht 'werden zu')."

"*Ḫpr* (is) not, indeed, a pseudoparticiple, but an authentic participle, after 𓏺🕊, as is brought to closure in Pepi. Then the following word for "masturbate" does not begin, as one has generally taken it . . . with *jw*, 'to come,' which would not be written without *w*, and possibly even ⟨𓏺𓂻𓅬⟩, but with 🕊 𓂻 'come,' thus is an expression like Vergissmeinnicht (Forget-me-not) or Noli me tangere, and the *m* is not therefore to be detached as the proposition, thus the *ḫpr* will be understood absolutely as 'to arise/originate' (not 'turn into')."

19. The glyph displays the dismemberment characteristic of hieroglyphics for animate objects (see Chap. 2, p. 75), but it is interesting to note the disposition of the left hand, held high in the air in the manner of the god Min, who is also commonly depicted with an erect phallus. The same posture is to be observed in certain representations of Osiris. This hieroglyph, however, is found apparently only in the pyramids of Meryre' Pepi I and Merenre' Nemtiemzaf I. In the third occurrence of the text, in the pyramid of Neferkare' Pepi II, it is replaced by the common glyph of an ejaculating phallus.

20. Redford, *Egypt, Canaan, and Israel*, pp. 396f.
21. See also Morenz, *Egyptian Religion*, p. 178.
22. Campbell, *Masks of God*, pp. 85–86.
23. See Quirke, *Ancient Egyptian Religion*, p. 25.
24. James P. Allen suggests that *jšš* means "sneeze," and I adopted his rendering in my earlier translation. Allen, *Genesis*, pp. 14 and 78. If this suggestion is correct, the word has a nice onomatopoetic force.
25. *Coffin Texts* 1.336, 338, 340, 354 (from Utterance 75), according to De Buck's text B2L, from the outer coffin of one Gw³ from el-Bersha, now in the British Museum (BM 38039), with minor restorations from others of the same group. See De Buck, *The Egyptian Coffin Texts*, 1: 336–54 passim.
26. Assmann, "Schöpfung," p. 679: "Die alte Vorstellung der Selbstbegattung und Ausscheidung wird aufgegriffen und zugleich widerrufen zugunsten einer besußten und 'geistigen' Schöpfung."
27. *Coffin Texts* 2.18 (from Utterance 77), according to De Buck's texts B1Bo, from the outer coffin of one Ḏḥwtnḫt from el-Bersha, now in Boston (20.1822–27) and De Buck's text G1T, the inner coffin of one Jqr from Gebelein, now in Turin. See De Buck, *Egyptian Coffin Texts*, 2: 18. Translation from Faulkner, *Ancient Egyptian Coffin Texts*, 1: 73.
28. First, since it is not possible to construct voice in the second person without constructing at the same time a voice in the first, the supposedly originary one is/are already two. And since sexual pleasure cannot be explicitly fig-

ured without reference to the gender of subject, a narration of (stricto sensu) origins in double sexual embrace must be narrated from yet a third position, that of an observer. Only thus could a "gender-neutral" position be articulated.

Compare in *Gita Govinda* the position of the singer, a subject position designated "Jayadeva," in the observation of Krishna and Radha. The relation of bhakti in this context is comparable to the third position in a cosmogony as outlined here, even though, of course, the lovemaking of Krishna and Radha is not explicitly cosmogenesis, however much one might argue it is the making of a certain kind of world.

In the case of the *Pyramid Texts*, there may have been an actual first person narrator in some of the passages we have been dealing with, but grammatical marking is far less important here than subject position as discussed below.

29. Jan Assmann, in "When Justice Fails," offers an instructive example of how the grammatical person of a given utterance may differ from the ontological person to whom the utterance applies, "This first set of curses [from Deuteronomy 27.11–13] begins with 'cursed be he who (ārûr),' then follows a specific crime. These curses are to be shouted before all the people and the people is to confirm everyone of them by responding 'Amen'; therefore, they are actually self-imprecations and the repeated 'cursed be he' has to be understood as 'cursed shall I be if I . . . '" (p. 161). These curses are performative language, and in that respect different from the language in question in *Pyramid Text* 1248, but the shift in person is the important point, and illustrates an important disjunction between grammatical category and subject position.

30. *Coffin Texts* 1.354 (from Utterance 75). See above, p. 116.

31. The name of Atum finds relatively frequent mention in various litanies, and he is occasionally represented as well—as a mummified god wearing the crowns of Upper and Lower Egypt (e.g., scenes of weighing the heart in pBM 9901 and 10470, the papyri of Hunefer and Ani). He is also given concrete form as any of a number of different animals. See Myśliwiec, *Studien zum Gott Atum*.

32. Plutarch, *Peri Isidos kai Osiridos* 18, 258B.

33. A more detailed account of the chapel can be found in David, *Religious Ritual*, pp. 178–82.

34. See, for example, Morenz, *Egyptian Religion*, pp. 262f.

35. Quirke, *Ancient Egyptian Religion*, p. 17.

36. Jakobsohn, "Kamutef": "Die Götter Min und Amun werden seit der 18. Dyn. häufig so genannt und ithyphallisch dargestellt. Der Kamutef steht in engem Zusammenhang mit dem göttlichen Königtum: ein Gott, der eine Göttin, vor allem die Königin, im gleichen Akt zu seiner Gattin wie zu seiner Mutter macht, indem sie den Zeugenden selbst wiedergebiert als 'Sohn.' Es handelt sich nicht um 'Selbstentstehung' des Urgottes, sondern um die stets sich wiederholende Gottes-Erneuerung (Inkarnation) in den wechselnden Erscheinungsformen der gott-menschlichen Dynastie. . . . Der Kamutef stellt die Wesenseinheit eines göttlichen Sohnes dar, so auch des Sonnengottes und

des Pharao, und damit auch die Wesenseinheit der gesamten gott-menschlichen Ahnenreihe mit dem Gott einerseits und dem jeweils regierenden König andererseits."

37. The most remarkable example may perhaps be the *Instruction for Merikare'*, which purports to be a testament from one king to his son and successor. A translation is readily available in Lichtheim, *Ancient Egyptian Literature*, 1: 97–109. So also *The Instruction of King Amenemhet I for His Son Sesostris I*, in *Ancient Egyptian Literature*, 1: 134–39.

38. A hieroglyphic transcription of the original hieratic is available in Gardiner, *Late Egyptian Stories*, pp. 37–60. The most readily available English translation is in Lichtheim, *Ancient Egyptian Literature*, 2: 214–23. Gustave Lefebvre's French translation and commentary with extensive notes is also very helpful, in *Romans et contes égyptiens*, pp. 178–203.

39. Attitudes regarding homosexuality in ancient Egypt have attracted a certain amount of scholarly attention. The best and most recent survey is Parkinson's "'Homosexual' Desire," pp. 57–76. Parkinson focuses on Middle Kingdom literature but has important insights on the construction of homosexuality in Egypt in a more general sense.

40. In "Further Notes on Phallism in Ancient Egypt," Hornblower discusses the occasion of the public display of the sodomization of a criminal as his punishment in Cairo with a strong orientalist fascination and exoticism, suggesting the highly implausible possibility of a historical connection between this phenomenon and ancient Egyptian attitudes vis-à-vis anal penetration.

41. That is, to be specific, the distaste for the anal penetration of one male by another. To define "homosexuality" by this particular act may be excessively restrictive, however, and similarly, to speak of an Egyptian distaste for homosexuality in broad terms may read too much into the scant and ambiguous references to the topic in extant texts. There is an earlier version of the homosexual episode from the conflict between Horus and Setekh in a Middle Kingdom papyrus from Kahun. There, Horus narrowly evades penetration by Setekh. In a fragmentary account of the last days of Pepi II, the pharaoh himself is severely criticized, apparently for consorting with one of his generals. Clearly, anal penetration brought derision on the passive participant. It may not have resulted in a particular stigma on the agent of penetration. If so, this construction of a certain species of homosexual behavior has much in common with classical Greek and subsequent constructions thereof. It is important to distinguish this particular attitude, however, from the abundantly evident celebration of the phallus between males (especially between a god and pharaoh), which might also be characterized as a type of homosexual or homosocial intimacy. See below, pp. 148.

42. A hieroglyphic transcription of the original hieratic is available in Gardiner, *Late Egyptian Stories*, pp. 9–29. Translations in Lichtheim, *Ancient Egyptian Literature*, 2: 203–10, and Lefebvre, *Romans et contes*, pp. 137–58. See also Hollis, *Two Brothers*, especially pp. 5–15.

43. The designation goes back to at least 1859, when W. Mannhardt so dubbed it. See Hollis, *Two Brothers*, p. 16.

44. Hollis gives an entertaining account thereof, in *Two Brothers*, pp. 16–48. See also the opening of Blumenthal's important article, "Die Erzählung des Papyrus d'Orbiney als Literaturwerk."

45. Lichtheim, *Ancient Egyptian Literature*, 2: 203.

46. Ibid., p. 204.

47. The pJumilhac (III, 12–25; I, x+4, to II, 20, and XX, 1–22, among others) contains versions and variations of the story, but makes the dubious equation of Bata with Setekh. See Hollis, *Two Brothers*, pp. 47–48, 171–76.

48. Lichtheim, *Ancient Egyptian Literature*, 2: 207.

49. *Papyrus d'Orbiney* (pBM 10183), sheet 9, line 8, in Gardiner, *Late Egyptian Stories*, p. 19. The pointed brackets indicate Gardiner's emendation, which Lichtheim incorporates into her translation.

50. Ibid., sheet 1, line 4, in Gardiner, *Late Egyptian Stories*, p. 10.

51. On the "Seven Hathors," see Redford, *Egypt, Canaan, and Israel*, p. 233, n. 101.

52. See above, pp. 000.

53. In *Egyptian Religion*, p. 26, Morenz notes other attempts to explain cosmogenesis from a sexually undifferentiated urgod.

54. The female as guardian finds expression not only in the myth of Osiris, but also in the funerary practices of the royal pharaohs. The internal organs retrieved during the process of mummification were, in the most elaborate burials, separately embalmed and eventually interred in "canopic jars," which were dedicated to the four sons of Horus, Imsety, Duamutef, Qebehsenuf, and Ha'py. The jars often incorporated busts of these four gods into their lids. Whereas the gods on the jars were all, of course, males, these jars themselves were then often secured in a canopic chest, the four corners of which were decorated with images of four *goddesses*, who held out their winged arms in protection of the organs enclosed in the chest. Similar deployments of these goddesses as protectors are sometimes found on the corners of stone sarcophagi or on mummy cases themselves.

55. Thutmose II died young. His mummy was found in a cache in Deir el-Bahari, and it is the body of a 25- to 30-year-old male. See Christine Meyer, "Thutmosis II.," pp. 539f.

56. At least two other women held the position of pharaoh apparently. The earliest example is Nitiqret (Manetho's "Nitocris") of the Sixth Dynasty; then again, in the Nineteenth Dynasty, the queen Twosre' (Sitre' Meritamun) was regent for her stepson Siptah.

57. *Urkunden des ägyptischen Altertums IV: Urkunden der 18. Dynastie*, pp. 219–20, discussed in Brunner, *Die Geburt des Gottkönigs*, pp. 42ff. The repeated use of "and" is intentional in translation of the Egyptian particle *sw*, and the expression "gave his heart into her" represents a slight alteration of the direct translation of the Egyptian *rdj jb=f r=s*, which, if translated as "gave

his heart to her" might erroneously evoke the romantic associations of that English expression without the daring sexual significance the phrase had in Egyptian. See Müller, "Die Zeugung durch das Herz."

"Punt" refers to a distant and exoticized land with which Egypt had sporadic trade relations. Hatshepsut had the Punt trade depicted carefully in friezes at her temple at Deir el-Bahari.

58. Gardiner, *Egyptian Grammar*, p. 448.

59. Ibid., pp. 442–49.

60. The reproductive life of animals, on the contrary, is a common subject on tomb walls and is probably related to notions of fecundity and rebirth.

61. Schäfer, *Principles of Egyptian Art*, p. 18.

62. Robins, *Women in Ancient Egypt*, p. 180. Exceptions can occasionally be found, as for instance in the female overseer of weavers pictured in the tomb of Khnumhotep at Beni Hasan. A facsimile of the painting by Norman DeGaris Davies can be found in Wilkinson and Hill, *Egyptian Wall Paintings*, p. 71, 33.8.16.

63. The tombs of Khety, Baqet III, and Amenemhet at Beni Hasan are famous for their wrestling scenes. Stick fighting scenes can be found in the tomb of Kheruef at Thebes (TT 192). An exception to the rule about fighting can be seen in the tomb of Menena in Thebes (TT 69), where in one register, two girls are tearing each other's hair out. In the lower register a girl removes a thorn from the foot of another girl.

64. The "subject" in question must, of course, be reconstructed by each individual viewer on each individual occasion, and the erotic content of a given representation must, of course, vary accordingly. We cannot, however, abandon all effort to historicize the constructions of "the erotic" and must try to cast the widest net possible to do so, cognizant all the time that our sample will always be incomplete. See remarks in Exerguer, pp. 5–9.

65. Kozloff, in Kozloff and Bryan, *Egypt's Dazzling Sun*, p. 271.

66. Ibid.: "Under this artist's brush adult female figures became more voluptuous and their drapery gauzier, Men[e]na's wife in the scene before Osiris being a perfect example."

67. W. Stevenson Smith, *Art and Architecture*, p. 255.

68. Ibid.

69. N. Davies, *The Tomb of Rekh-Mi-Reʿ at Thebes*, pp. 62f.

70. Schäfer, *Principles of Egyptian Art*, p. 264.

71. The perceived discrepancy between the depiction of the feet and that of the posterior may be interpreted as a positioning directed toward the gaze of Rekhmire'.

72. N. Davies, *The Tomb of Rekh-Mi-Reʿ at Thebes*, pl. 63: sḥm-jb mꜣ bw nfr ḥs(j) ḫbt šmʿ wrḥ ʿntyw.

73. Both formally, within the "closed" (Tefnin) system of the picture surface itself, and, more important, in the epistemological sense whereby the actual viewers of these scenes were predominantly male.

74. Or at least to homosexual penetration as passive participant. See Parkinson, "'Homosexual' Desire."

75. Milne, *History of Egypt*, p. 220.

76. Kemp, however, does picture an ostracon from the reign of Kha'sekhemwy of the Second Dynasty, ca. 2640 B.C.E., as the earliest recognizable image of Min, as well as a Sixth Dynasty representation of the god from a royal decree of Pepi I, ca. 2250 B.C.E. See Kemp, *Ancient Egypt*, p. 86, fig. 29.

Regarding the term "vajra-like," although my ambitions here do not encompass the temerity of trying to show a link between this symbol of Tantric Buddhism and the cult of Min, there is a tantalizing similarity between the vajra and the so-called Min symbol. The link between both these religious icons and the thunderbolt is well demonstrated, as is the relation to the erect phallus.

77. A near match for the representation of pharaoh is found as early as the Third Dynasty, among the few portrayals of King Netjerkhet (commonly known as Djoser) from under the Step Pyramid at Saqqara, but in the Saqqara relief, there is no representation of any god watching from the sidelines, much less an ithyphallic one.

78. The scene is on the second pillar from the east side in the northernmost row of pillars in the chapel. Lacau and Chévrier, in *Une Chapelle*, make it their "scène 22" and describe it on page 90 with further observations on the perplexing multiplicity it engages on pages 178ff. It is reproduced in Parkinson, *Voices from Ancient Egypt*, p. 122.

79. Consider as well the Restoration Stela of Tut'ankhamun, where the word *tw3*, "establish," "maintain," is written not with the usual determinative of a god holding up the sky glyph, but rather with the erect phallus glyph. See Chapter 4, pp. 205–6.

80. Kozloff and Bryan, *Egypt's Dazzling Sun*, p. 126.

81. Named for the modern name of the site of the ancient capital Akhetaten. The term has been widely used to refer to the reign of Nebkheperure' Amenhotep IV, or Akhenaten, and to the various distinctive cultural manifestations of that reign.

82. Aldred, *Akhenaten*, pp. 231–32.

83. As on, for example, the ivory label from among the finds relating to him at Abydos (British Museum, EA 55586).

84. Standing between the feet of a great falcon, for example, in a statue in the Metropolitan Museum.

85. Note the use of Amenhotep's facial features as a kind of hieroglyph which is stamped even on other figures in his reign. See Kozloff and Bryan, *Egypt's Dazzling Sun*, pp. 128f. and 237f.

86. I follow Jan Assmann's suggestion of this term, a suggestion he made after his lecture "Suppressed History—Repressed Memory? Moses and Akhenaten in Greek and Latin Texts," at Stanford University, March 1, 1995.

87. Such a suggestion has a certain plausibility, especially in an interpretive scheme which takes it together with two other types of colossus found at the same site. According to this scheme, the other two colossi would be seen as the gods Atum and Shu, instantiated in two aspects of Akhenaten himself, while the third, seemingly naked one, would be taken as Tefnut, instantiated as Nefertiti. And it is true that there are other plausible examples in which the divine triad of Atum, Shu, and Tefnut are given earthly form in a divine triad in Amarna, with Akhenaten and Nefertiti taking the part of the progeny. In those cases, though, the role of Atum is figured upon the solar disk, and not upon a second Akhenaten. If, moreover, the seemingly naked statue is not in fact a representation of Akhenaten at all, but rather, of Nefertiti, then how are we to explain its beard?

88. Redford, *Akhenaten*, p. 104.

89. Barry Kemp makes the interesting point that it is not only the feminizing representational strategies that are of significance. There is also a notable imbalance in the dramatis personae of Amarnan relief: "The composition of the royal family group is itself noteworthy. Apart from Akhenaten it is entirely female. For in addition to Nefertiti up to six daughters are shown as well.... It is possible that this exclusively female group is a faithful depiction of the full extent of Akhenaten's own family. Good evidence exists, however, for making Tut'ankhamun a son of Akhenaten, though not necessarily by Nefertiti, since Akhenaten is know to have had more than one wife. If this is so, emphasis on femininity may itself be a face of Akhenaten's ideology." Kemp, *Ancient Egypt*, p. 266.

A wonderful study of the archaeological context of the Nefertiti bust is to be found in Dorothea Arnold's recent catalog for an exhibition at the Metropolitan Museum of Art in New York, "The Workshop of the Sculptor Thutmose," in *Royal Women of Amarna*, pp. 41–84.

90. Paglia, *Sexual Personae*, pp. 68f.

91. Some of Paglia's assertions seem merely rhetorical. She states, for example, "The reign of Chephren ... gave Egypt its supreme style" (*Sexual Personae*, p. 57), and we must ask how "supreme" is to be understood. If she intends to refer to the full development of the canonical style, why does she skip over, say, Netjerkhet (Djoser)? At other times, she falls into the most conventional and outdated orientalisms: "An absolutist geography produced an absolutist politics and aesthetics" (p. 59). This is the line taken by Wittfogel in his discussions in "Oriental Despotism," but as Barry Kemp has pointed out (Kemp, *Ancient Egypt*, pp. 11–13), the assumption that early riverine civilizations needed strong centralized political organizations for the requisite irrigation schemes to work does not hold for ancient Egypt, with its reliable and relatively easily managed agricultural cycle based on the Nile floods. In Paglia's at times quite interesting revision of "our debt to the Greeks," she falls for the conventional contrast between Greece and Egypt and fails to recognize the continuity of many

Egyptian ideas in the subsequent east Mediterranean. She asserts, for example, "Words are the most removed of human inventions from things-as-they-are" (p. 61), aiming at a contrast between the Egyptians on the one hand and the Greeks and Hebrews on the other. Our examination of Egyptian notions of language above, however, undoes the polarity she intends to set up. It is worth noting that despite nearly a century of advances in Egyptology since, Paglia chooses to base her arguments on Budge's *Gods of the Egyptians*. Thus it is not surprising that she drags out his hackneyed characterization of Egyptian religion: "Chthonian mysteries are the secret of Egypt's perennial fascination. The gross and barbaric proliferated" (*Sexual Personae*, p. 62).

CHAPTER 4 ... *Three, Two, One, Zero*

1. More properly, *kršt* bread, which Herodotus calls *kullēstis*.
2. Alan H. Gardiner, *Ancient Egyptian Onomastica*, 2: 228–33.
3. Fascinating materials on the scientific classification of fish have been assembled by Gamer-Wallert in *Fische und Fischkulte im alten Ägypten*.
4. Kemp, *Ancient Egypt*, p. 29.
5. If there is a field in which names maintain a plausible reality status, it is the field of imprecation and slander, fighting words and vicious deprecation. Thus "nigger," "faggot," "cunt," and so on maintain a reality status by virtue of their emotional content, which cannot be ascribed to "circle," "apple tree," and "positivistic." And even here, of course, the reality status of such words is open to manipulation, and is thus not stable. Richard Pryor's use of "nigger" has a very different status from George Wallace's; the proponents of "queer theory" mean by "queer" something very different from those who intend it as a slightly less abrasive synonym for "faggot."
6. Kemp, *Ancient Egypt*, p. 29. I follow Kemp in rendering the scribe's name "Amenemope." Gardiner calls him "Amenopĕ." A similar predilection for lists can be found among the ancient Mesopotamians. See Bottéro, *Mesopotamia*, esp. pp. 29–32.
7. Kemp, *Ancient Egypt*, p. 29.
8. Baines, *Fecundity Figures*, p. 70.
9. Thus, how often have we heard that the Egyptians could not think abstractly, as the Greeks did, and so on. This contention not only confuses the presence of one thing with the absence of another, but also ignores the fact that our Greek sources come to us in a long and continuous tradition of transmission over the centuries, a tradition in which each generation took great pains to preserve texts of all kinds and make them intelligible to the next. The overwhelming majority of Egyptian texts, on the other hand, come to us after an extraordinary hiatus, and from the narrowly delineated sphere of the necropolis. Why should we expect to find extended "scientific" or "philosophical" speculation in such a corpus?

10. "Als Folge der Vorstellung von der Substanzierung einer höherwertigen Macht und Kraft in der Opfergabe kann sich die Übergabe des Opfer nicht als einfache Darreichung einer Gabe abspielen, sondern muß durch einen Ritus geheiligt werden." Altenmüller, "Opfer," p. 579.

"Die Weihe und Heiligung des Opfers erfolgt durch das Ritual. Während des Opfervorgangs werden Sprüche rezitiert, durch die die Opfergabe und die Handlung selbst mit mythischen Dingen und Ereignissen verbunden werden. Da der König kraft seines Amtes und seiner Legitimation allein für den Opferkult verantwortlich ist, übernimmt die Mythologisierung vor allem Themen aus dem Königsmythos, der eng auf die Götter Horus, Seth und Osiris bezogen ist." Ibid., p. 583.

11. One further corollary might be that ritual might itself constitute offerings without the accompaniment of either objects or images and words representing them. Such a possibility is not apparent in the extant evidence from Egypt, but there is no reason to believe, given the immaterial nature of such a process, that it would be apparent.

12. Hornung, *Conceptions of God*, pp. 33–65.

13. See, for instance, Loprieno's reconstruction in *Ancient Egyptian*, p. 35.

14. Hornung, *Conceptions of God*, p. 38.

15. More commonly, though, the $3h$ is written as a bird, illustrating a difference between the quotidian existence of humans and the beatified state of being the blessed dead were thought to attain.

16. Most famous is the Apis bull, sacred to Ptah and, of course, associated with Memphis, but at Aunu, the Mnevis bull, sacred to Re', was revered, and similarly, the Buchis bull had a cult following in Armant because of his association with the falcon-headed martial god Montu.

17. Morenz, *Egyptian Religion*, p. 156.

18. See now, Kemp, "How Religious Were the Ancient Egyptians?"

19. Morenz, *Egyptian Religion*, p. 142.

20. Hornung, *Conceptions of God*, p. 57.

21. See Assmann, *Re und Amun*.

22. Depending on the text in question, there is some variation in the characterizations of preexistence. See below, for instance, where hiddenness is replaced by pathlessness (p. 168). My point, however, remains the same.

23. Redford, *Egypt, Canaan, and Israel*, p. 39.

24. Gardiner, *Ancient Egyptian Onomastica*, 1: 13–98.

25. Leyden hymns 4.21–22, in Prichard, *Ancient Near Eastern Texts*, p. 369; quoted in Morenz, *Egyptian Religion*, p. 144.

26. *Coffin Texts* 2.39b–q (from Utterance 80), according to the text on the outer coffin of one Gw₃ from el-Bersha, now in the British Museum (BM 38039), with minor restorations from others of the same group in De Buck, *Egyptian Coffin Texts*, 2: 39. I cannot agree with Faulkner's reading of this text. He takes *jr.n* in *jr.n Tmw smw* as an independent verb in the *sḏm.n=f* form rather than as a relative *sḏm.n=f*. He then goes on to read the appositive

smsw, "elder," as an abstract noun, "eldership." But see Morenz, *Egyptian Religion,* p. 145.

27. Jan Assmann, "Schöpfung," pp. 678–79: "In den Sargtexten, und zwar der auf den Gott Schu bezogenen Spruchfolge 75–83, erscheint diese Theologie bereits in einer wesentlich elaborierteren Form. Der vorweltliche Zustand wird in vier Kategorien beschrieben: Nun (Urwasser), Huh (Endlosigkeit), Tenemu (Weglosigkeit) und Kuk (Finsternis). Atum 'schwimmt' ... 'müde' ... 'träge' ... im Nun, bewältigt in einem Akt der Autogenese ... den Übergang von der Präexistenz zur Existenz und gleichzeitig damit bereits zur Dreiheit: im selben 'Atemzug' entstehen aus dem selbstgestandenen Urgott Schu und Tefnut. Die alte Vorstellung der Selbstbegattung und Ausscheidung wird aufgegriffen und zugleich widerrufen zugunsten einer bewußten ... und 'geistigen' Schöpfung. Besonders wichtig ist für Spruch 80 die in Pyr. 1653 als Ka-Umarmung beschriebene Konstellation des 'zu Drei gewordenen' Einen mit seinen Kindern, die als Verkörperung kosmongonischer Prinzipien 'Leben' (*'nḫ*) und 'Maat' sowie 'Neheh' und 'Djet' genannt werden. Im gleichen Sinne kosmogonischer Prinzipien entstehen nach anderen Überlieferungen der Zaubergott Heka ... und das Paar Hu und Sia ('Befehlswort' und 'Erkenntnis') in dieser allersten kosmogonischen Phase."

28. Hornung, *Conceptions of God,* p. 176.
29. Erman, *Ein Denkmal memphitischer Theologie.*
30. Breasted, "Philosophy of a Memphite Priest."
31. Ibid., p. 40.
32. Ibid., p. 39.
33. Sethe, *Das "Denkmal memphitischer Theologie,"* and Junker, *Die Götterlehre von Memphis.*
34. Breasted, "Philosophy of a Memphite Priest," pp. 41f.
35. Thus Grimal states that "the third major Egyptian system of cosmology was by far the most sophisticated, from a theological point of view. This system is known from a unique document in the British Museum, dating to the reign of the Kushite ruler Shabaka, at the end of the seventh century B.C. It consists of a large granite slab from the temple of Ptah at Memphis, which bears an inscription claiming to be the copy of an old 'worm-eaten' papyrus: it combines the elements of the Heliopolitan and Hermopolitan systems in an attempt to establish the local god Ptah in the role of demiurge. The Heliopolitan and Osirid elements seem to dominate the text, but at the same time there is a clear movement towards greater abstraction in the description of the process of creation, which consists of the combined use of thought and word.

"*The original version of this text obviously dates to the Old Kingdom,* during which Memphis played a primary national role. It can probably be traced back more specifically to the Fifth Dynasty, when the Heliopolitan doctrine was definitively introduced." Grimal, *A History of Ancient Egypt,* p. 45 (my emphasis).

36. Junge, "Zur Fehldatierung."

37. Ibid., p. 201: "Man vergegenwärtige sich überdies die persönliche Lage Schabakos. Bokchoris und das neuerlich 'aufständische' Unterägypten (mit seinen zwar 'libyschen,' aber als Ägypter sicherlich 'etablierteren' Fürsten) hatte er unterwerfen müssen; Wege mußten gefunden werden, das Land zu 'befrieden.' Es konnte sicherlich als Geste gegenüber den traditionsbewußten Kreisen, die vielleicht eben noch im Aufstand gegen die Äthiopen standen, kaum etwas Wirkungsvolleres geben als eine Stele aufzustellen, die einen alten Text konservierte, der einmal die (endlich wieder erfolgte) Vereinigung von Ober- und Unterägypten unter einen Herrn, 'den rechtmäßigen Erben des ganzen Reiches,' auf mythischer Ebene abhandelte, und dies in der Beziehung Horus-Seth eher auf versöhnliche Weise, zum anderen auch das alte Memphis, die 'Waage der beiden Länder,' in den Vordergrund stellte, dessen Herr Schabako nun war und dessen Tradition er offenbar nicht nur zu achten, sondern gar zu fördern offensichtlich bereit war; dies alles unter den Augen des allmächtigen Schöpfergottes Ptah, dessen 'Wohlwollen' er für sich in Anspruch nehmen konnte, dem schon sein Bruder und Vorgänger Pije (Pianchi) besondere Ehrfurcht entgegengebracht hatte, aber auch Schabako selbst etwa durch Erweiterung des Ptahtempels in Karnak."

38. Ibid., p. 202: "Daß nämlich durchaus alte Texte, die sich möglicherweise 'wurmzerfressen' in den Bibliotheken befanden, sei es komplett oder in Form von 'Handbüchern,' als Quellen verschiedensten Gewichts in den Text eingegangen sind; die direkte Kompilation dürfte dabei eine geringere Rolle gespielt haben als die Adaption und freie Umformung im Sinne einer komplexeren und fortgeschritteneren Neugestaltung, so daß der Text nun wirklich 'schöner is als er früher war.'"

39. In J. P. Allen, *Genesis*, pp. 91–93.
40. Sauneron and Yoyotte, "La Naissance," pp. 62–64 and passim.
41. Breasted, "Philosophy of a Memphite Priest," p. 43.
42. For instance, much of the papyrus of Ani. The most extensive study of retrograde writing is Henry G. Fischer, *Egyptian Studies II*.
43. Fischer, "Hieroglyphen," p. 1192.
44. Breasted, "Philosophy of a Memphite Priest," p. 44.
45. Sauneron and Yoyotte, "La Naissance," p. 63: "Un des rares écrits égyptiens analysant de façon méthodique, non sans de remarkables raffinements en matière de psychologie expérimentale, la genèse de l'univers créé."
46. Redford, *Egypt, Canaan, and Israel*, p. 398.
47. Breasted, "Philosophy of a Memphite Priest," p. 45.
48. Ibid., p. 46.
49. The problem is exacerbated by the orthographical indeterminacy of the major verbal conjugation (the $sḏm=f$) and the general paucity of precise orthographical notation for inflection in verbs, even though it is clear enough that verbs were inflected and that subtle gradations of emphasis, contingency, and causality were indicated in this, as well as by other, means. For a sense of the state of the controversy, one might consult Englund and Frandsen, *Crossroad*.

50. This reading is not unique, but neither is it the only way to write the word. One might assume that had the writer wished to avoid the association with "heart," here, he would have used a purely phonetic spelling.

51. In this case, moreover, the scroll determinative, which might have encouraged a more abstract reading of the phallus, has been omitted.

52. Junker, *Die Götterlehre von Memphis*, p. 55: "Nach der Lehre von Heliopolis hat Atum sie auf unnatürliche Weise erzeugt, nach der Lehre von Memphis dagegen hat Ptaḥ sie durch sein Wort geschaffen. Wenn wir den in prägnanter Redeweise abgefaßten Text in ausführlicherer Sprachweise wiedergeben, lautet er, 'Seine Neunheit is vor ihm, geschaffen durch sein Wort = seine Zähne un Lippen, die dem Phallos und den Fingern des Atum entsprechen. Es soll ja (wie man in Heliopolis sagt) die Neunheit durch den Phallos und die Finger des Atum entstanden sein. In Wirklichkeit aber ist die Götterneunheit entstanden durch das Word = Zähne und Lippen in diesem Munde, der all Dinge benannte usw.'"

53. Ibid p. 56: "Es ist freilich etwas Eigenes um das Sinnbildhafte in der ägyptischen Religion, die Grenze zwischen Bild und Wirklichkeit verschwimmt hier sehr leicht, man hängt oft so stark am Bilde, daß sein sinnbildlicher Charakter darüber ganz in den Hintergrund tritt. Das ist vor allem da der Fall, wo kosmische Mächte verpersönlict und örtlichen Gottheiten gleichgesetzt werden, wie etwa Schu und Tefnut."

54. Breasted, "Philosophy of a Memphite Priest," pp. 50f.

55. Junge, "Zur Fehldatierung," p. 203: "Darüber hinaus verraten etwa die Vorstellungen Junkers von der Konzeption der Niederschrift eine wohl nur in der Nachfolge Ermans verstehbare Arroganz darin, den Ägypter für unfähig zu halten, seine eigene Sprache und seine eigenen Denkkategorien adäquat zu erfassen. Was wir von dem Text verstehen können, zeigt ein intellektuelles Niveau, das zur Vorsicht zwingen sollte gegenüber der Feststellung des 'befremdenen Mangels an Folgerichtigkeit': daß wir diese nicht voll erkennen, spricht eher gegen unsere 'Eindringtiefe' in die Logik und Komplexität 'bildhafter' Weltinterpretation."

"On top of that, Junker's ideas about the drafting of the copy sometime betray an arrogance fully comprehensible only in the succession of Erman, wherein one holds the Egyptian incapable of recording adequately his own language and his own categories of thought. What we can understand of this text shows an intellectual level which should compel us to caution against the establishment of a 'strange deficiency to logical consistency'; what we do not fully recognize speaks rather against our deep intrusion into the logic and complexity of a symbolic interpretation of the world."

56. As we can see from Breasted, "Philosophy of a Memphite Priest," p. 54: "The early Egyptian did much more and much better thinking on abstract subjects than we have hitherto believed, having formed a philosophical conception of the world of men and things, of which no people need be ashamed. . . . It is obvious that the above conception of the world forms quite a sufficient

basis for suggesting the later notions of νοῦς and λόγος, hitherto supposed to have been introduced into Egypt from abroad at a much later date. Thus the Greek tradition of the origin of their philosophy in Egypt undoubtedly contains more of truth than has in recent years been conceded. . . . The habit, later so prevalent among the Greeks of interpreting philosophically the functions and relations of the Egyptian gods, thus importing a profound significance which they originally never possessed, had already begun in Egypt, centuries before the earliest of the Greek philosophers was born; and it is not impossible that Greek practice of so interpreting their own gods, received its first impulse from Egypt."

57. John A. Wilson, in Frankfort et al., *Intellectual Adventure of Ancient Man*, p. 59.

58. Ibid., pp. 6of.

59. *Coffin Texts* (Utterance 261), De Buck, *Egyptian Coffin Texts*, 3: 382–89, according to De Buck's text S3C, from the coffin of one Jt-jb=j from Asyut (now Cairo 36444), with restorations from text S1C from the inner coffin of Msḫt, also of Asyut (now Cairo 28118).

60. As a verb, *ḫpr* has a range of meaning corresponding with the English spectrum of "come into being," "become," "change into," "grow up," "happen," "take place," "come to pass," "be effective," "be fully cooked," "transpire" (as of ages or time), "come" (again, of time), "accrue to," and "amount to." In a transitive sense, it can mean "bring about." Idiomatically, the term is found in the expressions *jrj mj ḫpr*, "to behave properly" (lit., "to do as becomes") and *jmj ḫpr*, "get it done!" (lit., "give the becoming of . . .").

61. Shortly before this passage is the very similar *ḫpr.j ḫpr ḫprw* (pBremner-Rhind 28, 20), "My coming into being is the coming into being of what is come into being."

62. We might plausibly assume that something is lost in translation, particularly something of the wit of the original. See also P. Vernus, "Formes 'emphatiques' en fonction non 'emphatique,'" *Göttinger Miszellen* 43 (1981) 73–74; and F. Junge, "A Study on Sequential Meaning and the Notion of 'Emphasis' in Middle Egyptian," and A. Loprieno, "Egyptian Grammar and Textual Features," both in Englund and Frandsen, *Crossroad*, pp. 195 and 271–72.

63. The most interesting recent addition to this literature is Assmann, *Moses the Egyptian*. Assmann discusses the possible remnant of an ancient Egyptian image of Akhenaten in subsequent characterizations of Moses and the Jews, with particular attention to the relation posited between Moses and Egypt in the Protestant Enlightenment in northern Europe.

64. Breasted, *Development of Religion and Thought*, pp. 342–43.

65. See, for instance, Redford's account in *Akhenaten*, p. 176.

66. Thus, the discovery of thousands of small stone blocks inside the second and ninth pylons at Karnak brought to light the remains of a major temple

to Akhenaten's god, "The Living Sundisk," in the very heart of the temple of His divine rival, Amun.

67. From the Great Hymn to Aten, after Sandman, "The Tomb of Eje," from *Texts from the Time of Akhenaten*, p. 94, ll. 3-10.

68. Ibid., ll. 13-16.

69. Although Assmann's work on New Kingdom solar religion provides an important corrective. See *Egyptian Solar Religion*, Anthony Alcock's translation of Assmann's *Re und Amun*.

70. Grimal, *A History of Ancient Egypt*, p. 230.

71. Breasted, *Development of Religion and Thought*, p. 331

72. Including the suffix pronoun =k, the enclitic pronoun tw, and the Late Egyptian independent pronoun tw.k.

73. Assmann, *Ägypten*, pp. 243-53.

74. Ibid., p. 246.

75. It might well be that just as the Egyptian writing systems, especially hieroglyphs, allow access to a range of figurative meaning impossible to attain with simple alphabets or syllabaries, they also constrain the antifiguralism of someone such as Akhenaten to an unavoidable reliance in some degree on figurality. Thus the common and perfectly understandable, but all the same mistaken, association of the Amarnan god with the sun disk proper.

76. Assmann, *Zeit und Ewigkeit*, p. 58 (his emphasis): "Der kosmische Gott is im Licht und in der Zeit das Leben selbst, demgegenüber bewußte Hingabe ebenso undenkbar ist wie deren Gegenteil. Die Frömmigkeit des Einzelnen kann sich nur in bezug auf den König manifestieren und differenzieren . . .

"Während der Gott Leben, Gedeihen, Wachsen, Werden und Vergehen *schlechthin* ist, ist der König Leben für den, der ihn verehrt, Tod für den, der ihn mißachtet."

77. J. P. Allen, "The Natural Philosophy of Akhenaten," pp. 97f.

78. Kemp, *Ancient Egypt*, pp. 264f.

79. One might well argue that this barrier had been a part of official religious belief in other times during Egyptian history, say, when the pyramids of Giza were erected, or under the reign of Senusert III, but there were clearly times during Egyptian history when the possibility of a much more direct relation between the individual subject and experience of the divine was accepted, and indeed, overall, the New Kingdom represents a time when such "personal piety" reached new levels of development, quite in contrast with the religious ideologies of Amarna.

80. Assmann, *Zeit und Ewigkeit*, p. 61: "Der König ist nicht die kosmische Quelle dieser Gaben, sondern die soziale Instanz, die über ihre individuelle Verteilung entscheidet, und zwar als Austausch für die individuelle Bewährung im Ganzen der gesellschaftlichen Kommunikation: 'Die Lebenszeit (ḥʿw) ist in deiner Hand, du gibst dem, den du liebst, sie leben von deiner Zuweisung'. Der Oberbegriff dieser ganzen vom König verwalteten und das Leben

des Einzelnen inhaltlich bestimmenden und gestaltenden Gegenleistunges ist *ḥzwt*, 'Gunst'. Obwohl dieses Wort einen der Zentralbegriffe der ägyptischen Kultur überhaupt darstellt und die Amarna-Theologie hier durchaus an z.T. uralte Traditionen anknüpft, kennzeichnet doch nichts vielleicht die Sonderstellung des Königs in Amarna und die polemische Abhebung dieser Richtung gegenüber allgemeinen Tendenzen des Neuen Reichs schärfer als die 'Monopolisierung' dieser *ḥzwt* in der Hand des Königs. Dadurch ergibt sich hier (und wohl nur hier in der ägyptischen Geistesgeschichte) diese scharfe, gewaltsam anmutende Trennung einer kosmisch-naturalen und einer sozial-personalen Ebene des Göttlichen. Auf der kosmischen Ebene ist *š3jj*, "Schicksal" der Anteil, der allem Seienden in der Zeit gewährt wird, die Entfaltung der Kreatur in der Zeitdimension; auf der sozialen Ebene, im Horizont der vom König verwalteten 'Gunst' ist *š3jj* das individuelle Wohlergehen als Lohn individueller Bewährung und 'Persönlicher Frömmigkeit'".

81. Kemp, *Ancient Egypt*, pp. 265f.

82. The body of, apparently, Smenekhkare' was found in a Theban tomb (TT 55) in 1907, first misidentified as that of a woman. It has subsequently been proved to be that of a man with, moreover, the same blood group as Tut'ankhamun and a skull shape remarkably close to his. It seems Smenekhkare' and Tut'ankhamun were brothers. See Redford, *Akhenaten*, pp. 188–93; Romer, *Valley of the Kings*, pp. 211–19; and Aldred, *Akhenaten*, passim, for (sometimes conflicting) accounts.

83. Recently translated as *Egyptian Solar Religion in the New Kingdom: Re, Amun, and the Crisis of Polytheism*.

84. After Sethe, "Restaurationsstele Tutenchamuns in Kairo," pp. 2027–28.

85. Ibid., pp. 2025–26.

86. John Bennett reports, moreover, that Tut'ankhamun's prenomen and nomen can as well be made out underneath the usurpers' cartouches. See Bennett, "Restoration Inscription," p. 15.

87. Schlögl, *Echnaton-Tutanchamun, Fakten und Texte*, p. 85.

88. Assmann, "Ewigkeit, " p. 48: "[Daraus] ergibt sich, daß *nḥḥ* die Zeit in ihrem diskontinuierlichen Aspekt bezeichnet, als die (unendliche) Zahl von Zyklen, *ḏt* dagegen den kontinuierlichen Aspekt der Zeit als Ausdehnung in einer mehr räumlich gedachten Dimension. *nḥḥ* als die aus unbegrenzter Zukunft in die Gegenwart einströmende Aktualisierung virtueller zyklischer Abläufe, *ḏt* als die sich in unbegrenzte Zukunft erstreckende Dauer eines in der Zeit Vollendeten. Diese Unterscheidung leitet sich vermutlich aus der Aspekt-Opposition her, die das Ägyptische mit der semitohamitischen Sprachfamilie zumindest ursprünglich gemein hat."

89. Hornung, *Conceptions of God*, pp. 172–73.

90. From the "Negative Confession," *Book of the Dead* 125, after De Buck, *Egyptian Readingbook*, p. 116.

91. The epistemological problem engaged here is strongly reminiscent, though in negative terms, of Anselm's argument for the existence of God: if He

is the greatest thing that can be imagined, then He must exist, because if He did not, then there would be something greater that could be imagined, i.e., the same object of thought carrying the attribute of "existence" as well. This of course has led to a long and intricate analysis of the nature of descriptives and the categorical potential of "existence."

92. Hornung, *Conceptions of God*, p. 183.
93. Ibid., p. 178.
94. Assmann, *Zeit und Ewigkeit*, pp. 18f.: "nḥḥ und ḏt, die beiden die ägyptische Ewigkeitsvorstellung in einem noch näher zu analysierenden Doppelaspekt bezeichnenden Lexeme, gehören seiner Auffassung nach eindeutig in das Diesseits dieses eschatologischen Horizonts, sie bezeichnen die Zeit, die dem Sein insgesamt gegeben ist. Diese "Welt-Zeit" wäre dann ebenfalls von der Art, die der Ägypter als ʿḥʿw bezeichnet, nur daß hier nicht Geburt und Tod, sondern Schöpfung und Weltend die Grenzen ihrer Erstreckung markieren. Die Unendlichkeit und Unbegrenzheit dieser Zeit sie nur scheinbar, die sich aus einer Art optischen Täuschung vom Standpunkt des vergänglichen individuellen Daseins aur ergibt; vom onto-bzw. kosmologischen Standpunkt aus erweisen sich auch nḥḥ und ḏt als endlich und innerweltlich."
95. Ibid., p. 19: "Die Negation von nḥḥ und ḏt weist nicht ins absolut Grenzenlose, sondern in das in anderer Weise Begrenzte. Das Jenseits, das wir im vorhergehenden Abschnitt als den durch nḥḥ und ḏt bestimmten Bereich dargestellt haben, ist eine durchaus innerweltliche Kategorie. Die Grenze, die ägyptischem Denken zur begrifflichen Unterscheidung von Zeit und Ewigkeit dient, verläuft innerhalb des Seins bzw. des Kosmos."
96. Ibid., p. 20: "Während wir nun auf der einen Seite die Gegensatzbildungen in der Zeitdimension in ähnlicher Weise zu verstehen suchen, schließt dagegen Hornungs ontologisches Verständnis der Zeit als "Sein" und Ewigkeit als "Nichtsein" eine dualistische Konzeption der Zeit (die in manchen an altiranische Motive erinnern würde) m. E. nicht deutlich genug aus."
97. Ibid., p. 25: "Welt und Zeit bilden ja gerade nicht eine 'Insel zwischen Nichts und Nichts', sondern eher ein Intervall der Vielheit, Differenziertheit und Wohlgeschiedenheit zwischen Einheit und Einheit."
98. Hornung, *Conceptions of God*, p. 177.

CHAPTER 5 *Post-ancient Ægyptians*

1. On the condition of the pharaohs' mummies, see Brier, *Egyptian Mummies*, especially pp. 194–97 and 270–71.
2. Consider, for example, the discourse of race. There, the search for "our" genetic home has turned back upon itself, imputing to nature the black, white, yellow, red, and brown chimeras of our current sociopolitical imagination.
3. Hamilton, *The Greek Way*, p. 15. The original book was supplemented by five chapters of new material to be published in 1942 as *The Great Age of*

Greek Literature, but it appeared in the same year as well under the previous title, *The Greek Way*.

4. Ibid., p. 16.

5. Ibid., pp. 18f.

6. Many of the eighteenth- and nineteenth-century hellenophiles from whom Hamilton has derived her arguments are themselves less extreme and simplistic in their understanding. Hegel, for instance, although he gives the Greeks clear pride of place in the ancient world, is still somewhat more subtle than Hamilton in understanding differences among the Chinese, the Persians, the Indians, the Egyptians, and other "oriental" civilizations.

Consider, as another, not-so-distant example, Kitto's *The Greeks*, a book we are told sold over 1,400,000 copies between 1951 and 1973: "The reader is asked, for the moment, to accept this as a reasonable statement of fact, that in a part of the world that had for centuries been civilized, and quite highly civilized, there gradually emerged a people, not very numerous, not very powerful, not very well organized, who had a totally new conception of what human life was for, and showed for the first time what the human mind was for" (p. 7). "While the older civilizations of the East were often extremely efficient in practical matters and, sometimes, in their art not inferior to the Greeks, yet they were intellectually barren. For centuries, millions of people had had experience of life—and what did they do with it? Nothing. The experience of each generation (except in certain purely practical matters) died with it—not like the leaves of the forest, for they at least enrich the soil" (p. 8).

7. Bernal, *Black Athena*, 1: 1.

8. Ibid., p. 2. Bernal has undertaken to fashion his arguments for plausibility (abandoning the possibility of proof), and his methodology is that of "thick description." This has required an extraordinarily impressive reach across disciplines as different as linguistics, paleoclimatology, ancient history, field archaeology, and philosophy, and there are mistakes in Bernal's representations, in certain details.

9. Lefkowitz and Rogers, *Black Athena Revisited*.

10. Lefkowitz, *Not Out of Africa*, p. xi.

11. Bernal, *Black Athena*, 1: 2.

12. Many of them were made, tellingly, in Alexandria, or other places in the far-flung Hellenistic empire.

13. "Greek" (which is really to say "Athenian") democracy has been eulogized numberless times as the still-beating heart of modern Western political institutions, but the comparison is rough at best. Greek democracy was not a continuous and stable political form throughout (even) the fifth century, and it did not extend to the majority of the population of (even) Athens: women, children, slaves, foreigners, Greeks from other city-states—a great many of the people whose lives were directly affected by this "democracy" had no voice in it. It has been argued, moreover, that the democracy of Athens could not have

existed without the wealth of Athens's colonies and allied states in the Delian league, and these entities were subject to the will of Athens under conditions that could hardly be called democratic.

Even as there are numerous caveats that must be raised about the quality of Greek democracy, we must admit that in some respects, it was more democratic than the modern states of the industrialized West. The voting population of Athens at its height has been estimated at some 40,000, and freeborn native Athenian men did indeed, for part of the fifth century, participate in the direct selection of their leaders. The Athenian democracy was immediately concerned with the details of everyday life in the agora. In both these respects, "Greek democracy" was more democratic than modern American or British or, say, Japanese democracies, which are representative, rather than direct, and which serve to govern nations whose size makes the comparison with the 40,000 enfranchised citizens of Athens highly dubious. (If comparisons are to be made at *this* level of precision, then surely it is worth debating that the large, and ethnically diverse, highly bureaucratized state of New Kingdom or Late Period Egypt bears a closer resemblance to the modern industrialized states of the West than the tiny city-state of Athens does.)

14. I recognize as well in Greek philosophy a strong tendency toward Idealism, whether of the overt sort advocated by Plato or the drier and less explicit sort that characterizes Aristotelian thought. (Such Idealism has had a remarkably tenacious hold on Western thought ever since, and its consequences will be touched upon below.)

The Greeks seem, moreover, to have been drawn irresistibly to struggle, to the *agon* as a painful but necessary part of the good life, a belief that has also characterized many varieties of Western thought. The Greeks loved violence, as we apparently do, to judge from popular entertainment, journalism, and sadly, government policy. The Greeks were often notoriously misogynist and ethnocentric. Is there a legacy to the modern West here as well, or just an unhappy coincidence?

15. I think, however, that it's difficult to speak in the present tense and at the same time deny that many of these things are also a legacy to "the East," or "the North," or "the South." The Pythagorean theorem certainly "belongs" to anyone who understands it, as does Euclid's Geometry or Sophocles' *Oidipous Tyrannos*.

16. Now it would probably be worth tracing the history of the very word "Judeo-Christian," given the many incompatibilities between Jewish and Christian thought. It sounds very much a coinage of twentieth-century rhetoric, more intended to forge a political consensus than describe a common cultural experience.

17. The inclusiveness of "Judeo-Christian" is dubious in its promiscuous combination of the strict monotheism of Jews with the complicated Trinitarianism of Christians. The exclusiveness of "Judeo-Christian" also raises serious

doubts because of its omission of Muslims from the group. Again, the problem of the Trinity, and especially the divinity of Jesus, separates Christianity from the monotheism of Jews and Muslims in a way in which the latter are not separated doctrinally from each other.

18. Though it is often attributed to Julius Caesar, with adjustments by Pope Gregory, the calendar we use throughout the world today is at heart Egyptian.

19. The Greek debt to Egyptian representational styles has been (grudgingly) acknowledged, and particularly in sculpture there are obvious links between representations of the human figure in archaic Greece and ancient Egypt.

Schäfer's important work on Egyptian representational styles notwithstanding, there is a strong link between Egyptian art and Greek art. The binarism of "pre-Greek" and "post-Greek" he insists upon is, moreover, patently orientalist and not sustainable with even the briefest consideration of, to name just one example, pre-Columbian relief, which makes skillful and frequent use of foreshortening. Schäfer's interest in Greek perspective and his projection of it throughout the Western tradition as a maturation of or an improvement upon the representational styles of those who went before is thrown open to refutation by the recent history of art in "the West." Cubism, Expressionism, and in some ways even Impressionism are notable for their departure from the illusionistic traditions Schäfer equates with the telos of Western art. The first of these, in particular, bears certain strong similarities to "the aspective" in Egyptian painting. See Schäfer, *Principles of Egyptian Art*.

20. Take, for instance, the fluted column, so much a part of the vocabulary of classical and neoclassical architectural styles. It has antecedents as far back as the Third Dynasty in Egypt (in the engaged columns of the pyramid complex at Saqqara).

21. Consider, first, an example generally used to delineate the difference between the Egyptians and us: their writing system. There is a long-standing prejudice that the alphabet is the goal toward which writing evolved between its inception around 3300 B.C.E. and the invention of the Greek alphabet in the eighth century B.C.E. (Bernal, however, argues for a much earlier invention of the alphabet. See *Black Athena*, 1: 34f.)

Both the logographic (e.g., Sumerian and Egyptian) and strictly consonantal phonetic (e.g., Phoenician and Hebrew) writing systems, which existed before the Greek alphabet, are seen, in this light, as immature or even primitive. Such a view, though, is vulnerable to several important criticisms. More important, though, it is necessary to recognize that the history of the alphabet is also the history of how the inadequacies of the alphabet have been supplemented by illustrations, oral performances, audio recordings, film, comic books, road signs, and even computer icons.

22. As read by Jean-Joseph Goux. I am indebted to Goux for his discussion of what he terms the Egyptian, the Greek, and the modern Osiris, although as

you will see, I come to differ with him eventually. See Goux, "The Phallus," pp. 40–75.

23. Ibid., p. 42.

24. Lacan, *Écrits*, p. 285, quoted in Goux, "The Phallus," p. 43.

25. Goux, "The Phallus," p. 43. In arguing for a lost phallus, Lacan is relying on readings of the Osirian myth by Plutarch and Herodotus and accepting the widespread Hellenistic and late classical association of Osiris with Dionysos. The loss instantiated in that reading allows a further development, however, which Goux characterizes as the "Greek Osiris," such that Dionysos gives up his place to Hermes. The replacement is important, in that it allows a link with the Hermetic tradition and an identification of the psychoanalytic paradigm within which Lacan is working with a Neoplatonist apperception most readily associated with Plotinus.

26. Lacan, *Écrits*, p. 291. Here the sublation of the penis into the Lacanian phallus finds a locus classicus given concrete expression in the characteristic statue called a "herm," which consists of the head of Hermes atop a rectangular block altogether limbless except for an erect phallus carved into the lower section of the front. This is explained in Plutarch as a symbol of the vigor of the *nous* in an old man even though his bodily powers have diminished: "That is the reason why they make the older Hermae without hands, or feet, but with their private parts stiff, indicating figuratively that there is no need whatsoever of old men who are active by their body's use, if they keep their mind [or their power of reason, logon energon], as it should be, active and fertile." *Moralia* 10.153; quoted in Goux, "The Phallus," p. 49.

27. A dualism of similar structure underlies not only the Neoplatonism of Plotinus, but Platonism itself and, in discussions of human conception, Aristotle's biology as well.

28. Hegel, *Lectures on the Philosophy of Religion*, p. 626; quoted in Goux, "The Phallus," p. 54.

29. Goux, "The Phallus," p. 54.

30. Ibid., pp. 55f.

31. In "The Phallus," Goux conjectures concerning Hegel's reasons for omitting all phallic reference: "Without asserting that Hegel, like the modern man Voltaire speaks of [in the *Philosophical Dictionary* under the entry "Ezekiel"], saw nothing but turpitude in the Egyptians' phallophorism (which is nevertheless likely), one can suspect that it is not without a certain anxiety and difficulty in accepting this and integrating it into his thought, that he discovered that *the most significant operation of his whole philosophy of Spirit: negation followed by reestablishment* could be figured in terms of castration and the phallus" (pp. 56f., Goux's emphasis).

32. Brown, *Augustine of Hippo*, p. 102.

33. Staten, "How the Spirit (Almost) Became Flesh," p. 35.

34. Ibid., p. 52.

35. Ibid., pp. 34f.
36. Ibid., p. 36.
37. Ibid., p. 35.
38. "If any one finds a difficulty in understanding why other sins do not alter human nature as it was altered by the transgression of those first human beings, . . . —if, I say, any one is moved by this, he ought not to think that that sin was a small and light one because it was committed about food, and that not bad or noxious, except because it was forbidden; . . . by the precept He gave, God commanded obedience. . . . And as this commandment enjoining abstinence from one kind of food in the midst of great abundance of other kinds was so easy to keep—so light a burden to the memory—and, above all, *found no resistance to its observance in lust,* which only afterwards sprung up as the penal consequence of sin, the iniquity of violating it was all the greater in proportion to the ease with which it might have been kept." Augustine, *The City of God* 14.11–12 (my emphasis).

39. "When the flesh is said to desire or to suffer, it is meant, as we have explained, that the man does so, or some part of the soul which is affected by the sensation of the flesh, whether a harsh sensation causing pain, or gentle, causing pleasure. But pain in the flesh is only a discomfort of the soul arising from the flesh. . . . But pleasure is preceded by a certain appetite which is felt in the flesh like a craving, as hunger and thirst and that generative appetite which is most commonly identified with the name "lust," though this is the generic word for all desires. . . .

Although . . . lust may have many objects, yet when no object is specified, the word lust usually suggests to the mind the lustful excitement of the organs of generation. And this lust not only takes possession of the whole body and outward members, but also makes itself felt within, and moves the whole man with a passion in which mental emotion is mingled with bodily appetite, so that the pleasure which results is the greatest of all bodily pleasures." Ibid., 14.15–16.

40. Ibid., 14.16.
41. Brown, *Augustine of Hippo*, p. 123 (my emphasis).
42. Steinberg, *The Sexuality of Christ*, esp. pp. 83–93, 183f., 298–325. These works are, in fact, quite rare. Half of Steinberg's eight pictured examples are by or after the style of one Maerten van Heemskerck (1498–1574), and the others all come from northwestern Europe from between 1515 and 1615.
43. Ibid., pp. 81–83.
44. Ibid., pp. 89f. Apparently the capacity of these paintings to shock is as potent as ever. My own request to reproduce the van Heemskerck owned by Bob Jones University (Steinberg's Fig. 97) was turned down for no stated reason other than that "we don't allow that painting to be reproduced anymore." I can only assume that in this case some sense of religious propriety has priority over the interests of intellectual inquiry at Bob Jones University.

45. So, as well, the *Pratimokṣa*, a code of behavioral restraints for monastic life in early Buddhism, prohibits the willful emission of semen, but allows involuntary ejaculation, as in wet dreams.
46. Steinberg, *The Sexuality of Christ*, p. 83.
47. Halbertal and Margalit, *Idolatry*, pp. 25-30.
48. As Howard Eilberg-Schwartz notes, "Theorists of religion have tended to assume that from the first Israel believed in the existence of only one God. But this belief developed only after a long period of evolution, and for a long part of its early history Israelite religion included more than one deity in its pantheon." *God's Phallus*, p. 245 n. 13.
49. Ibid., p. 109.   50. Ibid., pp. 14-15.
51. Even Michelangelo, who hardly ever passed up the chance to paint a naked man, could not quite manage to paint a full frontal nude of Christ. His *Entombment* may indeed be a new interpretation of a stage in the Passion, as the National Gallery (London) commentary informs us, but its icons are not entirely new. The body (at least the head and torso) of Christ has assumed that graceful and feminine position we recognize, knees bent slightly to one side, the head tilted likewise, the long smooth abdomen. The chest is partially hidden from view by a broad rope (improvised out of the shroud, perhaps?), but the shoulders still suggest how the arms of the corpse must have fallen, stiff to its sides when the body was pulled from the cross. It is an example of the centuries-old hieroglyph of the dead Jesus, such as you could easily find in countless paintings of the Crucifixion. Michelangelo's painting, however, is unfinished. A large area to your lower right is blank, left until later for technical reasons. Other details also remain to be filled in; most significant, the genitals of Christ remain unfinished. He is naked, and they lie near the center of the canvas. All contiguous areas are completed—indeed, the rest of Christ's body has been finished. Strange, then, that this alone has been left incomplete.

Michaelangelo did depict a fully naked, anatomically correct Christ in sculpture, in his *Risen Christ* of 1514-20. See Steinberg, *The Sexuality of Christ*, p. 20, fig. 19, for a reproduction.

52. In, of course, the prepositional phrase m-b^3h. See above, pp. 110.
53. In the myth of Osiris, the pattern of father-son (particularly in the context of royal succession) is given a reassuring cyclicality, especially in the explicate verbal designation of the dead pharaoh as Osiris So-and-so, and his successor as Horus So-and-so. Similarly, in the *kamutef* myth of Amun's self-engenderment, the supplementarity is countered by the perfect circularity of "the Bull of His Mother" (see above, p. 122). In the Eighteenth Dynasty construction whereby Hatshepsut, for example, is shown to be conceived by Amun, royal monopoly disarms any serious threat of proliferating supplementarity.
54. *Coffin Texts* 1.354 (from Utterance 75). See above, p. 116.
55. Eilberg-Schwartz's comments on a comparable displacement of the phallus to the word in archaic Judaism are worth considering here: "Because

the phallus of God had to remain unthought, the symbolic concerns that might normally be associated with the phallus were deflected onto the 'Godhead.' Recall, for example, how in Ezekiel, at the moment of union between God and Israel, an oral act (an oath) substitutes for a genital one. Moreover, as other interpreters have noted, in one version of the creation story, God creates the world by speaking. This theory of upper body displacement may suggest the origin of the Memra theology of the Aramaic translation of the Hebrew Bible. In these translations, references to God or God's presence are translated as 'God's Memra' [Word, Speech]" (Eilberg-Schwartz, *God's Phallus*, p. 126).

56. See above, pp. 113.

57. And indeed, comparison with Egyptian cases is illuminating: Atum's authority after the creation is shared with and subordinated to that of Shu, Geb, Osiris, Horus, etc., and although the Osirian pattern also establishes a kind of defense against supplementarity, that defense is possible only with the generational division and fragmentation of divine power—that power eventually becomes generalized to all the blessed dead, a situation that would be absolutely unacceptable in the absolutist theology of God's otherness characteristic of most strains of Christianity.

58. Has Islam been able to avoid the complications inherent in sexing the deity through its strong antifiguralist tradition? What is the relevance of gender to Allah?

59. Breasted, *Development of Religion and Thought*, p. 56.

60. If this is not so clear in Judaism, we find there as well an insistence on the importance of a specific individuated being. In both these cases, this seems to me to be at the most fundamental level of Western thought. Israelite religion seems to have invested primary significance not in immortality for the individual, but in the preservation of an absolute individual integrity during life. There is, apparently, considerable disagreement among modern Jews about immortality and a personal afterlife.

The Greeks for their part certainly subscribed to ideals of individual integrity and discrete personal identity (at least for freeborn Greek males), but their general rejection of an afterlife with such clear individuation places them outside the mainstream of "Western" thought even as it identifies the Egyptians as centered well within that mainstream. Consider this in connection with Bernal's proposed etymology of the Greek *makarios* (happy, blessed) from Egyptian *ma'a-kheru*.

61. Hegel, *Philosophie der Weltgeschichte*, 2: 487f.: "Die Zusammenstellung des menschlichen Lebenslaufes mit dem Nil, der Sonne, dem Osiris ist nicht etwa als Gleichnis aufzufassen, als ob das Geborenwerden, das Zunehmen der Kraft, die höchste Kräftigkeit und Fruchtbarkeit, die Abnahme und Schwäche sich in diesem Verschiedenen auf gleiche oder ähnliche Weise darstelle; sondern die Phantasie hat in diesem Verschiedenen ein Subjekt, eine

Lebendigkeit gesehen. Diese Einheit ist jedoch ganz abstrakt; das Heterogene zeigt sich darin als drängend und treibend und in einer Unklarheit, die von der griechischen Klarheit sehr absticht. Osiris stellt die Sonne, den Nil vor; und ebenso können wir sagen, Sonne und Nil seien Symbole des menschlichen Lebens und Geistes; eines ist des anderen Symbol. Bedeutung und Bild werden miteinander vertauscht; jedes ist Bedeutung, und jedes ist Bild. Osiris ist der Gott, der die Menschen belehrt, sie durch Einrichtungen beglückt; das Symbol ist der Nil, die Sonne; aber ebenso ist der geistige Inhalt ein Symbol des Nils und des Sonnenumlaufs. Es sind diese verschiedenen Vorstellungen in eine verknüpft, so daß aus jeder die andere erklärt werden kann. Das Symbol verkehrt sich zur Bedeutung, und diese ist Symbol des Symbols, das Bedeutung wird. Keine Bestimmung ist Bild, ohne nicht zugleich Bedeutung zu sein; jede ist jedes, aus einer erklärt sich die andere. Aber jede ist auch wesentlicher Inhalt, wesentliche Bestimmung. Diese Vorstellung haben wir als den Mittelpunkt der ägyptischen substanziellen Anschauung zu betrachten, die so reich ist und so sich in sich selbst widersprechend, daß ihre Momente sich ineinander drängen. Es ergibt sich so eine konkrete Vorstellung, die aus vielen Vorstellungen zusammengeknüpft ist, worin die Individualität der Grundknoten bleibt und nicht in das Allgemeine aufgelöst wird." See in this connection, Hulin, *Hegel et l'orient*, pp. 129–33.

62. Hegel, *Philosophie der Weltgeschichte*, 2: 509: "Plato erzählt, ein ägyptischer Priester habe gesagt, daß die Griechen ewig nur Kinder bleiben; umgekehrt können wir sagen, die Ägypter seien die kräftigen, in sich drängenden Knaben, die erst durch ideelle Form, durch die Klarheit über sich, zu Jünglingen werden."

63. In addition to the similarities between Hegel and the patristic tradition (represented by Augustine in our discussion), Hegel and late classical Idealism (exemplified by Plotinus), etc., we might mention here the evolutionary psychology of Julian Jaynes, who also saw the emergence of consciousness as, essentially, something that happened with the Greeks. Jaynes's pre-Greek human has a different wiring in the brain, indeed, and seems a different species altogether. See Jaynes, *The Origin of Consciousness in the Breakdown of the Bicameral Mind*.

64. Hegel, *Philosophie der Weltgeschichte*, 2: 510f.: "Sehr schön aber finden wir diesen Übergang ausgesprochen in der Erzälung von Ödipus. Eine Sphinx, das ägyptische Gebilde des Rätsels selbst, sei in Theben erschienen und habe ein Rätsel aufgegeben mit den Worten: 'Was ist das, was morgens auf vier Beinen geht, mittags auf zweien und abends auf dreien?' Der Grieche Ödipus habe das Rätsel gelöst und die Sphinx vom Felsen gestürzt, indem der aussprach, dies sei der Mensch. Dies ist richtig; das Rätsel der Ägypter ist der Geist, der Mensch, das Bewußtsein seines eigentümlichen Wesens. Aber mit dieser alten Lösung durch Ödipus, der sich so als Wissender zeigt, ist bei ihm die ungeheuerste Unwissenheit gepaart über sich selbst und über das, was er

tut. Der Aufgang geistiger Klarheit in dem alten Königshause ist noch mit Greueln aus Unwissenheit verbunden. Es ist die alte patriarchalische Herrschaft, der das Wissen ein Heterogene ist und die dadurch aufgelöst wird. Dies Wissen wird erst gereinigt durch politische Gesetze; unmittelbar ist es unheilbringend. Das Sebstbewußtsein muß sich noch, um zu wahrem Wissen und sittlicher Klarheit zu werden, durch bürgerliche Gesetze und politische Freiheit gestalten und zum schönen Geiste versöhnen."

65. Hulin's *Hegel et l'orient* is particularly helpful, as is the comparative perspective afforded by Haun Saussy, *The Problem of a Chinese Aesthetic*. See as well Spivak, "Time and Timing."

66. See, for example, Barry Kemp: "Mosaic Judaism, with its distinctive code of living, was a positive force for the host society, giving the Israelites a sense of identity in a hostile world. It became a means of rejecting the cultures of others. By contrast, the Aten robbed Egyptians of a tradition of explaining the phenomena of the universe through an extraordinarily rich imagery which, to those who studied it, managed to contain the concept that a unity, a oneness, could be found in the multiplicity of divine forms and names. Akhenaten was telling the Egyptians something that they knew already, but in a way that made further serious speculation pointless. It is easy to understand why the Egyptians rejected the king's religion after his death. He had tried to kill intellectual life." Kemp, *Ancient Egypt*, p. 264.

67. The strongly antifigural strains of traditional Judaism and Islam come immediately to mind, of course, but in Christianity as well (apart from antifigural phases in its development), we might point to the highly figural, but also tightly controlled, deployment of allegory in high medievalism.

68. Similarly, we must ask whether the presence of ibis-headed men, cattle with solar disks rising from their foreheads, and such in Egyptian representations means that Egyptians believed in a world where these hybrids existed.

It is more plausible that the Egyptians saw existence, whether eternal and divine or transient and human, whether phenomenal and material or shaped to some "fantastic" figurality, as parallel aspects of the same body of being; that the ibis-headed men, cattle with solar disks rising from their foreheads, and so on were never expected to materialize but nonetheless participated in a reality of religious meaning that was not separate from material reality, but merely another "reading" of it.

69. Kemp, *Ancient Egypt*, pp. 3f.

70. See above, p. 69.

BIBLIOGRAPHY

Frequently cited journals and series are abbreviated as follows:

JARCE   Journal of the American Research Center in Egypt
JEA   Journal of Egyptian Archaeology
LdÄ   Lexikon der Ägyptologie

Aldred, Cyril. *Akhenaten, King of Egypt*. London: Thames & Hudson, 1988.
Allen, James P. *Genesis in Egypt: The Philosophy of Ancient Egyptian Creation Accounts*. Yale Egyptological Studies 2. New Haven, Conn.: Yale Egyptological Seminar, 1988.
———. *Inflection of the Verb in the Pyramid Texts*. Bibliotheca Aegyptia 2. Malibu, Calif.: Undena, 1984.
———. "The Natural Philosophy of Akhenaten." In W. K. Simpson, ed., *Religion and Philosophy in Ancient Egypt*, pp. 89–101. New Haven, Conn.: Yale University Press, 1989.
Allen, Thomas George. *The Book of the Dead, or Going Forth by Day*. Studies in Ancient Oriental Civilization 37. Chicago: University of Chicago Press, 1974.
Altenmüller, Hartwig. "Denkmal memphitischer Theologie." *LdÄ* 1: 1065–69.
———. "Gliedervergottung." *LdÄ* 2: 624–27.
———. "Hand." *LdÄ* 2: 938–43.
———. "Hu." *LdÄ* 3: 65–68.
———. "Opfer." *LdÄ* 4: 579–84.
———. "Pyramidentexte." *LdÄ* 5: 5–23.

Ammianus Marcellinus. Translated by John C. Rolfe. Cambridge, Mass.: Harvard University Press, 1935.
Andrews, Carol. *Amulets of Ancient Egypt*. London: British Museum Press, 1994.
Anthes, Rudolph. "Note Concerning the Great Corporation of Heliopolis." *Journal of Near Eastern Studies* 13 (1954): 191–92.
Arnold, Dorothea. *Royal Women of Amarna*. New York: Abrams, 1996.
Assmann, Jan. *Ägypten—Theologie und Frömmigkeit einer frühen Hochkultur*. Stuttgart: W. Kohlhammer, 1984.
———. *Ägyptische Hymnen und Gebete*. Zurich: Artemis, 1975.
———. "Akhanyati's Theology of Light and Time." *Proceedings of the Israel Academy of Sciences and Humanities* 7, no. 4 (1992): 143–75.
———. "Ancient Egypt and the Materiality of the Sign." In Hans Ulrich Gumbrecht and K. Ludwig Pfeiffer, eds., *Materialities of Communication*, pp. 15–31. Stanford, Calif.: Stanford University Press, 1994.
———. "Aton." *LdÄ* 1: 526–40.
———. "Ewigkeit." *LdÄ* 2: 48–53.
———. *Maât, l'Égypte pharaonique et l'idée de justice sociale*. Conférences Essais et Leçons du Collège de France. Paris: Julliard, 1989.
———. *Moses the Egyptian: The Memory of Egypt in Western Monotheism*. Cambridge, Mass.: Harvard University Press, 1997.
———. *Re und Amun. Die Krise des polytheistischen Weltbilds im Ägypten der 18–20. Dynastie*. Orbis Biblicus et Orientalis 51. Göttingen: Vandenhoeck & Ruprecht; Freiburg, Switzerland: Universitätsverlag, 1983. Revised and enlarged for English translation by Anthony Alcock as *Egyptian Solar Religion in the New Kingdom: Re, Amun, and the Crisis of Polytheism*. London and New York: Kegan Paul International, 1995.
———. "Schöpfung." *LdÄ* 5: 677–90.
———. "When Justice Fails." *JEA* 78 (1992): 149–62.
———. *Zeit und Ewigkeit im alten Ägypten. Ein Beitrag zur Geschichte der literarischen Kommunikation*. Theorie und Geschichte der Literatur und der schönen Künste 55. Heidelberg: Carl Winter Universitätsverlag, 1975.
Augustine, Bishop of Hippo. *The City of God*. Translated by Marcus Dods. New York: Modern Library, 1950.
Baines, John. "Bnbn: Mythological and Linguistic Notes." *Orientalia*, n.s., 39 (1970): 389–404.
———. *Fecundity Figures: Egyptian Personification and the Iconology of a Genre*. Warminster: Aris & Phillips, 1985.
———. "Interpretations of Religion: Logic, Discourse, Rationality." *Göttinger Miszellen, Beiträge zur ägyptologischen Diskussion* 76 (1984): 25–54.
———. "Literacy and Ancient Egyptian Society." *Man*, n.s., 18 (September 1983): 572–99.
———. "Restricted Knowledge, Hierarchy, and Decorum: Modern Perceptions and Ancient Institutions." *JARCE* 27 (1990): 1–23.

———. "R. T. Rundle Clark's Papers on the Iconography of Osiris." *JEA* 58 (1972): 286–95.
Baines, John, and Christopher J. Eyre. "Four Notes on Literacy." *Göttinger Miszellen, Beiträge zur ägyptologischen Diskussion* 61 (1983): 65–96.
Baines, John, and Jaromir Málek. *Atlas of Ancient Egypt*. New York: Facts on File, 1980.
Barguet, Paul, ed. and trans. *Le Livre des morts des anciens Égyptiens*. Paris: Les Éditions du Cerf, 1967.
Barta, Winifred. "Opferformel." *LdÄ* 4: 584–86.
———. "Opferliste." *LdÄ* 4: 586–89.
———. "Re." *LdÄ* 5: 156–80.
Beckerath, Jürgen von. *Handbuch der ägyptischen Königsnamen*. Munich: Deutscher Kunstverlag, 1984.
Behrens, Peter. "Phallus." *LdÄ* 4: 1018–20.
Beinlich, Horst. "Reliquie." *LdÄ* 5: 230–32.
Bennett, John. "The Restoration Inscription of Tutʿankhamūn." *JEA* 25 (1939): 8–15.
Bergman, Jan. "Isis." *LdÄ* 3: 186–203.
Bernal, Martin. *Black Athena: The Afroasiatic Roots of Classical Civilization*. Vol. 1, *The Fabrication of Ancient Greece, 1785–1985*. London: Free Association Books; New Brunswick, N.J.: Rutgers University Press, 1987. Vol. 2, *The Archaeological and Documentary Evidence*. London: Free Association Books; New Brunswick, N.J.: Rutgers University Press, 1991.
Blumenthal, Elke. "Die Erzählung des Papyrus d'Orbiney als Literaturwerk." *Zeitschrift für ägyptische Sprache und Altertumskunde* 99 (1972): 1–17.
Bottéro, Jean. *Mesopotamia: Writing, Reasoning, and the Gods*. Translated by Zainab Bahrani and Marc Van De Mieroop. Chicago: University of Chicago Press, 1992.
Bowman, Alan K. *Egypt After the Pharaohs, 332 B.C.–A.D. 642: From Alexander to the Arab Conquest*. Berkeley: University of California Press, 1986.
Breasted, James Henry. *Development of Religion and Thought in Ancient Egypt: Lectures Delivered upon the Morse Foundation at Union Theological Seminary*. New York: Charles Scribner's Sons, 1912.
———. "The Philosophy of a Memphite Priest." *Zeitschrift für ägyptische Sprache und Altertumskunde* 39 (1901): 39–54. Reprint. Leipzig: Zentral Antiquariat der Deutschen Demokratischen Republik, 1967.
Brier, Bob. *Egyptian Mummies: Unraveling the Secrets of an Ancient Art*. New York: William Morrow, 1994.
Brown, Peter. *Augustine of Hippo*. Berkeley: University of California Press, 1967.
Brunner, Hellmut. *Die Geburt des Gottkönigs. Studien zur Überlieferung eines Altägyptischen Mythos*, Ägyptologische Abhandlungen 10. Wiesbaden: Otto Harrassowitz, 1964.
———. "Herz." *LdÄ* 2: 1158–68.

———. "Illustrierte Bücher im alten Ägypten." In *Wort und Bild, Symposion des Fachbereichs Altertums- und Kulturwissenschaften zum 500 jährigen Jubiläum der Eberhard-Karls-Universität Tübingen 1977*, pp. 201-18. Munich: Wilhelm Fink Verlag, 1979.

———. "Maʿa-cheru." *LdÄ* 3: 1107-10.

Brunner-Traut, Emma. "Domestikation (der Tiere)." *LdÄ* 1: 1120-27.

———. "Gesten." *LdÄ* 2: 574-85.

Bryson, Norman. *Vision and Painting: The Logic of the Gaze.* New Haven, Conn.: Yale University Press, 1983.

Buchberger, Hannes. "Sexualität und Harfenspiel, Notizen zur 'sexuellen' Konnotation der altägyptischen Ikonographie." *Göttinger Miszellen, Beiträge zur ägyptologischen Diskussion* 66 (1983): 11-43.

Budge, Sir E. A. Wallis. *The Egyptian Sudan.* London: K. Paul, Trench, Trübner, 1907.

———. *The Gods of the Egyptians.* London: Methuen, 1904.

———, ed. and trans. *The Book of the Dead. Facsimiles of the papyri of Hunefer, Anhai, Ķerāsher and Netchemet with supplementary text [in hieroglyphic type] from the papyrus of Nu, with transcripts, translations, etc.* London, British Museum, 1899.

———, ed. and trans. *The Egyptian Book of the Dead. Facsimile of the Papyrus of Ani in the British Museum.* London: Longmans; Asher; and Kegan Paul, Trench, Trübner, 1890.

Butler, Judith. "The Lesbian Phallus and the Morphological Imaginary." *Differences: A Journal of Feminist Cultural Studies,* "The Phallus Issue," 4 (Spring 1992): 133-71.

Caminos, Ricardo, and Henry G. Fischer. *Ancient Egyptian Epigraphy and Palaeography.* New York: Metropolitan Museum of Art, 1976.

Campbell, Joseph. *Oriental Mythology: The Masks of God.* Harmondsworth, U.K.: Penguin Books, 1976.

Champollion, Jean-François. *Principes généraux de l'écriture sacrée égyptienne appliquée à la représentation de la langue parlée.* 1836. Facsimile. Paris: Institut d'Orient / Michel Sidhom, 1984.

Chassinat, Émile. *Le Mystère d'Osiris au mois de Khoiak.* 2 vols. Cairo: Imprimerie de l'Institut Français d'Archéologie Orientale, 1966, 1968.

Commission des sciences et arts d'Égypte. *Description de l'Égypte, ou receuil des observations et des recherches qui ont été faites en Égypte pendant l'expédition de l'armée française.* 21 vols. + 2 atlases. Paris: L'Imprimerie Impériale, 1809-1828. Reprint of all plates from the Antiquités sections of volumes 1-5 in Charles Coulston Gillispie and Michel Dewachter, *Monuments of Egypt, the Napoleonic Edition: The Complete Archaeological Plates from "La Description de l'Égypte."* 2 vols. (Princeton: Princeton Architectural Press, 1987).

Cook, B. F. *Reading the Past: Greek Inscriptions.* Berkeley: University of

California Press, 1990. Originally published by the British Museum Press, London, 1987.

Corteggiani, Jean-Pierre. *L'Égypte des pharaons au musée du Caire*. With photographs by Jean-François Gout. Paris: Hachette, 1979.

David, A. Rosalie. *Religious Ritual at Abydos, c. 1300 B.C.* Warminster: Aris & Phillips, 1973.

Davies, Norman de Garis. *The Tomb of Rekh-Mi-Reᶜ at Thebes*. Reprint. New York: Arno Press, 1973.

Davies, W. V. *Reading the Past: Egyptian Hieroglyphs*. Berkeley: University of California Press, 1992. Originally published by the British Museum Press, London, 1987.

De Buck, Adriaan. *The Egyptian Coffin Texts*. 7 vols. Chicago: University of Chicago Press, 1935–1961.

———. *Egyptian Readingbook*. Chicago: Ares Publishers, 1982.

Depuydt, Leo. "On the Nature of Hieroglyphic Script." *Zeitschrift für ägyptische Sprache und Altertumskunde* 121 (1994): 17–36.

Derrida, Jacques. "La Pharmacie de Platon." In *La Dissémination*, pp. 71–197. Paris: Seuil, 1972. Translated, with an introduction and additional notes, by Barbara Johnson under the title "Plato's Pharmacy," in *Dissemination*, pp. 61–171 (Chicago: University of Chicago Press, 1981).

———. *Marges de la philosophie*. Paris: Les Éditions de Minuit, 1972.

Déscription de l'Égypt. Paris: Imprimerie Impériale, 1809–24.

Diodorus Siculus. *Bibliothecae Historicae Quae Supersunt*. Translated by Edwin Murphy under the title *The Antiquities of Egypt*. (New Brunswick, N.J.: Transaction Publishers, 1990).

Dover, Kenneth J. *Greek Homosexuality*. New York: Vintage Books, 1978.

Eilberg-Schwartz, Howard. *God's Phallus*. Boston: Beacon Press, 1994.

Englund, Gertie, and Paul John Frandsen, eds. *Crossroad: Chaos or the Beginning of a New Paradigm, Papers from the Conference on Egyptian Grammar, Helsingør, 28–30 May 1986*. Copenhagen: Carsten Niebuhr Institute of Ancient Near East Studies, 1986.

Erman, Adolf. *Ein Denkmal memphitischer Theologie, Sitzungsberichte der Preußischen Akademie der Wissenschaften, Philosophisch-historische Klasse*, 43. Berlin: Verlag der Akademie der Wissenschaften, 1911.

Erman, Adolf, and Hermann Grapow. *Wörterbuch der ägyptischen Sprache im Auftrage der deutschen Akademien*. 2d edition. Berlin: Akademie Verlag, 1957–63.

Estes, J. Worth. *The Medical Skills of Ancient Egypt*. Revised ed. Canton, Mass.: Science History Publications, 1993.

Ettlinger, Leopold D., and Helen S. Ettlinger. *Botticelli*. New York: Oxford University Press, 1977.

Eyre, Christopher. "The Semna Stelae: Quotation, Genre, and the Functions of Literature." In *Studies in Egyptology Presented to Miriam Lichtheim*, 1: 134–65. Jerusalem: The Magnes Press, 1990.

Fairservis, W. A., Jr. "A Revised View of the Naʿrmer Palette." *JARCE* 28 (1991): 1–20.

Faulkner, Raymond O., trans. *The Ancient Egyptian Book of the Dead*. Edited by Carol Andrews. New York: Macmillan, 1972.

———. *The Ancient Egyptian Coffin Texts*. 2 vols. Warminster, England: Aris & Phillips, 1973.

———. *The Ancient Egyptian Pyramid Texts*. Oxford: Oxford University Press, 1969.

———. *A Concise Dictionary of Middle Egyptian*. Oxford: Griffith Institute, 1962.

———. *The Papyrus Bremner-Rhind* (pBM 10188). Bibliotheca Ægyptiaca, III. Brussels: La Fondation Égyptologique Reine Élisabeth, 1933.

Fecht, G. *Wortakzent und Silbenstruktur*. Ägyptologische Forschungen 21. Glückstadt: Verlag J. J. Augustin, 1960.

Fischer, Henry G. *Ancient Egyptian Calligraphy: A Beginner's Guide to Writing Hieroglyphs*. New York, Metropolitan Museum of Art, 1988.

———. *Écriture et l'art de l'Égypte ancienne: Quatre leçons sur la paléographie et l'épigraphie pharaoniques*. Paris: Presses Universitaires de France: 1986.

———. *Egyptian Studies II: The Orientation of Hieroglyphs, Part 1: Reversals*. New York: The Metropolitan Museum of Art, 1977.

———. "Hieroglyphen." *LdÄ* 2: 1189–99.

Forman, Werner, and Stephen Quirke. *Hieroglyphs and the Afterlife in Ancient Egypt*. London: British Museum Press, 1996.

Fox, Michael V. *The Song of Songs and the Ancient Egyptian Love Songs*. Madison: University of Wisconsin Press, 1985.

France, Peter. *The Rape of Egypt*. London: Barrie & Jenkins, 1991.

Frankfort, H. A., John A. Wilson, Thorkild Jakobsen, and William A. Irwin. *The Intellectual Adventure of Ancient Man*. Chicago: University of Chicago Press, 1946.

Frazer, Sir James George. *The Golden Bough: A Study in Magic and Religion*. 1 vol., abridged. New York: Macmillan, 1922.

Gamer-Wallert, Ingrid. *Fische und Fischkulte im alten Ägypten*. Ägyptologische Abhandlungen 21. Wiesbaden: Otto Harrassowitz, 1970.

Gardiner, Sir Alan H. *The Admonitions of an Egyptian Sage from a Hieratic Papyrus in Leiden*. Leipzig: J. C. Hinrichs'sche Buchhandlung, 1909.

———. *Ancient Egyptian Onomastica*. 2 vols. Oxford: Oxford University Press, 1947.

———. *Egypt of the Pharaohs*. Oxford: Oxford University Press, 1961.

———. *Egyptian Grammar, Being an Introduction to the Study of Hieroglyphs*. 3d edition. London: Oxford University Press, 1957.

———. "The House of Life." *JEA* 23 (December 1937): 157–79.

———. *Late Egyptian Stories*. Bibliotheca Aegyptiaca 1. Brussels: La Fondation Égyptologique Reine Élisabeth, 1932.

Gardiner, Sir Alan H., and Nina de Garis Davies. *The Tomb of Amenemhēt*. The Theban Tombs Series 1. London: Egypt Exploration Fund, 1915.
Gombrich, E. H. "Botticelli's Mythologies." *Journal of the Warburg and Courtauld Institutes* 3 (1945). Reprinted in *Symbolic Images: Studies in the Art of the Renaissance* (London: Phaidon, 1972).
Goux, Jean-Joseph. "The Phallus: Masculine Identity and the 'Exchange of Women.'" Translated by Maria Amuchastegui, Caroline Benforado, Amy Hendrix, and Eleanor Kaufman. *Differences: A Journal of Feminist Cultural Studies*, "The Phallus Issue," 4 (Spring 1992): 40–75.
Grimal, Nicolas. *A History of Ancient Egypt*. Trans. Ian Shaw. Oxford: Blackwell Publishers, 1992.
Gumbrecht, Hans Ulrich. "A Farewell to Interpretation." In Hans Ulrich Gumbrecht and K. Ludwig Pfeiffer, eds., *Materialities of Communication*, pp. 389–402. Stanford, Calif.: Stanford University Press, 1994.
Gundlach, Rolf. "Min." *LdÄ* 4: 136–40.
Gwyn Griffiths, John. *The Conflict of Horus and Seth, from Egyptian and Classical Sources*. Liverpool: Liverpool University Press, 1960.
———. *The Divine Verdict: A Study of Divine Judgement in the Ancient Religions*. Leiden: E. J. Brill, 1991.
———. *The Origins of Osiris and His Cult*. Studies in the History of Religions (Supplements to *Numen*) 40. Leiden: E. J. Brill, 1980.
———. "Osiris." *LdÄ* 4: 624–33.
Halbertal, Moshe, and Avishai Margalit. *Idolatry*. Translated by Naomi Goldblum. Cambridge, Mass.: Harvard University Press, 1992.
Hamilton, Edith. *The Greek Way*. 2d edition. New York: W. W. Norton, 1930.
Hannig, Rainer. *Die Sprache der Pharaonen: Großes Handwörterbuch Ägyptisch-Deutsch (2800–950 v.Chr.)*. Kulturgeschichte der Antiken Welt, vol. 64. Mainz: Philipp von Zabern, 1995.
Hassan, Selim. *Excavations at Gîza, 1930–1931*. 2 vols. Cairo: Government Press, Bulâq, 1936.
Hegel, Georg Wilhelm Friedrich. *Enzyklopädie der philosophischen Wissenschaften im Grundrisse* (1827). In *Gesammelte Werke*, ed. Wolfgang Bonsiepen and Hans-Christian Lucas, vol. 19. Hamburg: Felix Meiner Verlag, 1989.
———. *Philosophie der Weltgeschichte II. Die orientalische Welt*. In *Sämtliche Werke*, vol. 9, edited by Georg Lasson. Leipzig: Felix Meiner Verlag, 1923.
Hollis, Susan Tower. *The Ancient Egyptian "Tale of Two Brothers," the Oldest Fairy Tale in the World*. Norman: University of Oklahoma Press, 1990.
Hornblower, G. D. "Further Notes on Phallism in Ancient Egypt." *Man* 27 (1927): 150–53.
Hornung, Erik. *Ägyptische Unterweltsbücher*. Reprint. Zurich: Artemis Verlag, 1984.
———. *Conceptions of God in Ancient Egypt: The One and the Many*. Translated by John Baines. Ithaca: Cornell University Press, 1982. Originally

published as *Der Eine und die Vielen* (Darmstadt: Wissen-schaftliche Buchge-sellschaft, 1971).

———. *Tal der Könige*. Zurich: Artemis Verlag, 1982. Translated by David Warburton under the title *Valley of the Kings: Horizon of Eternity* (New York: Timken Publishers, 1990).

———. "Zeitliches Jenseits im alten Ägypten." In *Zeit und Zeitlösigkeit, In Time and Out of Time, Le Temps et ses frontières*, ed. Adolf Portmann and Rudolf Ritsema. *Eranos* 47 (1981): 269–307.

Hulin, Michel. *Hegel et l'orient, suivi de la traduction annotée d'un essai de Hegel sur la Bhagavad-gîtâ*. Paris: Librairie Philosophique J. Vrin, 1979.

Ions, Veronica. *Egyptian Mythology*. New, revised edition. New York: Peter Bedrick Books, 1983.

Iversen, Erik. "Reflections on Some Ancient Egyptian Royal Names." In John Baines et al., eds., *Pyramid Studies and Other Essays Presented to I. E. S. Edwards*. Occasional Publications 7. London: Egypt Exploration Society, 1988.

Jakobsohn, Helmuth. "Kamutef." *LdÄ* 3: 308f.

Jaynes, Julian. *The Origin of Consciousness in the Breakdown of the Bicameral Mind*. Boston: Houghton Mifflin, 1972.

Johnson, Barbara. "Writing." In Frank Lentricchia and Thomas McLaughlin, eds., *Critical Terms for Literary Study*, pp. 39–49. Chicago: University of Chicago Press, 1990.

Junge, Friedrich. "Zur Fehldatierung des Sog. Denkmals memphitischer Theologie oder der Beitrag der ägyptischen Theologie zur Geistesgeschichte der Spätzeit." In *Mitteilungen des Deutschen archäologischen Instituts, Abteilung Kairo* 29, 2. Mainz: Philipp von Zabern, 1973.

Junker, Hermann. *Die Götterlehre von Memphis (Schabaka-Inschrift), Abhandlungen der Preußischen Akademie der Wissenschaften, Philosophisch-historische Klasse*, 23 (1939). Berlin: Verlag der Akademie der Wissenschaften, 1940.

Kakośy, László. "Atum." *LdÄ* 1: 550–52.

Kammerzell, Frank. "Zeichenverstümmelung." *LdÄ* 6: 1359–61.

Kaplony, Peter. *Die Inschriften der ägyptischen Frühzeit*. Ägyptologische Abhandlungen, vol. 8, nos. 1, 2, and 3 (1963), and vol. 9 (1964). Wiesbaden: Otto Harrassowitz, 1963.

———. "Königsring." *LdÄ* 3: 610–26.

———. "Königstitulatur." *LdÄ* 3: 641–59.

Kees, Hermann. *Der Götterglaube im alten Ägypten*. Berlin: Akademie Verlag, 1956.

Kemp, Barry. *Ancient Egypt: Anatomy of a Civilization*. London: Routledge, 1989.

———. "How Religious Were the Ancient Egyptians?" *Cambridge Archaeological Journal* 5 (April 1995): 25–54.

Kitto, H. D. F. *The Greeks*. Harmondsworth, U.K.: Penguin Books, 1951.
Kozloff, Arielle P., and Betsy M. Bryan, with Lawrence M. Berman. *Egypt's Dazzling Sun: Amenhotep III and His World*. Bloomington: Cleveland Museum of Art, in cooperation with the University of Indiana Press, 1992.
Lacan, Jacques. *Écrits: A Selection*. New York: Norton, 1977.
Lacau, Pierre. *Une Chapelle de Sesostris Ier a Karnak*. Cairo: Imprimerie de l'Institut Français d'Archéologie Orientale, 1956.
Lamy, Lucie. *New Light on Ancient Knowledge: Egyptian Mysteries*. London: Thames & Hudson, 1981.
Lanzone, R. V. *Dizionario di mitologia egizia*. Turin: Litografia Fratelli Doyen, 1884.
Leclant, Jean. "Gotteshand." *LdÄ* 2: 813–15.
———. "Schabaka." *LdÄ* 5: 499–513.
Lefebvre, Gustave. *Romans et contes égyptiens de l'époque pharaonique, traduction avec introduction, notices et commentaire*. Paris: Librairie d'Amérique et d'Orient, 1976.
Lefkowitz, Mary. *Not Out of Africa: How Afrocentrism Became an Excuse to Teach Myth as History*. New York: Basic Books, 1996.
Lefkowitz, Mary, and Guy MacLean Rogers, eds. *Black Athena Revisited*. Chapel Hill: University of North Carolina Press, 1996.
Lévi-Strauss, Claude. *Tristes Tropiques*. Translated by John and Doreen Weightman. New York: Pocket Books, 1977.
Lexikon der Ägyptologie. 6 vols. Edited by W. Helck et al. Wiesbaden: Otto Harrassowitz, 1972–1992.
Lichtheim, Miriam. *Ancient Egyptian Autobiographies Chiefly of the Middle Kingdom: A Study and an Anthology*. Orbis Biblicus et Orientalis 84. Freiburg: Universitätsverlag; Göttingen: Vandenhoeck & Ruprecht, 1988.
———. *Ancient Egyptian Literature*. 3 vols. Berkeley: University of California Press, 1975–1980.
———. "Have the Principles of Ancient Egyptian Metrics Been Discovered?" *JARCE* 9 (1971–72): 103–10.
Loprieno, Antonio. *Ancient Egyptian: A Linguistic Introduction*. Cambridge: Cambridge University Press, 1995.
Manetho. *Ægyptiaca (Epitome)*. Loeb Classical Library, 1980.
Meyer, Christine. "Thutmosis II." *LdÄ* 6: 539f.
Michalowski, Kazimierz. *Art of Ancient Egypt*. New York: Harry N. Abrams, 1968.
Milne, Joseph Grafton. *A History of Egypt Under Roman Rule*. London: Methuen, 1899. Reprint. Chicago: Ares Publications, 1924.
Möller, Georg. *Hieratische Paläographie, die ägyptische Buchschrift*. Osnabrück: Zeller, 1965.
Morenz, Siegfried. *Egyptian Religion*. Translated by Ann E. Keep. Ithaca: Cornell University Press, 1973.

Moret, Alexandre. "La Légende d'Osiris à l'époque thebaine d'après l'hymne à Osiris du Louvre." *Bulletin de l'Institut Français d'Archéologie Orientale* 30 (1930): 725–50.

Mudimbe, Valentin Y. *Parables and Fables: Exegesis, Textuality, and Politics in Central Africa.* Madison: University of Wisconsin Press, 1991.

Müller, Dieter. "Die Zeugung durch das Herz in Religion und Medizin der Ägypter." *Orientalia,* n.s., 35, no. 3 (1966): 247–74.

Myśliwiec, Karol. *Studien zum Gott Atum.* 2 vols. Hildesheim: Gerstenberg Verlag, 1978.

Naville, Edouard. *Deir el-Bahari.* Memoirs of the Egypt Exploration Fund. Vols. 12–16, 19, 27, 29. London: Egypt Exploration Fund, 1849–1908.

Niwiński, Andrzej. *Studies on the Illustrated Theban Funerary Papyri of the 11th and 10th Centuries B.C.* Freiburg: Universitätsverlag; Göttingen: Vandenhoeck & Ruprecht, 1989.

Ogden, Jorge. "Some Notes on the Iconography of the God Min." *Bulletin of the Egyptological Seminar* 7 (1985/6): 29–41.

Ogiwara, Asao, and Kōnosu Hayao, eds. *Kojiki, Jōdai kayō.* Nihon koten bungaku zenshū 1. Tokyo: Shōgakukan, 1973.

Otto, Eberhard. *Ancient Egyptian Art: The Cults of Osiris and Amon.* Translated by Kate Bosse Griffiths. New York: Harry N. Abrams, 1967. Originally published under the title *Osiris und Amun: Kult und heilige Stätten* (Munich: Hirmer, 1966).

Paglia, Camille. *Sexual Personae: Art and Decadence from Nefertiti to Emily Dickinson.* New York: Vintage Books, 1991.

Parker, Richard A., and Leonard H. Lesko. "The Khonsu Cosmogony." In *Pyramid Studies and Other Essays Presented to I. E. S. Edwards,* ed. John Baines, pp. 168–75 and plates 34–37. London: Egypt Exploration Society, 1988.

Parkinson, Richard. "'Homosexual' Desire and Middle Kingdom Literature." *JEA* 81 (1996): 57–76.

———. *Voices from Ancient Egypt.* Norman: University of Oklahoma Press, 1991.

Petrie, Sir William Matthew Flinders. *Koptos.* London: Egypt Exploration Society, 1896.

Plutarch. *Lives.* Loeb Classical Library. 1914–26.

———. *Peri Isidos kai Osiridos.* Translated and edited and with a commentary by Christian Froidefond. In *Plutarque, Oeuvres morales,* vol. 5, pt. 2. Paris: Les Belles Lettres, 1988.

———. *Peri Isidos kai Osiridos.* Translated and edited and with a commentary by J. Gwyn Griffiths. Cambridge: University of Wales Press, 1970.

Polotsky, Hans Jakob. "Egyptian." In *Collected Papers,* pp. 320–63. Jerusalem: The Magnes Press, Hebrew University, 1971.

———. "Egyptian Tenses." *Israel Academy of Sciences* II, 5: 71–96.

Prichard, James B., ed. *Ancient Near Eastern Texts Relating to the Old Testament.* 3d edition, with supplement. Princeton: Princeton Unversity Press, 1969.
Quirke, Stephen. *Ancient Egyptian Religion.* London: British Museum Press, 1992.
———. *Who Were the Pharaohs? A History of Their Names with a List of Cartouches.* New York: Dover Publications, 1990.
Quirke, Stephen and Carol Andrews. *The Rosetta Stone: Facsimile Drawing with an Introduction and Translations.* New York: Harry N. Abrams, 1988.
Redford, Donald. *Akhenaten, the Heretic King.* Princeton: Princeton University Press, 1984.
———. *Egypt, Canaan, and Israel in Ancient Times.* Princeton: Princeton University Press, 1992.
Reeves, Nicholas. *The Complete Tutankhamun: The King, the Tomb, the Royal Treasure.* London: Thames & Hudson, 1990.
Roaf, Michael. *Cultural Atlas of Mesopotamia and the Ancient Near East.* Oxford: Equinox, 1990.
Robins, Gay. *Proportion and Style in Ancient Egyptian Art.* Austin: University of Texas Press, 1994.
———. *Women in Ancient Egypt.* Cambridge, Mass.: Harvard University Press, 1993.
Romer, John. *Ancient Lives.* New York: Henry Holt, 1984.
———. *Valley of the Kings.* New York: Henry Holt, 1981.
Sandison, A. T. "Balsamierung." *LdÄ* 1: 610–14.
Sandman, Maj, ed. *Texts from the Time of Akhenaten.* Bibliotheca Aegyptiaca 8. Brussels: La Fondation Égyptologique Reine Élisabeth, 1938.
Satzinger, Helmut. "Hieratisch." *LdÄ* 2: 1187–89.
Sauneron, Serge. *The Priests of Ancient Egypt.* Translated by Ann Morrissett. New York: Grove Press, 1960.
Sauneron, Serge, and Jean Yoyotte. "La Naissance du monde selon l'Égypte ancienne." In *La Naissance du monde, sources orientales* 1. Paris: Editions du Seuil, 1959.
Saussure, Ferdinand de. *Cours de linguistique générale.* Paris: Payothéque, 1982.
Saussy, Haun. *The Problem of a Chinese Aesthetic.* Stanford, Calif.: Stanford University Press, 1993.
Schäfer, Heinrich. *Mysterien des Osiris in Abydos unter König Sesostris III nach dem Denkstein des Oberschatzmeisters I-cher-nofret im Berliner Museum, Untersuchungen zur Geschichte und Altertumskunde Ägyptens,* vol. 4, part 2, ed. Kurt Sethe. Leipzig: J. D. Hinrichs'sche Buchhandlung, 1904.
———. *Principles of Egyptian Art.* Edited, with an epilogue, by Emma Brunner-Traut. Translated and edited, with an introduction, by John Baines. 1974. Reprint. Oxford: Griffith Institute, 1986.

Schlögl, Hermann Alexander. *Echnaton-Tutanchamun, Fakten und Texte.* Wiesbaden: Otto Harrassowitz, 1983.

Schlott, Adelheid. *Schrift und Schreiber im alten Ägypten.* Munich: C. H. Beck, 1989.

Schmandt-Besserat, Denise. *Before Writing: From Counting to Cuneiform.* Austin: University of Texas Press, 1992.

Schott, Siegfried. "Zum Weltbild der Jenseitsführer des neuen Reiches." *Nachrichten der Akademie der Wissenschaften in Göttingen, I. Philologisch-historische Klasse* 11 (1965): 185–97.

Sedgwick, Eve Kosofsky. *Between Men: English Literature and Male Homosocial Desire.* New York: Columbia University Press, 1985.

Seeber, Christine. *Untersuchungen zur Darstellung des Totengerichts im alten Ägypten.* Munich: Deutscher Kunstverlag, 1976.

Sethe, Kurt. *Ägyptische Lesestücke: Texte des Mittleren Reiches.* Revised edition. Leipzig: J. C. Hinrichs Verlag, 1928.

———. *Das "Denkmal memphitischer Theologie," der Schabakostein des Britischen Museums.* Unters. z. Gesch. u. Altertumskunde Ägyptens, no. 10, part 1. Leipzig, 1928. Reprint. Hildesheim, 1964.

———. *Erläuterungen zu den ägyptischen Lesestücken.* Darmstadt: Wissenschaftliche Buchgesellschaft, 1976.

———. *Übersetzung und Kommentar zu den altägyptischen Pyramidentexten,* 6 vols. HamburgGlückstadt: J. J. Augustin, 1935–62.

———, ed. *Die altägyptischen Pyramidentexte.* 4 vols. Leipzig: J. C. Hinrichs'sche Buchhandlung, 1908.

———, ed. "Restaurationsstele Tutenchamuns in Kairo." In *Urkunden des ägyptisches Altertums,* 4: 2025–32. Leipzig: Akademie Verlag, 1961.

Seznec, Jean. *The Survival of the Pagan Gods: The Mythological Tradition and Its Place in Renaissance Humanism and Art.* Translated by Barbara Sessions. New York: Harper Torchbooks, The Bollingen Library, Harper & Row, 1953. Originally published under the title *La Survivance des dieux antiques.*

Shafer, Byron E., ed. *Religion in Ancient Egypt: Gods, Myths, and Personal Practice.* Ithaca: Cornell University Press, 1991.

Smither, Paul. "An Old Kingdom Letter Concerning the Crimes of Count Sabni." *JEA* 28 (1942): 16–19.

Spencer, A. J. *Death in Ancient Egypt.* London: Penguin Books, 1982.

Spivak, Gayatri. "Time and Timing: Law and History." In *Chronotypes: The Construction of Time,* ed. John Bender and David Wellbery. Stanford, Calif.: Stanford University Press, 1991.

Starobinski, Jean. *Jean-Jacques Rousseau: La Transparence et l'obstacle, suivi de sept essais sur Rousseau.* Paris: Gallimard, 1971.

Staten, Henry. "How the Spirit (Almost) Became Flesh: Gospel of John." *Representations* 41 (Winter 1993): 34–57.

Steinberg, Leo. *The Sexuality of Christ in Renaissance Art and in Modern Oblivion.* 2d edition, revised and expanded. New York: Pantheon, 1996.
Stevenson Smith, William. *The Art and Architecture of Ancient Egypt.* Revised by William Kelly Simpson. Pelican History of Art. New Haven, Conn.: Yale University Press, 1981.
——. *Egyptian Sculpture and Painting in the Old Kingdom.* London: Oxford University Press, 1946.
Störk, Lothar. "Erotik." *LdÄ* 2: 4–11.
——. "Rind." *LdÄ* 5: 258–63.
Tefnin, Roland. "Discours et iconicité dans l'art égyptien." *Göttinger Miszellen, Beiträge zur ägyptologischen Diskussion* 79 (1984): 55–72.
——. "Image, écriture, récit: À Propos des Représentations égyptiennes de la bataille de Qadesh." *Annales d'histore de l'art et d'archéologie, publication annuelle de la Section d'Histoire de l'Art et d'Archéologie de l'Université Libre de Bruxelles* 2 (1980): 7–24.
Torok, Maria. "The Meaning of 'Penis Envy' in Women (1963)." Translated by Nicholas Rand. *Differences: A Journal of Feminist Cultural Studies,* "The Phallus Issue," 4 (Spring 1992): 1–39.
Trigger, B. G., Barry J. Kemp, David O'Connor, and Allen B. Lloyd. *Ancient Egypt: A Social History.* Cambridge: Cambridge University Press, 1983.
Vandier, Jacques. *Le Papyrus Jumilhac.* Paris: Centre National de la Recherche Scientifique, 1962.
——. *La Religion égyptienne.* Paris: Presses Universitaires de France, 1949.
V.-David, Madeleine. *Le Débat sur les écritures et l'hiéroglyphe aux XVIIe et XVIIIe siècles et l'application de la notion de déchiffrement aux écritures mortes.* Paris: S.E.V.P.E.N., 1965.
Velde, Herman te. "Horus und Seth." *LdÄ* 3: 25–27.
——. "Ptah." *LdÄ* 4: 1178–80.
——. *Seth, God of Confusion: A Study of His Role in Egyptian Mythology and Religion.* Leiden: E. J. Brill, 1967.
Vernus, Pascal. "Formes 'emphatiques' en fonction non 'emphatique' dans la protase d'un système corrélatif." *Göttinger Miszellen* 43 (1981): 73–88.
——. "Name." *LdÄ* 4: 320–26.
Westendorf, Wolfhart. "Anatomie." *LdÄ* 1: 258–62.
——. "Die Anfänge der altägyptischen Hieroglyphen." In *Frühe Schriftzeugnisse der Menschheit,* pp. 57–87. Göttingen: Vandenhoeck & Ruprecht, 1969.
——. "Homosexualität." *LdÄ* 2: 1272–75.
——. *Painting, Sculpture, and Architecture of Ancient Egypt.* New York: Harry N. Abrams, 1968.
Wilkinson, Charles K., and Marsha Hill. *Egyptian Wall Paintings, The Metropolitan Museum of Art's Collection of Facsimiles.* New York: Metropolitan Museum of Art, 1983.
Wilkinson, Richard H. *Reading Egyptian Art: A Hieroglyphic Guide to*

Ancient Egyptian Painting and Sculpture. London: Thames & Hudson, 1992.

Williams, Bruce. "Narmer and the Coptos Colossi." *JARCE* 25 (1988): 35–59.

Ziegler, Christiane. *The Louvre: Egyptian Antiquities.* London: Scala Books, 1990.

———. "Des Signes sans secret." In *Hommage de L'Europe à Champollion: Mémoires d'Égypte,* pp. 81–109. Strasbourg: La Nuée Bleue/DNA and Fondation Mécénat Science et Art, 1990.

INDEX

In this index an "f" after a number indicates a separate reference on the next page, and an "ff" indicates separate references on the next two pages. A continuous discussion over two or more pages is indicated by a span of page numbers, e.g., "57–59." *Passim* is used for a cluster of references in close but not consecutive sequence. Pharaohs' names are listed first by nomen, with prenomen, when known, in parentheses.

Abbas Hilmi (II), Prince, 11, 250
Abedju (place-name), 13f. *See also* Abydos
Abstraction, 196
Abu Simbel, 54
Abydos, 19, 22, 34–35, 37–38, 93, 106, 120–21, 147, 212
Action, 76
Adam, 227f
Adultery, 234
Agency, 74–75, 137, 144, 189, 225, 236
Agon, 289
'Aha, King, 268
Ahmes, Queen, 135
Åkerblad, Johan, 49, 51
Akh, 161
Akhenaten, King (Neferkheperure'-Wa'enre'), 149–53, 190–201, 243–44, 277f, 285, 296
Akhetaten (place-name), 192, 277

Akhmim (place-name), 22, 145
Alchemy, 209
Alexander, 51
Alexandria, library at, 218
Alienation, 9, 228
Allah, 294
Allegory, 60–62, 114, 260
Allen, James, 111f, 175, 196, 198
Alphabet, 45–53 *passim*, 71, 263, 290
Amarna, 141, 148–53, 160, 189–201, 206, 212, 244, 278, 285; representational style, 201
Amaunet, 166f
Amduat (funerary text), 19
Amenemhet, tomb of, at Beni Hasan, 276
Amenemhet III, King (Nima'atre'), 84, 89
Amenemope, Onomasticon of, 157–58, 167, 279

312 INDEX

Amenemope, stela of, 250
Amenhotep III, King (Nebma'atre'), 136, 140f, 149, 204
Amenhotep IV, King (Neferkheperure'), see Akhenaten
American Sign Language (ASL), 59
Ammianus Marcellinus, 46
Amun, xix, 22, 110, 123, 135–36, 144–52 passim, 166f, 187, 191f, 194, 201–5 passim, 251; kamutef, 107, 122–23, 131–35 passim, 146–51 passim, 204, 235, 252, 285, 293; -Re', 147, 165, 203f
Analogy, 122, 181, 183, 241
"Ancient model" (Bernal), 217; Revised, 217–18
Androcentrism, 153
Ani, 9, 23, 245; papyrus of, 139, 249, 254, 273
Animal worship, 161–62
Animism, 118
'Anjety (place-name), 14
'Ankhesenpaaten, 196
'Ankhnesneferibre', 23
Anselm, 286
Anthropocentrism, of hieroglyphs, 19
Anthropomorphism, 161, 196, 240
Antifiguralism, 196f, 244, 296
Anubis, 127–33
Apep, 84, 125, 208
Apis bull, 162, 280
Apostrophe, 72, 260
Aristotle, 216, 218, 291
Arm, 112
Armant, 162, 280
Arnold, Matthew, 191
"Aryan model" (Bernal), 217f
'Ash tree, 129, 131
"Aspective," 97f, 269, 290
Assmann, Jan, 29–33, 70–71, 116, 165, 168, 196f, 201, 206–7, 209–10, 261, 271, 284
Assyria, 174
Aten, xix, 14, 194, 196–200, 243–44, 296
Athena, 226
Athothis, King, 11
Athribis (place-name), 14
Attis, 250
Atum, 8, 11, 85, 111–20, 123, 127, 133, 146f, 165–69 passim, 173, 177–82, 183–89 passim, 203, 211, 231, 236f, 243, 245, 252, 273, 278, 294
Atum-Shu-Tefnut, 167
Augustine of Hippo, 224, 227–28, 231, 235, 242ff, 292, 295; Confessions, 228
Aunu (Heliopolis), cosmogony of, 14, 111f, 117f, 123, 133, 147, 162, 173, 182, 203f, 236f, 271
Authority, 133f, 187, 189, 195, 225, 228, 233, 235ff, 241
Autobiography, 192
Autoeroticism, 113f
Autonomy, 134, 189
Ay, King (Kheperkheperure'-Irma'at), 201

Ba, 23, 28, 132, 238–39, 252–53
Baines, John, 77, 96, 113, 158, 207, 254
Baketaten, 196
Baqet III, 276
Barthélemy, Jean-Jacques, 47
Base ten, 220
"Basic Thought," 4
Bata, 127–33
Battlefield Palette, 77f
Being, 188f, 206–10, 214, 244
Beinlich, Horst, 251
Bellange, Jacques, 229
Beni Hasan (place-name), 156, 276
Bennett, John, 205
Berenike, 51f, 65
Bernal, Martin, 3, 216–18, 294; Black Athena I: The Fabrication of Ancient Greece, 1785–1985, 216, 218
Betrayal, 29
Bible, 47, 54, 130, 160, 190, 227, 294
Binarism, 210. See also Dualism
Body, 23–24, 27–28, 46, 63, 105, 108, 119, 131, 133, 137, 147, 179, 181, 184, 188, 222–28 passim, 233–39 passim, 242, 246, 260; phallic, 8, 64, 108, 116, 124, 137, 220, 227; of Osiris, 9, 17; constructions of, 23; parts, 26, 75, 87, 251, 253; female, 137, 141, 144; of Christ, 229; of the Deity, 234
Book of the Dead, 55, 114; Spell 175, 8, 249; Spell 142, 14; Spell 30B, 28–29, 243, 254
Botticelli, Sandro, 59, 64
Bread and beer, 8, 16, 95, 101, 104, 155
Breasted, James Henry, 114, 170–80

INDEX 313

passim, 182–83, 191–95 *passim*, 238–39
Bremner-Rhind Papyrus, 188
Bride of Yahweh, 234
Brothers, 124
Brown, Peter, 224, 228
Brugsch, Heinrich, 259
Brunner-Traut, Emma, 97
Buchis bull, 162, 280
Buddhism, 293
Budge, E. A. Wallis, 114
Bull Palette, 77, 79
Busiris, 251
Butchery, 26
Butler, Judith, 253
Buto (place-name), 17
Byblos, 17

Calendar, 220, 290
Campbell, Joseph, 115
Canon, 2; of representation, 139, 141, 144, 156
Canopic jars, 25, 275
Careers, 31
Carter, Howard, 200
Cartouche, 47, 51–52, 54–55, 64–65, 196, 204, 258
Castration, 223, 235, 237, 244, 291
Champollion, Jean-François, 49, 51–56, 64, 258f
Chauvinism, 214
Chephren, *see* Kha'fre'
Chinese, 47, 67, 78, 80, 263, 265, 288
Christ, 15, 221, 225–27, 229–33, 236f, 249, 293
Christianity, Christians, 15, 108, 114, 164, 219f, 224–33, 237–38, 239, 250, 294, 296
Church, Christian, 226, 231, 237
Church Fathers, 227
Clarity, 241–42
Cleopatra VII (Netjeret-merites), 45, 51f, 65, 191, 218
Coffin, 17
Coffin Texts, 133, 236; 1.336–54, 116; 2.39b–q, 168; 2.396b, 169; 3.383a, 169; 3.382–89, 185–86, 188
Complementarity, 19, 89
Conflict, 124
Consciousness, figuring of, 23, 113, 117, 241

Consumption, 155
Contendings of Horus and Setekh, 124
Coptic, 47, 53ff, 258
Coptos, 22, 106, 145, 270
Copts, 107
Corporeality, 181–82, 184, 226, 234, 243
Cosmogony, 85f, 111–18, 133, 166–70 *passim*, 177–81, 184, 186, 236, 273
Cosmology, 84, 211, 281
Creation, 111, 116, 134, 183–88 *passim*, 210, 236, 243, 294. *See also* Cosmogony
Creator, 187, 194
Crete, 216
"Crocodilicity," 257
Crucifixion, 226f
Cult of personality, 200
Cult shrine, 12

Davies, Norman de Garis, 143
Death, 11, 14, 44–45, 119, 131, 184, 223, 229, 236, 244, 250; of a God, 14–15, 249
Decipherment, 3, 47–56
Deconstruction, 8, 45
Defacement, 192
Deir el-Bahari, 135, 276
Deir el-Medina, 212
Democracy, 153, 218f, 288–89
Demotic, 48, 51, 55, 76, 258
Den, King, 149
Dendera, 53, 145, 256
Derrida, Jacques, 5–6, 44–45, 89, 159; "Plato's Pharmacy," 5
Description de l'Égypte, 55, 257
Desire, 9, 113–14, 115, 133, 144, 187, 189
Determinatives, 24, 30, 40, 42, 69–73, 76, 88, 108–12, 205, 211
Dialectic, 224, 233, 238, 243
Dictator, 200
Différance, 2, 44–45, 56, 153, 160, 168f, 211, 246
Differential meaning, 56, 63, 74, 98
Diodorus Siculus, 25f, 46
Dionysus, 10, 291
Disembodiment, *see* Dismemberment
Dismemberment, 9, 13, 21, 23, 24–25, 26, 27–29, 75, 108, 127, 131, 228, 272
Dissemination, 26

314 INDEX

Diversity, 155, 160, 163, 210
Divine Son, 226
Djed pillar, 251
Djedu (place-name), 14
Djet (figure of time), 169, 206, 271
Djet, King, *see* Serpent King
Djoser, King, *see* Netjerkhet, King
Dominance, political, 127
Dominion, 187, 195
"Double play" of writing, 89
Drowning, 13
Ḏt, *see Djet* (figure of time)
Dualism, 18f, 225, 241
Duamutef, 102, 253, 275

"East," 4, 191f, 213
Economics, 90
Economy, semiotic, 18, 23, 26, 39; of substitution, 95
Egg, 193–94
Egyptian Museum, Cairo, 11
Egyptology, 3f, 6f, 106, 113, 182f, 190
Eilberg-Schwartz, Howard, 233–35, 237, 293
Eileithyaspolis (place-name), 14
Ejaculation, 8f, 22, 26, 64, 111–17 *passim*, 231
Emasculation, 236, 242
Embodiment, 228, 237
Empire, 195
Emptiness, 245
Endowments, funerary, 104
Engenderment, 22, 228
Enlightenment, 217
Epistemology, 6, 154
Erasure, 233, 235f
Erection, 111–12, 121–23, 229–31, 233; -resurrection, 233
Erman, Adolf, 170f, 173, 183, 259, 283
Eroticism, 139f, 142, 144, 153
Eternal life, 11
Eternity, 209
Etymology, 11
Euclid, 289
Euripides, 216f
Eurocentrism, 2
Eve, 227
Expectoration, 116
Eye(s), 17, 20, 42, 185; glyph of, 71–72

Falcon, 20. *See also* Horus, as falcon

Fate, 199
Father, 111, 116, 124, 186, 221, 225f, 237, 293
Favor, 199
Fecundity, *see* Fertility
Female, 222
Feminism, 136
Feminist criticism, 235
Fertility, 9, 12, 15, 23, 110, 138, 141, 145, 147
Festival, 120
Fetishism, 161
"Fighting words," 279
Figurality, 8, 18f, 23, 34, 43, 50, 56, 59, 62, 64, 74–75, 80, 87–89, 110, 131, 138, 148, 153, 159–66 *passim*, 183, 197, 233–36 *passim*, 240–41, 243–46 *passim*, 262, 264, 272–73, 285, 296
First-person plural, 2f, 118, 153, 212, 272–73
"First Time," *see* Zep-tepy
Fish, 17, 23
Flesh, 225–26, 233, 237
Flood, 15
Forty-two negative avowals, 208
Fragmentation, 23, 29, 35, 118, 154, 221, 228, 236
Frazer, James George, 10, 249
Freedom, 242
French Revolution, 191
Freud, Sigmund, 108, 190, 235, 253
Frölich's syndrome, 149f
Funerary literature, 27, 32, 132, 254
Funerary practices, 17, 23, 138, 245, 275

Gardiner, Alan Henderson, 102, 137, 167, 259; *Egyptian Grammar*, xv, 71
Gaze, 276
Geb, 11, 13, 21, 32, 85, 119–23 *passim*, 168, 176f, 221, 294
Gempaaten, 151
Gender, 9, 118, 133, 142, 144, 148, 154, 166f, 229, 243, 273
Genealogy, 12
Generative command, *see* Hu
Genesis, Book of, 179
Gerzean period, 12
Gita Govinda, 273
Giza, 23
Glyphs, *see* Hieroglyphs

INDEX 315

Gnosticism, 209, 225f
God(s), 9, 160, 195, 223, 226, 231–37, 244. *See also individual gods by name*
Goux, Jean-Joseph, 222–24, 291
Grain, dying, 225
Grammaire égyptienne . . . (Champollion), 56
Grammar, 80
Graphical User Interface (GUI), 263
"Great He-She," 133
Greece, Greeks, 3, 45, 48, 153, 160–64 *passim*, 215–20, 227, 239–42 *passim*, 256, 274, 278–79, 288, 294f
Grimal, Nicolas, 194
Guignes, C. Joseph de, 47
Gunn, Battiscombe, 259

Ha, 77
Hamilton, Edith, 215–16, 218, 288
Ha'py, 102, 163, 253, 275
Hathor, xix, 125, 167, 256
Hatshepsut, King/Queen (Ma'atkare'), 134–36, 165, 276, 293
Hauhet, 166
Heart, 23, 25, 28–29, 32ff, 116, 129, 131, 135, 178–81, 189, 202, 254, 275–76
Heart scarab, 25, 28, 254
Hebrews, 190, 279, 294
Heb-Sed festival, 146
Heemskerck, Maerten van, 230–33, 292
Hegel, Georg Wilhelm Friedrich, 44–45, 132, 222–24, 235, 239–43, 244f, 257, 288, 291, 295
Heka, 169
Heliopolis, *see* Aunu
Hellenocentrism, 183, 216, 266. *See also* Greece
Henotheism, 165–67
Henuttawy, papyrus of, 85–86
Herm, 291
Hermeneutics, 220
Hermes, 222
Hermeticism, 3, 47
Hermopolis, *see* Khemenu
Herodotus, 25, 291
Herwer (place-name), 14
Hesire', 83, 94
Heterosexuality, 118, 148
Hierakonpolis, 12, 166
Hieratic, 25, 55

Hieroglyphika of "Horapollo," 46
Hieroglyphs, 12, 19, 24–30 *passim*, 35, 40, 45–56, 65–72, 74–78, 80, 82–85, 88–89, 94–103 *passim*, 108–10, 112, 137f, 145f, 156, 161, 175, 181, 197, 205, 246, 252, 258, 266, 274, 285; emblematic, 41f, 77, 83–85, 87, 265; retrograde, 175–76; disposition of, 176, 180
"His Beloved Son," 38–39, 42
History, 13, 23, 120, 221, 250
Hjelmslev, Leo, 259
Homoeroticism, 63, 144, 148, 234
Homonyms, 263
Homosexuality, 127, 145, 148f, 152, 274
Homosociality, 130, 132, 145
"Horapollo," 49. *See also Hieroglyphika* of "Horapollo"
Horemheb, King (Djeserkheperure'-Setepenre'), 201, 204
Hornub, 167
Hornung, Erik, 3, 19, 160, 164–65, 169, 206–10, 252
Horus, 11, 13, 16–17, 19, 21f, 26–33 *passim*, 39, 42, 78, 120–24 *passim*, 131–36 *passim*, 147, 163, 166–77 *passim*, 189, 196, 202ff, 231, 274f, 294; as falcon, 18; as pharaoh, 20, 23, 39, 82; of Behdet, 39–40, 41–42; "the Elder," 121; battle with Setekh, 37, 124–27
Hsi-Hsia, *see* Xixia
Hu, 169, 186–88 *passim*, 236
Humanity, 229
Hunefer, papyrus of, 101–3, 273
Hybridity of gods, 162, 296
Hymns, 192, 195, 205

Iconography, 18, 60, 240
Icons, iconicity, 19, 44, 65–67, 70, 81, 88, 108, 115, 158, 181, 261–64 *passim*; aural, 261–62
Idealism, 114, 222, 224, 240, 244, 246, 257, 289, 295
Identity, 9, 33, 42, 239; individual, 238, 245
Ideogram, xix, 50ff, 55–56, 59, 65, 68, 71–72, 74–75, 79, 88, 103, 111, 257, 264
Ideograph, *see* Ideogram

Idolatry, 162, 234
Idu, tomb of (G 7102), 23f, 252
Ihy, 167
Illusionism, 256
Immortality, 8
Imsety, 102, 253, 275
Incarnation, 226, 234
"Incorporation," 225
India, Indians, 47, 288
Indo-European, 47–48, 50, 217
Indo-Hittite, 218
Insemination, chain of, 231
Instruction of Merikare', 104, 274
Instrumentality, instrumentalism, 10
Intentionality, 189
Interclausal relationships, 259
Intersubjectivity, 1, 53
Irony, 132f
Isis, 13, 17–20 passim, 21–22, 27, 34, 102, 120–27 passim, 134, 144, 162, 167, 176f, 222, 231, 251, 261
Islam, 294, 296
Israel, 234, 237
Israelites, 190, 234–38 passim
Iykhernofret, Stela of, 34–43, 256

Jakobsohn, Helmuth, 122
Japanese, 263
Jayadeva, 273
Jaynes, Julian, 295
Jesus, 229, 236
Jews, see Judaism
Jmy-dȝt ("What Is in the Underworld"), 85
John, Gospel of, 179, 225f, 237
John, Saint, 224
Jones, William, 47–48
Joseph, 190
Judaism, 164, 219f, 226, 229, 233–34, 238, 290–96 passim
"Judeo-Christian tradition," 219f
Judgment, 9, 29, 32, 102f, 207
Jumilhac, papyrus, 127
Junge, Friedrich, 173–75, 183f
Junker, Hermann, 171–75 passim, 182f, 283
Justification, 9, 33f, 122, 207, 256
Juxtaposition, 262, 266

Ka, 23, 27f, 41f, 78, 113, 142, 165, 168, 186, 193, 252, 266

Kadesh reliefs, 89
Kamutef, see under Amun
Karnak, 22, 87, 107, 113, 123, 135, 145–51 passim, 174, 201, 203, 212, 267, 284
Katakana, 65
Kauket, 166
Kematef, 211
Kemp, Barry, 3–4, 5f, 157–58, 198, 245, 278, 296
Key, Willem, 229; *Pietà*, 230
Kha'fre', 278
Kha'kheperre'seneb, Sayings of, 28
Kha'sekhemwy, King, 18, 277
Khemenu (Hermopolis), 166f
Kheper, 187, 240, 284
Kher-aha (place-name), 14
Kheruef, tomb of (TT192), 276
Khety, 276
Khonsu, 167
Khnum, 165
Khnumhotep, tomb of (BH3), 156, 276
Kia, 200
Kircher, Athanasius, 47
Kite (bird), 22, 120
Knowledge, 155–59, 163
Kozloff, Arielle, 140–41, 144
Krishna, 273
Kush, see Nubia

Lacan, Jacques, 108, 221–22, 224, 228, 235f, 242ff, 291
Language, 7, 26, 57, 186, 188
Lefkowitz, Mary, 216, 217–18
Legacy, 212, 213–15, 219, 231, 238f, 243; Egyptian, 222
Legal documents, 35, 98, 100f
Legitimacy, 122
Leibniz, Gottfried Wilhelm, 257
Letopolis, 251
Letter, 44
Lettre à M. Dacier (Champollion), 52
Libya, 174, 195
Lichtheim, Miriam, 130
Light, 193, 196–98, 199
Likeness, sculpted, 26
Listening, 31
Lists, 158
Litany (of Osiris's titles), 14
Literalism, 78

Litigation, 32
"Living Sundisk," 198, 201. *See also* Pa-aten'ankh
Logic, 5, 67, 281
Logocentrism, 243
Logogram, 50, 59, 68–69, 70, 72, 79, 84, 88, 103, 109, 257, 262f, 290
Logograph, *see* Logogram
Logos, 51, 64, 222–28 passim, 236
Love, 119
Luke (New Testament), 228f
Lust, 227, 231, 292
Luxor, 107, 123

Ma'a-kheru ("True of Voice," "Justified"), 21, 27, 33, 294
Ma'at, xix, 19, 29–33, 169, 187, 204, 206, 245
Madame Bovary, 80
Magic, 9, 70, 185–86
Mailer, Norman, 10
"Man and his occupations" (Gardiner), 137
Manetho, 54
Man of Sorrows, 229–30, 232f
Many, 189
Mary, Virgin, 226, 229, 231
Masculinity, 231, 235
Masturbation, 22, 112, 114f, 133, 147, 236, 243, 271
Materialism, 222
Materiality, 238
Mathematical notation, 67, 262
Matter, 188
Matthew (New Testament), 228f
Meaning, 7, 59, 62, 79, 89; visually motivated, 66
Medical texts, 158
Medinet Habu, 107
Meidum, 89
Meketre', tomb of, 140
Memory, 31, 46, 105
Memphis, 14, 162f, 169–74 passim, 182, 201, 280, 281
"Memphite Theology," 170–75, 178–84, 224, 240
Menena, tomb of (TT69), 142, 276
Menes, 11
Menkaure', King, xix
Merenre', King (Nemtyemsaf), 75
Mesha'redwyseqeb, papyrus of, 87

Mesopotamia, 216, 234
Metaphor, 27, 46, 61–62, 72, 75, 114, 138, 240, 260
Metonymy, 27, 61–62, 72, 75, 138, 179, 260, 264
Michelangelo, 293
"Millions," 169, 186
Min, 22, 77, 106–7, 110, 122, 144ff, 235, 252, 270, 272, 277
Mind, 63, 180–81, 184, 187ff, 223, 236, 246
Misogyny, 133
Mnevis bull, 162, 280
Monotheism, 149, 154, 160, 164–65, 190, 194, 198, 200, 219, 228–38 passim, 244, 266, 289–90
Montu, 280
Morenz, Siegfried, 115, 162–64, 167
Moses, 190
Mouth, 185
Multiplicity, 8, 19, 67, 95, 115, 118, 121, 154, 159f, 166, 184–89 passim, 210, 220, 238, 245
Mummies, mummification, 9, 23–24, 26, 28, 101, 127, 190, 238, 253, 275
Murder, 12f, 17, 20, 119
Musical notation, 262
Muslims, 107, 290
Mut, 167
Mutilation, 131
Myth, 5, 7, 13, 19–26 passim, 43, 60, 115, 119–24 passim, 187, 221, 226
Mythological papyri, 84–87

Nakht, tomb of (TT52), 140–41, 143
Nakhthorheb, King (Snedjemibre'), 150
Nakhtnebef, King (Kheperkare'), 23
Name-dropping, 187
Names, naming, 23, 26–27, 92, 105, 149, 157–59, 172, 196f, 204, 238
Napata, 172
Naqada, 91, 93
Na'rmer, King, 94
Na'rmer Palette, 20, 70, 75f, 263, 265
Narrative, 10, 15, 17, 20, 119, 122, 132, 219f
Nationalism, 213
Nativity, 227
"Naturalism," 150, 192
"Natural Theology," 196
Naunet, 166

318 INDEX

Neb'ankh, 254
Nectanebo I, see Nakhtnebef
Nectanebo II, see Nakhthorheb
Nedjmemyt, 9
Nedyet (place-name), 13, 38, 251
Neferefre', King, 97, 100
Nefer-Hor, 167
Nefertem, 167
Nefertiti, Queen (Neferneferuraten), 149, 151ff, 192, 199f, 278
Negation, 211, 223, 245
Neheh (figure of time), 169, 206, 271
Nehmauit, 167
Neith, 91, 127
Neithhotep, Queen, 91–92, 268
Nekhen, 93
Neni-Nesu (place-name), 14
Neoplatonism, 224
Neper, 14, 15–16
Nephthys, 17f, 102, 176f, 251
Neshmet Barque, 38–39
Nespakashuty, papyrus of, 119
Netjer, 160–65; hieroglyphs, 161
Netjerkhet, King, 94, 277f. See also Djoser, King
New Testament, 22, 228, 233
Nfrw ("Beauty," "Goodness"), 39
Nḥḥ, see Neheh
Nicene Creed, 226, 228
Nile, 10–17 passim, 37, 240
Ninetjer, King, 18
Nitiqret, King/Queen, 275
Nonexistence, 207–11, 246
"Non-Western," 2
Nothingness, 207, 209
Nous, 222
Nubia, Nubians, 110f, 172, 174, 190, 195, 202
Nudity, 140–42, 143, 293
Number, 8, 92, 159, 169, 186
Numeral, see Number
Nut, 85, 119, 121, 140, 168, 186

Oedipus, 232, 241
Offering formula, see Offertory
Offerings, 17, 26, 93–96, 101, 103ff, 155, 159, 252, 280; economy of, 41–42
Offertory, 16, 27, 41, 159
Old Testament, 233
One, 118, 160, 169, 189, 209f, 222, 224

"Only begotten son," 226, 237
Onomastica, 155, 157–58
Ontology, 252
"Opening of the Mouth" ceremony, 162–63
Organization of knowledge, 156
Orient, 3
Orientalism, 3, 9, 48, 216, 242, 288, 290
Original Sin, 226f, 237
Origins, 118
Orthography, 282
Osiris, 8–43 passim, 64, 82, 102f, 108, 114, 118–27 passim, 131–36 passim, 142–45 passim, 155, 161, 167, 176, 194, 207f, 211, 220–23, 225, 231–36 passim, 240, 245, 251f, 260f, 272, 275, 290–94 passim; Festival of, at Abydos, 37–39; -Sokar, 107, 121
Ostentatio genitalium, 229
Ostentatio vulnerum, 229
Ouroboros snake, 208–9
Ousaphais, King, 11

Pa-aten'ankh, 197–98. See also Aten
Paganism, 190, 250
Paglia, Camille, 152–53, 278–79
Painting, 138, 140, 144, 290
Palace Facade, 18
Palestine, 174, 190f, 195, 234
Pantheism, 118
Paradox, 183
Paraskhistai, see "Slitters"
Passion, 221, 225f
Paternalist authoritarianism, 220
Paternity, 118f, 123, 137, 187, 225, 228, 233, 235f
Patriarchal rule, 242
Penis, 108, 112, 114, 125f, 128, 131, 147, 221ff, 227–28, 233–34, 236, 244, 291. See also Phallus
Pepi I, King (Meryre'), 277
Pepi II, King (Neferkare'), 274
Perception, 189
Performativity, 82, 273
Peribsen, King, 18
Persians, 288
"Personal piety," 199, 285
Perspective, 143
PerW'sir (place-name), 13
Petrie, W. M. Flinders, 106, 108, 145
Phallocentrism, 22, 64, 85f, 115, 123,

133, 135, 146–53 passim, 204, 206, 220, 225, 228, 235, 243
Phallus, 9, 17, 22–23, 25–26, 63, 106–12, 116–17, 120f, 123, 126f, 133, 145, 147f, 153f, 181f, 189, 205, 221, 223f, 228–36, 244f, 252, 261, 270–77 passim, 291–94 passim; and death, 22, 131; hieroglyphs of, 26, 108–12, 137
Φ, 220f, 224
Philae, 145
Philology, 7
Philosopher king, 190, 195
Philosophical Weltanschauung, 171
Philosophy, 182f
Phoenicia, 217
Phonetic structure, 73f, 261, 264
Phonetic writing systems, 57–58, 290
Phonogram, 50f, 56, 65–70 passim, 264
Pi'ankhy ("Piye"), King (Menkheperre'), 172, 174
"Picklers," 25f
Pictographs, 263
Pictures, 7, 70, 79, 94ff, 159
Piety, 200
Plato, Platonism, 15, 114, 218, 224, 241, 289, 291
Pleasure, sexual, 118, 221, 227, 236f, 243, 292
Plenitude, 214–15, 245
Plotinus, 222, 224, 243, 291, 295
Plurality, 167
Plutarch, 15, 17–18, 19, 23, 108, 120, 223f, 236, 291; Peri Isidos kai Osiridos, 10, 119
"Pneumaticism," 226
Polotsky, Hans, 259
"Polytheism," 108, 154, 160, 163, 169, 179, 194, 200, 206, 238
Potiphar's wife, 130, 132
Power, 126, 132, 137, 148, 153, 157, 186, 192, 225
Pratimokṣa, 293
Prayer, 10
Pre-Harakhti, 124f, 128
Presence, 45, 104, 111, 187, 236
Procreation, 231
Prodomus coptus sive ægyptiacus, 47
Prosopopoeia, 260
Protestantism, 250
Prt-m-hrw ("Going Forth by Day"), 85

Psalm 104, 194
Psychoanalytical discourse, 235
Psychology, 115
Ptah, 14, 113, 163–67 passim, 173, 177–89 passim, 280f; -South-of-His-Wall, 171, 203, 236
Ptahhotep, tomb of (Saqqara), 89
Ptah-Pre'-Horsiese, 167
Ptah-Sokar Chapel, temple of Osiris at Abydos, 120–21
Ptah-Sokar-Osiris, 167
Ptolemy, 51f
Puns, 115–16, 251
Punt, 135, 276
Pyramid, 44–45
Pyramid Texts, 11, 13, 17, 19, 33, 75, 124, 188, 250; 1248a–d, 111–12, 118, 134, 273; 1652–1653b, 112, 168; 1256a–b, 251, 273
Pythagorean theorem, 289

Qebehsenuf, 102, 253, 275
Quirke, Stephen, 33, 122

R', Papyrus of, 249
Race, 48, 195, 287
Racism, 114, 137, 214
Radha, 273
Ra'hotep, tomb of (Meidum), 89
Ramesses, 54f, 212
Ramesses II, King (Userma'atre'), 89
Ramesses V, King (Userma'atre'-Skheperenre'), 124
Re', xix, 14, 20, 27, 40, 84, 136, 167, 203, 251, 280
Reading, 6f, 39, 42, 96, 104
"Reason," 219
Redford, Donald, 115, 151, 166, 178f
Redundancy, 69
Re'-Horakhty, 196, 203
Rejuvenation, 221
Rekhmire', tomb of (TT 100), 23, 142–44
Relief, 97, 138, 146, 149, 192
Renaissance, 47
Replacement, 159
Representation, 7, 19, 23, 70, 77, 85, 89, 95–99 passim, 137, 139, 143, 149f, 152, 154, 158–62 passim, 219–23 passim, 228, 244, 269, 290; of men and women, 138

INDEX

Reserve heads, 25
Restitution, 21
Restoration, 191, 223; stela, 201–5, 277
Resurrection, 9, 14, 23, 25, 223–27 *passim*, 245, 250
Rhetoric, 219
Ritual, 163, 280
Robins, Gay, 138
Rosetau (place-name), 14
Rosetta Stone, 48–51
Rougé, Emmanuel de, 259
Rousseau, Jean-Jacques, 257

Sacrifice, 26, 221
Said, Edward, 3
Sanskrit, 47–48
Saqqara, 89, 212, 277
Satan, 250
Sauneron, Serge, 26, 175, 178
Saussure, Ferdinand de, 45, 56–59, 79–80, 257, 259
Scarab, 187, 240, 242
Schäfer, Heinrich, 96, 137–38, 143, 256, 290
Schenute, Bishop, 145
Schlögl, Hermann, 205
Schlott, Adelheid, 93
Schmandt-Besserat, Denise, 262
Scorpion, King, 94
Scribes kit, glyph of, 72–74
Sculpture, 138, 149, 152
Seal, 92ff
Sekhem (place-name), 14
Sekhmet, 167
Self, 9, 131, 134
Semen, 125–26, 178, 181
Seminal line, *see* Seminal trace
Seminal trace, 124, 131, 133, 153, 205, 226, 231
Semiotics, 6, 8, 19, 23, 30, 87, 97–98, 103, 108–9, 114, 126, 131, 136, 163
Semna Stela, 109–10, 111, 271
Sennedjem, tomb of (TT1), 139
Senusert, xix
Senusert I, King (Kheperkare'), 88, 113, 146f
Senusert III, King (Kha'kaure'), 35, 40f, 109ff
Sequence, 180, 188
Serdab, 104
Serekh, 18, 81

Serpent King, stela of, 81–82, 89, 91
Seshat, 167
Setekh, 11, 13, 17ff, 20–21, 22, 26–32 *passim*, 123–27 *passim*, 131, 134, 166, 174–77 *passim*, 251, 274; battle with Horus, 37, 124–27
Seth, *see* Setekh
Sethe, Kurt, 114, 171–76 *passim*, 259
Seti I, King (Menma'atre'), 19, 23, 101, 212; temple at Abydos, 19, 107, 120–22, 147, 260
Seven Hathors, 129, 132
Sexuality, 22, 61, 63, 113–18 *passim*, 124, 130ff, 137–38, 148, 225ff, 231, 236, 243, 261, 276. *See also* Pleasure, sexual
Sexual penetration, 126f
Shabaka ("Shebek-[tawy]"), King (Neferkare'), 172–74, 281
Shabaka Stone, xix, 171–80, 184, 187
Shadow, 23, 28
Shas-hotep (place-name), 14
Shu, 11, 111f, 115–16, 117ff, 123, 168f, 182f, 187, 189, 196–97, 236, 278, 294
Sia, 169, 189
Sign, signs, 27, 44, 57–58, 65, 79, 85; anthropomorphic, xix; theriomorphic, xix; abstract, 262
Significance, 240
Signified, 27, 57, 65, 89, 223, 241
Signifier, 27, 57, 65, 80, 90, 221–22, 223, 241
Silence, 187
Simulacrum, 10, 101, 221ff
Siptah, King (Akhenre' Setepenre'), 275
Slate palettes, 20, 76–78
Slaughter, 14
"Slitters," 25f
Smenekhkare', King ('Ankhkheperure'), 200, 286
Smith, Eliot, 149
Smith, W. Stevenson, 142–43
Snefru, King, 104, 270
Sobek, 83, 87
Sobek-iry, stela of, 251
Socrates, 218
Sokar, 14, 251
Sokar-Osiris, *see under* Osiris
Solar religion, 201. *See also* Aten; Re'
"Sole Lord," 185–86, 187
Solipsism, 8

Son of God, 232
Sons of Horus, 25, 34. *See also*
    Duamutef; Ha'py; Imsety;
    Qebehsenuf
Sophocles, 289
Soul, 238–39
Sovereignty, of subject, 188, 221, 236
Speech, 57f, 183, 186
Spelling, 53
Sphinx, 242
Spirit, 222, 224f, 241, 244
Standard, 77–78, 161
Staten, Henry, 225–26, 233
Steinberg, Leo, 229–31, 233; *The Sexuality of Christ in Renaissance Art and in Modern Oblivion*, 229
Steindorff, Georg, 259
Subject, subject position, 7–8, 23, 26–28, 39, 42–43, 104, 118, 124, 138f, 144, 153f, 184–89 *passim*, 195–96, 220–23, 227–28, 236–43 *passim*, 273, 276
Subjectivity, 7–8, 223, 233, 242, 244
Sublation, 244
Substitutes, substitution, 16, 25, 39–44 *passim*, 131, 238; economy of, 43, 127, 130
Sumer, *see* Sumeria
Sumeria, 83, 90
Sun, 193–94
Sun disk, *see* Aten
Sun god, 119, 123, 195
Supplementarity, 25, 68–73 *passim*, 88–99 *passim*, 102f, 122, 134, 159f, 184–89 *passim*, 210, 221, 231–37 *passim*, 242ff
Symbols, symbolism, 4f, 46, 50, 67, 77, 96, 122, 148, 161, 182, 221f, 231–35 *passim*, 241–45 *passim*, 262, 265, 281
Synecdoche, 75
Syntax, figural, 74, 85, 184
Syntax, spatial, 74, 176–77, 180–81
Syria, 174, 191, 195, 234

Tale of Two Brothers, 124, 127–33
Tangut, 263
Tantric Buddhism, 277
Tarikheutai, *see* "Picklers"
Tawer (place-name), 9
Taxonomy, 158

Tefnin, Roland, 88–89, 96, 102–4
Tefnut, 111f, 115–16, 117ff, 123, 168f, 182f, 187, 189, 236, 278
Temples, 161, 163
Ten Commandments, 219
Testicles, 17, 20
Theban priesthood, 192
Theocritus, 196
Theology, 84, 90, 124, 163–67 *passim*, 179, 198
"Thick description," 288
Thinis (place-name), 11
Thoth, 20, 34, 38, 54, 77, 125f, 167, 178, 189, 203
Thought, 183
Thutmose, xix, 54, 77
Thutmose I, King ('Aakheperkare'), xix, 135
Thutmose II, King ('Aakheperenre'), xix, 134, 275
Thutmose III, King (Menkheperre'), xix, 134f, 142
Thutmose IV, King (Menkheperure'), xix
Time, 198, 206, 208–11
Titles, titularies, 18, 35, 39–41, 94, 99, 105, 136, 146–75 *passim*, 196–97, 202, 204, 255–56, 257, 266
Tjenenet (place-name), 14
Tomb, 26, 31, 35, 90, 93ff, 98–99, 101–5 *passim*, 132, 138–39, 155–56, 159, 192, 200
Tongue, 178–81, 184, 189
Topography, 11
Torah, 233
Totalitarianism, 195
"Towns Palette," 76f
Trace, 6
Transformation, 22f, 42, 86, 132, 187, 210, 224f, 240ff
Transliteration, xvii–xix, 73
Transmission, paternal, 12
Triads, divine family, 167
Tribal ancestor, 12
Trinitarianism, 231, 289–90
Turin Papyrus 54065, 188
Tut'ankhamun, King (Nebkheperure'), 84, 152, 191, 200–206, 278, 286
Twelfth Dynasty, integration of text and pictures in, 83–84
Two, 118, 169, 252
Two-Mounds (place-name), 14

Twosre' King/Queen (Sitre' Meritamun), 275
Typhon, 11, 222
Typology of hieroglyphs, 137

Unas, King, 23, 250
"Underworld books," 84
"Universalism," Amarnan, 195

Vagina, 252
Vajra, 277
Valley of the 'Ash, 128f, 132
Valley of the Kings, 123
Valley of the Nobles, 123
Valley of the Queens, 123
Vandalism to monuments, 108
Venus and Mars (Botticelli), 59–64, 134, 260
Verbal inflection, 259
Vernus, Pascal, 26
Violence, 26f, 109, 127, 253, 289
Virgin, *see* Mary
Virtue, 32
Visible, 257
Visual portrayal, conventions of, 96
Vocalization, 57
Voice, 7–11 *passim*, 27, 32, 34, 39, 43, 53, 246; "True of Voice," *see* Ma'a-kheru

"We," 1, 213–14, 219–20, 238–39, 245. *See also* First-person plural
"Weighing of the Heart," 33f, 85, 139
Wenennofru (epithet of Osiris), 11, 38, 211

Wepemnefret, tomb of, 97–102, 138
Wepwawet, 38, 77
"West," "Western," 2ff, 9, 213, 215–20, 222, 243
"Western civilization," 10, 217f
"Western culture," 214, 237, 239
"Western thought," 222–31 *passim*
"White Chapel" at Karnak, 87–88, 89, 113, 146f, 267, 277
Wilson, John, 183
"Wisdom literature," 192
Wittfogel, Karl August, 278
Woman, women, 22, 134, 137–38, 153f, 224, 243. *See also* Gender
Word, 8f, 95, 104f, 182, 186, 189, 220, 224, 233, 237, 244; generative, 187. *See also* Hu
"Word-image," 58
Writing, 6, 12, 23, 26, 45, 52–56, 58, 64–80, 82–84, 87–92, 101, 113f, 127, 167, 171–75 *passim*, 188, 220, 240, 253, 264, 290

Xixia (Hsi-Hsia), 263

Yahweh, 234f
Young, Thomas, 49, 51, 64
Yoyotte, Jean, 175, 178

Zep-tepy ("First Time"), 168, 204, 206–7
Zero, 211
Zodiac of Dendera, 53f
Zoomorphism, 196

Library of Congress Cataloging-in-Publication Data
Hare, Tom
  ReMembering Osiris : number, gender, and the word in ancient Egyptian representational systems / Tom Hare.
      p.   cm.
  Includes biographical references and index.
  ISBN 0-8047-3178-0 (cloth : alk. paper) — ISBN 0-8047-3179-9 (pbk. : alk. paper)
  1. Osiris (Egyptian diety)   2. Egyptian language—Writing, Hieroglyphic.   3. Mythology, Egyptian.   4. Egypt—Religion. I. Title
BL2450.O7H3 1999
299'.31—DC21   98-17634
   CIP
   Rev.

◎ This book is printed on acid-free, recycled paper.
Original printing 1999
Last figure below indicates year of this printing:
08 07 06 05 04 03 02 01 00 99

The authorized representative in the EU for product safety and compliance is:
Mare Nostrum Group
B.V Doelen 72
4831 GR Breda
The Netherlands

www.ingramcontent.com/pod-product-compliance
Lightning Source LLC
Chambersburg PA
CBHW021818300426
44114CB00009BA/220